NOV - 9 1994

D1336811

EVOLUTIONARY ETHICS

SUNY Series in Philosophy and Biology
David Edward Shaner, editor, Furman University

EVOLUTIONARY ETHICS

edited by

Matthew H. Nitecki

and

Doris V. Nitecki

State University of New York Press

Cover illustration: From *Kreuterbuch...* by Adam Lonitzer, published in Germany in 1587.

Published by
State University of New York Press, Albany

© 1993 State University of New York

For information, address State University of New York Press,
State University Plaza, Albany, N.Y., 12246

Production by Marilyn P. Semerad
Marketing by Bernadette LaManna

Library of Congress Cataloging-in-Publication Data

Evolutionary ethics / edited by Matthew H. Nitecki and Doris
    V. Nitecki.
        p. cm. — (SUNY series in philosophy and biology)
    "Based on the Field Museum of Natural History Spring Systematics
Symposium held in Chicago on May 12, 1990."
    Includes index.
    ISBN 0-7914-1499-X (alk. paper). — ISBN 0-7914-1500-7 (pbk. :
alk. paper)
    1. Ethics, Evolutionary.   I. Nitecki, Matthew H.   II. Nitecki,
Doris V.   III. Series.
BJ1311.E96   1993
170'.9—dc20
                                                    92-47270
                                                    CIP

10   9   8   7   6   5   4   3   2   1

Table of Contents

Preface

This volume is based on the Field Museum of Natural History Spring Systematics Symposium, held in Chicago on May 12, 1990. The Symposium was sponsored by the Society for the Study of Evolution and was supported financially by the National Science Foundation. We are grateful to these institutions.

Lynn Margulis and Dorion Sagan withdrew their manuscript, and deprived us of the discussion of Gaia. George Williams requested permission to publish his paper simultaneously in *The Quarterly Review of Biology*. On the suggestion of David Shaner, editor of the SUNY *Philosophy and Biology* series, we have secured the contributions of Richard Alexander and Andrzej Elzanowski, which broaden the coverage of our book considerably. We are reprinting Thomas Huxley, Leslie Stephen, and John Dewey. Although Huxley and Dewey have been reprinted previously, all three papers are seminal. They are fundamental for the understanding of the history, and hence the origin, of evolutionary ethics. Perhaps even more important, they demonstrate that ideas and questions change, and that our arguments for or against Huxley are now from different bases and concepts. For these reasons, the reproduction of these papers is not only justified but necessary.

When we teach or write, we present only those elements that support our arguments. We avoid all weak points of our debate and all the uncertainties of our models. Thus, we offer hypotheses as facts. Multiauthored books, like ours, which simultaneously advocate and question diverse views, avoid these pitfalls and lessen the impact of indoctrination. In this volume we analyze the biological and philosophical disagreements and the positions taken on evolutionary ethics, point out the difficulties with the interpretations, and argue that the concept of evolutionary ethics has changed since the time of Huxley. The book is divided into four sections. The first, *Ethics and the Cosmic Order*, is the historical introduction to the origin of evolutionary ethics, and consists of three chapters by distinguished turn-of-the-century scholars. It shows how different evolutionary ethics was a hundred years ago, and how distant Huxley is from most of us now. The second section, *Philosophical Advocacy*, is the modern, almost classical, argument for the support of evolutionary ethics. A historian of evolution, a philosopher of evolution, and an evolutionary biologist, whose approaches reflect their respective fields, strongly argue for the sociobiological interpretation of evolutionary ethics. The third, *Philosophical Skepticism*, written by a philosopher of evolution, an evolutionary biologist, a philosopher, and an ethicist, is the exact opposite of the second section and rejects its interpretation. The fourth section, *Biosocial Debate*, perhaps the most novel section, deals unemotionally with many complex and fundamental issues. It is a diverse discussion from the perspectives of a bioethicist-ornithologist, physical anthropologists, a paleontologist-evolutionary biologist, an ecologist, a sociologist-historian and a zoologist, and a social anthropologist.

Humanity now and in the past has been governed by strong ethics, and to understand this we must understand biological origins of ethics. We must also face the future. We have tried very hard not to favor any viewpoint, but to present a symmetrical shape of the argument. We are neither advocating nor denying the reality of evolutionary ethics. We are aware that the great pendulum of intellectual fashion has swung toward sociobiology, and that evolutionary ethics may offer the resolution of our worldview of humanity and of human morality. We also know that new questions are being continuously asked. We hope that our approach to the complexities of evolutionary ethics, our attempt at providing both sides of the medal, will be of heuristic value.

December, 1991   Matthew H. Nitecki
University of Oslo   Doris V. Nitecki

Living Contributors

Richard D. Alexander, Museum of Zoology, The University of Michigan, Ann Arbor, MI 48109

Mary Catherine Bateson, 207 East Building, George Mason University, Fairfax, VA 22030

Andrzej Elzanowski, Max Planck Institut für Biochemie, 8033 Martinsried, Bei München, GERMANY

Margaret S. Ewing, Department of Zoology, Oklahoma State University, Stillwater, OK 74078

Alan Gewirth, Department of Philosophy, University of Chicago, 1010 East 59th Street, Chicago, IL 60637

Laurie R. Godfrey, Department of Anthropology, Machmer Hall, University of Massachusetts, Amherst, MA 01003

Evelyn Fox Keller, Department of Rhetoric, University of California, Berkeley, CA 94720

Doris V. Nitecki, Department of Geology, Field Museum of Natural History, Roosevelt Road at Lake Shore Drive, Chicago, IL 60605

Matthew H. Nitecki, Department of Geology, Field Museum of Natural History, Roosevelt Road at Lake Shore Drive, Chicago, IL 60605

Daniel J. Povinelli, Laboratory of Comparative Behavioral Biology, University of Southwestern Louisiana, 100 Avenue D, New Iberia, LA 70560

Robert J. Richards, Department of History, University of Chicago, 1126 East 59th Street, Chicago, IL 60637

Michael Ruse, Philosophy Department, University of Guelph, Guelph, ON N1G 2W1, CANADA

Lawrence B. Slobodkin, Department of Ecology and Evolution, State University of New York, Stony Brook, NY 11794

Elliott Sober, Department of Philosophy, University of Wisconsin, Madison, WI 53706

Adam Urbanek, Zaklad Paleobiologii PAN, Al. Zwirki i Wigury 93, 02-089 Warszawa, POLAND

George C. Williams, Department of Ecology and Evolution, State University of New York, Stony Brook, NY 11794

Patricia Williams, Department of History and International Studies, Hollins College, Box 24, Petersburg, VA 23803

Introduction

Problematic Worldviews of Evolutionary Ethics

Matthew H. Nitecki

The understanding and meaning of ethical judgment are of greatest importance, but should ethics be based on intuition, religion, or scientific knowledge? Is there a relation between ethics and evolution? Can moral behavior and motivation be genetically controlled, and does ethics evolve? If so, can a system of evolutionary ethics be perceived as a legitimate subject of analysis?

In the past these questions either have been answered in the positive or have been vehemently opposed. Evolutionary ethics derived its origin from Herbert Spencer's work in the 1850s and blossomed as Social Darwinism in the later part of the nineteenth and the beginning of the twentieth centuries. Spencer, in his 1892 *Principles of Ethics*, and Haeckel, in his 1899 *Die Welträthsel*, further developed the notion of evolutionary ethics. These ideas were almost immediately attacked by Thomas Huxley (below) and by G. E. Moore in his 1903 *Principia Ethica*. Huxley objected to Social Darwinism, while Moore's "naturalistic fallacy" claimed that *ought* cannot be derived from *is*, or *ethics* from *facts*.

In the 1940s and through the 1950s, Waddington, Dobzhansky, and particularly Julian Huxley attempted to resurrect evolutionary ethics. Now, probably strengthened by sociobiology and the associated controversies, there is a renewed interest in, and a reexamination of, the possibilities of evolutionary ethics. Presently a rigorous (and emotional) rethinking of evolutionary ethics cuts across political and feminist positions. On the one hand there exists an evolutionary, conservative political view based on evolutionary biology which supports the conservative views of evolutionary ethics (Wilson 1975, 1978, and 1984 sees a good connection between evolutionary ethics and the developments in human sociobiology), but, on the other hand, socialists and even communists have claimed an evolutionary moral ground.

Evolutionary ethics is as urgent now as it was a century ago. The more unknown, complex, and difficult the question is, the harder it becomes to resolve. Disagreement thus occurs before the resolution is reached. Evolutionary ethics is one of those eternal problems that is a subject of great conflict. While our daily ethical difficulties appear easy to resolve, evolutionary ethics stubbornly produces awkward problems, models and worldviews. In fact it is problematic. Different ethical views may represent different desires and not different values. Questions asked of evolutionary ethics are terribly complex, and many may be without answers, or at least without answers today. What greatly complicates the resolution of the controversies surrounding evolutionary ethics is the misconception that ideas, questions, the meanings of terms and our concepts of the cosmos remain unchanged, while in fact they age and evolve with time. When we will reject or change evolutionary ethics or our explanations of it is philosophically unimportant—that it will change or be rejected is, however, a historical certainty. Questions always change, or become extinct.

Birth of Inquiry

If we accept the theory of evolution, we cannot escape its philosophical conclusions. The origin of species (or rejection of creationism) and natural selection are now accepted concepts, but moral corollaries of the theory of evolution—in the deepest sense its most significant aspects—are still fiercely debated. The contribution of Darwin to biology must not overshadow his influence on ethics. Already in the late eighteenth century morals and behavior were beginning to be considered as subject to natural rather than divine laws, and after the Napoleonic wars the radical physiologists began to biologize ethics and to consider morality a subject for naturalists to examine (Desmond 1989). Thus, there were others before, but it was unquestionably Darwin who, implicitly in the *Origin* and explicitly in the *Descent of Man*, started the great ethical debate (see Richards 1988, 1989, and below). However, it was only in the second half of the twentieth century that Wilson (1975) finally biologized ethics. Now as we approach the end of the century, evolution is heavily influencing all aspects of our life, including ethics.

Thomas Huxley, the first major opponent of evolutionary ethics, sees humanity and the humblest weeds as products of the cosmic process. This process is the blind fury of the unethical universe, "the struggle for existence, the competition of each with all, the result of which is the selection, that is to say, the survival of those forms which, on the whole, are best adapted to the conditions which at any period obtain; and which are, therefore, in that respect, and only in that respect, the fittest" (this volume, p. 32). Humanity, ethics (meaning sympathies and cooperation), and aspirations are antithetic to the cosmic process. His ethical process is the "gradual strengthening of the social bond, which, though it arrests the struggle for existence inside society, up to a certain point improves the chances of society, as a corporate whole, in the cosmic struggle" (this volume, p. 46). He claims that once this process proceeds far enough, the struggle for existence (or the cosmic struggle or process) stops. He sees the "evolution of society" as an entirely different process from the "evolution of species." His two worldviews, "cosmic process" and "ethical process," are in mortal combat. The meaning of human life is to combat this cosmic process, whose purpose is the survival of the fittest, and to replace it with the human ethical process in which the victory will go to the *survival of ethically the best.* Man must work for the "State of Art" and build the artificial world of ethics within the cosmos, which is hostile to humans and to the human State of Art.

Leslie Stephen, best remembered for his later *The Science of Ethics* (1907), argues against Huxley's terribly pessimistic worldview. Like Huxley, he breaks down the world into macrocosmos versus microcosmos—evolution against human emotions. His reasoning and arguments foretell Dewey. He deals, differently from us, with many present-day problems: the anthropomorphism of terms, altruism and cooperation. His "typical" nineteenth-century racist attitudes are unfortunately similar to those now appearing in the letters-to-the-editor sections.

I have no objection to the use of anthropomorphic terms. Consider the word "parent." A turtle lays eggs; a bird sits on eggs; a domestic cat nurtures the young; a human remains a parent throughout the entire life of the offspring; all are parents, but each in a different sense. We know exactly what human parenting means, just as well as what fish parenting means. Many words, in all languages, have more than one meaning which can be deciphered only from the context they are used. By themselves most words are ambiguous. The fuss raised about their use from one discipline (or meaning) to another is nitpicking. The word most attacked is "altruism." But even human actions have many shades and scales of altruisms. We give Nobel Prizes for saving many lives, not for only one. So there is a "good" and a "very good" altruism. A more important problem is an a priori assumption that nonhumans do not "know" that they are altruistic. I, for one, do not know *whether animals know or do not know* whether they are altruistic. It is possible that many nonhumans "know" what they are doing, and if so their actions are purposeful, and their altruism real.

I am a Deweyan, and I find John Dewey's analysis of Huxley's arguments on evolutionary ethics most convincing. It is surprising how little known Dewey's article is. See, for example, the scholarly book by Rachels who thinks that Dewey "had little to say" about Darwinian evolution (1991:71). To Dewey, Huxley's ethical process is not opposing *all* cosmic purpose, but only that *part* of cosmic process which concerns human behavior in society as against the prehuman evolution. He interprets Huxley's argument of the garden and the gardener differently and reaches different conclusions. He agrees with Huxley that in ethics as in the garden there must be a constant struggle, but in the garden man is not against the entire state of the nature, but utilizes one part of nature to control another. Everything that gardener introduces—light, water, plants— may be foreign to the particular spot, but they are part of nature as a whole. The conflict is not "between the garden and the gardener; between the natural process and the process of art . . . [but] of reading the possibilities of a part through its place in the whole. Human intelligence and effort intervene, not as opposing forces but as making the connection . . . man is an organ of the cosmic process in effecting its *own* progress . . . making over a part of the environment by relating it more intimately to the environment as a whole; not . . . in man setting himself against that environment" (this volume, p. 98).

In the cosmic process fitness depends on the conditions which include the social structure and, therefore, unfit is antisocial. The struggle for existence and the survival of the fittest *do not* eliminate the weak and the insane, but, on the contrary, looking after the helpless develops those habits "to husband our means, which shall ultimately make us the most skilled in warfare. We shall foster habits of group loyalty, feelings of solidarity, which shall bind us together . . . that no [one] will be able to, withstand us" (this volume, pp. 98-99). It is fallacious to interpret fitness with reference to the past environment; the conditions have changed and "fit" must be now defined in the social environment. Dewey turns from the idea of *fitness* to the process, the *struggle for existence*, which is controlled by the environment where that struggle for life is constantly modified by the conditions.

Problems are usually not solved, but are left behind "not because any satisfactory solution has been reached; but interest [in them] is exhausted" (this volume, p. 95). Other things attracted attention, and the judgment and solutions reached are psychological, not logical. "Old ideas give way slowly; for they are more than abstract logical forms and categories. They are habits, predispositions, deeply ingrained attitudes of aversion and preference. Moreover, the conviction persists—though history shows it to be a hallucination—that all the questions that the human mind has asked are questions that can be answered in terms of the alternatives that the questions themselves present. But in fact intellectual progress usually occurs through sheer abandonment of questions together with both of the alternatives they assume—an abandonment that results from their decreasing vitality and a change of urgent interest. We do not solve them; we get over them. Old questions are solved by disappearing, evaporating, while new questions corresponding to the changed attitude of endeavor and preference take their place. Doubtless the greatest dissolvent in contemporary thought of old questions, the greatest precipitant of new methods, new intentions, new problems, is the one effected by the scientific revolution that found its climax in the 'Origin of Species'" (Dewey 1910:19).

New Believers

Almost one century separates us from Thomas Huxley, and while the concept of evolutionary ethics has changed, the controversy over it continues. The tone of the discussion is also different. Huxley's English is beautiful, literary, and even emotional, but he is considerate of others and avoids all personal references and attacks. In our next two sections, whether due to the ethos of the time or the personalities involved, the words are fighting and the tone is heated and polemical. The questions have changed so much that the meaning of evolutionary ethics is different. Not natural selection, but sociobiology, is a subject of disagreement.

To an evolutionary ethicist no organism exists alone; two or more organisms together generate a relationship, which when beneficial to the two (or to the group) is "good," and when disruptive is "bad"; the boundaries between the conscious and unconscious behavior are very hazy, or at least not clearly delineated; humans are not subject to any biological or physical law not applicable to other organisms, and all humans obey all biological and physical laws; no human society exists without a system of ethics, which is an internal societal system of control; and, therefore, all human behavior can be reduced to biology. Thus, to an evolutionary ethicist, an animal is comparable to a cell that lives a double life as an independent individual and as an unseparable component of the organism. Humans also lead a "free" life as individuals and a life constrained by society. Neither a cell nor a human can survive alone and neither is independent or free. A cell must obey the rules of the organism, and a human those of the society, including the moral rules. Neither can violate the rules. Moral rules cannot exist among solitary organisms, and are fully developed only in the social life. How an individual (or a cell), ought to behave is determined by the society (or the body). Therefore, to the evolutionary ethicist, humans are, at least in this sense, *animals*.

Robert J. Richards, who has written extensively on evolutionary ethics (1986a, 1986b, 1988, 1989 and references therein), thinks that some contemporary biologists, Gould and Lewontin for example, detect Social Darwinism in evolutionary ethics for good reason. The interpretation of evolutionized ethics by sociobiologists Wilson, Ruse, and Alexander is not entirely logical to him. However, their feelings about the human condition are humane and their goal of bringing evolution to bear on moral behavior perfectly reasonable. Although Richards somewhat doubts their logic, he believes that their logic can be revitalized and the promise of joining ethics with science can be resurrected. He argues that his version of evolutionary ethics can save it philosophically.

He thinks evolutionary ethics is now a legitimate subject for ethical analysis. He attempts to overcome the objections of the naturalistic fallacies and to show how evolutionary *is* can proceed to moral *ought*. His "revised version" does not commit a naturalistic fallacy and his evolutionary properties motivate us to abide for the good of the community; each person abides for the community good, thus each ought to act altruistically. Moral sense plus social instincts equal moral animals. He links morality to altruism in order for evolutionary *is* to lead to moral *ought*. For a spirited discussion of Richards's (1986a, 1986b) views, see Cela-Conde (1986), Gewirth (1986), Hughes (1986), Thomas (1986) and Trigg (1986).

I would go further than Richards. It is assumed by the opponents of evolutionary ethics that we cannot extrapolate human ethics from animal behavior. But we never do that anyway. Our observations on nonhumans are based on a model that we have of human behavior, which we later extrapolate and apply to animals. Just as the terms inheritance and heredity came to biology from law and tradition, and not the other way around, so the term altruism came from humans to termites.

Michael Ruse, who has produced a great share of ideas on evolutionary ethics (Ruse 1984, 1986a, 1986b, 1987; Ruse and Wilson 1985, 1986, etc.), again argues that the time has come to take the biological origins of morality seriously. Ethics is nothing but a collective illusion of our genes, put in place to make us successful cooperators. This has serious implications for our sense of obligation to strangers.

Michael Ruse proposes that in biology, morality has no rational justification but is used to make us good cooperators. Morality has no objective foundation; we objectify—we think it is objective. He claims that there is an impassable gulf between *is* and *ought*, because our system of ethics is merely an *illusion* used to justify the strong moral objections we feel towards individuals in our own group. Like Richards, Ruse confines evolutionary ethics mostly to altruistic behavior.

Richard Alexander enlarges his earlier ideas (1980, 1987) further. He deals with the biological analysis of morality and the history of sociobiological conflict, and how evolution can be applied to humans and their ethics. He discusses group selection and ontogeny in depth, and also the nature of organisms, the evolutionary view of morality, and the problem of intent. Efforts by evolutionary biologists to understand human tendencies and abilities encounter many obstacles. The workings of natural selection and the underlying ontogenetic and physiological mechanisms of behavior are difficult and imperfectly understood topics. Students of human behavior typically have little training in biology, and may reject natural selection as a guiding force in the evolution of humans even though accepting it for other organisms. Human efforts for self-understanding are convoluted not only because the properties to be analyzed must be used to conduct the analyses, but because selection seems to have designed human motivation in social matters to be resistant to conscious analysis. Oh, how right he is that moral behavior sometimes demands absence of conscious knowledge or intent, and those who seek to discover how kindness, beneficence, and good fellowship might have been reproductively selfish may be viewed as unduly crediting the dark side of human motivation. The most difficult problems in understanding morality may turn out to be the play between conscious and nonconscious motivation, especially as revealed in expressions of the emotions. Therefore, Alexander's thesis is that evolution poses great problems for ethics. First, how selection serves the interest of others; second, how evolved tendencies can be moral and how to understand them; third, how is ethical intent related to behavior; and fourth, since emotions have evolved why is our control over them so poor? He defends his ideas logically and persuasively argues for the role and control of natural selection.

I believe that learning, observations, and experience are as imprinted upon our minds as genetic factors, and for an equal length of time. However, how they are imprinted and how retained is unknown. What and how we know, and what and how we remember, are secrets we have not yet deciphered. Yet the mind is the only source of knowledge of the cosmos and of our inner world. The knowledge is transmitted to our mind by sense organs; we know a lot about them and about transmission of the information, and we even know the speed with which this transfer is accomplished. But how these are transferred into the "image" of the mind, into the "understanding," the "knowledge" of the cosmos we do not know. Was calculus invented from experience or reason? In fact we are most ignorant of the mind and how it works, and of the nature of our mental life. We cannot tell which of our thoughts are conscious and which subconscious; of which we have control, and which we do not; which are learned and which are rational; and which are free and which are not.

Eddington (1929) taught us that our common sense and our observations may not be right after all, that the cosmos is different from the reality that our senses comprehend, and that the table on which we write is an illusion. Dawkins (1976) told us that what matters is within the gene. What was complexity to early observers, for example, the metamorphosis of the flea to Leeuwenhoek, is simplicity today. Now Dawkins resolves the human complexity to the simplicity of genes. These are microscopic explanations of macroscopic phenomena.

Our knowledge of the "minds" of other species is an even greater *tabula rasa.* Unless we learn more about the workings of minds of animals we cannot be certain whether ethics is the sole property of humans. The cosmos may not be as it seems to us at all, perhaps it is only our imperfect interpretation. Everything that we know of cosmos we know only through our senses, and *we understand and interpret the behavior of other species in terms of, and in comparison with, our own behavior.* The interpretation of the behavior of nonhumans, therefore, depends on how well we understand the human mind, and how closely we relate animals to us.

Old Skeptics

Sociobiologists search for the ethical universals in biology. It is certainly now a received wisdom that there are biological bases to human behavior. What is questioned by the opponents of evolutionary ethics is whether human ethical behavior can be reduced to biology, and whether it can be compared with nonhuman behavior. Humans and apes may be similar enough for this comparison to be acceptable, but comparisons with termites, bees, colonial bryozoans, or sponges is a taboo to them.

We recognize and understand intuitively what ethics is; the meaning of the word is clear, and irrespective of the language we speak, we understand it in similar ways. We know and agree what is, and what is not, ethical. Ethics of all people are very similar. Arab ethics is not different from Jewish. There is very little variation and little difference from one people to another in the use and application of ethics, except that humans possess an "inventiveness" in many aspects of ethical behavior which can be called "ethics acquisition." While we learn in childhood to differentiate good from bad, we are able to make ethical judgments on *all* ethical questions only later in life when we make this judgment irrespective of their novelty or complexity. We may either have an *innate* built-in mechanism to make future judgments, or they may be learned, or they may only represent potentialities which develop later in life. But the ability to recognize ethics must be a common property of all humans, a universal property of human mind. There may be ethical criteria and issues that are shared by all humans and at all times. Therefore, these may be called *universal properties* recognizable by all human beings.

Anthropologists also search for universals. Goldschmidt (1957:67) does not find universal ethics in any culture, except perhaps the universal "general-welfare principle," that is the universal forbidding of anything inimical to the general welfare of the society. Linton (1957), however, accepts the almost unlimited variety of ethical principles, and a fundamental uniformity underlying human cultures, the uniformity of the basic physiological needs. All human societies are based on the same societal organization, operation and perpetuation of the community. While there are differences, Cortez and Pizarro were impressed with the presence of familiar ethical principles. In universal ethical principles the frame of reference must be on society and not on the individual. When society has a particular ethical stand it means that the large majority of the people, and not individuals, accept it. It is the society, not individual who are units of ethics, and "the ethical system functions only in terms of in-groups" (Linton 1957:75), the smaller the social unit, the greater the ethical considerations of the unit. There is a hierarchy of emphasis—the nuclear family, distant relatives, village, etc.—and the ethical standards and enforcement are also hierarchical. Ethical standards are a function of closeness of the group, or its members. Sexual behavior, marriage, parents and children relationship, obligation of siblings, the respect of property, and finally a united front toward outsiders are universal ethical principles. These universals basically concern sexual and family behavior. "Thou shalt not kill" seems also to be a universal ethical property (Linton 1957:82).

Ethical behavior is the behavior which is considered good (that is, approved) at the time of judgment, and, therefore, ethics also differs from one time to another. It was morally wrong for Adam and Eve to eat from the tree of knowledge, but is mandatory now. It was morally right for Abraham to sacrifice his son, but Abraham's obedience to the voice of God would be today considered hallucinations, or an attempted murder, as it is no longer acceptable to sacrifice human beings. Abraham's God was vengeful, and this kind of God is today unacceptable. Can we imagine our baseball or soccer players replaced by gladiators? In the past it was ethically correct to arrange marriages for financial considerations, today we disapprove. All of us respond differently to our ethical demands, however, the pool of the responses is limited by nature and nurture.

Ethical judgments also differ geographically. Consider the opposing views of Israelis and Palestinians. Menachem Begin, a patriotic terrorist, was elected a Prime Minister of Israel, and Yasir Arafat is his Palestinian counterpart. The same action, the infitada, is held evil by some and virtuous by others. There are no absolute rights or wrongs, but only differences in community ethics at the particular time and place.

Thus, I think that despite the most persuasive and logical arguments of Degler (1991), ethics can be considered universal only in a sense that all humans have ethics. One can argue that all ethics has a common pattern, and that the differences are only superficial reflections of time or geography. Each time and place may superimpose its own function, but not the structure, of ethics. Ethics evolves through time, but ethics of primitive peoples are not qualitatively different from ours; they are only different responses to different needs expressed differently in different times. There are thus many ethics, and many degrees of relatedness and responsibilities, and many hierarchies of these relationships. There may be basic "ethical principles," "ethical instincts," and "wills to ethics." Ethics prescribes the behavior of individuals necessary for the stability and survival of society. Whether ethical thoughts have evolutionary origins, and whether an evolutionary mechanism, or model, can explain the origin of ethics still remains open. Our minds are the same, whoever we are, thus human ethics must be the same. This does not imply universal ethics, but rather common human characteristics.

Elliott Sober has also thought deeply about evolutionary ethics (1984, 1988), and he believes that evolutionary biologists use the terms "altruism" and "selfishness" in a very different way from the way those terms are used in everyday life. The evolutionary concepts have to do with survival and reproduction, but do not imply that the agent has a mind. In contrast, the everyday concepts are psychological in their subject matter and have nothing essentially to do with survival and reproduction.

After having separated the two ideas, Sober considers how they are related. Psychological egoism is the thesis that people are selfish (in the everyday sense of the term). Some recent evolutionary theorists have argued that a characteristic that is altruistic (in the evolutionary sense of the term) cannot evolve and be maintained in a population of organisms. Does this evolutionary thesis imply that psychological egoism is true?

What does it mean to attribute a moral code to someone, and is having a morality the same as being inclined to act altruistically? Sober's general goal is to clarify the question of whether evolutionary theory can help explain facts about human motivation and morality. He is concerned with the relevance of the evolutionary discussion of units of selection to the origin of ethics. He also argues about taboos. In human beings, the behavior is frequently mediated by a system of beliefs, by an incest taboo. An important distinction is between simple altruism and true ethics, and Sober is pulling the rug from beneath the logics of Richards and Ruse by arguing that ethics cannot be confined to altruism alone.

I agree. Certainly, Sober *must* be right in claiming that there is much more to altruism than acting on a genetic impulse, or satisfying the selfishness of the gene. It is much more, as being human is much more than being a mammal with a certain dental formula. Humanness is above biology. If altruism is an element of cooperation, then it may have evolved by gradual natural selection. Altruistic behavior, whether giving one's life for another or giving breast to the child, is, by definition, detrimental to the donor; energy to produce milk could be spent in other ways. At a certain stage (in social animals, whether corals, ants or humans) the will to reproduce requires "altruism." Energy is spent for existence of future generations. As Mayr states, "the shift from an instinctive altruism based on inclusive fitness to an ethics based on decision making was perhaps the most important step in humanization" (1988:77). It is this shift that marks the demarcation point between *Homo sapiens* and other animals. But much of altruistic human behavior may be automatic. Soldiers seldom make a conscious choice, neither do army units opposing each other. One will be defeated, the other will be victorious, therefore, one made a more rational decision then the other.

George C. Williams knows Huxley well (see Paradis and Williams 1989). He is as pessimistic as Huxley (above) in accepting that the cosmos is hostile to human ethical standards. Natural selection, as Shaw recognized, is to him a morally unacceptable process. None of the conceptual advances of recent decades ameliorate these conclusions. Williams's examination of animal behavior, tribal human behavior, and other biological processes shows that gross violations of ethical norms are the general rule. This he illustrates by a few examples of mammalian infanticide.

George Williams holds that it is equally true that the cosmos in general, and even the earth in general, is hostile to the origin and maintenance of life. Organisms exist only because of their adaptation to a mainly hostile environment. Henderson's (1913) *The Fitness of the Environment*, and recent works in the same tradition, are based on grossly biased data and failure to appreciate the one-sided nature of biological adaptation. Williams argues this point from the data of physics, chemistry, and astronomy, and from community trophic structure.

Evolution (i.e., natural selection) is not ethical. Williams answers in the negative the big question of whether nature can provide analog and guidance to ethical decisions or, otherwise whether human moral impulses evolved.

Patricia Williams believes that Ruse and Wilson have developed a theory which suggests that at least some human ethical dispositions are the products of evolution. They recommend that we follow those dispositions, at least in part, because our evolved ethical dispositions are sufficiently strong so that not following them will lead to psychological and social stress. Patricia Williams challenges that recommendation philosophically, in two connected paths. First, if our evolved ethical dispositions are so strong that we are constrained to follow them, then we are not free agents. But beings who are not free cannot be ethical, for freedom to chart one's course is the fundamental requirement for being ethical. Beings who have great difficulty sailing except with the evolutionary current, therefore, can hardly be ethical. Secondly, if we are not strongly constrained to follow our evolved ethical dispositions, then not following them will produce, at most, only minimal psychological and social stress. In this second path, we are free to choose, and, therefore, are ethical. But if we have the freedom to chart our own course, then reason may tell us where to sail, and whether our heading is with or against the evolutionary current need not be relevant to our chosen direction.

I think that we only accept conscious behavior as ethical and rational. However, much human "ethical" behavior may be intuitive, not the result of thoughtful deliberations and, therefore, subject to physiological analysis. There are two components to this problem: behavior, and the interpretation of the behavior. Behavior is not ethical or unethical, it is ethically neutral. What is ethical is our interpretation that assigns ethical values to behavior. Ethics is in the eyes of the judge. The things that are uniquely human are by definition biological properties of *Homo sapiens*. If all humans have them, they have scientific meaning. The unquestionable moral behavior is that which is directed by love, hardly a rational motivation. Therefore, the deep meaning of ethics is not in the behavior, but in thoughtfulness, intentions, or a state of mind. Repentance, and listening to one's consciousness may be enough. Patricia Williams is right that for action to be moral there must be no coercion into doing it, and it must be done on free will. But it is less certain whether, as the critics of evolutionary ethics claim, acting under the constraints of evolution cannot be free because genetic determinants are outside of our control and thus we cannot take responsibility for them. Just because our hearts or our legs may restrain our freedom they are still ours and part of us, and, therefore, whether or not we depend on them they do not deprive us of moral choices. Whether or not we need oxygen to breathe is irrelevant to our moral choice.

It may be an error to think that because biology restrains us we cannot be responsible, or moral. We can be moral whether or not biology controls us. We can be moral whatever sex we are.

Alan Gewirth has thought about ethics for a long time (Gewirth 1978, 1982). To him evolutionary ethics provides, at most, necessary conditions of human morality, and not sufficient conditions. The explanations offered by evolutionary ethics fail to accommodate the intentionality that is characteristic of moral *oughts* and to give determinate answers to either the distributive or the substantive questions of human morality.

He describes the discontinuities between evolutionary ethics and human morality. We have evolved the power of choice but what we choose is indeterminate. Since voluntary choice is excluded from natural selection, evolutionary ethics is nonethical because we do retain voluntary choice. He argues that evolutionary ethics can only judge moral conduct by stretching beyond evolution and into culture. He argues against those who impose the human altruism onto animals by pointing out that according to Kant, *ought* implies both *can* and *may not*.

Because we have relegated progress, and with it the considerations of moral progress to the dustbins of history, I also find it difficult to see the issues of evolutionary ethics clearly. With rejection of progress we reject faith in the future. Questions answered correctly imply progress. For evolutionary ethics to remain alive, we must ask questions, seek answers, and progress intellectually. There are no answers to ethical questions without progress. Ethics, including evolutionary ethics, is based on faith in a better world, and in the belief that humans can act better. Behavior, to be ethical, requires, as Patricia Williams argues, the presence of at least two alternative paths of behavior—existence of choice, and the freedom to make this choice. Those are the prerequisites for ethical action. There must be also a strong temporary block of such powerful instincts as hunger or self-preservation; the chosen path must benefit the recipient (or the group) more than the donor; and the system of behavior that we call ethical cannot be static (or else it will become instinctive like termites). By definition it is "for others," therefore, it must continuously improve and be progressive. Absence of free will, for example, will knock the whole concept down. We believe in correctness of ethical prescriptions only when we see that there will be, or is, progress in human behavior. Thus evolutionary ethics has an unspoken, and hidden, claim to a meaning or a direction to biological process. Since, according to evolutionary ethicists, natural selection is responsible for morality, the more moral will be selected, and hence there is progress in morality. If evolutionary biology rejects progress then it must also reject evolutionary ethics. Just as to remain alive requires regeneration, or repair, so evolutionary ethics requires progress. Progress is a process that produces improvement. It is a process that must continue and cannot end. By definition, the process that ends, dies. Thus progress reflects the drama of the evolutionary intellectual, who must either accept evolutionary ethics *and* progress or must reject both—to many of us a difficult choice. But I am not certain that progress must be rejected.

Biosocial Debate

There is much talk nowadays about ethics. New professions, such as the medical ethicists, advise what should or should not be done, judge and set limits on the medical and biological research, and influence the acquisition of knowledge itself. Evolutionary ethics crosses the boundaries of anatomy, anthropology, biology, ethics, ethology, evolution, genetics, medicine, metaphysics, philosophy, politics, psychology, sociology, systematics, and zoology. Even lawyers call for the involvement of sociobiology in courts and legislations (Beckstrom 1985). This diversity of approaches produces diversity of meanings; almost everyone who studies different aspects of evolutionary ethics narrows the scope and defines evolutionary ethics differently. It also produces a somewhat hazy focus, and makes definition of evolutionary ethics difficult. But perhaps the definition is not possible.

Andrzej Elzanowski, who hunts for evolutionary ethics at the base of the phylogenetic tree, shows why bioethics is important. He combs the vertebrate primordial behavior for bioethics, and claims that humans must have inherited most of their primary, experienced values from their mammalian ancestors. He demonstrates the continuity of the primary value experience in humans and other vertebrates by a number of motivational phenomena such as intracranial self-stimulation and learned avoidance of electrical brain stimulation, effective contrasts, value-dependent interaction and value-dependent categorization of incentives as well as play, curiosity and other evidence for the activity-derived reward.

Through the development of empathy, Elzanowski believes, humans became liable to feel good or bad for other individuals, both human and animal. Vicarious value experience is the primary factor of moral evaluation and motivation in evolution and ontogeny (but not necessarily in microgeny). The exercise of empathy is limited by the preemptive devaluation of others, leading to discrimination of some people and animals and disregarding their value experience. Values specific for humans may counterbalance and sometimes overrule but not supersede the common vertebrate values. By the logic of valuative deduction (Pugh 1977), the value experience provides an objective moral standard applicable to behavior toward people and other higher vertebrates.

Daniel Povinelli and Laurie R. Godfrey climb up the phylogenetic tree to examine primates for evolutionary ethics. Ethical systems are uniquely human, and they show how a primatologist can develop a framework for understanding the emergence of human morality from a comparative perspective. They have been developing a model to do exactly this. They identify shared characteristics of the cognitive-emotional systems of apes and humans, and reconstruct the cognitive-emotional system of their common ancestor. Certain features of human cognition underlie, or allow for, the expression of the multitude of ethical belief systems that are found cross-culturally. Recent research on chimpanzee cognition suggests that some of these abilities were, in fact, present in the common ancestor of humans and apes. In particular, the ability to project emotions, intentions, and states of belief onto others evolved long before the emergence of *Homo sapiens*, and these attributional capabilities, along with some others that are unique to humans, underlie the expression of ethics in humans. Yet they exist in animals that do not *have* morals in the human sense. Clearly, these attributional skills did not evolve to support ethical systems *per se*. A key evolutionary problem is to discover what behavioral patterns or expressions they do support in chimpanzees and other apes.

Two sets of questions are central to developing an understanding of the evolution of ethics. First, what evolved? What cognitive-emotional abilities can be regarded as supporting or motivating the enormous range of expressed behaviors that comprises human ethical systems? Second, when did these abilities evolve? What can we infer about the distribution of these abilities in humans and nonhuman primates? Can we begin to evaluate these characters as primitive or derived for humans and for hominoids? Positing the cognitive-emotional characters of the common ancestor of humans and apes represents a stage of evolutionary hypothesis formulation that should precede the formulation of more complex explanatory models such as scenarios. Our current state of knowledge does not justify scenario-building for the evolution of ethics. But tackling the problem from an ape's eye view does give us a novel and potentially very productive point of entry into this fascinating evolutionary problem.

Povinelli and Godfrey provide examples of ethical behavior in humans and compare them with nonhuman primates, and place the issue of ethics in a broad perspective of nonhuman primates and in a cross-cultural perspective. Their conclusions are based on comparative primate material. Some of the questions that have been asked about ethics, particularly those equating altruism with ethics, are perhaps oversimplifications. Ethics is based on much more than altruism, for example, power structure and group behavior and how these are used to manipulate and shape morality. Finally can we identify a genetic basis for ethics?

Povinelli and Godfrey maintain that "morality depends on the ability to contribute values, intentions, and motives to others." They have conducted studies on chimpanzees to determine whether social attributions evolved before *H. sapiens*. Their research leads them to the conclusion that "social attribution in chimpanzees does exist but in a limited form," thus there is a contention that certain features of ethics are common to both humans and apes which may have evolved from their common ancestors. Ethical thought is basically a by-product of the development of cognitive processes. Ethics or altruism were not in themselves competitive advantages, because selfishness and altruism were unavoidably tied together and thus would cancel each other out. There are basic cognitive processes that have served as competitive advantages, and these cognitive processes can be seen in "lower" primates at a somewhat cruder level. These processes allow human choice and ethical thought, but such ethics in themselves have no evolutionary basis. Thus their mechanism for the development of ethics is evolutionary, but does not rely on the idea of altruism or correct ethical action as a competitive advantage. They illustrate a mechanism for ethics without having to use altruism as a competitive advantage. The cognitive capacity for altruism exists in animals which do not live according to any kind of ethical system, such as humans. We will never understand the origin of morality or altruism until we understand "social attributional capacities."

Adam Urbanek claims that human culture may be understood as a species-specific mode of psychosocial adaptation to the environment. It is expressed through a complex system functioning in the sphere of consciousness and in the sphere of material products. Formation of a worldview is one of the adaptive functions of culture, providing a comprehensive insight into the structure and history of the world and suggesting a deeper sense of human life. The worldview also implies the general goals to be achieved and specifies the admissible means to be used. Thus, the worldview determines the general strategy of behavior. Wierciński (1988) believes that, for effective steering of the society, the worldview should be linked with social institutions (i.e., power structures, religious and political organizations, educational systems). It is important that they dispose of material products of culture which may be used as information carriers (art, public announcements, press, and other modern mass media). Both the social institutions and the material products of culture control and support certain moral norms (expressed in characteristic attitudes and beliefs), that, in turn, provide the basis and justification for the norms of conduct of individuals and groups. Due to the educational and normative influence of the worldview, an individual is determined not only by genetic endowment and experience (that is, the past), but in a certain sense also by the future, as defined by the far-reaching goals set by culture. While Wierciński attempted to describe the functioning of the norms within the worldview system, Krzywicki (1951) suggested an explanation of their origin. The primary role of the norms of conduct (and moral principles as their justification) is that of regulators of individual and group conflicts. They decrease the severity of the conflicts and provide a means for their solution. Hence, the norms of conduct and ritualized behavior minimize the intragroup competition as well as stimulate cooperation. According to Krzywicki, the mechanism of a moral norms fixation involves elimination of nonconformist individuals from the group. The evolution of moral values also implies substitution of the old norms by the new, fitting better the existing level of social organization and development of material culture. Competition, combined with cooperation and controlled by a system of moral norms, is the driving force of cultural evolution.

Urbanek combines the theories of the East European thinkers, Kropotkin, Krzywicki and Wierciński, to create a sociobiological theory of evolutionary ethics in which moral norms control competition and cooperation, and create a force which derives culture through evolution. In this sense, it seems that ethics did not evolve, but rather helped evolution to progress.

To Lawrence Slobodkin, answers to the controversies associated with evolutionary ethics depend as much on the types of questions as on empirical facts or laws. He sees four obvious categories of questions about the association of evolution with ethics. First, are human ethical decisions constrained by a "biological human nature" because of either the nature of evolution itself or particular properties of human phylogeny? To the extent that these questions are empirically posed, he answers "No!" Second, is nature in some sense ethical? This is a projection from human ethics to nature and the answers are nonempirical, contingent on culture-bound definitions, and likely not to be definitive. Third, was the origin or development of the theory of evolution bound by the conscious or subconscious ethical assumptions of the developers? This is answered by the methodology of social and intellectual historians and historians of science. To some degree these methodologies are neither compatible nor even intertranslatable. Fourth, should ethical codes or decisions take cognizance of the facts of evolution and of evolutionary and ecological law? This involves two main subgroups of questions. First, what are the ethical criteria for dealing with the biological world in all its complexity, fragility and diversity? This leads to real questions of biology and management. Second, should we look to natural evolutionary and ecological laws for suggestions in the formulation of general ethical codes? This itself is an ethical question, which, in the context of this book, opens the recursion of how evolution should or should not help us deal with ethical questions, which is an ethical question, and so on.

Slobodkin suggests that the polemics in this area written by biologists, historians of science, philosophers, and historiographers usually relate either to only one of the above questions, which leaves the studies incomplete, or combines aspects of several of them, which leaves the studies confused. Ethics are culturally bound, and it is coincidental that many cultural differences coincide with genetic differencs.

Evelyn Fox Keller and Margaret S. Ewing believe that the difficulties and ambiguities inherent in the common-sense notion of a biological "individual" are notorious, and have been well laid out by Hull (1980). In popular parlance, a biological "individual" is an organism, more or less like ourselves—at the very least, an animal, and usually, a vertebrate. Yet, despite the obvious inadequacy of this definition for the range of living forms encountered in the natural world, it is precisely to this common-sense understanding that biologists (and biology texts) tacitly appeal in their most conventional uses of the term. From its inadequacy, some would argue for the elimination of this common-sense notion of "individual" from biological discourse; from its ubiquity, by contrast, Keller and Ewing argue for further examination. It may not be possible either to salvage or to eliminate the "idea of individuality" from biological discourse; it may, however, be possible to sort out the different ideas which that term, in fact, subsumes, and the ways in which different criteria of individuality depend on disciplinary and other interests. Both what counts and how one counts depend on spatial and temporal stances as well as on the purposes for which one needs to count; they also depend on metaphysical and ideological commitments. Furthermore, by no existing criteria will the resulting tally be unambiguous. Even that paradigm of common-sensical individuality, "man," is an idealization only approximately realized in nature. Neither physiologically nor reproductively autonomous, he is also not necessarily genetically unique.

I think that there is a difference between the behavior of species and of individuals. We never (or almost never) consider ants as individuals, but instead we think of them as a colony. Ethologists may work with individuals, but sociobiologists study populations. When speaking of the human behavior we think of ourself, or, at best, about an individual. We are thinking statistically about ants, but not about humans. Thinking about human behavior statistically may discover some pattern which, nevertheless, will break down when thinking about individuals. An individual is not an isolated being, but although separate, forms a part of the community. Thus the individual behaves in response to the law of the community and its ethics. If, as cladists claim, a species is an individual, then selection will work on species. Therefore, in species or in individuals certain members (e.g., red blood cells) will always act at a certain time and in certain circumstances (or all the time) for the benefit of other members. Darwin abolished species, and in the *Origin* his species exists only in a particular time slice. It is strange, therefore, that evolutionists now concerned with species as individuals call themselves Darwinians, and believe species to be not only real, but even individuals.

Keller and Ewing address these basic problems from a somewhat different angle. They are not concerned with "who we are," but they argue that it is difficult to define an individual, and hence humans.

Mary Catherine Bateson claims that the human domain of ethics involves those areas where choice is possible, and this domain is changed both by technical capability and by factors which structure the understanding of these possibilities, such as attention. The evolving pattern of human adaptation involves changes at both these levels. The human capacity to act with ever-increasing impact on the natural environment has led to whole new areas of ethical concern which propose changes in patterns of human attention and in the formulation of purposes.

Her chapter explores the hypothesis, put forward twenty years ago by Gregory Bateson, that the human capacity for conscious purpose involves a structuring of attention such that, in the service of conscious purpose, decisions are made based on a biased selection of environmental information. The focus is on the relationship between a gender-based division of labor and the development of complementary patterns of purposiveness and attention in relation to sex roles. It explores the implications for human adaptation of cognitive differences in how the ethical implications of decisions and the range of phenomena relevant to them are conceptualized.

Who Are We?

Dualism seems to be a part of human nature. The unresolved dichotomy between the rationalists and the empiricists is a subset of the nature versus nurture dichotomy. Nature is innate, unacquirable and unalterable. Nurture is the acquired product of culture. To a rationalist, knowledge is derived from mind or nature, and, therefore, acquisition of knowledge is genetic. To an empiricist, knowledge is derived from experience or environment, and, therefore, is acquired. Who is right cannot be resolved until we learn how our brain works, and how we invented calculus. It is possible that our dual interpretations of nature versus nurture have deep biological bases in bilateral symmetry, two sexes, or in being bimanus. This great dichotomy in our worldview may be at the base of the controversy in evolutionary ethics. I think, however, that the search for evolutionary ethics represents our deep and profound yearning to resolve *who we are*, and thus, to discover our place in the universe. This search has been scientific and philosophical, but also has involved a myth of the origin and definition of humanity.

First, the question of the relationship of man to "lower animals" had to be asked; in our dichotomous view, either the similarities were seen or the differences were magnifying the big fault between humans and nonhumans. As Dewey (below) shows, one school claimed that our physical, intellectual, and moral characteristics evolved gradually from apes, and, therefore, our ethics also evolved from animals. The other school made the difference between us and all other animals so large that the gap was unbridgeable, and hence morality was a uniquely human trait. This controversy has not been resolved, it has only shifted. There was (and still is, in some parts of the world and in the science fiction of the West) a myth that humans and animals were once a single family, that the metamorphosis from human to animal and vice versa was common, that some were part animal and part human (centaurs), and that they could easily talk to each other. A wolf could assume a human shape; a witch could fly; a devil was half-human and half-animal, often entirely animal, and sometimes with goat feet; an angel had bird wings. This was a traditional, mythical explanation of truths of natural phenomena, events, and beliefs. Because such beliefs were associated with religion, they are now held in low esteem. Society (or population) acts and thinks collectively and for itself. It has its own memory, history, ethics, and myths. While it is true that it is an individual who initiates the first action or behavior that later becomes a myth or a part of the ethical system, it is the population that accepts, modifies, and inherits it by passing it from generation to generation. These myths are passed down without known authorship, are deeply ingrained in social practices and ethics, and become part of the history. They express the population's wishes and thinking. They were the ethics of the day. In the future the red shift of light may become a myth, the big bang itself may become the sterile barrier to the inquiry into the myth of the pre-big bang universe. Our evolutionary ethics may also turn to myth.

Our question, *What is human?*, involves the reduction of ethics to biology. I will try, with some liberty, to rephrase, however simply, Hempel's (1966: chap. 8) argument on reducibility. Hempel argues that reducibility of biology to physics and to chemistry is not easy. For example, you may resolve penicillin to a chemical equation, but not as a substance produced by a living fungus *Penicillium notatum*. Reduction of morality to biology is even more difficult. To say that a person is moral is to say that he acts in a certain way in certain circumstances. But both behavior and circumstances vary in time and in space. We can neither define all possibilities of moral behavior, nor construe a definition that would include all moral behavior. Nor can we define moral behavior in terms of biology. Moral behavior does not depend on facts, but on what the agent knows and believes. The man who distracts the murderer from killing and thus exposes himself to danger, does not act morally if he does not *know* that the murderer was about to commit a murder. Thus moral behavior hinges on *beliefs and wants* of what to accomplish. These concepts are not definable in terms of biology. At least, not yet.

The differences between humans and animals are much greater than in their anatomy. The characters that separate humans from all the other animals are more than smoothness of skin, shape and size of finger nails, or dental formulae. Such anatomical characters are trivial and separate all species from each other, not only humans from nonhumans. Systematists may also see the differences in genetics and evolution, but even these are not enough to determine the boundary of humanity. By humanity we also mean a state or quality of being humane, being sympathetic and compassionate, being *ethical*. We must see in humanness the opposite of animalism, the opposite of amorality. We cannot, and we must not, think of humanity in terms of biology only.

Thus, consciously or unconsciously, we are asking "what is it to be human?" Are humans only bipedal talking mammals? Or should we place humans in the genus *Homo*, and *Homo* in the family Hominidae, or in a level above the animals? Is it *Homo bimanus? H. sapiens? H. economicus? H. ethicus?* Where is the pigeonhole to place humans? systematics, zoology, or ethics? in all of them? or in a return to the very primordial basic myth?

To Huxley the conflict between the two worldviews exists, and must exist. It is the conflict that makes us human! If the conflict will be resolved we will lose humanity. We will either become *Rex omnium creatorum* or animals. However, we no longer see the limits of humanity between angels and animals. Instead we limit the definition to a few criteria: anthropologists to behavior, systematists to anatomy, ethicists to moral behavior. What then would ethical behavior become? The sum total of all human traits. This will be a return to myths of the meaning and purpose of life. These are profound questions. To Huxley all the cosmos condemns us to be animals, and places us in a world that knows nothing of love, virtue, or ethics. He assumes that happiness, love, and goodness as well as suffering, tragedy, and terror are strictly human properties, that human nature is unique, and that only humans have consciousness. Huxley revolted against this worldview that he himself created. His is a deep conflict against the cosmos, the deep desire to separate humanness from animalism. I agree that it is this which differentiates us from animals. To Huxley, to be human means the separation from the cosmos, the revolt against the cosmos. To be human is to be in conflict with the cosmos. But this conflict that makes us humans will not resolve the question of who we are. We can only delineate the boundary of humanity broadly, but we cannot define it exactly. To Huxley, being human is not genetic, but humanness must be acquired through a painful fight against the cosmos.

Terminalia. Kuhn's explanation of paradigm, and of paradigm shift, does not apply to evolutionary ethics. Although Arthur Fisher (1991) has eloquently demonstrated the thesis that sociobiology has passed the Kuhnian paradigm test, I am not certain that evolutionary ethics has reached that stage. Neither do I accept the directional development of ideas, nor that this directionality leads to a new and radical worldview based on a continuation of the previous ideas. Ideas are very complex products of the human mind and social influences. They never follow a single line, nor, as Dewey (below) points out, are they developed in a straight line, but are rather like a sailboat on high seas with constantly changing winds. Not a single problem is followed from the beginning to the end. As soon as a problem is defined and the battle lines are drawn, the topography changes.

Huxley warns that two very different questions that people fail to discriminate are whether evolution accounts for morality, and whether the theory of evolution in general can be adopted as an ethical principle. He advocates the first, but emphatically rejects the second, the evolutionary ethics based upon it (1900:382).

When we are born we are dropped onto the big wheel of history, dropped on it without our consent or knowledge, dropped into history to form a part of it. To be human is to have a consciousness of self, of nature, and of history, and to fight for humanity against cosmos. Humanity is an abstraction—a concept, at the very bottom of which is animalism. Evolutionary ethics is an introduction to the great monograph on what is human.

References

Alexander, R. D. 1980. *Darwinism and Human Affairs*. Seattle, WA: University of Washington Press.

Alexander, R. D. 1987. *The Biology of Moral Systems*. Hawthorne, NY: Aldine de Gruyter.

Beckstrom, J. H. 1985. *Sociobiology and the Law. The Biology of Altruism in the Courtroom of the Future*. Urbana: University of Illinois Press.

Cela-Conde, C. J. 1986. The challenge of evolutionary ethics. *Biology & Philosophy* 1: 293-97.

Dawkins, R. 1976. *The Selfish Gene*. Oxford: Oxford University Press.

Degler, C. N. 1991. *In Search of Human Nature. The Decline and Revival of Darwinism in American Social Thought*. New York: Oxford.

Desmond, A. 1989. *The Politics of Evolution*. Chicago: University of Chicago Press.

Dewey, J. 1910. *The Influence of Darwin on Philosophy*. New York: Henry Holt and Co.

Eddington, A. S. 1929. *The Nature of the Physical World*. New York: Cambridge University Press.

Fisher, A. 1991. A new synthesis comes of age. *Mosaic* 22(1):2-17.

Gewirth, A. 1978. *Reason and Morality*. Chicago: University of Chicago Press.

Gewirth, A. 1982. *Human Rights: Essays on Justification and Application*. Chicago: University of Chicago Press.

Gewirth, A. 1986. The problem of specificity in evolutionary ethics. *Biology & Philosophy* 1:297-305.

Goldschmidt, W., ed. 1957. *Ways of Mankind*. Boston: The Beacon Press.

Hempel, C. G. 1966. *Philosophy of Natural Science*. Foundations of Philosophy Series, ed. E. and M. Beardsley. Englewood Cliffs, NJ: Prentice-Hall.

Henderson, L. J. 1913. *The Fitness of the Environment*. New York: Macmillan.

Hughes, W. 1986. Richards' defense of evolutionary ethics. *Biology and History* 1:306-15.

Hull, D. 1980. Individuality and selection. *Annual Reviews of Ecology and Systematics* 11:311-32.

Huxley, L. 1900. *Life and Letters of Thomas Henry Huxley*. Vol. 2. New York: Appleton and Co.

Krzywicki, L. 1951. Rozwój moralności (Development of morality), 233-95. In *Studia Socjologiczne. Wybór (Sociological Studies. A Selection of Papers)*. Warsaw: PIW.

Linton, R. 1957. Universal ethical principles, 72-83. In *Ways of Mankind*, ed. W. Goldschmidt. Boston: The Beacon Press.

Mayr, E. 1988. *Toward a New Philosophy of Biology. Observations of an Evolutionist*. Cambridge, MA: Belknap Press.

Paradis, J. G., and G. C. Williams, eds. 1989. *Evolution and Ethics*. Princeton, NJ: Princeton University Press.

Pugh, G. E. 1977. *The Biological Origin of Human Values*. New York: Basic Books.

Rachels, J. 1991. *Created from Animals. The Moral Implications of Darwinism*. Oxford: Oxford University Press.

Richards, R. J. 1986a. A defense of evolutionary ethics. *Biology & Philosophy* 1:265-93.

Richards, R. J. 1986b. Justification through biological faith: A rejoinder. *Biology & Philosophy* 1:337-54.

Richards, R. J. 1988. The moral foundations of the idea of evolutionary progress: Darwin, Spencer, and the neo-Darwinians, 129-48. In *Evolutionary Progress*, ed. M. H. Nitecki. Chicago: University of Chicago Press.

Richards, R. J. 1989. *Darwin and the Emergence of Evolutionary Theories of Mind and Behavior*. Chicago: University of Chicago Press.

Ruse, M. 1984. The morality of the gene. *Monist* 67:167-99.

Ruse, M. 1986a. Evolutionary ethics: A Phoenix arisen. *Zygon* 21(1):95-112.

Ruse, M. 1986b. *Homosexuality: A Philosophical Inquiry*. Oxford: Blackwell.

Ruse, M. 1987. Darwinism and determinism. *Zygon* 22(4):419-42.

Ruse, M., and E. O. Wilson. 1985. The evolution of ethics. *New Scientist* 1478 (17th October):50-52.

Ruse, M., and E. O. Wilson. 1986. Moral philosophy as applied science. *Philosophy* 61:173-92.

Sober, E. 1984. *The Nature of Selection*. Cambridge, MA: MIT Press.

Sober, E. 1988. What is evolutionary altruism? 75-99. In *New Essays on Philosophy of Biology*, ed. B. Linsky and M. Matthen. *Canadian Journal of Philosophy*. Suppl. Vol. 14.

Stephen, L. 1907. *The Science of Ethics*. 2d. ed. London: Smith, Elder & Co.

Thomas, L. 1986. Biological moralism. *Biology & Philosophy* 1:316-25.

Trigg, R. 1986. Evolutionary ethics. *Biology & Philosophy* 1:325-35.

Wierciński, A. 1988. Antropologiczna koncepcja rozwoju światopogladu (An anthropological concept of the world view of development). *Seria Antropologia* 12:30-41.

Wilson, E. O. 1975. *Sociobiology: The New Synthesis*. Cambridge, MA: Harvard University Press.

Wilson, E. O. 1978. *On Human Nature*. Cambridge, MA: Harvard University Press.

Wilson, E. O. 1984. *Biophilia*. Cambridge, MA: Harvard University Press.

Ethics and the Cosmic Order

Evolution and Ethics

Thomas H. Huxley

Evolution & Ethics and Other Essays, pp. v-ix, 1-116, are reprinted with minor format changes from *Collected Essays* [1894] 1898. Vol. IX. London: Macmillan. The Latin and Greek quotations, but not the French, are translated into English.

Preface

The discourse on "Evolution and Ethics," reprinted in the first half of the present volume, was delivered before the University of Oxford, as the second of the annual lectures founded by Mr. Romanes: whose name I may not write without deploring the untimely death, in the flower of his age, of a friend endeared to me, as to so many others, by his kindly nature; and justly valued by all his colleagues for his powers of investigation and his zeal for the advancement of knowledge. I well remember, when Mr. Romanes' early work came into my hands, as one of the secretaries of the Royal Society, how much I rejoiced in the accession to the ranks of the little army of workers in science of a recruit so well qualified to take a high place among us.

It was at my friend's urgent request that I agreed to undertake the lecture, should I be honoured with an official proposal to give it, though I confess not without misgivings, if only on account of the serious fatigue and hoarseness which public speaking has for some years caused me; while I knew that it would be my fate to follow the most accomplished and facile orator of our time, whose indomitable youth is in no matter more manifest than in his penetrating and musical voice. A certain saying about comparisons intruded itself somewhat importunately.

And even if I disregarded the weakness of my body in the matter of voice, and that of my mind in the matter of vanity, there remained a third difficulty. For several reasons, my attention, during a number of years, has been much directed to the bearing of modern scientific thought on the problems of morals and of politics, and I did not care to be diverted from that topic. Moreover, I thought it the most important and the worthiest which, at the present time, could engage the attention even of an ancient and renowned University.

But it is a condition of the Romanes foundation that the lecturer shall abstain from treating of either Religion or Politics; and it appeared to me that, more than most, perhaps, I was bound to act, not merely up to the letter, but in the spirit, of that prohibition. Yet Ethical Science is, on all sides, so entangled with Religion and Politics, that the lecturer who essays to touch the former without coming into contact with either of the latter, needs all the dexterity of an egg-dancer; and may even discover that his sense of clearness and his sense of propriety come into conflict, by no means to the advantage of the former.

I had little notion of the real magnitude of these difficulties when I set about my task; but I am consoled for my pains and anxiety by observing that none of the multitudinous criticisms with which I have been favoured and, often, instructed, find fault with me on the score of having strayed out of bounds.

Among my critics there are not a few to whom I feel deeply indebted for the careful attention which they have given to the exposition thus hampered; and further weakened, I am afraid, by my forgetfulness of a maxim touching lectures of a popular character, which has descended to me from that prince of lecturers, Mr. Faraday. He was once asked by a beginner, called upon to address a highly select and cultivated audience, what he might suppose his hearers to know already. Whereupon the past master of the art of exposition emphatically replied "Nothing!"

To my shame as a retired veteran, who has all his life profited by this great precept of lecturing strategy, I forgot all about it just when it would have been most useful. I was fatuous enough to imagine that a number of propositions, which I thought established, and which, in fact, I had advanced without challenge on former occasions, needed no repetition.

I have endeavoured to repair my error by prefacing the lecture with some matter—chiefly elementary or recapitulatory—to which I have given the title of "Prolegomena." I wish I could have hit upon a heading of less pedantic aspect which would have served my purpose; and if it be urged that the new building looks over large for the edifice to which it is added, I can only plead the precedent of the ancient architects, who always made the adytum the smallest part of the temple.

If I had attempted to reply in full to the criticisms to which I have referred, I know not what extent of ground would have been covered by my *pronaos.* All I have endeavoured to do, at present, is to remove that which seems to have proved a stumbling-block to many—namely, the apparent paradox that ethical nature, while born of cosmic nature, is necessarily at enmity with its parent. Unless the arguments set forth in the Prolegomena, in the simplest language at my command, have some flaw which I am unable to discern, this seeming paradox is a truth, as great as it is plain, the recognition of which is fundamental for the ethical philosopher.

We cannot do without our inheritance from the forefathers who were the puppets of the cosmic process; the society which renounces it must be destroyed from without. Still less can we do with too much of it; the society in which it dominates must be destroyed from within.

The motive of the drama of human life is the necessity, laid upon every man who comes into the world, of discovering the mean between self-assertion and self-restraint suited to his character and his circumstances. And the eternally tragic aspect of the drama lies in this: that the problem set before us is one the elements of which can be but imperfectly known, and of which even an approximately right solution rarely presents itself, until that stern critic, aged experience, has been furnished with ample justification for venting his sarcastic humour upon the irreparable blunders we have already made.

Prolegomena
[1894]

It may be safely assumed that, two thousand years ago, before Cæsar set foot in southern Britain, the whole country-side visible from the windows of the room in which I write, was in what is called "the state of nature." Except, it may be, by raising a few sepulchral mounds, such as those which still, here and there, break the flowing contours of the downs, man's hands had made no mark upon it; and the thin veil of vegetation which overspread the broad-backed heights and the shelving sides of the coombs was unaffected by his industry. The native grasses and weeds, the scattered patches of gorse, contended with one another for the possession of the scanty surface soil; they fought against the droughts of summer, the frosts of winter, and the furious gales which swept, with unbroken force, now from the Atlantic, and now from the North Sea, at all times of the year; they filled up, as they best might, the gaps made in their ranks by all sorts of underground and overground animal ravagers. One year with another, an average population, the floating balance of the unceasing struggle for existence among the indigenous plants, maintained itself. It is as little to be doubted, that an essentially similar state of nature prevailed, in this region, for many thousand years before the coming of Cæsar; and there is no assignable reason for denying that it might continue to exist through an equally prolonged futurity, except for the intervention of man.

Reckoned by our customary standards of duration, the native vegetation, like the "everlasting hills" which it clothes, seems a type of permanence. The little Amarella Gentians, which abound in some places to-day, are the descendants of those that were trodden underfoot by the prehistoric savages who have left their flint tools about, here and there; and they followed ancestors which, in the climate of the glacial epoch, probably flourished better than they do now. Compared with the long past of this humble plant, all the history of civilized men is but an episode.

Yet nothing is more certain than that, measured by the liberal scale of time-keeping of the universe, this present state of nature, however it may seem to have gone and to go on for ever, is but a fleeting phase of her infinite variety; merely the last of the series of changes which the earth's surface has undergone in the course of the millions of years of its existence. Turn back a square foot of the thin turf, and the solid foundation of the land, exposed in cliffs of chalk five hundred feet high on the adjacent shore, yields full assurance of a time when the sea covered the site of the "everlasting hills"; and when the vegetation of what land lay nearest, was as different from the present Flora of the Sussex downs, as that of Central Africa now is.[1] No less certain is it that, between the time during which the chalk was formed and that at which the original turf came into existence, thousands of centuries elapsed, in the course of which, the state of nature of the ages during which the chalk was deposited, passed into that which now is, by changes so slow that, in the coming and going of the generations of men, had such witnessed them, the contemporary conditions would have seemed to be unchanging and unchangeable.

But it is also certain that, before the deposition of the chalk, a vastly longer period had elapsed, throughout which it is easy to follow the traces of the same process of ceaseless modification and of the internecine struggle for existence of living things; and that even when we can get no further back, it is not because there is any reason to think we have reached the beginning, but because the trail of the most ancient life remains hidden, or has become obliterated.

Thus that state of nature of the world of plants, which we began by considering, is far from possessing the attribute of permanence. Rather its very essence is imper-manence. It may have lasted twenty or thirty thousand years, it may last for twenty or thirty thousand years more, without obvious change; but, as surely as it has followed upon a very different state, so it will be followed by an equally different condition. That which endures is not one or another association of living forms, but the process of which the cosmos is the product, and of which these are among the transitory expres-sions. And in the living world, one of the most characteristic features of this cosmic process is the struggle for existence, the competition of each with all, the result of which is the selection, that is to say, the survival of those forms which, on the whole, are best adapted to the conditions which at any period obtain; and which are, therefore, in that respect, and only in that respect, the fittest.[2] The acme reached by the cosmic process in the vegetation of the downs is seen in the turf, with its weeds and gorse. Under the conditions, they have come out of the struggle victorious; and, by surviving, have proved that they are the fittest to survive.

That the state of nature, at any time, is a temporary phase of a process of incessant change, which has been going on for innumerable ages, appears to me to be a proposition as well established as any in modern history. Paleontology assures us, in addition, that the ancient philosophers who, with less reason, held the same doctrine, erred in supposing that the phases formed a cycle, exactly repeating the past, exactly foreshadowing the future, in their rotations. On the contrary, it furnishes us with conclusive reasons for thinking that, if every link in the ancestry of these humble indigenous plants had been preserved and were accessible to us, the whole would present a converging series of forms of gradually diminishing complexity, until, at some period in the history of thc earth, far more remote than any of which organic remains have yet been discovered, they would merge in those low groups among which the boundaries between animal and vegetable life become effaced.[3]

The word "evolution," now generally applied to the cosmic process, has had a singular history, and is used in various senses.[4] Taken in its popular signification it means progressive development, that is, gradual change from a condition of relative uniformity to one of relative complexity; but its connotation has been widened to include the phenomena of retrogressive metamorphosis, that is, of progress from a condition of relative complexity to one of relative uniformity.

As a natural process, of the same character as the development of a tree from its seed, or of a fowl from its egg, evolution excludes creation and all other kinds of supernatural intervention. As the expression of a fixed order, every stage of which is the effect of causes operating according to definite rules, the conception of evolution no less excludes that of chance. It is very desirable to remember that evolution is not an explanation of the cosmic process, but merely a generalized statement of the method and results of that process. And, further, that, if there is proof that the cosmic process was set going by any agent, then that agent will be the creator of it and of all its products, although supernatural intervention may remain strictly excluded from its further course.

So far as that limited revelation of the nature of things, which we call scientific knowledge, has yet gone, it tends, with constantly increasing emphasis, to the belief that, not merely the world of plants, but that of animals; not merely living things, but the whole fabric of the earth; not merely our planet, but the whole solar system; not merely our star and its satellites, but the millions of similar bodies which bear witness to the order which pervades boundless space, and has endured through boundless time; are all working out their predestined courses of evolution.

With none of these have I anything to do, at present, except with that exhibited by the forms of life which tenant the earth. All plants and animals exhibit the tendency to vary, the causes of which have yet to be ascertained; it is the tendency of the conditions of life, at any given time, while favouring the existence of the variations best adapted to them, to oppose that of the rest and thus to exercise selection; and all living things tend to multiply without limit, while the means of support are limited; the obvious cause of which is the production of offspring more numerous than their progenitors, but with equal expectation of life in the actuarial sense. Without the first tendency there could be no evolution. Without the second, there would be no good reason why one variation should disappear and another take its place; that is to say, there would be no selection. Without the third, the struggle for existence, the agent of the selective process in the state of nature, would vanish.[5]

Granting the existence of these tendencies, all the known facts of the history of plants and of animals may be brought into rational correlation. And this is more than can be said for any other hypothesis that I know of. Such hypotheses, for example, as that of the existence of a primitive, orderless chaos; of a passive and sluggish eternal matter moulded, with but partial success, by archetypal ideas; of a brand-new world-stuff suddenly created and swiftly shaped by a supernatural power; receive no encouragement, but the contrary, from our present knowledge. That our earth may once have formed part of a nebulous cosmic magma is certainly possible, indeed seems highly probable; but there is no reason to doubt that order reigned there, as completely as amidst what we regard as the most finished works of nature or of man.[6] The faith which is born of knowledge, finds its object in an eternal order, bringing forth ceaseless change, through endless time, in endless space; the manifestations of the cosmic energy alternating between phases of potentiality and phases of explication. It may be that, as Kant suggests,[7] every cosmic magma predestined to evolve into a new world, has been the no less predestined end of a vanished predecessor.

Three or four years have elapsed since the state of nature, to which I have referred, was brought to an end, so far as a small patch of the soil is concerned, by the intervention of man. The patch was cut off from the rest by a wall; within the area thus protected, the native vegetation was, as far as possible, extirpated; while a colony of strange plants was imported and set down in its place. In short, it was made into a garden. At the present time, this artificially treated area presents an aspect extraordinarily different from that of so much of the land as remains in the state of nature, outside the wall. Trees, shrubs, and herbs, many of them appertaining to the state of nature of remote parts of the globe, abound and flourish. Moreover, considerable quantities of vegetables, fruits, and flowers are produced, of kinds which neither now exist, nor have ever existed, except under conditions such as obtain in the garden; and which, therefore, are as much works of the art of man as the frames and glass-houses in which some of them are raised. That the "state of Art," thus created in the state of nature by man, is sustained by and dependent on him, would at once become apparent, if the watchful supervision of the gardener were withdrawn, and the antagonistic influences of the general cosmic process were no longer sedulously warded off, or counteracted. The walls and gates would decay; quadrupedal and bipedal intruders would devour and tread down the useful and beautiful plants; birds, insects, blight, and mildew would work their will; the seeds of the native plants, carried by winds or other agencies, would immigrate, and in virtue of their long-earned special adaptation to the local conditions, these despised native weeds would soon choke their choice exotic rivals. A century or two hence, little beyond the foundations of the wall and of the houses and frames would be left, in evidence of the victory of the cosmic powers at work in the state of nature, over the temporary obstacles to their supremacy, set up by the art of the horticulturist.

It will be admitted that the garden is as much a work of art,[8] or artifice, as anything that can be mentioned. The energy localised in certain human bodies, directed by similarly localised intellects has produced a collocation of other material bodies which could not be brought about in the state of nature. The same proposition is true of all the works of man's hands, from a flint implement to a cathedral or a chronometer; and it is because it is true, that we call these things artificial, term them works of art, or artifice, by way of distinguishing them from the products of the cosmic process, working outside man, which we call natural, or works of nature. The distinction thus drawn between the works of nature and those of man, is universally recognised; and it is, as I conceive, both useful and justifiable.

No doubt, it may be properly urged that the operation of human energy and intelligence, which has brought into existence and maintains the garden, by what I have called "the horticultural process," is, strictly speaking, part and parcel of the cosmic process. And no one could more readily agree to that proposition than I. In fact, I do not know that any one has taken more pains than I have, during the last thirty years, to insist upon the doctrine, so much reviled in the early part of that period, that man, physical, intellectual, and moral, is as much a part of nature, as purely a product of the cosmic process, as the humblest weed.[9]

But if, following up this admission, it is urged that, such being the case, the cosmic process cannot be in antagonism with that horticultural process which is part of itself—I can only reply, that if the conclusion that the two are antagonistic is logically absurd, I am sorry for logic, because, as we have seen, the fact is so. The garden is in the same position as every other work of man's art; it is a result of the cosmic process working through and by human energy and intelligence; and, as is the case with every other artificial thing set up in the state of nature, the influences of the latter are constantly tending to break it down and destroy it. No doubt, the Forth bridge and an ironclad in the offing, are, in ultimate resort, products of the cosmic process; as much so as the river which flows under the one, or the seawater on which the other floats. Nevertheless, every breeze strains the bridge a little, every tide does something to weaken its foundations; every change of temperature alters the adjustment of its parts, produces friction and consequent wear and tear. From time to time, the bridge must be repaired, just as the ironclad must go into dock; simply because nature is always tending to reclaim that which her child, man, has borrowed from her and has arranged in combinations which are not those favoured by the general cosmic process.

Thus, it is not only true that the cosmic energy, working through man upon a portion of the plant world, opposes the same energy as it works through the state of nature, but a similar antagonism is everywhere manifest between the artificial and the natural. Even in the state of nature itself, what is the struggle for existence but the antagonism of the results of the cosmic process in the region of life, one to another?[10]

Not only is the state of nature hostile to the state of art of the garden; but the principle of the horticultural process, by which the latter is created and maintained, is antithetic to that of the cosmic process. The characteristic feature of the latter is the intense and unceasing competition of the struggle for existence. The characteristic of the former is the elimination of that struggle, by the removal of the conditions which give rise to it. The tendency of the cosmic process is to bring about the adjustment of the forms of plant life to the current conditions; the tendency of the horticultural process is the adjustment of the conditions to the needs of the forms of plant life which the gardener desires to raise.

The cosmic process uses unrestricted multiplication as the means whereby hundreds compete for the place and nourishment adequate for one; it employs frost and drought to cut off the weak and unfortunate; to survive, there is need not only of strength, but of flexibility and of good fortune.

The gardener, on the other hand, restricts multiplication; provides that each plant shall have sufficient space and nourishment; protects from frost and drought; and, in every other way, attempts to modify the conditions, in such a manner as to bring about the survival of those forms which most nearly approach the standard of the useful, or the beautiful, which he has in his mind.

If the fruits and the tubers, the foliage and the flowers thus obtained, reach, or sufficiently approach, that ideal, there is no reason why the *status quo* attained should not be indefinitely prolonged. So long as the state of nature remains approximately the same, so long will the energy and intelligence which created the garden suffice to maintain it. However, the limits within which this mastery of man over nature can be maintained are narrow. If the conditions of the cretaceous epoch returned, I fear the most skilful of gardeners would have to give up the cultivation of apples and goose-berries; while, if those of the glacial period once again obtained, open asparagus beds would be superfluous, and the training of fruit trees against the most favourable of south walls, a waste of time and trouble.

But it is extremely important to note that, the state of nature remaining the same, if the produce does not satisfy the gardener, it may be made to approach his ideal more closely. Although the struggle for existence may be at end, the possibility of progress remains. In discussions on these topics, it is often strangely forgotten that the essential conditions of the modification, or evolution, of living things are variation and hereditary transmission. Selection is the means by which certain variations are favoured and their progeny preserved. But the struggle for existence is only one of the means by which selection may be effected. The endless varieties of cultivated flowers, fruits, roots, tubers, and bulbs are not products of selection by means of the struggle for existence, but of direct selection, in view of an ideal of utility or beauty. Amidst a multitude of plants, occupyiug thc same station and subjected to the same conditions, in the garden, varieties arise. The varieties tending in a given direction are preserved, and the rest are destroyed. And the same process takes place among the varieties until, for example, the wild kale becomes a cabbage, or the wild *Viola tricolor* a prize pansy.

The process of colonization presents analogies to the formation of a garden which are highly instructive. Suppose a shipload of English colonists sent to form a settlement, in such a country as Tasmania was in the middle of the last century. On landing, they find themselves in the midst of a state of nature, widely different from that left behind them in everything but the most general physical conditions. The common plants, the common birds and quadrupeds, are as totally distinct as the men from anything to be seen on the side of the globe from which they come. The colonists proceed to put an end to this state of things over as large an area as they desire to occupy. They clear away the native vegetation, extirpate or drive out the animal population, so far as may be necessary, and take measures to defend themselves from the re-immigration of either. In their place, they introduce English grain and fruit trees; English dogs, sheep, cattle, horses; and English men; in fact, they set up a new Flora and Fauna and a new variety of mankind, within the old state of nature. Their farms and pastures represent a garden on a great scale, and themselves the gardeners who have to keep it up, in watchful antagonism to the old *regime*. Considered as a whole, the colony is a composite unit introduced into the old state of nature; and, thenceforward, a competitor in the struggle for existence, to conquer or be vanquished.

Under the conditions supposed, there is no doubt of the result, if the work of the colonists be carried out energetically and with intelligent combination of all their forces. On the other hand, if they are slothful, stupid, and careless; or if they waste their energies in contests with one another, the chances are that the old state of nature will have the best of it. The native savage will destroy the immigrant civilized man; of the English animals and plants some will be extirpated by their indigenous rivals, others will pass into the feral state and themselves become components of the state of nature. In a few decades, all other traces of the settlement will have vanished.

Let us now imagine that some administrative authority, as far superior in power and intelligence to men, as men are to their cattle, is set over the colony, charged to deal with its human elements in such a manner as to assure the victory of the settlement over the antagonistic influences of the state of nature in which it is set down. He would proceed in the same fashion as that in which the gardener dealt with his garden. In the first place, he would, as far as possible, put a stop to the influence of external competition by thoroughly extirpating and excluding the native rivals, whether men, beasts, or plants. And our administrator would select his human agents, with a view to his ideal of a successful colony, just as the gardener selects his plants with a view to his ideal of useful or beautiful products.

In the second place, in order that no struggle for the means of existence between these human agents should weaken the efficiency of the corporate whole in the battle with the state of nature, he would make arrangements by which each would be provided with those means; and would be relieved from the fear of being deprived of them by his stronger or more cunning fellows. Laws, sanctioned by the combined force of the colony, would restrain the self-assertion of each man within the limits required for the maintenance of peace. In other words, the cosmic struggle for existence, as between man and man, would be rigorously suppressed; and selection, by its means, would be as completely excluded as it is from the garden.

At the same time, the obstacles to the full development of the capacities of the colonists by other conditions of the state of nature than those already mentioned, would be removed by the creation of artificial conditions of existence of a more favourable character. Protection against extremes of heat and cold would be afforded by houses and clothing; drainage and irrigation works would antagonise the effects of excessive rain and excessive drought; roads, bridges, canals, carriages, and ships would overcome the natural obstacles to locomotion and transport; mechanical engines would supplement the natural strength of men and of their draught animals; hygienic precautions would check, or remove, the natural causes of disease. With every step of this progress in civilization, the colonists would become more and more independent of the state of nature; more and more, their lives would be conditioned by a state of art. In order to attain his ends, the administrator would have to avail himself of the courage, industry, and co-operative intelligence of the settlers; and it is plain that the interest of the community would be best served by increasing the proportion of persons who possess such qualities, and diminishing that of persons devoid of them. In other words, by selection directed towards an ideal.

Thus the administrator might look to the establishment of an earthly paradise, a true garden of Eden, in which all things should work together towards the well-being of the gardeners: within which the cosmic process, the coarse struggle for existence of the state of nature should be abolished; in which that state should be replaced by a state of art; where every plant and every lower animal should be adapted to human wants, and would perish if human supervision and protection were withdrawn; where men themselves should have been selected, with a view to their efficiency as organs for the performance of the functions of a perfected society. And this ideal polity would have been brought about, not by gradually adjusting the men to the conditions around them, but by creating artificial conditions for them; not by allowing the free play of the struggle for existence, but by excluding that struggle; and by substituting selection directed towards the administrator's ideal for the selection it exercises.

But the Eden would have its serpent, and a very subtle beast too. Man shares with the rest of the living world the mighty instinct of reproduction and its consequence, the tendency to multiply with great rapidity. The better the measures of the administrator achieved their object, the more completely the destructive agencies of the state of nature were defeated, the less would that multiplication be checked.

On the other hand, within the colony, the enforcement of peace, which deprives every man of the power to take away the means of existence from another, simply because he is the stronger, would have put an end to the struggle for existence between the colonists, and the competition for the commodities of existence, which would alone remain, is no check upon population.

Thus, as soon as the colonists began to multiply, the administrator would have to face the tendency to the reintroduction of the cosmic struggle into his artificial fabric, in consequence of the competition, not merely for the commodities, but for the means of existence. When the colony reached the limit of possible expansion, the surplus population must be disposed of somehow; or the fierce struggle for existence must recommence and destroy that peace, which is the fundamental condition of the maintenance of the state of art against the state of nature.

Supposing the administrator to be guided by purely scientific considerations, he would, like the gardener, meet this most serious difficulty by systematic extirpation, or exclusion, of the superfluous. The hopelessly diseased, the infirm aged, the weak or deformed in body or in mind, the excess of infants born, would be put away, as the gardener pulls up defective and superfluous plants, or the breeder destroys undesirable cattle. Only the strong and the healthy, carefully matched, with a view to the progeny best adapted to the purposes of the administrator, would be permitted to perpetuate their kind.

Of the more thoroughgoing of the multitudinous attempts to apply the principles of cosmic evolution, or what are supposed to be such, to social and political problems, which have appeared of late years, a considerable proportion appear to me to be based upon the notion that human society is competent to furnish, from its own resources, an administrator of the kind I have imagined. The pigeons, in short, are to be their own Sir John Sebright.[11] A despotic government, whether individual or collective, is to be endowed with the preternatural intelligence, and with what, I am afraid, many will consider the preternatural ruthlessness, required for the purpose of carrying out the principle of improvement by selection, with the somewhat drastic thoroughness upon which the success of the method depends. Experience certainly does not justify us in limiting the ruthlessness of individual "saviours of society"; and, on the well-known grounds of the aphorism which denies both body and soul to corporations, it seems probable (indeed the belief is not without support in history) that a collective despotism, a mob got to believe in its own divine right by demagogic missionaries, would be capable of more thorough work in this direction than any single tyrant, puffed up with the same illusion, has ever achieved. But intelligence is another affair. The fact that "saviours of society" take to that trade is evidence enough that they have none to spare. And such as they possess is generally sold to the capitalists of physical force on whose resources they depend. However, I doubt whether even the keenest judge of character, if he had before him a hundred boys and girls under fourteen, could pick out, with the least chance of success, those who should be kept, as certain to be serviceable members of the polity, and those who should be chloroformed, as equally sure to be stupid, idle, or vicious. The "points" of a good or of a bad citizen are really far harder to discern than those of a puppy or a short-horn calf; many do not show themselves before the practical difficulties of life stimulate manhood to full exertion. And by that time the mischief is done. The evil stock, if it be one, has had time to multiply, and selection is nullified.

I have other reasons for fearing that this logical ideal of evolutionary regimentation—this pigeon-fanciers' polity—is unattainable. In the absence of any such a severely scientific administrator as we have been dreaming of, human society is kept together by bonds of such a singular character, that the attempt to perfect society after his fashion would run serious risk of loosening them.

Social organization is not peculiar to men. Other societies, such as those constituted by bees and ants, have also arisen out of the advantage of cooperation in the struggle for existence; and their resemblances to, and their differences from, human society are alike instructive. The society formed by the hive bee fulfils the ideal of the communistic aphorism "to each according to his needs, from each according to his capacity." Within it, the struggle for existence is strictly limited. Queen, drones, and workers have each their allotted sufficiency of food; each performs the function assigned to it in the economy of the hive, and all contribute to the success of the whole cooperative society in its competition with rival collectors of nectar and pollen and with other enemies, in the state of nature without. In the same sense as the garden, or the colony, is a work of human art, the bee polity is a work of apiarian art, brought about by the cosmic process, working through the organization of the hymenopterous type.

Now this society is the direct product of an organic necessity, impelling every member of it to a course of action which tends to the good of the whole. Each bee has its duty and none has any rights. Whether bees are susceptible of feeling and capable of thought is a question which cannot be dogmatically answered. As a pious opinion, I am disposed to deny them more than the merest rudiments of consciousness.[12] But it is curious to reflect that a thoughtful drone (workers and queens would have no leisure for speculation) with a turn for ethical philosophy, must needs profess himself an intuitive moralist of the purest water. He would point out, with perfect justice, that the devotion of the workers to a life of ceaseless toil for a mere subsistence wage, cannot be accounted for either by enlightened selfishness, or by any other sort of utilitarian motives; since these bees begin to work, without experience or reflection, as they emerge from the cell in which they are hatched. Plainly, an eternal and immutable principle, innate in each bee, can alone account for the phenomena. On the other hand, the biologist, who traces out all the extant stages of gradation between solitary and hive bees, as clearly sees in the latter, simply the perfection of an automatic mechanism, hammered out by the blows of the struggle for existence upon the progeny of the former, during long ages of constant variation.

I see no reason to doubt that, at its origin, human society was as much a product of organic necessity as that of the bees.[13] The human family, to begin with, rested upon exactly the same conditions as those which gave rise to similar associations among animals lower in the scale. Further, it is easy to see that every increase in the duration of the family ties, with the resulting co-operation of a larger and larger number of descendants for protection and defence, would give the families in which such modification took place a distinct advantage over the others. And, as in the hive, the progressive limitation of the struggle for existence between the members of the family would involve increasing efficiency as regards outside competition.

But there is this vast and fundamental difference between bee society and human society. In the former, the members of the society are each organically predestined to the performance of one particular class of functions only. If they were endowed with desires, each could desire to perform none but those offices for which its organization specially fits it; and which, in view of the good of the whole, it is proper it should do. So long as a new queen does not make her appearance, rivalries and competition are absent from the bee polity.

Among mankind, on the contrary, there is no such predestination to a sharply defined place in the social organism. However much men may differ in the quality of their intellects, the intensity of their passions, and the delicacy of their sensations, it cannot be said that one is fitted by his organization to be an agricultural labourer and nothing else, and another to be a landowner and nothing else. Moreover, with all their enormous differences in natural endowment, men agree in one thing, and that is their innate desire to enjoy the pleasures and to escape the pains of life; and, in short, to do nothing but that which it pleases them to do, without the least reference to the welfare of the society into which they are born. That is their inheritance (the reality at the bottom of the doctrine of original sin) from the long series of ancestors, human and semi-human and brutal, in whom the strength of this innate tendency to self-assertion was the condition of victory in the struggle for existence. That is the reason of the *aviditas vitæ*[14]—the insatiable hunger for enjoyment—of all mankind, which is one of the essential conditions of success in the war with the state of nature outside; and yet the sure agent of the destruction of society if allowed free play within.

The check upon this free play of self-assertion, or natural liberty, which is the necessary condition for the origin of human society, is the product of organic necessities of a different kind from those upon which the constitution of the hive depends. One of these is the mutual affection of parent and offspring, intensified by the long infancy of the human species. But the most important is the tendency, so strongly developed in man, to reproduce in himself actions and feelings similar to, or correlated with, those of other men. Man is the most consummate of all mimics in the animal world; none but himself can draw or model; none comes near him in the scope, variety, and exactness of vocal imitation; none is such a master of gesture; while he seems to be impelled thus to imitate for the pure pleasure of it. And there is no such another emotional chameleon. By a purely reflex operation of the mind, we take the hue of passion of those who are about us, or, it may be, the complementary colour. It is not by any conscious "putting one's self in the place" of a joyful or a suffering person that the state of mind we call sympathy usually arises;[15] indeed, it is often contrary to one's sense of right, and in spite of one's will, that "fellow-feeling makes us wondrous kind," or the reverse. However complete may be the indifference to public opinion, in a cool, intellectual view, of the traditional sage, it has not yet been my fortune to meet with any actual sage who took its hostile manifestations with entire equanimity. Indeed, I doubt if the philosopher lives, or ever has lived, who could know himself to be heartily despised by a street boy without some irritation. And, though one cannot justify Haman for wishing to hang Mordecai on such a very high gibbet, yet, really, the consciousness of the Vizier of Ahasuerus, as he went in and out of the gate, that this obscure Jew had no respect for him, must have been very annoying.[16]

It is needful only to look around us, to see that the greatest restrainer of the anti-social tendencies of men is fear, not of the law, but of the opinion of their fellows. The conventions of honour bind men who break legal, moral, and religious bonds; and while people endure the extremity of physical pain rather than part with life, shame drives the weakest to suicide.

Every forward step of social progress brings men into closer relations with their fellows, and increases the importance of the pleasures and pains derived from sympathy. We judge the acts of others by our own sympathies, and we judge our own acts by the sympathies of others, every day and all day long, from childhood upwards, until associations, as indissoluble as those of language, are formed between certain acts and the feelings of approbation or disapprobation. It becomes impossible to imagine some acts without disapprobation, or others without approbation of the actor, whether he be one's self, or any one else. We come to think in the acquired dialect of morals. An artificial personality, the "man within," as Adam Smith[17] calls conscience, is built up beside the natural personality. He is the watchman of society, charged to restrain the anti-social tendencies of the natural man within the limits required by social welfare.

I have termed this evolution of the feelings out of which the primitive bonds of human society are so largely forged, into the organized and personified sympathy we call conscience, the ethical process.[18] So far as it tends to make any human society more efficient in the struggle for existence with the state of nature, or with other societies, it works in harmonious contrast with the cosmic process. But it is none the less true that, since law and morals are restraints upon the struggle for existence between men in society, the ethical process is in opposition to the principle of the cosmic process, and tends to the suppression of the qualities best fitted for success in that struggle.[19]

It is further to be observed that, just as the self-assertion, necessary to the maintenance of society against the state of nature, will destroy that society if it is allowed free operation within; so the self-restraint, the essence of the ethical process, which is no less an essential condition of the existence of every polity, may, by excess, become ruinous to it.

Moralists of all ages and of all faiths, attending only to the relations of men towards one another in an ideal society, have agreed upon the "golden rule," "Do as you would be done by." In other words, let sympathy be your guide; put yourself in the place of the man towards whom your action is directed; and do to him what you would like to have done to yourself under the circumstances. However much one may admire the generosity of such a rule of conduct; however confident one may be that average men may be thoroughly depended upon not to carry it out to its full logical consequences; it is nevertheless desirable to recognise the fact that these consequences are incompatible with the existence of a civil state, under any circumstances of this world which have obtained, or, so far as one can see, are, likely to come to pass.

For I imagine there can be no doubt that the great desire of every wrongdoer is to escape from the painful consequences of his actions. If I put myself in the place of the man who has robbed me, I find that I am possessed by an exceeding desire not to be fined or imprisoned; if in that of the man who has smitten me on one cheek, I contemplate with satisfaction the absence of any worse result than the turning of the other cheek for like treatment. Strictly observed, the "golden rule" involves the negation of law by the refusal to put it in motion against law-breakers; and, as regards the external relations of a polity, it is the refusal to continue the struggle for existence. It can be obeyed, even partially, only under the protection of a society which repudiates it.

Without such shelter, the followers of the "golden rule" may indulge in hopes of heaven, but they must reckon with the certainty that other people will be masters of the earth.

What would become of the garden if the gardener treated all the weeds and slugs and birds and trespassers as he would like to be treated, if he were in their place?

Under the preceding heads, I have endeavoured to represent in broad, but I hope faithful, outlines the essential features of the state of nature and of that cosmic process of which it is the outcome, so far as was needful for my argument; I have contrasted with the state of nature the state of art, produced by human intelligence and energy, as it is exemplified by a garden; and I have shown that the state of art, here and else-where, can be maintained only by the constant counteraction of the hostile influences of the state of nature. Further, I have pointed out that the "horticultural process" which thus sets itself against the "cosmic process" is opposed to the latter in principle, in so far as it tends to arrest the struggle for existence, by restraining the multiplication which is one of the chief causes of that struggle, and by creating artificial conditions of life, better adapted to the cultivated plants than are the conditions of the state of nature. And I have dwelt upon the fact that, though the progressive modification, which is the consequence of the struggle for existence in the state of nature, is at an end such modification may still be effected by that selection, in view of an ideal of usefulness, or of pleasantness, to man, of which the state of nature knows nothing.

I have proceeded to show that a colony, set down in a country in the state of nature, presents close analogies with a garden; and I have indicated the course of action which an administrator, able and willing to carry out horticultural principles, would adopt, in order to secure the success of such a newly formed polity, supposing it to be capable of indefinite expansion. In the contrary case, I have shown that difficulties must arise; that the unlimited increase of the population over a limited area must, sooner or later, reintroduce into the that struggle for the means of existence between the colonists, which it was the primary object of the administrator to exclude, insomuch as it is fatal to the mutual peace which is the prime condition of the union of men in society.

I have briefly described the nature of the only radical cure, known to me, for the disease which would thus threaten the existence of the colony; and, however regretfully, I have been obliged to admit that this rigorously scientific method of applying the principles of evolution to human society hardly comes within the region of practical politics, not for want of will on the part of a great many people; but because, for one reason, there is no hope that mere human beings will ever possess enough intelligence to select the fittest. And I have adduced other grounds for arriving at the same conclusion.

I have pointed out that human society took its rise in the organic necessities expressed by imitation and by the sympathetic emotions; and that, in the struggle for existence with the state of nature and with other societies, as part of it, those in which men were thus led to close cooperation had a great advantage.[20] But, since each man retained more or less of the faculties common to all the rest, and especially a full share of the desire for unlimited selfgratification, the struggle for existence within society could only be gradually eliminated. So long as any of it remained, society continued to be an imperfect instrument of the struggle for existence and, consequently, was improvable by the selective influence of that struggle. Other things being alike, the tribe of savages in which order was best maintained; in which there was most security within the tribe and the most loyal mutual support outside it, would be the survivors.

I have termed this gradual strengthening of the social bond, which, though it arrests the struggle for existence inside society, up to a certain point improves the chances of society, as a corporate whole, in the cosmic struggle—the ethical process. I have endeavoured to show, that, when the ethical process has advanced so far as to secure every member of the society in the possession of the means of existence, the struggle for existence, as between man and man, within that society is, *ipso facto,* at an end. And, as it is undeniable that the most highly civilized societies have substantially reached this position, it follows that, so far as they are concerned, the struggle for existence can play no important part within them.[21] In other words, the kind of evolution which is brought about in the state of nature cannot take place.

I have further shown cause for the belief that direct selection, after the fashion of the horticulturist and the breeder, neither has played, nor can play, any important part in the evolution of society; apart from other reasons, because I do not see how such selection could be practised without a serious weakening, it may be the destruction, of the bonds which hold society together. It strikes me that men who are accustomed to contemplate the active or passive extirpation of the weak, the unfortunate, and the superfluous; who justify that conduct on the ground that it has the sanction of the cosmic process, and is the only way of ensuring the progress of the race; who, if they are consistent, must rank medicine among the black arts and count the physician a mischievous preserver of the unfit; on whose matrimonial undertakings the principles of the stud have the chief influence; whose whole lives, therefore, are an education in the noble art of suppressing natural affection and sympathy, are not likely to have any large stock of these commodities left. But, without them, there is no conscience, nor any restraint on the conduct of men, except the calculation of self-interest, the balancing of certain present gratifications against doubtful future pains; and experience tells us how much that is worth. Every day, we see firm believers in the hell of the theologians commit acts by which, as they believe when cool, they risk eternal punishment; while they hold back from those which are opposed to the sympathies of their associates.

That progressive modification of civilization which passes by the name of the "evolution of society," is, in fact, a process of an essentially different character, both from that which brings about the evolution of species, in the state of nature, and from that which gives rise to the evolution of varieties, in the state of art.

There can be no doubt that vast changes have taken place in English civilization since the reign of the Tudors. But I am not aware of a particle of evidence in favour of the conclusion that this evolutionary process has been accompanied by any modification of the physical, or the mental, characters of the men who have been the subjects of it. I have not met with any grounds for suspecting that the average Englishmen of today are sensibly different from those that Shakspere knew and drew. We look into his magic mirror of the Elizabethan age, and behold, nowise darkly, the presentment of ourselves.

During these three centuries, from the reign of Elizabeth to that of Victoria, the struggle for existence between man and man has been so largely restrained among the great mass of the population (except for one or two short intervals of civil war), that it can have had little, or no, selective operation. As to anything comparable to direct selection, it has been practised on so small a scale that it may also be neglected. The criminal law, in so far as by putting to death, or by subjecting to long periods of imprisonment, those who infringe its provisions, it prevents the propagation of hereditary criminal tendencies; and the poor-law, in so far as it separates married couples, whose destitution arises from hereditary defects of character, are doubtless selective agents operating in favour of the non-criminal and the more effective members of society. But the proportion of the population which they infiuence is very small; and, generally, the hereditary criminal and the hereditary pauper have propagated their kind before the law affects them. In a large proportion of cases, crime and pauperism have nothing to do with heredity; but are the consequence, partly, of circumstances and, partly, of the possession of qualities, which, under different conditions of life, might have excited esteem and even admiration. It was a shrewd man of the world who, in discussing sewage problems, remarked that dirt is riches in the wrong place; and that sound aphorism has moral applications. The benevolence and open-handed generosity which adorn a rich man, may make a pauper of a poor one; the energy and courage to which the successful soldier owes his rise, the cool and daring subtlety to which the great financier owes his fortune, may very easily, under unfavourable conditions, lead their possessors to the gallows, or to the hulks. Moreover, it is fairly probable that the children of a "failure" will receive from their other parent just that little modification of character which makes all the difference. I sometimes wonder whether people, who talk so freely about extirpating the unfit, ever dispassionately consider their own history. Surely, one must be very "fit," indeed, not to know of an occasion, or perhaps two, in one's life, when it would have been only too easy to qualify for a place among the "unfit."

In my belief the innate qualities, physical, intellectual, and moral, of our nation have remained substantially the same for the last four or five centuries. If the struggle for existence has affected us to any serious extent (and I doubt it) it has been, indirectly, through our military and industrial wars with other nations.

What is often called the struggle for existence in society (I plead guilty to having used the term too loosely myself), is a contest, not for the means of existence, but for the means of enjoyment. Those who occupy the first places in this practical competitive examination are the rich and the influential; those who fail, more or less, occupy the lower places, down to the squalid obscurity of the pauper and the criminal. Upon the most liberal estimate, I suppose the former group will not amount to two per cent of the population. I doubt if the latter exceeds another two per cent; but let it be supposed, for the sake of argument, that it is as great as five per cent.[22]

As it is only in the latter group that anything comparable to the struggle for existence in the state of nature can take place; as it is only among this twentieth of the whole people that numerous men, women, and children die of rapid or slow starvation, or of the diseases incidental to permanently bad conditions of life; and as there is nothing to prevent their multiplication before they are killed off, while, in spite of greater infant mortality, they increase faster than the rich; it seems clear that the struggle for existence in this class can have no appreciable selective influence upon the other 95 per cent of the population.

What sort of a sheep breeder would he be who should content himself with picking out the worst fifty out of a thousand, leaving them on a barren common till the weakest starved, and then letting the survivors go back to mix with the rest? And the parallel is too favourable; since in a large number of cases, the actual poor and the convicted criminals are neither the weakest nor the worst.

In the struggle for the means of enjoyment, the qualities which ensure success are energy, industry, intellectual capacity, tenacity of purpose, and, at least as much sympathy as is necessary to make a man understand the feelings of his fellows. Were there none of those artificial arrangements by which fools and knaves are kept at the top of society instead of sinking to their natural place at the bottom,[23] the struggle for the means of enjoyment would ensure a constant circulation of the human units of te social compound, from the bottom to the top and from the top to the bottom. The survivors of the contest, those who continued to form the great bulk of the polity, would not be those "fittest" who got to the very top, but the great body of the moderately "fit," whose numbers and superior propagative power, enable them always to swamp the exceptionally endowed minority.

I think it must be obvious to every one, that, whether we consider the internal or the external interests of society, it is desirable they should be in the hands of those who are endowed with the largest share of energy, of industry, of intellectual capacity, of tenacity of purpose, while they are not devoid of sympathetic humanity; and, in so far as the struggle for the means of enjoyment tends to place such men in possession of wealth and influence, it is a process which tends to the good of society. But the process, as we have seen, has no real resemblance to that which adapts living beings to current conditions in the state of nature; nor any to the artificial selection of the horticulturist.

To return, once more, to the parallel of horticulture. In the modern world, the gardening of men by themselves is practically restricted to the performance, not of selection, but of that other function of the gardener, the creation of conditions more favourable than those of the state of nature; to the end of facilitating the free expansion of the innate faculties of the citizen, so far as it is consistent with the general good. And the business of the moral and political philosopher appears to me to be the ascertainment, by the same method of observation, experiment, and ratiocination, as is practised in other kinds of scientific work, of the course of conduct which will best conduce to that end.

But, supposing this course of conduct to be scientifically determined and carefully followed out, it cannot put an end to the struggle for existence in the state of nature; and it will not so much as tend, in any way, to the adaptation of man to that state. Even should the whole human race be absorbed in one vast polity, within which "absolute political justice" reigns, the struggle for existence with the state of nature outside it, and the tendency to the return of the struggle within, in consequence of over-multiplication, will remain; and, unless men's inheritance from the ancestors who fought a good fight in the state of nature, their dose of original sin, is rooted out by some method at present unrevealed, at any rate to disbelievers in supernaturalism, every child born into the world will still bring with him the instinct of unlimited self-assertion. He will have to learn the lesson of self-restraint and renunciation. But the practice of self-restraint and renunciation is not happiness, though it may be something much better.

That man, as a "political animal," is susceptible of a vast amount of improvement, by education, by instruction, and by the application of his intelligence to the adaptation of the conditions of life to his higher needs, I entertain not the slightest doubt. But, so long as he remains liable to error, intellectual or moral; so long as he is compelled to be perpetually on guard against the cosmic forces, whose ends are not his ends, without and within himself; so long as he is haunted by inexpugnable memories and hopeless aspirations; so long as the recognition of his intellectual limitations forces him to acknowledge his incapacity to penetrate the mystery of existence; the prospect of attaining untroubled happiness, or of a state which can, even remotely, deserve the title of perfection, appears to me to be as misleading an illusion as ever was dangled before the eyes of poor humanity. And there have been many of them.

That which lies before the human race is a constant struggle to maintain and improve, in opposition to the State of Nature, the State of Art of an organized polity; in which, and by which, man may develop a worthy civilization, capable of maintaining and constantly improving itself, until the evolution of our globe shall have entered so far upon its downward course that the cosmic process resumes its sway; and, once more, the State of Nature prevails over the surface of our planet.[24]

Evolution and Ethics
[*The Romanes Lecture*, 1893]

I make a practice of going over to the enemy's camp, not as a deserter, but for reconnaissance.
(L. ANNÆI SENECÆ EPIST. II. 4.)

There is a delightful child's story, known by the title of "Jack and the Beanstalk," with which my contemporaries who are present will be familiar. But so many of our grave and reverend juniors have been brought up on severer intellectual diet, and, perhaps, have become acquainted with fairyland only through primers of comparative mythology, that it may be needful to give an outline of the tale. It is a legend of a bean-plant, which grows and grows until it reaches the high heavens and there spreads out into a vast canopy of foliage. The hero, being moved to climb the stalk, discovers that the leafy expanse supports a world composed of the same elements as that below, but yet strangely new; and his adventures there, on which I may not dwell, must have completely changed his views of the nature of things; though the story, not having been composed by, or for, philosophers, has nothing to say about views.

My present enterprise has a certain analogy to that of the daring adventurer. I beg you to accompany me in an attempt to reach a world which, to many, is probably strange, by the help of a bean. It is, as you know, a simple, inert-looking thing. Yet, if planted under proper conditions, of which sufficient warmth is one of the most important, it manifests active powers of a very remarkable kind. A small green seedling emerges, rises to the surface of the soil, rapidly increases in size and, at the same time, undergoes a series of metamorphoses which do not excite our wonder as much as those which meet us in legendary history, merely because they are to be seen every day and all day long.

By insensible steps, the plant builds itself up into a large and various fabric of root, stem, leaves, flowers, and fruit, every one moulded within and without in accordance with an extremely complex but, at the same time, minutely defined pattern. In each of these complicated structures, as in their smallest constituents, there is an immanent energy which, in harmony with that resident in all the others, incessantly works towards the maintenance of the whole and the efficient performance of the part which it has to play in the economy of nature. But no sooner has the edifice, reared with such exact elaboration, attained completeness, than it begins to crumble. By degrees, the plant withers and disappears from view, leaving behind more or fewer apparently inert and simple bodies, just like the bean from which it sprang; and, like it, endowed with the potentiality of giving rise to a similar cycle of manifestations.

Neither the poetic nor the scientific imagination is put to much strain in the search after analogies with this process of going forth and, as it were, returning to the starting point. It may be likened to the ascent and descent of a slung stone, or the course of an arrow along its trajectory. Or we may say that the living energy takes first an upward and then a downward road. Or it may seem preferable to compare the expansion of the germ into the full-grown plant, to the unfolding of a fan, or to the rolling forth and widening of a stream; and thus to arrive at the conception of "development," or "evolution." Here as elsewhere, names are "noise and smoke"; the important point is to have a clear and adequate conception of the fact signified by a name. And, in this case, the fact is the Sisyphæan process, in the course of which the living and growing plant passes from the relative simplicity and latent potentiality of the seed to the full epiphany of a highly differentiated type, thence to fall back to simplicity and potentiality.

The value of a strong intellectual grasp of the nature of this process lies in the circumstance that what is true of the bean is true of living things in general. From very low forms up to the highest—in the animal no less than in the vegetable kingdom—the process of life presents the same appearance[25] of cyclical evolution. Nay, we have but to cast our eyes over the rest of the world and cyclical change presents itself on all sides. It meets us in the water that flows to the sea and returns to the springs; in the heavenly bodies that wax and wane, go and return to their places; in the inexorable sequence of the ages of man's life; in that successive rise, apogee, and fall of dynasties and of states which is the most prominent topic of civil history.

As no man fording a swift stream can dip his foot twice into the same water, so no man can with exactness, affirm of anything in the sensible world that it is.[26] As he utters the words, nay as he thinks them, the predicate ceases to be applicable; the present has become the past; the "is" should be "was." And the more we learn of the nature of things, the more evident is it that what we call rest is only unperceived activity; that seeming peace is silent but strenuous battle. In every part, at every moment, the state of the cosmos is the expression of a transitory adjustment of contending forces; a scene of strife, in which all the combatants fall in turn. What is true of each part, is true of the whole. Natural knowledge tends more and more to the conclusion that "all the choir of heaven and furniture of the earth" are the transitory forms of parcels of cosmic substance wending along the road of evolution, from nebulous potentiality, through endless growths of sun and planet and satellite; through all varieties of matter; through infinite diversities of life and thought; possibly, through modes of being of which we neither have a conception, nor are competent to form any, back to the indefinable latency from which they arose. Thus the most obvious attribute of the cosmos is its impermanence. It assumes the aspect not so much of a permanent entity as of a changeful process, in which naught endures save the flow of energy and the rational order which pervades it.

We have climbed our beanstalk and have reached a wonderland in which the common and the familiar become things new and strange. In the exploration of the cosmic process thus typified, the highest intelligence of man finds inexhaustible employment; giants are subdued to our service; and the spiritual affections of the contemplative philosopher are engaged by beauties worthy of eternal constancy.

But there is another aspect of the cosmic process, so perfect as a mechanism, so beautiful as a work of art. Where the cosmopoietic energy works through sentient beings, there arises, among its other manifestations, that which we call pain or suffering. This baleful product of evolution increases in quantity and in intensity, with advancing grades of animal organization, until it attains its highest level in man. Further, the consummation is not reached in man, the mere animal; nor in man, the whole or half savage; but only in man, the member of an organized polity. And it is a necessary consequence of his attempt to live in this way; that is, under those conditions which are essential to the full development of his noblest powers.

Man, the animal, in fact, has worked his way to the headship of the sentient world, and has become the superb animal which he is, in virtue of his success in the struggle for existence. The conditions having been of a certain order, man's organization has adjusted itself to them better than that of his competitors in the cosmic strife. In the case of mankind, the self-assertion, the unscrupulous seizing upon all that can be grasped, the tenacious holding of all that can be kept, which constitute the essence of the struggle for existence, have answered. For his successful progress, throughout the savage state, man has been largely indebted to those qualities which he shares with the ape and the tiger; his exceptional physical organization; his cunning, his sociability, his curiosity, and his imitativeness; his ruthless and ferocious destructiveness when his anger is roused by opposition.

But, in proportion as men have passed from anarchy to social organization, and in proportion as civilization has grown in worth, these deeply ingrained serviceable qualities have become defects. After the manner of successful persons, civilized man would gladly kick down the ladder by which he has climbed. He would be only too pleased to see "the ape and tiger die." But they decline to suit his convenience; and the unwelcome intrusion of these boon companions of his hot youth into the ranged existence of civil life adds pains and griefs, innumerable and immeasurably great, to those which the cosmic process necessarily brings on the mere animal. In fact, civilized man brands all these ape and tiger promptings with the name of sins; he punishes many of the acts which flow from them as crimes; and, in extreme cases, he does his best to put an end to the survival of the fittest of former days by axe and rope.

I have said that civilized man has reached this point; the assertion is perhaps too broad and general, I had better put it that ethical man has attained thereto. The science of ethics professes to furnish us with a reasoned rule of life; to tell us what is right action and why it is so. Whatever differences of opinion may exist among experts, there is a general consensus that the ape and tiger methods of the struggle for existence are not reconcilable with sound ethical principles.

The hero of our story descended the beanstalk, and came back to the common world, where fare and work were alike hard; where ugly competitors were much commoner than beautiful princesses; and where the everlasting battle with self was much less sure to be crowned with victory than a turn-to with a giant. We have done the like. Thousands upon thousands of our fellows, thousands of years ago, have preceded us in finding themselves face to face with the same dread problem of evil. They also have seen that the cosmic process is evolution; that it is full of wonder, full of beauty, and, at the same time, full of pain. They have sought to discover the bearing of these great facts on ethics; to find out whether there is, or is not, a sanction for morality in the ways of the cosmos.

Theories of the universe, in which the conception of evolution plays a leading part, were extant at least six centuries before our era. Certain knowledge of them, in the fifth century, reaches us from localities as distant as the valley of the Ganges and the Asiatic coasts of the Ægean. To the early philosophers of Hindostan, no less than to those of Ionia, the salient and characteristic feature of the phenomenal world was its changefulness; the unresting flow of all things, through birth to visible being and thence to not being, in which they could discern no sign of a beginning and for which they saw no prospect of all ending. It was no less plain to some of these antique forerunners of modern philosophy that suffering is the badge of all the tribe of sentient things; that it is no accidental accompaniment, but an essential constituent of the cosmic process. The energetic Greek might find fierce joys in a world in which "strife is father and king"; but the old Aryan spirit was subdued to quietism in the Indian sage; the mist of suffering which spread over humanity hid everything else from his view; to him life was one with suffering and suffering with life.

In Hindostan, as in Ionia, a period of relatively high and tolerably stable civilization had succeeded long ages of semi-barbarism and struggle. Out of wealth and security had come leisure and refinement, and, close at their heels, had followed the malady of thought. To the struggle for bare existence, which never ends, though it may be alleviated and partially disguised for a fortunate few, succeeded the struggle to make existence intelligible and to bring the order of things into harmony with the moral sense of man, which also never ends, but, for the thinking few, becomes keener with every increase of knowledge and with every step towards the realization of a worthy ideal of life.

Two thousand five hundred years ago, the value of civilization was as apparent as it is now; then, as now, it was obvious that only in the garden of an orderly polity can the finest fruits humanity is capable of bearing be produced. But it had also become evident that the blessings of culture were not unmixed. The garden was apt to turn into a hothouse. The stimulation of the senses, the pampering of the emotions, endlessly multiplied the sources of pleasure. The constant widening of the intellectual field indefinitely extended the range of that especially human faculty of looking before and after, which adds to the fleeting present those old and new worlds of the past and the future, wherein men dwell the more the higher their culture. But that very sharpening of the sense and that subtle refinement of emotion, which brought such a wealth of pleasures, were fatally attended by a proportional enlargement of the capacity for suffering; and the divine faculty of imagination, while it created new heavens and new earths, provided them with the corresponding hells of futile regret for the past and morbid anxiety for the future.[27] Finally, the inevitable penalty of over-stimulation, exhaustion, opened the gates of civilization to its great enemy, ennui; the stale and flat weariness when man delights not, nor woman neither; when all things are vanity and vexation; and life seems not worth living except to escape the bore of dying.

Even purely intellectual progress brings about its revenges. Problems settled in a rough and ready way by rude men, absorbed in action, demand renewed attention and show themselves to be still unread riddles when men have time to think. The beneficent demon, doubt, whose name is Legion and who dwells amongst the tombs of old faiths, enters into mankind and thenceforth refuses to be cast out. Sacred customs, venerable dooms of ancestral wisdom, hallowed by tradition and professing to hold good for all time, are put to the question. Cultured reflection asks for their credentials; judges them by its own standards; finally, gathers those of which it approves into ethical systems, in which the reasoning is rarely much more than a decent pretext for the adoption of foregone conclusions.

One of the oldest and most important elements in such systems is the conception of justice. Society is impossible unless those who are associated agree to observe certain rules of conduct towards one another; its stability depends on the steadiness with which they abide by that agreement; and, so far as they waver, that mutual trust which is the bond of society is weakened or destroyed. Wolves could not hunt in packs except for the real, though unexpressed, understanding that they should not attack one another during the chase. The most rudimentary polity is a pack of men living under the like tacit, or expressed, understanding; and having made the very important advance upon wolf society, that they agree to use the force of the whole body against individuals who violate it and in favour of those who observe it. This observance of a common understanding, with the consequent distribution of punishments and rewards according to accepted rules, received the name of justice, while the contrary was called injustice. Early ethics did not take much note of the animus of the violator of the rules. But civilization could not advance far, without the establishment of a capital distinction between the case of involuntary and that of wilful misdeed; between a merely wrong action and a guilty one. And, with increasing refinement of moral appreciation, the problem of desert, which arises out of this distinction, acquired more and more theoretical and practical importance. If life must be given for life, yet it was recognized that the unintentional slayer did not altogether deserve death; and, by a sort of compromise between the public and the private conception of justice, a sanctuary was provided in which he might take refuge from the avenger of blood.

The idea of justice thus underwent a gradual sublimation from punishment and reward according to acts, to punishment and reward according to desert; or, in other words, according to motive. Righteousness, that is, action from right motive, not only became synonymous with justice, but the positive constituent of innocence and the very heart of goodness.

Now when the ancient sage, whether Indian or Greek, who had attained to this conception of goodness, looked the world, and especially human life, in the face, he found it as hard as we do to bring the course of evolution into harmony with even the elementary requirements of the ethical ideal of the just and the good.

If there is one thing plainer than another, it is that neither the pleasures nor the pains of life, in the merely animal world, are distributed according to desert; for it is admittedly impossible for the lower orders of sentient beings to deserve either the one or the other. If there is a generalization from the facts of human life which has the assent of thoughtful men in every age and country, it is that the violator of ethical rules constantly escapes the punishment which he deserves; that the wicked flourishes like a green bay tree, while the righteous begs his bread; that the sins of the fathers are visited upon the children; that, in the realm of nature, ignorance is punished just as severely as wilful wrong; and that thousands upon thousands of innocent beings suffer for the crime, or the unintentional trespass, of one.

Greek and Semite and Indian are agreed upon this subject. The book of Job is at one with the "Works and Days" and the Buddhist Sutras; the Psalmist and the Preacher of Israel, with the Tragic Poets of Greece. What is a more common motive of the ancient tragedy in fact, than the unfathomable injustice of the nature of things; what is more deeply felt to be true than its presentation of the destruction of the blameless by the work of his own hands, or by the fatal operation of the sins of others? Surely Œdipus was pure of heart; it was the natural sequence of events—the cosmic process—which drove him, in all innocence, to slay his father and become the husband of his mother, to the desolation of his people and his own headlong ruin. Or to step, for a moment, beyond the chronological limits I have set myself, what constitutes the sempiternal attraction of Hamlet but the appeal to deepest experience of that history of a no less blameless dreamer, dragged, in spite of himself, into a world out of joint; involved in a tangle of crime and misery, created by one of the prime agents of the cosmic process as it works in and through man?

Thus, brought before the tribunal of ethics, the cosmos might well seem to stand condemned. The conscience of man revolted against the moral indifference of nature, and the microcosmic atom should have found the illimitable macrocosm guilty. But few, or none, ventured to record that verdict.

In the great Semitic trial of this issue, Job takes refuge in silence and submission; the Indian and the Greek, less wise perhaps, attempt to reconcile the irreconcilable and plead for the defendant. To this end, the Greeks invented Theodicies; while the Indians devised what, in its ultimate form, must rather be termed a Cosmodicy. For, though Buddhism recognizes gods many and lords many, they are products of the cosmic process; and transitory, however long enduring, manifestations of its eternal activity. In the doctrine of transmigration, whatever its origin, Brahminical and Buddhist speculation found, ready to hand,[28] the means of constructing a plausible vindication of the ways of the cosmos to man. If this world is full of pain and sorrow; if grief and evil fall, like the rain, upon both the just and the unjust; it is because, like the rain, they are links in the endless chain of natural causation by which past, present, and future are indissolubly connected; and there is no more injustice in the one case than in the other. Every sentient being is reaping as it has sown; if not in this life, then in one or other of the infinite series of antecedent existences of which it is the latest term. The present distribution of good and evil is, therefore, the algebraical sum of accumulated positive and negative deserts; or, rather, it depends on the floating balance of the account. For it was not thought necessary that a complete settlement should ever take place. Arrears might stand over as a sort of "hanging gale"; a period of celestial happiness just earned might be succeeded by ages of torment in a hideous nether world, the balance still overdue for some remote ancestral error.[29]

Whether the cosmic process looks any more moral than at first, after such a vindication, may perhaps be questioned. Yet this plea of justification is not less plausible than others; and none but very hasty thinkers will reject it on the ground of inherent absurdity. Like the doctrine of evolution itself, that of transmigration has its roots in the world of reality; and it may claim such support as the great argument from analogy is capable of supplying.

Everyday experience familiarizes us with the facts which are grouped under the name of heredity. Every one of us bears upon him obvious marks of his parentage,

perhaps of remoter relationships. More particularly, the sum of tendencies to act in a
certain way, which we call "character," is often to be traced through a long series of
progenitors and collaterals. So we may justly say that this "character"—this moral and
intellectual essence of a man—does veritably pass over from one fleshly tabernacle to
another, and does really transmigrate from generation to generation. In the new-born
infant, the character of the stock lies latent, and the Ego is little more than a bundle of
potentialities. But, very early, these become actualities; from childhood to age they
manifest themselves in dulness or brightness, weakness or strength, viciousness or
uprightness; and with each feature modified by confluence with another character, if by
nothing else, the character passes on to its incarnation in new bodies.

The Indian philosophers called character, as thus defined, "karma."[30] It is this
karma which passed from life to life and linked them in the chain of transmigrations;
and they held that it is modified in each life, not merely by confluence of parentage, but
by its own acts. They were, in fact, strong believers in the theory, so much disputed
just at present, of the hereditary transmission of acquired characters. That the manifestation of the tendencies of a character may be greatly facilitated, or impeded, by conditions, of which self-discipline, or the absence of it, are among the most important, is
indubitable; but that the character itself is modified in this way is by no means so
certain; it is not so sure that the transmitted character of an evil liver is worse, or that
of a righteous man better, than that which he received. Indian philosophy, however, did
not admit of any doubt on this subject; the belief in the influence of conditions, notably
of selfdiscipline, on the karma was not merely a necessary postulate of its theory of
retribution but it presented the only way of escape from the endless round of transmigrations.

The earlier forms of Indian philosophy agreed with those prevalent in our own
times, in supposing the existence of a permanent reality, or "substance," beneath the
shifting series of phenomena, whether of matter or of mind. The substance of the
cosmos was "Brahma," that of the individual man "Atman"; and the latter was separated
from the former only, if I may so speak, by its phenomenal envelope, by the easing of
sensations, thoughts and desires, pleasures and pains, which make up the illusive
phantasmagoria of life. This the ignorant take for reality; their "Atman" therefore
remains eternally imprisoned in delusions, bound by the fetters of desire and scourged
by the whip of misery. But the man who has attained enlightenment sees that the
apparent reality is mere illusion, or, as was said a couple of thousand years later, that
there is nothing good nor bad but thinking makes it so. If the cosmos "is just and of
our pleasant vices makes instruments to scourge us," it would seem that the only way

to escape from our heritage of evil is to destroy that fountain of desire whence our vices flow; to refuse any longer to be the instruments of the evolutionary process, and withdraw from the struggle for existence. If the karma is modifiable by self-discipline, if its coarser desires, one after another, can be extinguished, the ultimate fundamental desire of self-assertion, or the desire to be, may also be destroyed.[31] Then the bubble of illusion will burst, and the freed individual "Atman" will lose itself in the universal "Brahma."

Such seems to have been the pre-Buddhistic conception of salvation, and of the way to be followed by those who would attain thereto. No more thorough mortification of the flesh has ever been attempted than that achieved by the Indian ascetic anchorite; no later monachism has so nearly succeeded in reducing the human mind to that condition of impassive quasi-somnambulism, which, but for its acknowledged holiness, might run the risk of being confounded with idiocy.

And this salvation, it will be observed, was to be attained through knowledge, and by action based on that knowledge; just as the experimenter, who would obtain a certain physical or chemical result, must have a knowledge of the natural laws involved and the persistent disciplined will adequate to carry out all the various operations required. The supernatural, in our sense of the term, was entirely excluded. There was no external power which could affect the sequence of cause and effect which gives rise to karma; none but the will of the subject of the karma which could put an end to it.

Only one rule of conduct could be based upon the remarkable theory of which I have endeavoured to give a reasoned outline. It was folly to continue to exist when an overplus of pain was certain; and the probabilities in favour of the increase of misery with the prolongation of existence, were so overwhelming. Slaying the body only made matters worse; there was nothing for it but to slay the soul by the voluntary arrest of all its activities. Property, social ties, family affections, common compnnionship, must be abandoned; the most natural appetites, even that for food, must be suppressed, or at least minimized; until all that remained of a man was the impassive, extenuated, mendicant monk, self-hypnotised into cataleptic trances, which the deluded mystic took for foretastes of the final union with Brahma.

The founder of Buddhism accepted the chief postulates demanded by his predecessors. But he was not satisfied with the practical annihilation involved in merging the individual existence in the unconditioned—the Atman in Brahma. It would seem that the admission of the existence of any substance whatever—even of the tenuity of that which has neither quality nor energy and of which no predicate whatever can be asserted—appeared to him to be a danger and a snare. Though reduced to a hypostatized negation, Brahma was not to be trusted; so long as entity was there, it might conceivably resume the weary round of evolution, with all its train of immeasurable miseries. Gautama got rid of even that shade of a shadow of permanent existence by a metaphysical *tour de force* of great interest to the student of philosophy, seeing that it supplies the wanting half of Bishop Berkeley's well-known idealistic argument.

Granting the premises, I am not aware of any escape from Berkeley's conclusion, that the "substance" of matter is a metaphysical unknown quantity, of the existence of which there is no proof. What Berkeley does not seem to have so clearly perceived is that the non-existence of a substance of mind is equally arguable; and that the result of the impartial applications of his reasonings is the reduction of the All to coexistences and sequences of phemonena, beneath and beyond which there is nothing cognoscible. It is a remarkable indication of the subtlety of Indian speculation that Gautama should have seen deeper than the greatest of modern idealists; though it must be admitted that, if some of Berkeley's reasonings respecting the nature of spirit are pushed home, they reach pretty much the same conclusion.[32]

Accepting the prevalent Brahminical doctrine that the whole cosmos, celestial, terrestrial, and infernal, with its population of gods and other celestial beings, of sentient animals, of Mara and his devils, is incessantly shifting through recurring cycles of production and destruction, in each of which every human being has his transmigratory representative, Gautama proceeded to eliminate substance altogether; and to reduce the cosmos to a mere flow of sensations, emotions, volitions, and thoughts, devoid of any substratum. As, on the surface of a stream of water, we see ripples and whirlpools, which last for a while and then vanish with the causes that gave rise to them, so what seem individual existences are mere temporary associations of phenomena circling round a centre, "like a dog tied to a post." In the whole universe there is nothing permanent, no eternal substance either of mind or of matter. Personality is a metaphysical fancy; and in very truth, not only we, but all things, in the worlds without end of the cosmic phantasmagoria, are such stuff as dreams are made of.

What then becomes of karma? Karma remains untouched. As the peculiar form of energy we call magnetism may be transmitted from a loadstone to a piece of steel, from the steel to a piece of nickel, as it may be strengthened or weakened by the conditions to which it is subjected while resident in each piece, so it seems to have been conceived that karma might be transmitted from one phenomenal association to another by a sort of induction. However this may be, Gautama doubtless had a better guarantee for the abolition of transmigration, when no wrack of substance, either of Atman or of Brahma, was left behind when, in short, a man had but to dream that he willed not to dream, to put an end to all dreaming.

This end of life's dream is Nirvana. What Nirvana is the learned do not agree. But, since the best original authorities tell us there is neither desire nor activity, nor any possibility of phenomenal reappearance for the sage who has entered Nirvana, it may be safely said of this acme of Buddhistic philosophy—"the rest is silence."[33]

Thus there is no very great practical disagreement between Gautama and his predecessors with respect to the end of action; but it is otherwise as regards the means to that end. With just insight into human nature, Gautama declared extreme ascetic practices to be useless and indeed harmful. The appetites and the passions are not to be abolished by mere mortification of the body; they must, in addition, be attacked on their own ground and conquered by steady cultivation of the mental habits which oppose them; by universal benevolence; by the return of good for evil; by humility; by abstinence from evil thought; in short, by total renunciation of that self-assertion which is the essence of the cosmic process.

Doubtless, it is to these ethical qualities that Buddhism owes its marvellous success.[34] A system which knows no God in the western sense; which denies a soul to man; which counts the belief in immortality a blunder and the hope of it a sin; which refuses any efficacy to prayer and sacrifice; which bids men look to nothing but their own efforts for salvation; which, in its original purity, knew nothing of vows of obedience, abhorred intolerance, and never sought the aid of the secular arm; yet spread over a considerable moiety of the Old World with marvellous rapidity, and is still, with whatever base admixture of foreign superstitions, the dominant creed of a large fraction of mankind.

Let us now set our faces westwards, towards Asia Minor and Greece and Italy, to view the rise and progress of another philosophy, apparently independent, but no less pervaded by the conception of evolution.[35]

The sages of Miletus were pronounced evolutionists; and, however dark may be some of the sayings of Heraclitus of Ephesus, who was probably a contemporary of Gautama, no better expressions of the essence of the modern doctrine of evolution can be found than are presented by some of his pithy aphorisms and striking metaphors.[36] Indeed, many of my present auditors must have observed that, more than once, I have borrowed from him in the brief exposition of the theory of evolution with which this discourse commenced.

But when the focus of Greek intellectual activity shifted to Athens, the leading minds concentrated their attention upon ethical problems. Forsaking the study of the macrocosm for that of the microcosm, they lost the key to the thought of the great

Ephesian, which, I imagine, is more intelligible to us than it was to Socrates, or to Plato. Socrates, more especially, set the fashion of a kind of inverse agnosticism, by teaching that the problems of physics lie beyond the reach of the human intellect; that the attempt to solve them is essentially vain; that the one worthy object of investigation is the problem of ethical life; and his example was followed by the Cynics and the later Stoics. Even the comprehensive knowledge and the penetrating intellect of Aristotle failed to suggest to him that in holding the eternity of the world, within its present range of mutation, he was making a retrogressive step. The scientific heritage of Heraclitus passed into the hands neither of Plato nor of Aristotle, but into those of Democritus. But the world was not yet ready to receive the great conceptions of the philosopher of Abdera. It was reserved for the Stoics to return to the track marked out by the earlier philosophers; and, professing themselves disciples of Heraclitus, to develop the idea of evolution systematically. In doing this, they not only omitted some characteristic features of their master's teaching, but they made additions altogether foreign to it. One of the most influential of these importations was the transcendental theism which had come into vogue. The restless, fiery energy, operating according to law, out of which all things emerge and into which they return, in the endless successive cycles of the great year; which creates and destroys worlds as a wanton child builds up, and anon levels, sand castles on the seashore; was metamorphosed into a material world--soul and decked out with all the attributes of ideal Divinity; not merely with infinite power and transcendent wisdom, but with absolute goodness.

The consequences of this step were momentous. For if the cosmos is the effect of an immanent, omnipotent, and infinitely beneficent cause, the existence in it of real evil, still less of necessarily inherent evil, is plainly inadmissible.[37] Yet the universal experience of mankind testified then, as now, that, whether we look within us or without us, evil stares us in the face on all sides; that if anything is real, pain and sorrow aud wrong are realities.

It would be a new thing in history if *à priori* philosophers were daunted by the factious opposition of experience; and the Stoics were the last men to allow themselves to be beaten by mere facts. "Give me a doctrine and I will find the reasons for it," said Chrysippus. So they perfected, if they did not invent, that ingenious and plausible form of pleading, the Theodicy; for the purpose of showing firstly, that there is no such thing as evil; secondly, that if there is, it is the necessary correlate of good; and, moreover, that it is either due to our own fault, or inflicted for our benefit. Theodicies have been very popular in their time, and I believe that a numerous, though somewhat dwarfed, progeny of them still survives. So far as I know, they are all variations of the theme set forth in those famous six lines of the "Essay on Man," in which Pope sums up Bolingbroke's reminiscences of stoical and other speculations of this kind—

> "All nature is but art, unknown to thee;
> All chance, direction which thou canst not see;
> All discord, harmony not understood;
> All partial evil, universal good;
> And spite of pride, in erring reason's spite
> One truth is clear: whatever is is right."

Yet, surely, if there are few more important truths than those enunciated in the first triad, the second is open to very grave objections. That there is a "soul of good in things evil" is unquestionable; nor will any wise man deny the disciplinary value of pain and sorrow. But these considerations do not help us to see why the immense multitude of irresponsible sentient beings, which cannot profit by such discipline, should suffer; nor why, among the endless possibilities open to omnipotence—that of sinless, happy existence among the rest—the actuality in which sin and misery abound should be that selected. Surely it is mere cheap rhetoric to call arguments which have never yet been answered by even the meekest and the least rational of Optimists, suggestions of the pride of reason. As to the concluding aphorism, its fittest place would be as an inscription in letters of mud over the portal of some "stye of Epicurus";[38] for that is where the logical application of it to practice would land men, with every aspiration stifled and every effort paralyzed. Why try to set right what is right already? Why strive to improve the best of all possible worlds? Let us eat and drink, for as today all is right, so to-morrow all will be.

But the attempt of the Stoics to blind themselves to the reality of evil, as a necessary concomitant of the cosmic process, had less success than that of the Indian philosophers to exclude the reality of good from their purview. Unfortunately, it is much easier to shut one's eyes to good than to evil. Pain and sorrow knock at our doors more loudly than pleasure and happiness; and the prints of their heavy footsteps are less easily effaced. Before the grim realities of practical life the pleasant fictions of optimism vanished. If this were the best of all possible worlds, it nevertheless proved itself a very inconvenient habitation for the ideal sage.

The stoical summary of the whole duty of man, "Live according to nature," would seem to imply that the cosmic process is an exemplar for human conduct. Ethics would thus become applied Natural History. In fact, a confused employment of the maxim, in this sense, has done immeasurable mischief in later times. It has furnished an axiomatic foundation for the philosophy of philosophasters and for the moralizing of sentimentalists. But the Stoics were, at bottom, not merely noble, but sane, men; and if we look closely into what they really meant by this ill-used phrase, it will be found to present no justification for the mischievous conclusions that have been deduced from it.

In the language of the Stoa, "Nature" was a word of many meanings. There was the "Nature" of the cosmos and the "Nature" of man. In the latter, the animal "nature," which man shares with a moiety of the living part of the cosmos, was distinguished from a higher "nature." Even in this higher nature there were grades of rank. The logical faculty is an instrument which may be turned to account for any purpose. The passions and the emotions are so closely tied to the lower nature that they may be considered to be pathological, rather than normal, phenomena. The one supreme, hegemonic, faculty, which constitutes the essential "nature" of man, is most nearly represented by that which, in the language of of a later philosophy, has been called the pure reason. It is this "nature" which holds up the ideal of the supreme good and demands absolute submission of the will to its behests. It is this which commands all men to love one another, to return good for evil, to regard one another as fellow-citizens of one great state. Indeed, seeing that the progress towards perfection of a civilized state, or polity, depends on the obedience of its members to these commands, the Stoics sometimes termed the pure reason the "political" nature. Unfortunately, the sense of the adjective has undergone so much modification, that the application of it to that which commands the sacrifice of self to the common good would now sound almost grotesque.[39]

But what part is played by the theory of evolution in this view of ethics? So far as I can discern, the ethical system of the Stoics, which is essentially intuitive, and reverences the categorical imperative as strongly as that of any later moralists, might have been just what it was if they had held any other theory; whether that of special creation, on the one side, or that of the eternal existence of the present order, on the other.[40] To the Stoic, the cosmos had no importance for the conscience, except in so far as he chose to think it a pedagogue to virtue. The pertinacious optimism of our philosophers hid from them the actual state of the case. It prevented them from seeing that cosmic nature is no school of virtue, but the headquarters of the enemy of ethical nature. The logic of facts was necessary to convince them that the cosmos works through the lower nature of man, not for righteousness, but against it. And it finally drove them to confess that the existence of their ideal "wise man" was incompatible with the nature of things; that even a passable approximation to that ideal was to be attained only at the cost of renunciation of the world and mortification, not merely of the flesh, but of all human affections. The state of perfection was that "apatheia"[41] in which desire, though it may still be felt, is powerless to move the will, reduced to the sole function of executing the commands of pure reason. Even this residuum of activity was to be regarded as a temporary loan, as an efflux of the divine world-pervading spirit, chafing at its imprisonment in the flesh, until such time as death enabled it to return to its source in the all-pervading logos.

I find it difficult to discover any very great difference between Apatheia and Nirvana, except that stoical speculation agrees with pre-Buddhistic philosophy, rather than with the teachings of Gautama, in so far as it postulates a permanent substance equivalent to "Brahma" and "Atman"; and that, in stoical practice, the adoption of the life of the mendicant cynic was held to be more a counsel of perfection than an indispensable condition of the higher life.

Thus the extremes touch. Greek thought and Indian thought set out from ground common to both, diverge widely, develop under very different physical and moral conditions, and finally converge to practically the same end.

The Vedas and the Homeric epos set before us a world of rich and vigorous life, full of joyous fighting men

> That ever with a frolic welcome took
> The thunder and the sunshine . . . .

and who were ready to brave the very Gods themselves when their blood was up. A few centuries pass away, and under the influence of civilization the descendants of these men are "sicklied o'er with the pale cast of thought"—frank pessimists, or, at best, make-believe optimists. The courage of the warlike stock may be as hardly tried as before, perhaps more hardly, but the enemy is self. The hero has become a monk. The man of action is replaced by the quietist, whose highest aspiration is to be the passive instrument of the divine Reason. By the Tiber, as by the Ganges, ethical man admits that the cosmos is too strong for him; and, destroying every bond which ties him to it by ascetic discipline, he seeks salvation in absolute renunciation.[42]

Modern thought is making a fresh start from the base whence Indian and Greek philosophy set out; and, the human mind being very much what it was six-and-twenty centuries ago, there is no ground for wonder if it presents indications of a tendency to move along the old lines to the same results.

We are more than sufficiently familiar with modern pessimism, at least as a speculation; for I cannot call to mind that any of its present votaries have sealed their faith by assuming the rags and the bowl of the mendicant Bhikku, or the cloak and the

wallet of the Cynic. The obstacles placed in the way of sturdy vagrancy by an unphilo-
sophical police have, perhaps, proved too formidable for philosophical consistency. We
also know modern speculative optimism, with its perfectibility of the species, reign of
peace, and lion and lamb transformation scenes; but one does not hear so much of it as
one did forty years ago; indeed, I imagine it is to be met with more commonly at the
tables of the healthy and wealthy, than in the congregations of the wise. The majority
of us, I apprehend, profess neither pessimism nor optimism. We hold that the world is
neither so good, nor so bad, as it conceivably might be; and, as most of us have reason,
now and again, to discover that it can be. Those who have failed to experience the joys
that make life worth living are, probably, in as small a minority as those who have
never known the griefs that rob existence of its savour and turn its richest fruits into
mere dust and ashes.

Further, I think I do not err in assuming that, however diverse their views on
philosophical and religious matters, most men are agreed that the proportion of good
and evil in life may be very sensibly affected by human action. I never heard anybody
doupt that the evil may be thus increased, or diminished; and it would seem to follow
that good must be similarly susceptible of addition or subtraction. Finally, to my
knowledge, nobody professes to doubt that, so far forth as we possess a power of
bettering things, it is our paramount duty to use it and to train all our intellect and
energy to this supreme service of our kind.

Hence the pressing interest of the question, to what extent modern progress in
natural knowledge, and, more especially, the general outcome of that progress in the
doctrine of evolution, is competent to help us in the great work of helping one another?

The propounders of what are called the "ethics of evolution," when the "evolution of ethics" would usually better express the object of their speculations, adduce a
number of more or less interesting facts and more or less sound arguments, in favour
of the origin of the moral sentiments, in the same way as other natural phenomena, by
a process of evolution. I have little doubt, for my own part, that they are on the right
track; but as the immoral sentiments have no less been evolved, there is, so far, as
much natural sanction for the one as the other. The thief and the murderer follow
nature just as much as the philanthropist. Cosmic evolution may teach us how the good
and the evil tendencies of man may have come about; but, in itself, it is incompetent to
furnish any better reason why what we call good is preferable to what we call evil than
we had before. Some day, I doubt not, we shall arrive at an understanding of the
evolution of the æsthetic faculty; but all the understanding in the world will neither
increase nor diminish the force of the intuition that this is beautiful and that is ugly.

There is another fallacy which appears to me to pervade the so-called "ethics of evolution." It is the notion that because, on the whole, animals and plants have advanced in perfection of organization by means of the struggle for existence and the consequent "survival of the fittest"; therefore men in society, men as ethical beings, must look to the same process to help them towards perfection. I suspect that this fallacy has arisen out of the unfortunate ambiguity of the phrase "survival of the fittest." "Fittest" has a connotation of "best"; and about "best" there hangs a moral flavour. In cosmic nature, however, what is "fittest" depends upon the conditions. Long since,[43] I ventured to point out that if our hemisphere were to cool again, the survival of the fittest might bring about, in the vegetable kingdom, a population of more and more stunted and humbler and humbler organisms, until the "fittest" that survived might be nothing but lichens, diatoms, and such microscopic organisms as those which give red snow its colour; while, if it became hotter, the pleasant valleys of the Thames and Isis might be uninhabitable by any animated beings save those that flourish in a tropical jungle. They, as the fittest, the best adapted to the changed conditions, would survive.

Men in society are undoubtedly subject to the cosmic process. As among other animals, multiplication goes on without cessation, and involves severe competition for the means of support. The struggle for existence tends to eliminate those less fitted to adapt themselves to the circumstances of their existence. The strongest, the most self-assertive, tend to tread down the weaker. But the influence of the cosmic process on the evolution of society is the greater the more rudimentary its civilization. Social progress means a checking of the cosmic process at every step and the substitution for it of another, which may be called the ethical process; the end of which is not the survival of those who may happen to be the fittest, in respect of the whole of the conditions which obtain, but of those who are ethically the best.[44]

As I have already urged, the practice of that which is ethically best—what we call goodness or virtue—involves a course of conduct which, in all respects, is opposed to that which leads to success in the cosmic struggle for existence. In place of ruthless self-assertion it demands self-restraint; in place of thrusting aside, or treading down, all competitors, it requires that the individual shall not merely respect, but shall help his fellows; its influence is directed, not so much to the survival of the fittest, as to the fitting of as many as possible to survive. It repudiates the gladiatorial theory of existence. It demands that each man who enters into the enjoyment of the advantages of a polity shall be mindful of his debt to those who have laboriously constructed it; and shall take heed that no act of his weakens the fabric in which he has been permitted to live. Laws and moral precepts are directed to the end of curbing the cosmic process and reminding the individual of his duty to the community, to the protection and influence of which he owes, if not existence itself, at least the life of something better than a brutal savage.

It is from neglect of these plain considerations that the fanatical individualism[45] of our time attempts to apply the analogy of cosmic nature to society. Once more we have a misapplication of the stoical injunction to follow nature; the duties of the individual to the state are forgotten, and his tendencies to self-assertion are dignified by the name of rights. It is seriously debated whether the members of a community are justified in using their combined strength to constrain one of their number to contribute his share to the maintenance of it; or even to prevent him from doing his best to destroy it. The struggle for existence which has done such admirable work in cosmic nature, must, it appears, be equally beneficent in the ethical sphere. Yet if that which I have insisted upon is true; if the cosmic process has no sort of relation to moral ends; if the imitation of it by man is inconsistent with the first principles of ethics; what becomes of this surprising theory?

Let us understand, once for all, that the ethical progress of society depends, not on imitating the cosmic process, still less in running away from it but in combating it. It may seem an audacious proposal thus to pit the microcosm against the macrocosm and to set man to subdue nature to his higher ends; but I venture to think that the great intellectual difference between the ancient times with which we have been occupied and our day, lies in the solid foundation we have acquired for the hope that such an enterprise may meet with a certain measure of success.

The history of civilization details the steps by which men have succeeded in building up an artificial world within the cosmos. Fragile reed as he may be, man, as Pascal says, is a thinking reed:[46] there lies within him a fund of energy, operating intelligently and so far akin to that which pervades the universe, that it is competent to influence and modify the cosmic process. In virtue of his intelligence, the dwarf bends the Titan to his will. In every family, in every polity that has been established, the cosmic process in man has been restrained and otherwise modified by law and custom; in surrounding nature, it has been similarly influenced by the art of the shepherd, the agriculturist, the artisan. As civilization has advanced, so has the extent of this interference increased; until the organized and highly developed sciences and arts of the present day have endowed man with a command over the course of non-human nature greater than that once attributed to the magicians. The most impressive, I might say startling, of these changes have been brought about in the course of the last two centuries; while a right comprehension of the process of life and of the means of influencing its manifestations is only just dawning upon us. We do not yet see our way beyond generalities; and we are befogged by the obtrusion of false analogies and crude anticipations. But Astronomy, Physics, Chemistry, have all had to pass through similar phases, before they reached the stage at which their influence became an important factor in human affairs. Physiology, Psychology, Ethics, Political Science, must submit to the same ordeal. Yet it seems to me irrational to doubt that, at no distant period, they will work as great a revolution in the sphere of practice.

The theory of evolution encourages no millennial anticipations. If, for millions of years, our globe has taken the upward road, yet, some time, the summit will be reached and the downward route will be commenced. The most daring imagination will hardly venture upon the suggestion that the power and the intelligence of man can ever arrest the procession of the great year.

Moreover, the cosmic nature born with us and, to a large extent, necessary for our maintenance, is the outcome of millions of years of severe training, and it would be folly to imagine that a few centuries will suffice to subdue its masterfulness to purely ethical ends. Ethical nature may count upon having to reckon with a tenacious and powerful enemy as long as the world lasts. But, on the other hand, I see no limit to the extent to which intelligence and will, guided by sound principles of investigation, and organized in common effort, may modify the conditions of existence, for a period longer than that now covered by history. And much may be done to change the nature of man himself.[47] The intelligence which has converted the brother of the wolf into the faithful guardian of the flock ought to be able to do something towards curbing the instincts of savagery in civilized men.

But if we may permit ourselves a larger hope of abatement of the essential evil of the world than was possible to those who, in the infancy of exact knowledge, face the problem of existence more than a score of centuries ago, I deem it an essential condition of the realization of that hope that we should cast aside the notion that the escape from pain and sorrow is the proper object of life.

We have long since emerged from the heroic childhood of our race, when good and evil could be met with the same "frolic welcome"; the attempts to escape from evil, whether Indian or Greek, have ended in flight from the battle-field; it remains to us to throw aside the youthful overconfidence and the no less youthful discouragement of nonage. We are grown men, and must play the man

strong in will
To strive, to seek, to find, and not to yield,

cherishing the good that falls in our way, and bearing the evil, in and around us, with stout hearts set on diminishing it. So far, we all may strive in one faith towards one hope:

> It may be that the gulfs will wash us down,
> It may be we shall touch the Happy Isles,
>
> . . . . but something ere the end,
> Some work of noble note may yet be done. [48]

Notes

1. See "On a piece of Chalk" in the preceding volume of these Essays (vol. viii, p. 1).

2. That every theory of evolution must be consistent not merely with progressive development, but with indefinite persistence in the same condition and with retrogressive modification, is a point which I have insisted upon repeatedly from the year 1862 till now. See *Collected Essays*, vol ii, pp. 461-89; vol. iii, p. 33; vol. viii, p. 304. In the address on "Geological Contemporaneity and Persistent Types" (1862), the paleontological proofs of this proposition were, I believe, first set forth.

3. "On the Border Territory between the Animal and the Vegetable Kingdoms," Essays, vol. viii, p. 162.

4. See "Evolution in Biology," Essays, vol. ii, p. 187.

5. *Collected Essays*, vol. ii, *passim.*

6. *Ibid.*, vol iv, p. 138; vol. v, pp. 71-73.

7. *Ibid.*, vol. viii, p. 321.

8. The sense of the term "Art" is becoming narrowed; "work of Art" to most people means a picture, a statue, or a piece of *bijouterie*; by way of compensation "artist" has included in its wide embrace cooks and ballet girls, no less than painters and sculptors.

9. See "Man's Place in Nature," *Collected Essays*, vol. vii, and "On the Struggle for Existence in Human Society" (1888), below.

10. Or to put the case still more simply. When a man lays hold of the two ends of a piece of string and pulls them, with intent to break it, the right arm is certainly exerted in antagonism to the left arm; yet both arms derive their energy from the same original source.

11. Not that the conception of such a society is necessarily based upon the idea of evolution. The Platonic state testifies to the contrary.

12. *Collected Essays*, vol. i, "Animal Automatism"; vol. v, "Prologue," pp. 45 *et seq.*

13. *Collected Essays*, vol. v, Prologue, pp. 50-54.

14. See below. Romanes' Lecture, note [31, p. 74].

15. Adam Smith makes the pithy observation that the man who sympathises with a woman in childbed, cannot be said to put himself in her place. ("The Theory of the Moral Sentiments," Part vii. sec. iii. chap. i.) Perhaps there is more humour than force in the example; and in spite of this and other observations

of the same tenor, I think that the one defect of the remarkable work in which it occurs is that it lays too much stress on conscious substitution, too little on purely reflex sympathy.

16. Esther v: 9-13 ". . . but when Haman saw Mordecai in the king's gate, that he stood up, nor moved for him, he was full of indignation against Mordecai. . . . And Haman told them of the glory of his riches. . . . and all the things wherein the king had promoted him. . . . Yet all this availeth me nothing, so long as I see Mordecai the Jew sitting at the king's gate." What a shrewd exposure of human weakness it is!

17. "Theory of the Moral Sentiments," Part iii, chap. 3. *On the influence and authority of conscience.*

18. Worked out, in its essential features, chiefly by Hartley and Adam Smith, long before the modern doctrine of evolution was thought of. See *Note* below, note [24].

19. See the essay "On the Struggle for Existence in Human Society" below; and *Collected Essays*, in vol. i, p. 276, for Kant's recognition of these facts.

20. *Collected Essays*, vol. v, Prologue, p. 52.

21. Whether the struggle for existence with the state of nature and with other societies, so far as they stand in the relation of the state of nature with it, exerts a selective influence upon modern society, and in what direction, are questions not easy to answer. The problem of the effect of military and industrial warfare upon those who wage it is very complicated.

22. Those who read the last Essay in this volume will not accuse me of wishing to attenuate the evil of the existence of this group, whether great or small.

23. I have elsewhere lamented the absence from society of a machinery for facilitating the descent of incapacity. "Administrative Nihilism," *Collected Essays*, vol. i, p. 54.

24. *Note* (see note [18]).—It seems the fashion nowadays to ignore Hartley; though, a century and a half ago, he not only laid the foundations but built up much of the superstructure of a true theory of the Evolution of the intellectual and moral faculties. He speaks of what I have termed the ethical process as "our Progress from Self-interest to Self-annihilation." *Observations on Man* (1749), vol. ii, p. 281.

25. I have been careful to speak of the "appearance" of cylical evolution presented by living things; for, on critical examination, it will be found that the course of vegetable and of animal life is not exactly represented by the figure of a cycle which returns into itself. What actually happens, in all but the lowest organisms, is that one part of the growing germ (*A*) gives rise to tissues and organs; while another part (*B*) remains in its primitive condition, or is but slightly modified. The moiety *A* becomes the body of the adult and, sooner or later, perishes, while portions of the moiety *B* are detached and, as offspring, continue the life of the species. Thus, if we trace back an organism along the direct line of descent from its remotest ancestor, *B*, as a whole, has never suffered death; portions of it, only, have been cast off and died in each individual offspring.

Everybody is familiar with the way in which the "suckers" of a strawberry plant behave. A thin cylinder of living tissue keeps on growing at its free end, until it attains a considerable length. At successive intervals, it develops buds which grow into strawberry plants; and these become independent by the death of the parts of the sucker which connect them. The rest of the sucker, however, may go on living and growing indefinitely, and, circumstances remaining favourable, there is no obvious reason why it should ever die. The living substance *B*, in a manner, answers to the sucker. If we could restore the continuity which was once possessed by the portions of *B*, contained in all the individuals of a direct line of descent, they would form a sucker, or stolon, on which these individuals would be strung, and which would never have wholly died.

A species remains unchanged so long as the potentiality of development resident in *B* remains unaltered; so long, *e.g.*, as the buds of the strawberry sucker tend to become typical strawberry plants. In the case of the progressive evolution of a species, the developmental potentiality of *B* becomes of a higher and higher order. In retrogressive evolution, the contrary would be the case. The phenomena of atavism seem to show that retrogressive evolution, that is, the return of a species to one or other of its earlier forms, is a possibility to be reckoned with. The simplification of structure, which is so common in the parasitic members of a group, however, does not properly come under this head. The worm-like, limbless *Lernœa* has no resemblance to any of the stages of development of the many-limbed active animals of the group to which it belongs.

26. Heraclitus says, "It is impossible to reenter the same river"; but, to be strictly accurate, the river remains, though the water of which it is composed changes—just as a man retains his identity though the whole substance of his body is constantly shifting.

This is put very well by Seneca (Ep. lviii, 22): "Our bodies are carried along like flowing waters; everything goes with time in its flight. None of the visible things are fixed. Even I, as I am speaking about this change, am changed. This is exactly what Heraclitus says: 'We cannot enter the same river twice.' The river is called by the same name, but the water has already gone by. This is more evident in rivers than in humans. We are also carried in no less rapid a course. . ."

27. "Many of our blessings harm us, because the agony of fear is brought back by memory, while foresight brings it too early. No one keeps his unhappiness to the present" (Seneca, Ep. v, 7).

Among the many wise and weighty aphorisms of the Roman Bacon, few sound the realities of life more deeply than "Many of our blessings harm us." If there is a soul of good in things evil, it is at least equally true that there is a soul of evil in things good: for things, like men, have "les défauts de leurs qualités." It is one of the last lessons one learns from experience, but not the least important, that a heavy tax is levied upon all forms of success; and that failure is one of the commonest disguises assumed by blessings.

28. "There is within the body of every man a soul which, at the death of the body, flies away from it like a bird out of a cage, and enters upon a new life . . . either in one of the heavens or one of the hells or on this earth. The only exception is the rare case of a man having in this life acquired a true knowledge of God. According to the pre-Buddhistic theory, the soul of such a man goes along the path of the Gods to God, and, being united with Him, enters upon an immortal life in which his individuality is not extinguished. In the latter theory, his soul is directly absorbed into the Great Soul, is lost in it, and has no longer any independent existence. The souls of all other men enter, after the death of the body, upon a new existence in one or other of the many different modes of being. If in heaven or hell, the soul itself becomes a god or demon without entering a body; all superhuman beings, save the great gods, being looked upon as not eternal, but merely temporary creatures. If the soul returns to earth it may or may not enter a new body; and this either of a human being, an animal, a plant, or even a material object. For all these are possessed of souls, and there is no essential difference between these souls and the souls of men—all being alike mere sparks of the Great Spirit, who is the only real existence" (Rhys Davids, *Hibbert Lectures*, 1881, p. 83).

For what I have said about Indian Philosophy, I am particularly indebted to the luminous exposition of primitive Buddhism and its relations to earlier Hindu thought, which is given by Prof. Rhys Davids in his remarkable *Hibbert Lectures* for 1881, and *Buddhism* (1890). The only apology I can offer for the freedom with which I have borrowed from him in these notes, is my desire to leave no doubt as to my indebtedness. I have also found Dr. Oldenberg's *Buddha* (Ed. 2, 1890) very helpful. The origin of the theory of transmigration stated in the above extract is an unsolved problem. That it differs widely from the Egyptian metempsychosis is clear. In fact, since men usually people the other world with phantoms of this, the Egyptian doctrine would seem to presuppose the Indian as a more archaic belief.

Prof. Rhys Davids has fully insisted upon the ethical importance of the transmigration theory. "One of the latest speculations now being put forward among ourselves would seek to explain each man's character, and even his outward condition in life, by the character he inherited from his ancestors, a character gradually formed during a practically endless series of past existences, modified only by the conditions into which he was born, those very conditions being also, in like manner, the last result of a practically endless series of past causes. Gotama's speculation might be stated in the same words. But it attempted also to explain, in a way different from that which would be adopted by the exponents of the modern theory, that strange problem which it is also the motive of the wonderful drama of the book of Job to explain—the fact that the actual distribution here of good fortune or misery, is entirely independent of the moral qualities which men call good or bad. We cannot wonder that a teacher, whose whole system was so essentially an ethical reformation, should have felt it incumbent upon him to seek an explanation of this apparent injustice. And all the more so, since the belief he had inherited, the theory of the transmigration of souls, had provided a solution perfectly sufficient to any one who could accept that belief" (*Hibbert Lectures*, p. 93). I should venture to suggest the substitution of "largely" for "entirely" in the foregoing passage. Whether a ship makes a good or a bad voyage is largely independent of the conduct of the captain, but it is largely affected by that conduct. Though powerless before a hurricane he may weather many a bad gale.

29. The outward condition of the soul is, in each new birth, determined by its actions in a previous birth; but by each action in succession, and not by the balance struck after the evil has been reckoned off against the good. A good man who has once uttered a slander may spend a hundred thousand years as a god, in consequence of his goodness, and when the power of his good actions is exhausted, may be born as a dumb man on account of his transgression; and a robber who has once done an act of mercy, may come to life in a king's body as the result of his virtue, and then suffer torments for ages in hell or as a ghost without a body, or be re-born many times as a slave or an outcast, in consequence of his evil life.

"There is no escape, according to this theory, from the result of any act; though it is only the consequences of its own acts that each soul has to endure. The force has been set in motion by itself and can never stop; and its effect can never be foretold. If evil, it can never be modified or prevented, for it depends on a cause already completed, that is now for ever beyond the soul's control. There is even no continuing consciousness, no memory of the past that could guide the soul to any knowledge of its fate. The only advantage open to it is to add in this life to the sum of its good actions, that it may bear fruit with the rest. And even this can only happen in some future life under essentially the same conditions as the present one: subject, like the present one, to old age, decay, and death; and affording opportunity, like the present one, for the commission of errors, ignorances, or sins, which in their turn must inevitably produce their due effect of sickness, disability, or woe. Thus is the soul tossed about from life to life, from billow to billow in the great ocean of transmigration. And there is no escape save for the very few, who, during their birth as men, attain to a right knowledge of the Great Spirit: and thus enter into immortality, or, as the later philosophers taught, are absorbed into the Divine Essence" (Rhys Davids, *Hibbert Lectures*, pp. 85, 86).

The state after death thus imagined by the Hindu philosophers has a certain analogy to the purgatory of the Roman Church; except that escape from it is dependent, not on a divine decree modified, it may be, by sacerdotal or saintly intercession, but by the acts of the individual himself; and that while ultimate emergence into heavenly bliss of the good, or well-prayed for, Catholic is professedly assured, the chances in favour of the attainment of absorption, or of Nirvana, by any individual Hindu are extremely small.

30. "That part of the then prevalent transmigration theory which could not be proved false seemed to meet a deeply felt necessity, seemed to supply a moral cause which would explain the unequal distribution here of happinesss or woe, so utterly inconsistent with the present characters of men." Gautama "still therefore talked of men's previous existence, but by no means in the way that he is generally represented to have done." What he taught was "the transmigration of character." He held that after the death of any being, whether human or not, there survived nothing at all but that being's "Karma," the result, that is, of its mental and bodily actions. Every individual, whether human or divine, was the last inheritor and the last result of the Karma of a long series of past individuals—a series so long that its beginning is beyond the reach of calculation, and its end will be coincident with the destruction of the world" (Rhys Davids, *Hibbert Lectures*, p. 92).

In the theory of evolution, the tendency of a germ to develop according to a certain specific type, *e.g.*, of the kidney bean seed to grow into a plant having all the characters of *Phaseolus vulgaris*, is its "Karma." It is the "last inheritor and the last result" of all the conditions that have affected a line of ancestry which goes back for many millions of years to the time when life first appeared on the earth. The moiety B of the substance of the bean plant (see *Note* 25) is the last link in a once continuous chain extending from the primitive living substance: and the characters of the successive species to which it has given rise are the manifestations of its gradually modified Karma. As Prof. Rhys Davids aptly says, the snowdrop "is a snowdrop and not an oak, and just that kind of snowdrop, because it is the outcome of the

Karma of an endless series of past existences" (*Hibbert Lectures*, p. 114).

31. "It is interesting to notice that the very point which is the weakness of the theory—the supposed concentration of the effect of the Karma in one new being—presented itself to the early Buddhists themselves as a difficulty. They avoided it, partly by explaining that it was a particular thirst in the creature dying (a craving, Tanha, which plays otherwise a great part in the Buddhist theory) which actually caused the birth of the new individual who was to inherit the Karma of the former one. But, how this took place, how the craving desire produced this effect, was acknowledged to be a mystery patent only to a Buddha" (Rhys Davids, *Hibbert Lectures*, p. 95).

Among the many parallelisms of Stoicism and Buddhism, it is curious to find one for this Tanha, "thirst," or "craving desire" for life. Seneca writes (Epist. lxxvi 18): " If there is other than honorable goodness, we will be hounded by greed for life and life's comforts. But this is undefinable, boundless, and intolerable."

32. "The distinguishing characteristic of Buddhism was that it started a new line, that it looked upon the deepest questions men have to solve from an entirely different standpoint. It swept away from the field of its vision the whole of the great soul-theory which had hitherto so completely filled and dominated the minds of the superstitious and the thoughtful alike. For the first time in the history of the world, it proclaimed a salvation which each man could gain for himself and by himself, in this world, during this life, without any the least reference to God, or to Gods, either great or small. Like the Upanishads, it placed the first importance on knowledge; but it was no longer a knowledge of God, it was a clear perception of the real nature, as they supposed it to be, of men and things. And it added to the necessity of knowledge, the necessity of purity, of courtesy, of uprightness, of peace and of a universal love far reaching, grown great and beyond measure" (Rhys Davids, *Hibbert Lectures*, p. 29).

The contemporary Greek philosophy takes an analogous direction. According to Heraclitus, the universe was made neither by Gods nor men; but, from all eternity, has been, and to all eternity, will be, immortal fire, glowing and fading in due measure (Mullach, *Heracliti Fragmenta*, 27). And the part assigned by his successors, the Stoics, to the knowledge and the volition of the "wise man" made their Divinity (for logical thinkers) a subject for compliments, rather than a power to be reckoned with. In Hindu speculation the "Arahat," still more the "Buddha," becomes the superior of Brahma; the stoical "wise man" is, at least, the equal of Zeus.

Berkeley affirms over and over again that no idea can be formed of a soul or spirit—"If any man shall doubt of the truth of what is here delivered, let him but reflect and try if he can form any idea of power or active being; and whether he hath ideas of two principal powers marked by the names of *will* and *understanding* distinct from each other, as well as from a third idea of substance or being in general, with a relative notion of its supporting or being the subject of the aforesaid power, which is signified by the name *soul* or *spirit*. This is what some hold: but, so far as I can see, the words *will, soul, spirit*, do not stand for different ideas or, in truth, for any idea at all, but for something which is very different from ideas, and which, being an agent, cannot be like unto or represented by any idea whatever [though it must be owned at the same time, that we have some notion of soul, spirit, and the operations of the mind, such as willing, loving, hating, inasmuch as we know or understand the meaning of these words]" (*The Principles of Human Knowledge*, lxxvi. See also §§ lxxxix, cxxxv, cxlv.).

It is open to discussion, I think, whether it is possible to have "some notion" of that of which we can form no "idea."

Berkeley attaches several predicates to the "perceiving active being mind, spirit, soul or myself" (Parts I, II) It is said, for example, to be "indivisible, incorporeal, unextended, and incorruptible." The predicate indivisible, though negative in form, has highly positive consequences. For, if "perceiving active being" is strictly indivisible, man's soul must be one with the Divine spirit: which is good Hindu or Stoical doctrine, but hardly orthodox Christian philosophy. If, on the other hand, the "substance" of active perceiving "being" is actually divided into the one Divine and innumerable human entities, how can the predicate "indivisible" be rigorously applicable to it?

Taking the words cited, as they stand, they amount to the denial of the possibility of any knowledge of substance. "Matter" having been resolved into mere affections of "spirit," "spirit" melts away into an admittedly inconceivable and unknowable hypostasis of thought and power—consequently the existence of anything in the universe beyond a flow of phenomena is a purely hypothetical assumption. Indeed a pyrrhonist might raise the objection that if "esse" is "percipi" spirit itself can have no existence except as a perception, hypostatized into a "self," or as a perception of some other spirit. In the former case, objective reality vanishes; in the latter, there would seem to be the need of an infinite series of spirits each perceiving the others.

It is curious to observe how very closely the phraseology of Berkeley sometimes approaches that of the Stoics: thus (cxlviii) "It seems to be a *general pretence of the unthinking* herd that *they cannot see God* . . . . But, alas, we need only open our eyes to see the Sovereign Lord of all things with a more full and clear view, than we do any of our fellow-creatures . . . . we do at all times and in all places perceive manifest tokens of the Divinity: everything we see, hear, feel, or any wise perceive by sense, being a sign or effect of the power of God" . . . . cxlix. "It is therefore plain, that *nothing can be more evident* to any one that is capable of the least reflection, *than the existence of God*, or a spirit who is intimately present to our minds, producing in them all that variety of ideas or sensations which continually affect us, on whom we have an absolute and entire dependence, in short, *in whom we live and move and have our being*." cl. [But you will say hath Nature no share in the production of natural things, and must they be all ascribed to the immediate and sole operation of God? . . . . if by *Nature* is meant some being distinct from God, as well as from the laws of nature and things perceived by sense, I must confess that word is to me an empty sound, without any intelligible meaning annexed to it.] Nature in this acceptation is a vain *Chimæra* introduced by those heathens, who had not just notions of the omnipresence and infinite perfection of God."

Compare Seneca (*De Beneficiis*, iv, 7): "You say that it is nature who gives me these things. But do you not understand that this is only another name for God? For what is nature if not God and the divine reason that penetrates the whole cosmos and all its parts? You can call, as frequently as you desire, this creator of our world by different names; it will be correct to call him Jupiter the Best and the Greatest, and the Thunderer and the Stayer, a name derived, not from the historical fact that the Roman battle-line stayed its flight in answer to prayer, but from the fact that everything is stayed by his grace, that he is their stayer and stabilizer. Or should you call him fate, it would not be wrong, because fate is no more than a connected chain of causes, and he is the first cause on which all the others depend." It would appear, therefore, that the good Bishop is somewhat hard upon the "heathen," of whose words his own might be a paraphrase.

There is yet another direction in which Berkeley's philosophy, I will not say agrees with Gautama's, but at any rate helps to make a fundamental dogma of Buddhism intelligible. "I find I can excite ideas in my mind at pleasure, and vary and shift the scene as often as I think fit. It is no more than willing, and straightway this or that idea arises in my fancy: and by the same power, it is obliterated, and makes way for another. This making and unmaking of ideas doth very properly denominate the mind active. This much is certain and grounded on experience . . ." (*Principles*, xxviii).

A good many of us, I fancy, have reason to think that experience tells them very much the contrary; and are painfully familiar with the obsession of the mind by ideas which cannot be obliterated by any effort of the will and steadily refuse to make way for others. But what I desire to point out is that if Gautama was equally confident that he could "make and unmake" ideas—then, since he had resolved self into a group of ideal phantoms—the possibility of abolishing self by volition naturally followed.

33. According to Buddhism, the relation of one life to the next is merely that borne by the flame of one lamp to the flame of another lamp which is set alight by it. To the "Arahat" or adept "no outward form, no compound thing, no creature, no creator, no existence of any kind, must appear to be other than a temporary collocation of its component parts, fated inevitably to be dissolved." Rhys Davids, *Hibbert Lectures*, p. 211).

The self is nothing but a group of phenomena held together by the desire of life; when that desire shall have ceased, "the Karma of that particular chain of lives will cease to influence any longer any distinct individual, and there will be no more birth; for birth, decay, and death, grief, lamentation, and despair will have come, so far as regards that chain of lives, for ever to an end."

The state of mind of the Arahat in which the desire of life has ceased is Nirvana. Dr. Oldenberg has very acutely and patiently considered the various interpretations which have been attached to "Nirvana" in the work to which I have referred (pp. 285 *et seq.*). The result of his and other discussions of the question may I think be briefly stated thus:

1. Logical deduction from the predicates attached to the term "Nirvana" strips it of all reality, conceivability, or perceivability, whether by Gods or men. For all practical purposes, therefore, it comes to exactly the same thing as annihilation.

2. But it is not annihilation in the ordinary sense, inasmuch as it could take place in the living Arahat or Buddha.

3. And, since, for the faithful Buddhist, that which was abolished in the Arahat was the possibility of further pain, sorrow, or sin; and that which was attained was perfect peace; his mind directed itself exclusively to this joyful consummation, and personified the negation of all conceivable existence and of all pain into a positive bliss. This was all the more easy, as Gautama refused to give any dogmatic definition of Nirvana. There is something analogous in the way in which people commonly talk of the "happy release" of a man who has been long suffering from mortal disease. According to their own views, it must always be extremely doubtful whether the man will be any happier after the "release" than before. But they do not choose to look at the matter in this light. A Buddhist would hesitate.

The popular notion that, with practical if not metaphysical, annihilation in view, Buddhism must needs be a sad and gloomy faith seems to be inconsistent with fact; on the contrary, the prospect of Nirvana fills the true believer, not merely with cheerfulness, but with an ecstatic desire to reach it.

34. The influence of the picture of the personal qualities of Gautama, afforded by the legendary anecdotes which rapidly grew into a biography of the Buddha; and by the birth stories, which coalesced with the current folk-lore, and were intelligible to all the world, doubtless played a great part. Further, although Gautama appears not to have meddled with the caste system, he refused to recognize any distinction, save that of perfection in the way of salvation, among his followers; and by such teaching, no less than by the inculcation of love and benevolence to all sentient beings, he practically levelled every social, political, and racial barrier. A third important condition was the organization of the Buddhists into monastic communities for the stricter professors, while the laity were permitted a wide indulgence in practice and were allowed to hope for accommodation in some of the temporary abodes of bliss. With a few hundred thousand years of immediate paradise in sight, the average man could be content to shut his eyes to what might follow.

35. In ancient times it was the fashion, even among the Greeks themselves, to derive all Greek wisdom from Eastern sources; not long ago it was as generally denied that Greek philosophy had any connection with Oriental speculation; it seems probable, however, that the truth lies between these extremes.

The Ionian intellectual movement does not stand alone. It is only one of several sporadic indications of the working of some powerful mental ferment over the whole of the area comprised between the Ægean and Northern Hindostan during the eighth, seventh, and sixth centuries before our era. In these three hundred years, prophetism attained its apogee among the Semites of Palestine; Zoroasterism grew and became the creed of a conquering race, the Iranic Aryans; Buddhism rose and spread with marvellous rapidity among the Aryans of Hindostan; while scientific naturalism took its rise among the Aryans of Ionia. It would be difficult to find another three centuries which have given birth to four events of equal importance. All the principal existing religions of mankind have grown out of the first three: while the fourth is the little spring, now swollen into the great stream of positive science. So far as physical possibilities go, the prophet Jeremiah and the oldest Ionian philosopher might have met and conversed. If they had done so, they would probably have disagreed a good deal; and it is interesting to reflect that their discussions might have embraced questions which, at the present day, are still hotly controverted.

The old Ionian philosophy, then, seems to be only one of many results of a stirring of the moral and intellectual life of the Aryan and the Semitic populations of Western Asia. The conditions of this general awakening were doubtless manifold; but there is one which modern research has brought into great prominence. This is the existence of extremely ancient and highly advanced societies in the valleys of the Euphrates and of the Nile.

It is now known that, more than a thousand—perhaps more than two thousand—years before the sixth century B.C., civilization had attained a relatively high pitch among the Babylonians and the Egyptians. Not only had painting, sculpture, architecture, and the industrial arts reached a remarkable development; but in Chaldæa, at any rate, a vast amount of knowledge had been accumulated and methodized, in the departments of grammar, mathematics, astronomy, and natural history. Where such traces of the scientific spirit are visible, naturalistic speculation is rarely far off, though, so far as I know, no remains of an Accadian, or Egyptian, philosophy, properly so called, have yet been recovered.

Geographically, Chaldæa occupied a central position among the oldest seats of civilization. Commerce, largely aided by the intervention of those colossal pedlars, the Phœnicians, had brought

Chaldæa into connection with all of them, for a thousand years before the epoch at present under consideration. And in the ninth, eighth, and seventh centuries, the Assyrian, the depositary of Chaldæan civilization, as the Macedonian and the Roman, at a later date, were the depositaries of Greek culture, had added irresistible force to the other agencies for the wide distribution of Chaldæan literature, art, and science.

I confess that I find it difficult to imagine that the Greek immigrants—who stood in somewhat the same relation to the Babylonians and the Egyptians as the later Germanic barbarians to the Romans of the Empire—should not have been immensely influenced by the new life with which they became acquainted. But there is abundant direct evidence of the magnitude of this influence in certain spheres. I suppose it is not doubted that the Greek went to school with the Oriental for his primary instruction in reading, writing, and arithmetic; and that Semitic theology supplied him with some of his mythological lore. Nor does there now seem to be any question about the large indebtedness of Greek art to that of Chaldæa and that of Egypt.

But the manner of that indebtedness is very instructive. The obligation is clear, but its limits are no less definite. Nothing better exemplifies the indomitable originality of the Greeks than the relations of their art to that of the Orientals. Far from being subdued into mere imitators by the technical excellence of their teachers, they lost no time in bettering the instruction they received, using their models as mere stepping stones on the way to those unsurpassed and unsurpassable achievements which are all their own. The shibboleth of Art is the human figure. The ancient Chaldæans and Egyptians, like the modern Japanese, did wonders in the representation of birds and quadrupeds; they even attained to something more than respectability in human portraiture. But their utmost efforts never brought them within range of the best Greek embodiments of the grace of womanhood, or of the severer beauty of manhood.

It is worth while to consider the probable effect upon the acute and critical Greek mind of the conflict of ideas, social, political, and theological, which arose out of the conditions of life in the Asiatic colonies. The Ionian polities had passed through the whole gamut of social and political changes, from patriarchal and occasionally oppressive kingship to rowdy and still more burdensome mobship—no doubt with infinitely eloquent and copious argumentation, on both sides, at every stage of their progress towards that arbitrament of force which settles most political questions. The marvellous speculative faculty, latent in the Ionian, had come in contact with Mesopotamian, Egyptian, Phœnician theologies and cosmogonies; with the illuminati of Orphism and the fanatics and dreamers of the Mysteries; possibly with Buddhism and Zoroasterism; possibly even with Judaism. And it has been observed that the mutual contradictions of antagonistic supernaturalisms are apt to play a large part among the generative agencies of naturalism.

Thus, various external influences may have contributed to the rise of philosophy among the Ionian Greeks of the sixth century. But the assimilative capacity of the Greek mind—its power of Hellenizing whatever it touched—has here worked so effectually, that, so far as I can learn, no indubitable traces of such extraneous contributions are now allowed to exist by the most authoritative historians of Philosophy. Nevertheless, I think it must be admitted that the coincidences between the Heraclito-stoical doctrines and those of the older Hindu philosophy are extremely remarkable. In both, the cosmos pursues an eternal succession of cyclical changes. The great year, answering to the Kalpa, covers an entire cycle from the origin of the universe as a fluid to its dissolution in fire—"Humor initium, ignis exitus mundi," as Seneca has it. In both systems, there is immanent in the cosmos a source of energy, Brahma, or the Logos, which works according to fixed laws. The individual soul is an efflux of this world-spirit, and returns to it. Perfection is attainable only by individual effort, through ascetic discipline, and is rather a state of painlessness than of happiness; if indeed it can be said to be a state of anything, save the negation of perturbing emotion. The hatchment motto "In Cœlo Quies" would serve both Hindu and Stoic; and absolute quiet is not easily distinguishable from annihilation.

Zoroasterism, which, geographically, occupies a position intermediate between Hellenism and Hinduism, agrees with the latter in recognizing the essential evil of the cosmos; but differs from both in its intensely anthropomorphic personification of the two antagonistic principles, to the one of which it ascribes all the good; and, to the other, all the evil. In fact, it assumes the existence of two worlds, one good and one bad; the latter created by the evil power for the purpose of damaging the former. The existing cosmos is a mere mixture of the two, and the "last judgment" is a root-and-branch extirpation of the work of Ahriman.

36. There is no snare in which the feet of a modern student of ancient lore are more easily entangled, than that which is spread by the similarity of the language of antiquity to modern modes of expression.

I do not presume to interpret the obscurest of Greek philosophers; all I wish is to point out, that his words, in the sense accepted by competent interpreters, fit modern ideas singularly well.

So far as the general theory of evolution goes there is no difficulty. The aphorism about the river; the figure of the child playing on the shore; the kingship and fatherhood of strife, seem decisive. The "road up and down is the same" expresses, with singular aptness, the cyclical aspect of the one process of organic evolution in individual plants and animals: yet it may be a question whether the Heraclitean strife included any distinct conception of the struggle for existence. Again, it is tempting to compare the part played by the Heraclitean "fire" with that ascribed by the moderns to heat, or rather to that cause of motion of which heat is one expression; and a little ingenuity might find a foreshadowing of the doctrine of the conservation of energy, in the saying that all the things are changed into fire and fire into all things, as gold into goods and goods into gold.

37. Pope's lines in the *Essay on Man* (Ep. i, 267-8),

> "All are but parts of one stupendous whole,
> Whose body Nature is, and God the soul,"

simply paraphrase Seneca—(Ep. lxv, 24); which again is a Latin version of the old Stoical doctrine.

So far as the testimony for the universality of what ordinary people call "evil" goes, there is nothing better than the writings of the Stoics themselves. They might serve as a storehouse for the epigrams of the ultra-pessimists. Heraclitus (*circa* 500 B.C.) says just as hard things about ordinary humanity as his disciples centuries later; and there really seems no need to seek for the causes of this dark view of life in the circumstances of the time of Alexander"s successors or of the early Emperors of Rome. To the man with an ethical ideal, the world, including himself, will always seem full of evil.

38. I use the well-known phrase, but decline responsibility for the libel upon Epicurus whose doctrines were far less compatible with existence in a stye than those of the Cynics. If it were steadily borne in mind that the conception of the "flesh" as the source of evil, and the great saying "The beginning of salvation is the knowledge of sin," are the property of Epicurus, fewer illusions about Epicureanism would pass muster for accepted truth.

39. The Stoics said that man was a rational, a political, and an altruistic or philanthropic animal. In their view, his higher nature tended to develop in these three directions, as a plant tends to grow up into its typical form. Since, without the introduction of any consideration of pleasure or pain, whatever thwarted the realization of its type by the plant might be said to be bad, and whatever helped it good; so virtue, in the Stoical sense, as the conduct which tended to the attainment of the rational, political, and philanthropic ideal, was good in itself, and irrespectively of its emotional concomitants.

Man is a "social animal born for the common good." The safety of society depends upon practical recognition of the fact. "A society can only be secure by guard and the sympathy of the parties," says Seneca (*De. Ira*, ii, 31).

40. The importance of the physical doctrine of the Stoics lies in its clear recognition of the universality of the law of causation, with its corollary, the order of nature: the exact form of that order is an altogether secondary consideration.

Many ingenious persons now appear to consider that the incompatibility of pantheism, of materialism, and of any doubt about the immortality of the soul, with religion and morality, is to be held as an axiomatic truth. I confess that I have a certain difficulty in accepting this dogma. For the Stoics were notoriously materialists and pantheists of the most extreme character; and while no strict Stoic believed in the eternal duration of the individual soul, some even denied its persistence after death. Yet it is equally certain that of all gentile philosophies, Stoicism exhibits the highest ethical development, is animated by the most religious spirit, and has exerted the profoundest influence upon the moral and religious development not merely of the best men among the Romans, but among the moderns down to our own day.

Seneca was claimed as a Christian and placed among the saints by the fathers of the early Christian church; and the genuineness of a correspondence between him and the apostle Paul has been hotly maintained in our own time, by orthodox writers. That the letters, as we possess them, are worthless forgeries is obvious; and writers as wide apart as Baur and Lightfoot agree that the whole story is devoid of foundation.

The dissertation of the late bishop of Durham (*Epistle to the Philippians*) is particularly worthy of study, apart from this question, on account of the evidence which it supplies of the numerous similarities of thought between Seneca and the writer of the Pauline epistles. When it is remembered that the writer of the Acts puts a quotation from Aratus, or Cleanthes, into the mouth of the apostle; and that Tarsus was a great seat of philosophical and especially stoical learning (Chrysippus himself was a native of the adjacent town of Sôli), there is no difficulty in understanding the origin of these resemblances. See, on this subject, Sir Alexander Grant's dissertation in his edition of *The Ethics of Aristotle* (where there is an interesting reference to the stoical character of Bishop Butler's ethics), the concluding pages of Dr. Weygoldt's instructive little work *Die Philosophie der Stoa*, and Aubertin's *Sénèque et Saint Paul*.

It is surprising that a writer of Dr. Lightfoot's stamp should speak of Stoicism as a philosophy of "despair." Surely, rather, it was a philosophy of men who, having cast off all illusions, and the childishness of despair among them, were minded to endure in patience whatever conditions the cosmic process might create, so long as those conditions were compatible with the progress towards virtue, which alone, for them, conferred a worthy object on existence. There is no note of despair in the stoical declaration that the perfected "wise man" is the equal of Zeus in everything but the duration of his existence. And, in my judgment, there is as little pride about it, often as it serves for the text of discourses on stoical arrogance. Grant the stoical postulate that there is no good except virtue; grant that the perfected wise man is altogether virtuous, in consequence of being guided in all things by the reason, which is an effluence of Zeus, and there seems no escape from the stoical conclusion.

41. Our "Apathy" carries such a different set of connotations from its Greek original that I have ventured on using the latter as a technical term.

42. Many of the stoical philosophers recommended their disciples to take an active share in public affairs; and in the Roman world, for several centuries, the best public men were strongly inclined to Stoicism. Nevertheless, the logical tendency of Stoicism seems to me to be fulfilled only in such men as Diogenes and Epictetus.

43. "Criticisms on the Origin of Species," 1864. *Collected Essays*, vol. ii, p. 91 [1894].

44. Of course, strictly speaking, social life, and the ethical process in virtue of which it advances towards perfection, are part and parcel of the general process of evolution, just as the gregarious habit of innumerable plants and animals, which has been of immense advantage to them, is so. A hive of bees is an organic polity, a society in which the part played by each member is determined by organic necessities. Queens, workers, and drones are, so to speak, castes, divided from one another by marked physical barriers. Among birds and mammals, societies are formed, of which the bond in many cases seems to be purely psychological; that is to say, it appears to depend upon the liking of the individuals for one another's company. The tendency of individuals to over self-assertion is kept down by fighting. Even in these rudimentary forms of society, love and fear come into play, and enforce a greater or less renunciation of self-will. To this extent the general cosmic process begins to be checked by a rudimentary ethical process, which is, strictly speaking, part of the former, just as the "governor" in a steam-engine is part of the mechanism of the engine.

45. See "Government: Anarchy or Regimentation," *Collected Essays*, vol. i, pp. 413-18. It is this form of political philosophy to which I conceive the epithet of "reasoned savagery" to be strictly applicable [1894].

46. "L'homme n'est qu'un roseau, le plus faible de la nature, mais c'est un roseau pensant. Il ne faut pas que l'univers entier s'arme pour l'écraser. Une vapeur, une goutte d'eau, suffit pour le tuer. Mais quand l'univers l'écraserait, l'homme serait encore plus noble que ce qui le tue, parce qu'il sait qu'il meurt; et l'avantage que l'univers a sur lui, l'univers n'en sait rien."—*Pensées de Pascal.*

47. The use of the word "Nature" here may be criticised. Yet the manifestation of the natural tendencies of men is so profoundly modified by training that it is hardly too strong. Consider the suppression of the

sexual instinct between near relations.

48. A great proportion of poetry is addressed by the young to the young; only the great masters of the art are capable of divining, or think it worth while to enter into, the feelings of retrospective age. The two great poets whom we have so lately lost, Tennyson and Browning, have done this, each in his own inimitable way; the one in the *Ulysses,* from which I have borrowed; the other in that wonderful fragment "Childe Roland to the dark Tower came."

Ethics and the Struggle for Existence

Leslie Stephen

Reprinted from *The Contemporary Review* 64 (August 1893): 157-70.

In his deeply-interesting Romanes lecture, Professor Huxley has stated the opinion that the ethical progress of society depends upon our combating the "cosmic process" which we call the struggle for existence. Since, as he adds, we inherit the "cosmic nature" which is the outcome of millions of years of severe training, it follows that the "ethical nature" may count upon having to reckon with a tenacious and powerful enemy as long as the world lasts. This is not a cheerful prospect. It is, as he admits, an audacious proposal to pit the microcosm against the macrocosm. We cannot help fearing that the microcosm may get the worst of it. Professor Huxley has not fully expanded his meaning, and says much to which I could cordially subscribe. But I think that the facts upon which he relies admit or require an interpretation which avoids the awkward conclusion.

Pain and suffering, as Professor Huxley tells us, are always with us, and even increase in quantity and intensity as evolution advances. The fact has been recognised in remote ages long before theories of evolution had taken their modern form. Pessimism, from the time of the ancient Hindoo philosophers to the time of their disciple, Schopenhauer, has been in no want of evidence to support its melancholy conclusions. It would be idle to waste rhetoric in the attempt to recapitulate so familiar a position. Though I am not a pessimist, I cannot doubt that there is more plausibility in the doctrine than I could wish. Moreover, it may be granted that any attempt to explain or to justify the existence of evil is undeniably futile. It is not so much that the problem cannot be answered as that it cannot even be asked in any intelligible sense. To "explain" a fact is to assign its causes—that is, to give the preceding set of facts out of which it arose. However far we might go backwards, we should get no nearer to perceiving any reason for the original fact. If we explain the fall of man by Adam's eating the apple we are quite unable to say why the apple should have been created. If we could discover a general theory of pain, showing, say, that it implied certain physiological conditions, we should be no nearer to knowing why those physiological conditions should have been what they are. The existence of pain, in short, is one of the primary data of our problem, not one of the accidents for which we can hope in any intelligible sense to account. To give any "justification" is equally impossible. The book of Job really suggests an impossible, one may almost say a meaningless, problem. We can give an intelligible meaning to a demand for justice when we can suppose that a man has certain antecedent rights which another man may respect or neglect. But this has no meaning as between the abstraction "Nature" and the concrete facts which are themselves nature. It is unjust to treat equal claims differently. But it is not "unjust" in any intelligible sense that one being should be a monkey and another a man, any more than that one part of me should be a hand and another a head. The question would only arise if we supposed that the man and the monkey had existed before they were created, and had then possessed claims to equal treatment. The most logical theologians indeed admit that as between creature and creator there can be properly no question of justice. The pot and the potter cannot complain of each other. If the writer of Job had been able to show that the virtuous were rewarded and the vicious punished, he would only have transferred the problem to another issue. The judge might be justified but the creator would be condemned. How can it be just to place a being where he is certain to sin and then to damn him for sinning? That is the problem to which no answer can be given; and which already implies a confusion of ideas. We apply the conception of justice in a sphere where it is not applicable, and naturally fail to get any intelligible answer.

The question therefore really resolves itself into a different one. We can neither explain nor justify the existence of pain; but of course we can ask whether, as a matter of fact, pain predominates over pleasure, and we can ask whether, as a matter of fact, the "cosmic processes" tend to promote or discourage virtuous conduct. Does the theory of the "struggle for existence" throw any new light upon the general problem? I am quite unable to see, for my own part, that it really makes any difference: evil exists; and the question whether evil predominates over good can only, I should say, be decided by an appeal to experience. One source of evil is the conflict of interests. Every beast preys upon others, and man, according to the old saying, is a wolf to man. All that the Darwinian theory can do is to enable us to trace the consequences of this fact in certain directions, but it neither reveals the fact nor makes it more or less an essential part of the process. It "explains" certain phenomena, in the sense of showing their connection with previous phenomena, but does not show why the phenomena should present themselves at all. If we indulge our minds in purely fanciful construc-tions, we may regard the actual system as good or bad, just as we choose to imagine for its alternative a better or a worse system. If everybody had been put into a world where there was no pain, or where each man could get all he wanted without interfering with his neighbours, we may fancy that things would have been pleasanter. If the struggle, which we all know to exist, had no effect in promoting the "survival of the fittest," things—so at least some of us may think—would have been worse. But such fancies have nothing to do with scientific inquiries. We have to take things as they are and make the best of them.

The common feeling, no doubt, is different. The incessant struggle between different races suggests a painful view of the universe, as Hobbes' natural state of war suggested painful theories as to human nature. War is evidently immoral, we think; and a doctrine which makes the whole process of evolution a process of war must be radically immoral too. The struggle, it is said, demands "ruthless self-assertion," and the hunting down of all competitors; and such phrases certainly have an unpleasant sound. But, in the first place, the use of the epithets implies an anthropomorphism to which we have no right so long as we are dealing with the inferior species. We are then in a region to which moral ideas have no direct application, and where the moral sentiments exist only in germ, if they can properly be said to exist at all. Is it fair to call a wolf "ruthless" because it eats a sheep and fails to consider the transaction from the sheep's point of view? We must surely admit that if the wolf is without mercy he is also without malice. We call an animal ferocious because a man who acted in the same way would be ferocious. But the man is really ferocious because he is really aware of the pain which he inflicts. The wolf, I suppose, has no more recognition of the sheep's feelings than a man has of feelings in the oyster or the potato. For him, they are simply non-existent; and it is just as inappropriate to think of the wolf as cruel as it would be to call the sheep cruel for eating grass. Are we, then, to say that "nature" is cruel because the arrangement increases the sum of general suffering? That is a problem which I do not feel able to answer; but it is at least obvious that it cannot be answered off-hand in the affirmative. To the individual sheep it matters nothing whether he is eaten by the wolf or dies of disease or starvation. He has to die anyway, and the particular way is unimportant. The wolf is simply one of the limiting forces upon sheep, and, if he were removed, others would come into play. The sheep, left to himself, would still have a practical illustration of the doctrine of Malthus. If, as evolutionists tell us, the hostility of the wolf tends to improve the breed of sheep, to encourage him to climb better and to sharpen his wits, the sheep may be, on the whole, the better for the wolf: in this sense, at least, thus the sheep of a wolfless region might lead a more wretched existence, and be less capable animals and more subject to disease and starvation than the sheep in a wolf-haunted region. The wolf may, so far, be a blessing in disguise.

This suggests another obvious remark. When we speak of the struggle for existence, the popular view seems to construe this into the theory that the world is a mere cockpit, in which one race carries on an internecine struggle with the other. If the wolves are turned in with the sheep, the first result will be that all the sheep will become mutton, and the last that there will be one big wolf with all the others inside him. But this is contrary to the essence of the doctrine. Every race depends, we all hold, upon its environment, and the environment includes all the other races. If some, therefore, are in conflict, others are mutually necessary. If the wolf ate all the sheep, and the sheep ate all the grass, the result would be the extirpation of all the sheep and all the wolves, as well as all the grass. The struggle necessarily implies reciprocal dependence in a countless variety of ways. There is not only a conflict, but a system of tacit alliances. One species is necessary to the existence of others, though the multiplication of some implies also the dying out of particular rivals. The conflict implies no cruelty, as I have said, and the alliance no goodwill. The wolf neither loves the sheep (except as mutton) nor hates him; but he depends upon him as absolutely as if he were aware of the fact. The sheep is one of the wolf's necessaries of life. When we speak of the struggle for existence we mean, of course, that there is at any given period a certain equilibrium between all the existing species; it changes, though it changes so slowly that the process is imperceptible and difficult to realise even to the scientific imagination. The survival of any species involves the disappearance of rivals no more than the preservation of allies. The struggle, therefore, is so far from internecine that it necessarily involves co-operation. It cannot even be said that it necessarily implies suffering. People, indeed, speak as though the extinction of a race involved suffering in the same way as the slaughter of an individual. It is plain that this is not a necessary, though it may sometimes be the actual result. A corporation may be suppressed without injury to its members. Every individual will die before long, struggle or no struggle. If the rate of reproduction fails to keep up with the rate of extinction, the species must diminish. But this might happen without any increase of suffering. If the boys in a district discovered how to take birds' eggs, they might soon extirpate a species; but it does not follow that the birds would individually suffer. Perhaps they would feel themselves relieved from a disagreeable responsibility. The process by which a species is improved, the dying out of the least fit, implies no more suffering than we know to exist independently of any doctrine as to a struggle. When we use anthropomorphic language, we may speak of "self-assertion." But "self-assertion," minus the anthropomorphism, means self-preservation; and that is merely a way of describing the fact that an animal or plant which is well adapted to its conditions of life is more likely to live than an animal which is ill-adapted. I have some difficulty in imagining how any other arrangement can even be supposed possible. It seems to be almost an identical proposition that the healthiest and strongest will generally live longest; and the conception of a "struggle for existence" only enables us to understand how this results in certain progressive modifications of the species. If we could even for a moment have fancied that there was no pain and disease, and that some beings were not more liable than others to those evils, I might admit that the new doctrine has made the world darker. As it is, it seems to me that it leaves the data just what they were before, and only shows us that they have certain previously unsuspected bearings upon the history of the world.

One other point must be mentioned. Not only are species interdependent as well as partly in competition, but there is an absolute dependence in all the higher species between its different members which may be said to imply a *de facto* altruism, as the dependence upon other species implies a *de facto* co-operation. Every animal, to say nothing else, is absolutely dependent for a considerable part of its existence upon its parents. The young bird or beast could not grow up unless its mother took care of it for a certain period. There is, therefore, no struggle as between mother and progeny, but, on the contrary, the closest possible alliance. Otherwise life would be impossible. The young being defenceless, their parents could exterminate them if they pleased, and by so doing would exterminate the race. This, of course, constantly involves a mutual sacrifice of the mother to her young. She has to go through a whole series of operations, which strain her own strength and endanger her own existence, but which are absolutely essential to the continuance of the race. It may be anthropomorphic to attribute any maternal emotions of the human kind to the animal. The bird, perhaps, sits upon her eggs because they give her an agreeable sensation, or, if you please, from a blind instinct which somehow determines her to the practice. She does not look forward, we may suppose, to bringing up a family, or speculate upon the delights of domestic affection. I only say that as a fact she behaves in a way which is at once injurious to her own chances of survival and absolutely necessary to the survival of the species. The abnormal bird who deserts her nest escapes many dangers; but if all birds were devoid of the instinct, the birds would not survive a generation.

Now, I ask, what is the difference which takes place when the monkey gradually loses his tail and sets up a superior brain? Is it properly to be described as a development or improvement of the "cosmic process," or as the beginning of a prolonged contest against it?

In the first place, so far as man becomes a reasonable being, capable of foresight and of the adoption of means to ends, he recognises the necessity of these tacit alliances. He believes it to be his interest not to exterminate everything, but to exterminate those species alone whose existence is incompatible with his own. The wolf eats every sheep that he comes across as long as his appetite lasts. If there are too many wolves, the process is checked by the starvation of the supernumerary eaters. Man can preserve as many sheep as he wants, and may also proportion the numbers of his own species to the possibilities of future supply. Many of the lower species thus become subordinate parts of the social organism—that is to say, of the new equilibrium which has been established. There is so far a reciprocal advantage. The sheep who is preserved with a view to mutton gets the advantage, though he is not kept with a view to his own advantage. Of all arguments for vegetarianism, none is so weak as the argument from humanity. The pig has a stronger interest than any one in the demand for bacon. If all the world were Jewish, there would be no pigs at all. He has to pay for his privileges by an early death; but he makes a good bargain of it. He dies young, and, though we can hardly infer the "love of the gods," we must admit that he gets a superior race of beings to attend to his comforts, moved by the strongest possible interest in his health and vigour, and induced by its own needs, perhaps, to make him a little too fat for comfort, but certainly also to see that he has a good sty, and plenty to eat every day of his life. Other races, again, are extirpated as "ruthlessly" as in the merely instinctive struggle for existence. We get rid of wolves and snakes as well as we can, and more systematically than can be done by their animal competitors. The process does not necessarily involve cruelty, and certainly does not involve a diminution of the total of happiness. The struggle for existence means the substitution of a new system of equilibrium, in which one of the old discords has been removed, and the survivors live in greater harmony. If the wolf is extirpated as an internecine enemy, it is that there may be more sheep when sheep have become our allies and the objects of our earthly providence. The result may be, perhaps I might say must be, a state in which, on the whole, there is a greater amount of life supported on the planet: and therefore, as those will think who are not pessimists, a decided gain on the balance. At any rate, the difference so far is that the condition which was in all cases necessary, is now consciously recognised as necessary; and that we deliberately aim at a result which always had to be achieved on penalty of destruction. So far, again, as morality can be established on purely prudential grounds, the same holds good of relations between human beings themselves. Men begin to perceive that, even from a purely personal point of view, peace is preferable to war. If war is unhappily still prevalent, it is at least not war in which every clan is fighting with its neighbours, and where conquest means slavery or extirpation. Millions of men are at peace within the limits of a modern State, and can go about their business without cutting each other's throats. When they fight with other nations they do not enslave nor massacre their prisoners. Taking the purely selfish ground, a Hobbes can prove conclusively that everybody has benefited by the social compact which substituted peace and order for the original state of war. Is this, then, a reversal of the old state of things—a combating of a "cosmic process"? I should rather say that it is a development of the tacit alliances, and a modification so far of the direct or internecine conflict. Both were equally implied in the older conditions, and both still exist. Some races form alliances, while others are crowded out of existence. Of course, I cease to do some things which I should have done before. I don't attack the first man I meet in the street and take his scalp. The reason is that I don't expect that he will take mine; for, if I did, I fear that even as a civilised being, I should try to anticipate his intentions. This merely means that we have both come to see that we have a common interest in keeping the peace. And this, again, merely means that the alliance which was always an absolutely necessary condition of the survival of the species has now been extended through a wider area. The species could not have got on at all if there had not been so much alliance as is necessary for its reproduction and for the preservation of its young for some years of helplessness. The change is simply that the small circle which included only the primitive family or class has extended, so that we can meet members of the same race on terms which were previously confined to the minuter group. We have still to exterminate and still to preserve. The mode of employing our energies has changed, but not the essential nature.

Morality proper, however, has so far not emerged. It begins when sympathy begins; when we really desire the happiness of others; or, as Kant says, when we treat other men as an end and not simply as a means. Undoubtedly this involves a new principle, no less than the essential principle of all true morality. Still I have to ask whether it implies a combating or a continuation of a cosmic process. Now, as I have observed, even the animal mother shows what I have called a de facto altruism. She has instincts which, though dangerous to the individual, are essential for the race. The human mother sacrifices herself with a consciousness of the results to herself, and her personal fears are overcome by the strength of her affections. She will endure a painful death to save her children from suffering. The animal sacrifices herself but without consciousness and therefore without moral worth. This is merely the most striking exemplification of the general process of the development of morality. Conduct is first regarded purely with a view to the effects upon the agent, and is therefore enforced by extrinsic penalties, by consequences, that is, supposed to be attached to it by the will of some ruler, natural or supernatural. The instinct which comes to regard such conduct as bad in itself, which implies a dislike of giving pain to others, not merely a dislike to the gallows, grows up under such protection, and in the really moralised being acquires a strength which makes the external penalty superfluous. This, indubitably, is the greatest of all changes, the critical fact which decides whether we are to regard conduct simply as useful or also to regard it as moral in the strictest sense. But I should still call it a development and not a reversal of the previous process. The conduct which we call virtuous is the same conduct externally which we before regarded as useful. The difference is that the simple fact of its utility—that is, of its utility to others and to the race in general—has now become the sufficient motive for the action as well as the implicit cause of the action. In the earlier stages, when no true sympathy existed, men and animals were still forced to act in a certain way because it was beneficial to others. They now act in that way because they perceive it to be beneficial to others. The whole history of moral evolution seems to imply this. We may go back to a period at which the moral law is identified with the general customs of the race; at which there is no perception of any clear distinction between that which is moral and that which is simply customary; between that which is imposed by a law in the strict sense and that which is dictated by general moral principles. In such a state of things, the motives for obedience partake of the nature of "blind instincts." No definite reason for them is present to the mind of the agent, and it does not occur to him even to demand a reason. "Our father did so and we do so" is the sole and sufficient explanation of their conduct. Thus instinct again may be traced back by evolutionists to the earliest period at which the instincts implied in the relations between the sexes, or between parents and offspring, existed. They were the germ from which has sprung all morality such as we now recognise.

Morality, then, implies the development of certain instincts which are essential to the race, but which may in an indefinite number of cases be injurious to the individual. The particular mother is killed because she obeys her natural instincts; but if it were not for mothers and their instincts, the race would come to an end. Professor Huxley speaks of the "fanatical individualism" of our time as failing to construct morality from the analogy of the cosmic process. An individualism which regards the cosmic process as equivalent simply to an internecine struggle of each against all must certainly fail to construct a satisfactory morality, and I will add that any individualism which fails to recognise fully the social factor, which regards society as an aggregate instead of an organism, will, in my opinion, find itself in difficulties. But I also submit that the development of the instincts which directly correspond to the needs of the race, is merely another case in which we aim consciously at an end which was before an unintentional result of our actions. Every race, above the lowest, has instincts which are only intelligible by the requirements of the race; and has both to compete with some and to form alliances with others of its fellow-occupants of the planet. Both in the unmoralised condition and in that in which morality has become most developed, these instincts have the common characteristics that they may be regarded as conditions of the power of the race to maintain its position in the world, and so, speaking roughly, to preserve or increase its own vitality.

I will not pause to insist upon this so far as regards many qualities which are certainly moral, though they may be said to refer primarily to the individual. That chastity and temperance, truthfulness and energy, are, on the whole, advantages both to the individual and to the race, does not, I fancy, require elaborate proof; nor need I argue at length that the races in which they are common will therefore have inevitable advantages in the struggle for existence. Of all qualities which enable a race to hold its own, none is more important than the power of organising ecclesiastically, politically, and socially, and that power implies the prevalence of justice and the existence of mutual confidence, and therefore of all the social virtues. The difficulty seems to be felt in regard to those purely altruistic impulses which, at first glance at any rate, make it apparently our duty to preserve those who would otherwise be unfit to live. Virtue, says Professor Huxley, is directed "not so much to the survival of the fittest," as to the "fitting of as many as possible to survive." I do not dispute the statement, I think it true in a sense; but I have a difficulty as to its application.

Morality, it is obvious, must be limited by the conditions in which we are placed. What is impossible is not a duty. One condition plainly is that the planet is limited. There is only room for a certain number of living beings. It is one consequence that we do in fact go on suppressing the unfit, and cannot help going on suppressing them. Is it desirable that it should be otherwise? Should we wish, for example, that America could still be a hunting-ground for savages? Is it better that a country should contain a million red men or twenty millions of civilised whites? Undoubtedly the moralist will say with truth that the methods of extirpation adopted by Spaniards and Englishmen were detestable. I need not say that I agree with him and hope that such methods may be abolished wherever any remnant of them exists. But I say so partly just because I believe in the struggle for existence. This process underlies morality, and operates whether we are moral or not. The most civilised race—that which has the greatest knowledge, skill, power of organisation—will, I hold, have an inevitable advantage in the struggle, even if it does not use the brutal means which are superfluous as well as cruel. All the natives who lived in America a hundred years ago would be dead now in any case, even if they had invariably been treated with the greatest humanity, fairness, and consideration. Had they been unable to suit themselves to new conditions of life, they would have suffered a euthanasia instead of a partial extirpation; and had they suited themselves they would either have been absorbed or become a useful part of the population. To abolish the old brutal method is not to abolish the struggle for existence, but to make the result depend upon a higher order of qualities than those of the mere piratical viking.

Mr. Pearson has been telling us in his most interesting book that the negro may not improbably hold his own in Africa. I cannot say I regard this as an unmixed evil. Why should there not be parts of the world in which races of inferior intelligence or energy should hold their own? I am not so anxious to see the whole earth covered by an indefinite multiplication of the cockney type. But I only quote the suggestion for another reason. Till recent years the struggle for existence was carried on as between Europeans and negroes by simple violence and brutality. The slave-trade and its consequences have condemned the whole continent to barbarism. That undoubtedly was part of the struggle for existence. But if Mr. Pearson's guess should be verified, the results have been so far futile as well as disastrous. The negro has been degraded, and yet, after all our brutality, we cannot take his place. Therefore, besides the enormous evils to slave-trading countries themselves, the lowering of their moral tone, the substitution of piracy for legitimate commerce, and the degradation of the countries which bought the slaves, the superior race has not even been able to suppress the inferior. But the abolition of this monstrous evil does not involve the abolition but the humanisation of the struggle. The white man, however merciful he becomes, may gradually extend over such parts of the country as are suitable to him, and the black man will hold the rest, and acquire such arts and civilisation as he is capable of appropriating. The absence of cruelty would not alter the fact that the fittest race would extend; but it may ensure that whatever is good in the negro may have a chance of development in his own sphere, and that success in the struggle will be decided by more valuable qualities.

Without venturing further into a rather speculative region, I need only indicate the bearing of such considerations upon problems nearer home. It is often complained that the tendency of modern civilisation is to preserve the weakly, and therefore to lower the vitality of the race. This seems to involve inadmissible assumptions. In the first place, the process by which the weaker are preserved, consists in suppressing various conditions unfavourable to human life in general. Sanitary legislation, for example, aims at destroying the causes of many of the diseases from which our forefathers suffered. If we can suppress the small-pox, we of course save many weakly children, who would have died had they been attacked. But we also remove one of the causes which weakened the constitutions of many of the survivors. I do not know by what right we can say that such legislation, or again the legislation which prevents the excessive labour of children, does more harm by preserving the weak than it does good by preventing the weakening of the strong. But one thing is at any rate clear. To preserve life is to increase the population, and therefore to increase the competition, and, in other words, to intensify the struggle for existence. The process is as broad as it is long. If we could ensure that every child born should grow up to maturity, the result would be to double the severity of the competition for support. What we should have to show, therefore, in order to justify the inference of a deterioration due to this process, would be, not that it simply increased the number of the candidates for living, but that it gave to feebler candidates a differential advantage; that they are now more fitted than they were before for ousting their superior neighbours from the chances of support. But I can see no reason for supposing such a consequence to be probable or even possible. The struggle for existence, as I have suggested, rests upon the unalterable facts, that the world is limited and population elastic, and under all conceivable circumstances we shall still have in some way or other to proportion our numbers to our supplies, and under all circumstances those who are fittest by reason of intellectual or moral or physical qualities will have the best chance of occupying good places, and leaving descendants to supply the next generation. It is surely not less true that in the civilised as much as in the most barbarous race, the healthiest are the most likely to live, and the most likely to be ancestors. If so, the struggle will still be carried on upon the same principles, though certainly in a different shape.

It is true that this suggests one of the most difficult questions of the time. It is suggested, for example, that in some respects the "highest" specimens of the race are not the healthiest or the fittest. Genius, according to some people, is a variety of disease, and intellectual power is won by a diminution of reproductive power. A lower race, again, if we measure "high" and "low" by intellectual capacity, may oust a higher race, because it can support itself more cheaply, or, in other words, because it is more efficient for industrial purposes. Without presuming to pronounce upon such questions, I will simply ask whether this does not interpret Professor Huxley's remark about that "cosmic nature" which, he says, is still so strong, and which is likely to be strong so long as men require stomachs. The fact is simply that we have not to suppress it, but to adapt it to new circumstances. We are engaged in working out a gigantic problem: What is the best, in the sense of the most efficient, type of human being? What is the best combination of brains and stomach? We turn out saints who are "too good to live," and philosophers who have run too rapidly to brains. They do not answer in practice, because they are instruments too delicate for the rough work of daily life. They may give a foretaste of qualities which will be some day possible for the average man; of intellectual and moral qualities which, though now exceptional, may become commonplace. But the best stock for the race are those in whom we have been lucky enough to strike out the happy combination in which greater intellectual power is gained without the loss of physical vigour. Such men, it is probable, will not deviate so widely from the average type. The reconciliation of the two conditions can only be effected by a very gradual process of slowly edging onwards is the right direction. Meanwhile the theory of a struggle for existence justifies us, instead of condemning us, for preserving the delicate child, who may turn out to be a Newton or a Keats, because he will leave to us the advantage of his discoveries or his poems, while his physical feebleness assures us that he will not propagate his race.

This may lead to a final question. Does the morality of a race strengthen or weaken it; fit it to hold its own in the general equilibrium, or make its extirpation by lower races more probable? I do not suppose that anybody would deny what I have already suggested that the more moral the race, the more harmonious and the better organised, the better it is fitted for holding its own. But if this be admitted, we must also admit that the change is not that it has ceased to struggle, but that it struggles by different means. It holds its own, not merely by brute force, but by justice, humanity, and intelligence, while, it may be added, the possession of such qualities does not weaken the brute force, where such a quality is still required. The most civilised races are, of course, also the most formidable in war. But, if we take the opposite alternative, I must ask how any quality which really weakens the vitality of the race can properly be called moral? I should entirely repudiate any rule of conduct which could be shown to have such a tendency. This, indeed, indicates what seems to me to be the chief difficulty with most people. Charity, you say, is a virtue; charity increases beggary, and so far tends to produce a feebler population; therefore, a moral quality clearly tends to diminish the vigour of a nation. The answer is, of course, obvious, and I am confident that Professor Huxley would so far agree with me. It is that all charity which fosters a degraded class is therefore immoral. The "fanatical individualism" of today has its weaknesses; but in this matter it seems to me that we see the weakness of the not less fanatical "collectivism."

The question, in fact, how far any of the socialistic or religious schemes of today are right or wrong, depends upon our answer to the question how far they tend to produce a vigorous or an enervated population. If I am asked to subscribe to General Booth's scheme, I inquire first whether the scheme is likely to increase or diminish the number of helpless hangers-on upon the efficient part of society. Will the whole nation consist in larger proportions of active and responsible workers, or of people who are simply burthens upon the real workers? The answer decides not only the question whether it is expedient, but also the question whether it is right or wrong, to support the proposed scheme. Every charitable action is so far a good action that it implies sympathy for suffering; but if it implies such want of prudence that it increases the evil which it means to remedy, it becomes for that reason a bad action. To develop sympathy without developing foresight is just one of the one-sided developments which fail to constitute a real advance in morality, though I will not deny that it may incidentally lead to an advance.

I hold, then, that the "struggle for existence" belongs to an underlying order of facts to which moral epithets cannot be properly applied. It denotes a condition of which the moralist has to take account, and to which morality has to be adapted, but which, just because it is a "cosmic process," cannot be altered, however much we may alter the conduct which it dictates. Under all conceivable circumstances, the race has to adapt itself to the environment, and that necessarily implies a conflict as well as an alliance. The preservation of the fittest, which is surely a good thing, is merely another aspect of the dying out of the unfit, which is hardly a bad thing. The feast which Nature spreads before us, according to Malthus' metaphor, is only sufficient for a limited number of guests, and the one question is how to select them. The use of morality is to humanize the struggle; to minimise the suffering of those who lose the game; and to offer the prizes to the qualities which are advantageous to all rather than to those which serve to intensify the bitterness of the conflict. This implies the growth of foresight, which is an extension of the earlier instinct, and enables men to adapt themselves to the future, and to learn from the past, as well as to act upon the immediate impulse of present events. It implies still more the development of the sympathy which makes every man feel for the sufferings of all, and which, as social organisation becomes closer, and the dependence of each constituent atom upon the whole organisation is more vividly realised, extends the range of a man's interests beyond his own private needs. In that, sense, again, it must stimulate "collectivism" at the expense of a crude individualism, and condemns the doctrine which, as Professor Huxley puts it, would forbid us to restrain the member of a community from doing his best to destroy it. If it be right to restrain such conduct, it is right to carry on the conflict against all anti-social agents or tendencies. I should certainly hold any form of collectivism to be immoral which denied the essential doctrine of the abused individualist, the necessity, that is, for individual responsibility. We have surely to suppress the murderer as our ancestors suppressed the wolf. We have to suppress both the external enemies, the noxious animals whose existence is incompatible with our own, and the internal enemies which are injurious elements in the society itself. That is, we have to work for the same end of eliminating the least fit. Our methods are changed; we desire to suppress poverty, not to extirpate the poor man. We give inferior races a chance of taking whatever place they are fit for, and try to supplant them with the least possible severity if they are unfit for any place. But the suppression of poverty supposes not the confiscation of wealth, which would hardly suppress poverty in the long run, nor even the adoption of a system of living which would make it easier for the idle and the good-for-nothing to survive. The progress of civilisation depends, I should say, on the extension of the sense of duty which each man owes to society at large. That involves a constitution of society which, although we abandon the old methods of hanging, and flogging, and shooting down—methods which corrupted the inflicters of punishment by diminishing their own sense of responsibility—may give an advantage to the prudent and industrious and make it more probable that they will be the ancestors of the next generation. A system which should equalise the advantages of the energetic and the helpless would begin by demoralising, and would very soon lead to an unprecedented intensification of the struggle for existence. The probable result of a ruthless socialism would be the adoption of very severe means for suppressing those who did not contribute their share of work. But in any case, as it seems, we never get away or break away from the inevitable fact. If individual ends could be suppressed, if every man worked for the good of society as energetically as for his own, we should still feel the absolute necessity of proportioning the whole body to the whole supplies obtainable from the planet, and to preserve the equilibrium of mankind relatively to the rest of nature. That day is probably distant, but even upon that hypothesis the struggle for existence would still be with us, and there would be the same necessity for preserving the fittest and suppressing, as gently as might be, those who were unfit.

Evolution and Ethics[1]

John Dewey

Reprinted, with minor format changes, from *The Monist*, Vol. VIII, April 1898, No. 3, pp. 321-41.

To a strictly logical mind the method of the development of thought must be a perplexing, even irritating matter. Its course is not so much like the simple curve described by a bullet as it speeds its way to a mark, as it is like the devious tacking of a sail boat upon a heavy sea with changeable winds. It would be difficult to find a single problem during the whole record of reflective thought which has been pursued consistently until some definite result was reached. It generally happens that just as the problem becomes defined, and the order of battle is drawn, with contestants determined on each side, the whole scene changes; interest is transferred to another phase of the question, and the old problem is left apparently suspended in mid air. It is left, not because any satisfactory solution has been reached; but interest is exhausted. Another question which seems more important has claimed attention. If one, after a generation or a century, reviews the controversy and finds that some consensus of judgment has finally been reached, he discovers that this has come about, not so much through exhaustive logical discussion, as through a change in men's points of view. The solution is psychologically, rather than logically, justified.

This general reflexion is called to mind as I undertake the discussion of the question of the relation of evolution and ethics. A generation ago the entire interest was in the exact relation between man and the lower animals. We had one school concerned with reducing this difference to the lowest possible limits and urging that the consciousness of man, intellectual and moral, as well as his physical nature, might be considered a direct inheritance through easy gradations from some form of the anthropoid ape. We had another school equally concerned with magnifying the difference, making it, if possible, an unbridgeable chasm. It would be a bold man who would say that this controversy has been settled by the actual weight of concrete detailed evidence, or even that it has been very far advanced. The writings which really throw light on the question, in either direction (so far as the facts are concerned and not merely general considerations), can probably be easily numbered on the fingers of the two hands. Yet suddenly we find that discussion of this question has practically ceased, and that what engages controversy is the relation of what I may call the evolutionary concepts in general to the ethical concepts. Points of agreement and disagreement between the ideas involved in the notion of evolution and those involved in the notion of moral conduct are searched for. It is the state of the imagination and the direction of interest which have changed.

It is the latter question which I purpose to discuss today. This particular phase of the problem was precipitated, if not initiated, by the late Professor Huxley in his Romanes lecture for 1893 on "Evolution and Ethics." It is some points in that address which I shall take as my text—not for the sake of directly controverting them, but as convenient points of departure for raising the questions which seem to me fundamental. In that lecture, as you will all remember, Mr. Huxley points out in his incisive and sweeping language certain differences between what he terms the cosmic and the ethical processes. Those who recall the discussion following the lecture will remember that many felt as if they had received a blow knocking the breath out of their bodies. To some it appeared that Mr. Huxley had executed a sudden *volte-face* and had given up his belief in the unity of the evolutionary process, accepting the very dualistic idea of the separation between the animal and the human, against which he had previously directed so many hard blows. To some conservative thinkers it appeared that Saul had finally shown himself among the prophets. The lecture was deplored or welcomed according to the way one interpreted it with reference to his own prepossessions.

The position taken by Huxley, so far as it concerns us here, may be summed up as follows: The *rule* of the cosmic process is struggle and strife. The rule of the ethical process is sympathy and co-operation. The *end* of the cosmic process is the survival of the fittest; that of the ethical, the fitting of as many as possible to survive. Before the ethical tribunal the cosmic process stands condemned. The two processes are not only incompatible but even opposed to each other. "Social progress means the checking of the cosmic process at every step and the substitution for it of another, which may be called the ethical process; the end of which is not the survival of those who happen to be the fittest in respect of the whole of the conditions which exist, but of those who are ethically the best. The practice of that which is ethically best—which we call goodness or virtue—involves a course of conduct which in all respects is opposed to that which leads to success in the cosmic struggle for existence. . . . The cosmic process has no sort of relation to moral ends. The imitation by man is inconsistent with the first principles of ethics. Let us understand once for all that the ethical progress of society depends, not on imitating the cosmic process, still less in running away from it, but in combating it" (*Ethics and Evolution*, pp. 67-68 above, *et passim*).

Even in the lecture, however, Mr. Huxley used certain expressions which show that he did not hold to this opposition in a sense which meant the surrender of his previous evolutionary convictions. Thus he says that the ethical process, "strictly speaking, is part of the general cosmic process, just as the governor in a steam engine is part of the mechanism of the engine" (Note 44, p. 79 above). In a later essay (published as Prolegomena), aroused somewhat by the clamour which the lecture had called forth, he makes his position even clearer. Here he illustrates his meaning by referring to the two hands as used in stretching or pulling. Each is opposed to the other, and yet both are manifestations of the same original force (p. 70, note 10 above). It is not that the ethical process is opposed to the entire cosmic process, but that *part* of the cosmic process which is maintained in the conduct of men in society, is radically opposed both in its methods and its aims to that *part* of the cosmic process which is exhibited in the stages of evolution prior to the appearance of socialised man upon the scene.

He makes this point clearer by reference to the analogy of a garden (pp. 34-35 above). Through the cosmic process, independent of man, certain plants have taken possession of a piece of soil because they are adapted to that particular environment. Man enters and roots out these plants as noxious weeds, or at least as useless for his purposes. He introduces other plants agreeable to his own wants and aims, and proceeds at once to modify the environment; if necessary, changing the soil by fertilisation, building walls, altering conditions of sunlight and moisture so as to maintain his garden as a work of art—an artifice. This artificial structure, the one mediated by man's aims and efforts, is so opposed to the natural state of things that if man lets up in the ardor, the continuity, of his labors, the natural forces and conditions reassert themselves, the wall crumbles, the soil deteriorates, and the garden is finally once more overgrown with weeds.

Mr. Huxley is a trenchant writer, and his illustrations hold the mind captive. But possibly further consideration of this very illustration will point to a different conclusion. Illustrations are two-edged swords. There is no doubt in my mind of the justness of the analogy. The ethical process, like the activity of the gardener, is one of constant struggle. We can never allow things simply to go on of themselves. If we do, the result is retrogression. Oversight, vigilance, constant interference with conditions as they are, are necessary to maintain the ethical order, as they are to keep up the garden. The problem, however, is to locate this opposition and interference—to interpret it, to say what it means in the light of our idea of the evolutionary process as a whole.

Thus considering the illustration, the thought suggests itself that we do not have here in reality a conflict of man as man with his entire natural environment. We have rather the modification by man of one part of the environment with reference to another part. Man does not set himself against the state of nature. He utilises one part of this state in order to control another part. It still holds that "nature is made better by no mean, but nature makes that mean." The plants which the gardener introduces, the vegetables and fruits he wishes to cultivate, may indeed be foreign to this particular environment; but they are not alien to man's environment as a whole. He introduces and maintains by art conditions of sunlight and moisture to which this particular plot of ground is unaccustomed; but these conditions fall within the wont and use of nature as a whole.

These may appear as too obvious considerations to be worth mentioning. Surely they could not have escaped Mr. Huxley for a moment. Yet it is possible that their bearing escaped him; for, if I mistake not, when we allow our mind to dwell upon such considerations as these, the entire import of the illustration changes. We are led to conceive, not of the conflict between the garden and the gardener; between the natural process and the process of art dependent upon human consciousness and effort. Our attention is directed to the possibility of interpreting a narrow and limited environment in the light of a wider and more complete one—of reading the possibilities of a part through its place in the whole. Human intelligence and effort intervene, not as opposing forces but as making this connexion. When Huxley says that "the macrocosm is pitted against the microcosm; that man is subduing nature to his higher ends; that the history of civilisation details the steps by which we have succeeded in building up an artificial world within the cosmos; that there lies within man a fund of energy operating intelligently and so far akin to that which pervades the universe that it is competent to influence and modify the cosmic process"—he says to my mind that man is an organ of the cosmic process in effecting its *own* progress. This progress consists essentially in making over a part of the environment by relating it more intimately to the environment as a whole; not, once more, in man setting himself against that environment.

Huxley himself defines the issue in words already quoted in which he contrasts the survival of those who "may happen to be the fittest *in respect of the whole of the conditions which exist*, to the survival of those who are ethically the best." The clause italicised sums up the whole problem. It is granted without argument that the fittest with respect to a limited part of the environment are not identical with the ethically best. Can we make this concession, however, when we have in mind the whole of the existing conditions? Is not the extent to which Mr. Huxley pushes his dualistic opposition, are not many of the popular contrasts between the natural and the ethical, results of taking a limited view of the conditions with respect to which the term "fit" is used?

In cosmic nature, as Mr. Huxley says, what is fittest depends upon the conditions. If our hemisphere were to cool again, the "survival of the fittest might leave us with nothing but lichens, diatomes, and such microscopic organisms as that which gives red snow its color." We cannot work this idea one way without being willing to work it in the other. The conditions with respect to which the term "fit" must *now* be used include the existing social structure with all the habits, demands, and ideals which are found in it. If so, we have reason to conclude that the "fittest with respect to the whole of the conditions" is the best; that, indeed, the only standard we have of the best is the discovery of that which maintains these conditions in their integrity. The unfit is practically the antisocial.

Loose popular argument—Mr. Huxley himself hardly falls into the pit—is accustomed to suppose that if the principle of the struggle for existence and survival of the fittest were rigorously carried out, it would result in the destruction of the weak, the sickly, the defective, and the insane. An examination of this popular assumption may serve to illuminate the point just made. We are all familiar with Fiske's generalisation that civilisation is a product of the prolongation of the period of infancy; that the necessity of caring for offspring not able to take care of themselves, during a continually lengthening period, stimulated the affection and care, the moral germs of social life, and required the foresight and providence that were the germs of the industrial arts upon which society depends. Mr. Fiske's contention, whether true or false, is worth putting over against the popular assumption. How far are we to go in the destruction of the helpless and dependent in order that the "fit" may survive? Clearly in this case the infant was one who was "fit," not only in ethical terms but in terms of furthering the evolutionary process. Is there any reason to suppose that the dependent classes are not equally "fit" at present, when measured by the whole of the conditions as a standard?

We may imagine a leader in an early social group, when the question had arisen of putting to death the feeble, the sickly, and the aged, in order to give that group an advantage in the struggle for existence with other groups;—we may imagine him, I say, speaking as follows: "No. In order that we may secure this advantage, let us preserve these classes. It is true for the moment that they make an additional drain upon our resources, and an additional tax upon the energies which might otherwise be engaged in fighting our foes. But in looking after these helpless we shall develop habits of foresight and forethought, powers of looking before and after, tendencies to husband our means, which shall ultimately make us the most skilled in warfare. We shall foster habits of group loyalty, feelings of solidarity, which shall bind us together by such close ties that no social group which has not cultivated like feelings through caring for all its members, will be able to withstand us." In a word, such conduct would pay in the struggle for existence as well as be morally commendable.

If the group to which he spoke saw any way to tide over the immediate emergency, no one can gainsay the logic of this speech. Not only the prolongation of the period of dependence, but the multiplication of its forms, has meant historically increase of intelligent foresight and planning, and increase of the bonds of social unity. Who shall say that such qualities are not positive instruments in the struggle for existence, and that those who stimulate and call out such powers are not among those "fit to survive"? If the deer had never developed his timidity and skill in running away, the tiger and the wolf had never shown their full resources in the way of courage and power of attack. Again, prevention is better than cure, but it has been through trying to cure the sick that we have learned how to protect the well.

I have discussed this particular case in the hope of enlarging somewhat our conception of what is meant by the term "fit"; to suggest that we are in the habit of interpreting it with reference to an environment which long ago ceased to be. That which was fit among the animals is not fit among human beings, not merely because the animals were nonmoral and man is moral; but because the conditions of life have changed, and because there is no way to define the term "fit" excepting through these conditions. The environment is now distinctly a social one, and the content of the term "fit" has to be made with reference to social adaptation. Moreover, the environment in which we now live is a changing and progressive one. Every one must have his fitness judged by the whole, including the anticipated change; not merely by reference to the conditions of today, because these may be gone tomorrow. If one is fitted simply to the present, he is not fitted to survive. He is sure to go under. A part of his fitness will consist in that very flexibility which enables him to adjust himself without too much loss to sudden and unexpected changes in his surroundings. We have then no reason here to oppose the ethical process to the natural process. The demand is for those who are fit for the conditions of existence in one case as well as in the other. It is the conditions which have changed.[2]

Let us turn our attention from the idea of "fitness" to that of the process or method—the "struggle for existence." Is it true that in the moral sphere the struggle must cease, or that we must turn ourselves resolutely upon it, branding it as immoral? Or, as in the case of the idea of fitness, is this struggle as necessary to the ethical as it is to the biological? In reality, the idea of struggle for existence is controlled by the environment in which that struggle is put forth. That which is struggle for life, and successful struggle, at one time, would be inert supineness or suicidal mania at another. This is as true of varying periods in animal development as it is of the human contrasted with the animal. The nature of the struggle for existence is constantly modifying itself, not because something else is substituted for it, much less opposed to it; but because as the conditions of life change, the modes of living must change also. That which would count in the Carboniferous period will not count in the Neozoic. Why should we expect that which counts among the carnivora to count with man—a social animal? If we do not find the same qualities effective (and hence to be maintained) in both cases; or if we find that opposed qualities are called for, what right have we to assume that what was once effected by the struggle for existence has now to be accomplished by another and opposed force?

The term "struggle for existence" seems to be used in two quite different senses by Mr. Huxley. In one case it means practically simply self-assertion. I do not see that the *struggle* for existence is anything more than living existence itself. Life tends to maintain itself because it is life. The particular acts which are put forth are the outcome of the life that is there; they are its expression, its manifestation.

Self-assertion in this sense carries with it no immoral connotation, unless life by its very nature is immoral. But Huxley also uses "struggle for existence" with a distinctly selfish meaning. He speaks of the "ape and tiger promptings" as branded with the name of sins (p. 53). He identifies self-assertion with "the unscrupulous seizing upon all that can be grasped; the tenacious holding of all that can be kept" (p. 53). It is "ruthless." It "thrusts aside or treads down all competitors." It "involves the gladiatorial theory of existence" (p. 67). Hence it is a "powerful and tenacious enemy to the ethical" (p. 69).

Surely, all this is rhetoric rather than philosophy or science. We inherit our impulses and our tendencies from our ancestors. These impulses and tendencies need to be modified. They need to be curbed and restrained. So much goes without saying. The question is regarding the nature of the modification; the nature of the restraint, and its relation to the original impulses of self-assertion. Surely, we do not want to suppress our animal inheritance; nor do we wish to restrain it absolutely—that is, for the mere sake of restraint. It is not an enemy to the moral life, simply because without it no life is possible. Whatever is necessary to life we may fairly assume to have some relevancy to moral living. More than this is true. That self-assertion which we may call life is not only negatively, but positively a factor in the ethical process. What are courage, persistence, patience, enterprise, initiation, but forms of the self-assertion of those impulses which make up the life process? So much, I suppose, all would grant;

but are temperance, chastity, benevolence, self-sacrifice itself, any less forms of self-assertion? Is not more, rather than less strength, involved in their exercise? Does the man who definitely and resolutely sets about obtaining some needed reform and with reference to that need sacrifices all the common comforts and luxuries of life, even for the time being social approval and reputation, fail in the exercise of self-assertion?

The simple fact of the case is of course that these promptings, even the promptings of the "tiger and the ape," are, simply as promptings, neither moral nor immoral; no more sins than they are saintly attributes. They are the basis and material of all acts whatsoever, good and bad. They become good when trained in a certain way, just as they become bad when trained in another way. The man who regards his animal inheritance as evil in and of itself apart from its relation to aims proposed by his intelligence, has logically but one recourse—to seek Nirvana.[3] With him the principle of self-negation becomes absolute. But with all others, the men and women whom Mr. Huxley is presumably addressing, self-restraint is simply a factor within self-assertion. It relates to the particular ways in which self-assertion is made.

I may appear here to have ignored Huxley's distinction between the struggle for existence and the struggle for happiness (p. 48). The former it will be said, he uses in a definite technical sense as meaning simply the struggle for the perpetuation of life, apart from the kind of life led, and as exhibiting itself in direct conflict with others, leading to the elimination of some. That struggle for existence it may be surely said, is not to be continued within the ethical process. The struggle for existence relates, he says, simply to the "means of living." Besides that we have the struggle for happiness, having to do with the uses to which these means are put—the values which are got out of them, the ends.

I reply in the first place, that Mr. Huxley contradicts himself on this point in such a way that one would be quite justified in ignoring the distinction; and in the second place, that I am not able to see the validity of the distinction.

As to Mr. Huxley's self-contradiction, he asserts in a number of places that the struggle for existence as such (as distinct from the struggle for happiness) has now come to an end. It held only in the lower social forms when living was so precarious that people actually killed each other, if not for food, at least to secure the scanty store of food available. If it holds now at all it is simply among the small criminal class in society (p. 48). Now Mr. Huxley not only takes this position, but from a certain point of view is bound to take it. If the struggle is still going on, selection is still occurring, and there is every reason to suppose that as heretofore, it is a distinct agent in social progress; and Mr. Huxley is bound to hold that natural selection no longer operates in social progress and that therefore we must have recourse to other means. But if the struggle for existence has thus ceased of itself within any given human society, what sense is there in saying that it is now "a tenacious and powerful enemy with which ethical nature has to reckon"? If it has died out because of the change of conditions, why should the ethical process have to spend all its energy in combating it? "Let the dead bury their dead."[4]

In other words, Mr. Huxley himself is practically unable to limit the meaning of the phrase "struggle for existence" to this narrow import. He has himself to widen it so as to include not only the struggle for mere continuance of physical existence, but also whatever makes that life what it is. The distinction between the struggle for existence and the struggle for happiness breaks down. It breaks down, I take it, none the less in animal life itself than it does in social life. If the struggle for existence on the part of the wolf meant simply the struggle on his part to keep from dying, I do not doubt that the sheep would gladly have compromised at any time upon the basis of furnishing him with the necessary food—including even an occasional bowl of mutton broth. The fact is the wolf asserted himself as a wolf. It was not mere life he wished, but the life of the wolf. No agent can draw this distinction between desire for mere life and desire for happy life for himself; and no more can the spectator intelligently draw it for another.

What then is the conflict, the tension, which is a necessary factor in the moral life—for be it remembered there is no difference of opinion with Mr. Huxley upon this point? The sole question is whether the combat is between the ethical process as such, and the cosmic, natural process as such.

The outcome of our previous discussion is that it cannot be the latter because the natural process, the so-called inherited animal instincts and promptings, are not only the stimuli, but also the materials, of moral conduct. To weaken them absolutely, as distinct from giving them a definite turn or direction, is to lessen the efficiency of moral conduct. Where then does the struggle come in? Evidently in the particular turn or direction which is given to the powers of the animal nature making up the immediate content of self-assertion. But once more, what does this turn or direction mean? Simply, I take it, that an act which was once adapted to given conditions must now be adapted to other conditions. The effort, the struggle, is a name for the necessity of this re-adaptation.[5] The conditions which originally called the power forth, which led to its "selection," under which it got its origin, and formation, have ceased to exist, not indeed, wholly, but in such part that the power is now more or less irrelevant. Indeed, it is not now a "power" in the sense of being a function which can without transformation operate successfully with reference to the whole set of existing conditions. Mr.

Huxley states the whole case when he says that "in extreme cases man does his best to put an end to the survival of the fittest of former days by the axe and rope." The phrase, "the fittest of *former* days" contains the matter in a nut-shell. Just because the acts of which the promptings and impulses are the survival, were the fittest for by-gone days they are not the fittest now. The struggle comes, not in suppressing them nor in substituting something else for them; but in reconstituting them, in adapting them, so that they will function with reference to the existing situation.

This, I take it, is the truth, and the whole truth, contained in Mr. Huxley's opposition of the moral and the natural order. The tension is between an organ adjusted to a past state and the functioning required by present conditions. And this tension demands reconstruction. This opposition of the structure of the past and the deeds of the present is precisely that suggested in the discussion of the illustrative garden. The past environment is related to the present as a part to a whole. When animal life began on land, water became only one factor in the conditions of life, and the animal attitude towards it was changed. It certainly could not now get along without a water environment, much less could it turn against it; but its relations to moisture as a condition of life were profoundly modified. An embryonic Huxley might then have argued that the future success of animal life depended upon combating the natural process which had previously maintained and furthered it. In reality the demand was, that which was only a part should be treated as such, and thus subordinated to the whole set of conditions.

Thus when Mr. Huxley says (p. 36) that "nature is always tending to reclaim that which her child, man, has borrowed from her and has arranged in combinations which are not those favored by the general cosmic process," this only means that the environment *minus* man is not the same environment as the one that includes man. In any other sense these "combinations" *are* favored by the general cosmic process—in witness whereof man through whom that process works has set his sign and seal. That *if* you took man out of this process things would change, is much like saying that if they were different they would not be the same; or, that a part is not its own whole.

There are many signs that Mr. Huxley had Mr. Spencer in mind in many of his contentions; that what he is really aiming at is the supposition on the part of Mr. Spencer that the goal of evolution is a complete state of final adaptation in which all is peace and bliss and in which the pains of effort and of reconstruction are known no more. As against this insipid millennium, Mr. Huxley is certainly right in calling attention to the fact that the ethical process implies continual struggle, conquest, and the defeats that go with conquest. But when Mr. Huxley asserts that the struggle is between the natural process and the ethical, we must part company with him. He seems to assert that in some far century it may be possible for the ape and the tiger to be so thoroughly subjugated by man that the "inveterate enemy of the moral process" shall finally be put under foot. Then the struggle will occur against the environment because of a shortage of food. But we must insist that Mr. Huxley is here falling into the very charges which he has brought against Mr. Spencer's school. The very highest habits and ideals which are organising today with reference to existing conditions will be just as much, and just as little, an obstacle to the moral conduct of man millions of years from now, as those of the ape and the tiger are to us. So far as they represent the survival of outworn conditions, they will demand re-constitution and readaptation, and that modification will be accompanied by pain. Growth always costs something. It costs the making over of the old in order to meet the demands of the new.

This struggle, then, is not more characteristic of the ethical process than it is of the biological. Long before man came upon the earth, long before any talk was heard of right and wrong, it happened that those who clung persistently to modes of action which were adapted to an environment that had passed away, were at a disadvantage in the struggle for existence, and tended to die out. The factors of the conflict upon which Mr. Huxley lays so much stress have been present ever since the beginning of life and will continue to be present as long as we live in a moving, and not a static world. What he insists upon is reconstruction and readaptation—modification of the present with reference to the conditions of the future.

With the animal it was simply the happy guess—the chance. In society there is anticipation; with man it is the intelligent and controlled foresight, the necessity of maintaining the institutions which have come down to us, while we make over these institutions so that they serve under changing conditions. To give up the institutions is chaos and anarchy; to maintain the institutions unchanged is death and fossilisation. The problem is the reconciliation of unbridled radicalism and inert conservatism, in a movement of reasonable reform. Psychologically the tension manifests itself as the conflict between habits and aims: a conflict necessary, so far as we can see, to the maintenance of conscious life. Without habits we can do nothing. Yet if habits become so fixed that they cannot be adapted to the ends suggested by new situations, they are barriers to conduct and enemies to life. It is conflict with the end or ideal which keeps the habit working, a flexible and efficient instrument of action. Without this conflict with habits, the end becomes vague, empty, and sentimental. Defining it so that the habits may be utilised in realising it makes it of practical value. This definition would never occur were it not that habits resist it.

Just as habits and aims are co-operating factors in the maintenance of conscious experience, just as institutions and plans of reform are co-workers in our social life, just as the relative antagonism between the two is necessary to their valuable final co-adaptation; so impulse, call it animal if we will, and ideal, call it holy though we may, are mutually necessary in themselves and in their mutual opposition—necessary for the ethical process. It is well for the ideal that it meet the opposition of the impulse, as it is for the animal prompting to be held to the function suggested by the ideal.

In locating and interpreting this tension, this opposition between the natural and the moral, I have done what I set out to do. There is one other point which it seems worth while to touch upon before leaving the matter. Three terms are always found together in all discussions of evolution—natural selection, struggle for existence, and the fit. The latter two of these ideas we have discussed in their bearings upon moral life. It remains to say a word or two upon natural selection. Mr. Huxley's position on this point is not quite clear. As has been already suggested, it seems to be varying, if not actually self-contradictory. At times he seems to hold that since the struggle for existence has ceased in the social sphere, selection has ceased also to act, and therefore the work formerly done by it (if we may for the moment personify it as an agent) now has to be done in other ways. (See the passages referred to on p. 101.) At other times he seems to hold that it is still going on but that its tendency upon the whole is bad, judged from the ethical standpoint, and therefore requires to be consciously counter-acted.

Certainly the question of the scope of selection in the sphere of social life is confused. Does it still continue or does it not? If it does operate, what are its modes of working? Many seem to suppose that we do not have it excepting where we inten-tionally isolate those whom we consider unfit, and prevent them from reproducing offspring; or that it is found only if we artificially regulate marriage in such a way as to attempt to select social and animal types considered higher at the expense of the lower. Mr. Huxley naturally considers selection in this sense, not only practically impossible, but intrinsically undesirable. But is this the only or the chief meaning of natural selection? Does it follow that social selection, to use a term employed by late writers, is something radically different from natural selection?

The belief that natural selection has ceased to operate rests upon the assumption that there is only one form of such selection: that where improvement is indirectly effected by the failure of species of a certain type to continue to reproduce; carrying with it as its correlative that certain variations continue to multiply, and finally come to possess the land. This ordeal by death is an extremely important phase of natural selection, so called. That it has been the chief form in pre-human life will be here admitted without discussion; though doubtless those having competent knowledge of details have good reason for qualifying this admission. However, to identify this procedure absolutely with selection, seems to me to indicate a somewhat gross and narrow vision. Not only is one form of life as a whole selected at the expense of other forms, but one mode of action in the same individual is constantly selected at the expense of others. There is not only the trial by death, but there is the trial by the success or failure of special acts — the counterpart, I suppose, of physiological selection so called. We do not need to go here into the vexed question of the inheritance of acquired characters. We know that through what we call public opinion and education certain forms of action are constantly stimulated and encouraged, while other types are as constantly objected to, repressed, and punished. What difference in principle exists between this mediation of the acts of the individual by society and what is ordinarily called natural selection, I am unable to see. In each case there is the reaction of the conditions of life back into the agents in such a way as to modify the function of living. That in one case this modification takes place through changes in the structure of the organ, say the eye, requiring many generations to become active; while in the other case it operates within the life of one and the same individual, and affects the uses to which the eye is put rather than (so far as we can tell) the structure of the eye itself, is not a reason for refusing to use the term "natural selection." Or if we have limited that term to a narrower technical meaning, it is certainly no reason for refusing to say that the same kind of forces are at work bringing about the same sort of results. If we personify Nature, we may say that the influences of education and social approval and disapproval in modifying the behavior of the agent, mark simply the discovery on the part of Nature of a shorter and more economical form of selection than she had previously known. The modification of structure is certainly not an end in itself. It is simply one device for changing function. If other means can be devised which do the work more efficiently, then so much the better. Certainly it marks a distinct gain to accomplish this modification in one and the same generation rather than to have to trust to the dying out of the series of forms through a sequence of generations. It is certainly implied in the idea of natural selection that the most effective modes of variation should themselves be finally selected.

But Mr. Huxley insists upon another distinction. Stated in terms of the garden illustration, it is that: "The tendency of the cosmic process is to bring about the adjustment of the forms of plant life to the current conditions; the tendency of the horticultural process is the adjustment of the needs of the forms of plant life which the gardner desires to raise." This is a very common antithesis. But is it as absolute and sweeping

as we generally affect to believe? Every living form is dynamically, not simply stat-
ically, adapted to its environment. I mean by this it subjects conditions about it to its
own needs. This is the very meaning of "adjustment"; it does not mean that the life-
form passively accepts or submits to the conditions just as they are, but that it functionally subordinates these natural circumstances to its own food needs.

But this principle is of especial importance with reference to the forms in which
are found the lines of progressive variation. It is, relatively speaking, true of the weeds
and gorse of the patch of soil from which Mr. Huxley draws his illustration, that they
are adjusted to current conditions. But that is simply because they mark the result, the
relatively finished outcome of a given process of selection. They are arrested forms.
Just because the patch has got into equilibrium with surrounding conditions progressive
variation along that line has ceased. If this were all the life in existence, there would
be no more evolution. Something, in other words, did *not* adapt itself to "current conditions," and so development continued.

It would be ungrateful in any discussion of this subject not to refer to Malthus's
classic illustration of the feast spread by nature—not big enough for the invited guests.
It is supposed, in its application to struggle for existence and selection, that this means
that the life-forms present struggle just to get a share of the food that is already there.
Such a struggle for a quota of food already in existence, might result, through selection,
in perfecting a species already in existence, and thus in fixing it. It could not give rise
to a new species. The selection which marks progress is that of a variation which
creates a new food supply or amplifies an old one. The advantage which the variation
gives, if it tends towards a new species, is an organ which opens up a wider food
environment, detects new supplies within the old, or which makes it possible to utilise
as food something hitherto indifferent or alien. The greater the number of varieties on
a given piece of soil, the more individuals that can maintain a vigorous life. *The new
species means a new environment to which it adjusts itself without interfering with
others.* So far as the progressive varieties are concerned, it is not in the least true that
they simply adapt themselves to current conditions; evolution is a continued development of new conditions which are better suited to the needs of organisms than the old.
The unwritten chapter in natural selection is that of the evolution of environments.

Now, in man we have this power of variation and consequent discovery and
constitution of new environments set free. All biological process has been effected
through this, and so every tendency which forms this power is selected; in man it
reaches its climax. So far as the individual is concerned, the environment (the specific
conditions which relate to his life) is highly variable at present. The growth of science,

its application in invention to industrial life, the multiplication and acceleration of means of transportation and intercommunication, have created a peculiarly unstable environment. It shifts constantly within itself, or qualitatively, and as to its range, or quantitatively. Simply as an affair of nature, not of art (using these terms in Mr. Huxley's sense) it is a profitable, an advantageous thing that structural changes, if any occur, should not get too set. They would limit unduly the possibility of change in adaptation. In the present environment, flexibility of function, the enlargement of the range of uses to which one and the same organ, grossly considered, may be put, is a great, almost the supreme, condition of success. As such, any change in that direction is a favorable variation which must be selected. In a word, the difference between man and animal is not that selection has ceased, but that selection along the line of variations which enlarge and intensify the environment is active as never before.

We reach precisely the same conclusion with respect to "selection" that we have reached with reference to the cognate ideas—"fit" and "struggle for existence." It is found in the ethical process as it is in the cosmic, and it operates in the same way. So far as conditions have changed, so far as the environment is indefinitely more complex, wider, and more variable, so far of necessity and as a biological and cosmic matter, not merely an ethical one, the functions selected differ.

There are no doubt sufficiently profound distinctions between the ethical process and the cosmic process as it existed prior to man and to the formation of human society. So far as I know, however, all of these differences are summed up in the fact that the process and the forces bound up with the cosmic have come to consciousness in man. That which was instinct in the animal is conscious impulse in man. That which was "tendency to vary" in the animal is conscious foresight in man. That which was unconscious adaptation and survival in the animal, taking place by the "cut and try" method until it worked itself out, is with man conscious deliberation and experimentation. That this transfer from unconsciousness to consciousness has immense importance, need hardly be argued. It is enough to say that it means the whole distinction of the moral from the unmoral. We have, however, no reason to suppose that the cosmic process has become arrested or that some new force has supervened to struggle against the cosmic. Some theologians and moralists, to be sure, welcomed Huxley's apparent return to the idea of a dualism between the cosmic and the ethical as likely to inure favorably to the spiritual life. But I question whether the spiritual life does not get its surest and most ample guarantees when is is learned that the laws and conditions of righteousness are implicated in the working processes of the universe; when it is found that man in his conscious struggles, in his doubts, temptations, and defeats, in his aspirations and successes, is moved on and buoyed up by the forces which have developed nature; and that in this moral struggle he acts not as a mere individual but as an organ in maintaining and carrying forward the universal process.

Notes

1. This paper was delivered as a public lecture during the Summer Quarter's work of the University of Chicago. This will account for the lack of reference to other articles bearing on the subject. I would call special attention, however, to Mr. Leslie Stephen on "Natural Selection and Ethics," in the *Contemporary Review* [reprinted above], and the article by Dr. Carus in *The Monist*, Vol. IV, No. 3, on "Ethics and the Cosmic Order."

2. Precisely it may be said, and that is just the reason that Mr. Huxley insists upon the opposition of the natural and the ethical. I cannot avoid believing that this is what Mr. Huxley really had in mind at the bottom of his conciousness. But what he says is not that the form and content of fitness, of struggle for existence, and of selection, change with the change of conditions, but that these concepts lose all applicability. And this is just the point under discussion.

3. It is passing strange that Mr. Huxley should not have seen that the logical conclusion from his premises of this extreme opposition are just those which he has himself set forth with such literary power earlier in his essay (pp. 58-61 above). That he did not shows, to my mind, how much he takes the opposition in a rhetorical, not a practical, sense.

4. Here is his flat contradiction: "Men in society are undoubtedly subject to the cosmic process . . . . The struggle for existence tends to eliminate those less fitted to adapt themselves to the circumstances of their existence" (p. 67). Compare this with pp. 37, 46, 47 (above), and the other passages referred to above.

5. I have developed this conception psychologically in the *Philosophical Review* for Jan. 1897, in an article upon the Psychology of Effort.

Philosophical Advocacy

Birth, Death, and Resurrection
of Evolutionary Ethics

Robert J. Richards

Darwin's Ethical Theory and Its Critics

In 1871, even before he had read one word of Darwin's explanation of moral behavior in the *Descent of Man*, St. George Jackson Mivart diagnosed altruism as the terminal infection ravaging Darwin's general theory. Mivart argued that "on strict utilitarian principles," of which he thought natural selection merely the biological expression, acts of altruism, which had to be useless to the individual, could not evolve. Natural selection, after all, operated only to promote the good of the individual, and so could not explain traits in the organism that are beneficial to others. The impulse of the soldier to lay down his life for his comrades could not be the result of a biological principle of utility. So we had to conclude, Mivart insisted, "that the admiration which all feel for acts of self-denial done for the good of others, and tending even toward the destruction of the actor, could hardly be accounted for on Darwinian principles alone" (Mivart 1871:207-8).

Notwithstanding Mivart's presumption of his adversary's lack of conceptual sensitivity, Darwin indeed felt acutely the problem of how other-regarding sentiments, moral attitudes, might have evolved. The difficulties of explaining altruism lodged beneath the skin of Darwin's developing theory and remained a constant irritant. His earliest speculations on species change, beginning just after his *Beagle* voyage in the late 1830s, also included hypotheses about an evolutionary ethics (see Richards 1987: 110-24). From the first, Darwin recognized that the moral sense could not be selfish. An evolutionary theory of morality could not be, as for instance Paley's moral theory was, a version of utilitarianism, which supposed that pleasure for self seduced all behavior, including moral behavior. From his own reflections on the common moral wisdom and from the work of his older relative, Sir James Mackintosh, Darwin had become convinced that any behavior correctly described as moral had to be altruistic.

Darwin was able to resolve the difficulty of how natural selection could produce an altruistic sense only after he had solved a more fundamental problem that captured his attention during the mid-1840s. This problem concerned the social insects—how to explain their behavior and anatomy. Worker ants and bees have anatomical traits and behaviors that differ considerably from those characterizing other members of their nests or hives. According to Darwin's emerging theory, these traits must have evolved under selection. But worker bees and ants are nature's eunuchs. They toil for the welfare of the entire group, but themselves leave no offspring to inherit any advantageous traits that they might have acquired. Theirs is parabolic altruism, bending, as in traditional lore, away from low existence toward Divinity.

Darwin's solution to the problem of how natural selection could produce the anatomical and behavioral traits of sterile insects has been recovered in our time and now forms a main strut of sociobiological doctrine. Darwin worked slowly, watched several weak hypotheses collapse, but finally achieved a brilliant solution, namely, that selection operated, not on the individual, but on the whole hive or colony. Selection preserved communities that chanced to have members whose traits gave advantage to the group but eliminated societies of selfish individualists (see Richards 1987:127-56). Darwin detailed this solution in Chapter 7 of the *Origin of Species*. His theory also yielded the conceptual materials he required to construct a natural-selection account of human altruism.

In the *Descent of Man*, published a dozen years after the *Origin*, Darwin argued that protohumans formed small tribal units upon which natural selection might operate. As these groups would be in competition with one another, selection would act favorably on those showing any advantage. If individuals instinctively acted for the common good, for the benefit of the community—a community, incidentally, which because it was small, would be bound together by ties of kinship—such unselfish behaviors would give one tribe a competitive edge in relation to others, and thus genuine altruistic sentiments might evolve. As Darwin fashioned his theory in the *Descent of Man* (1871, 1:166):

> It must not be forgotten that although a high standard of morality gives but a slight or no advantage to each individual man and his children over the other men of the same tribe, yet that an advancement in the standard of morality and an increase in the number of well-endowed men will certainly give an immense advantage to one tribe over another. There can be no doubt that a tribe including many members who, from possessing in a high degree the spirit of patriotism, fidelity, obedience, courage, and sympathy, were always ready to give aid to each other and to sacrifice themselves for the common good, would be victorious over most other tribes; and this would be natural selection.

Darwin urged that the chief feature of his naturalistic theory of morality was that it removed "the reproach of laying the foundation of the most noble part of our nature in the base principle of selfishness" (1871, 1:98). Darwin would thus have been rather surprised to learn that his theory, in our time, has been transmuted into a base scheme of selfish genes.

In Darwin's view, when a member of a primitive tribe, or a citizen of an advanced society, acted altruistically, especially in circumstances requiring an immediate response, that person's conscience would be impelled by a deeply embedded social instinct, one that answered neither to a calculus of pleasure nor a judgment of reciprocity. Rather, the individual so moved would act simply for the common good. Even if we now placed Darwin's theory within the framework of modern genetics, genes lying at the root of altruistic behavior would have been selected because of their utility for the group (especially the kin group), not for the welfare of the particular individual. Blind, dumb bits of DNA can neither be selfish nor caring; they can only be casually efficacious or not.

Consider, if you will, poor, underrated Herbert Spencer. As in many other aspects of his own theory of evolution, he had anticipated Darwin's concern with morality, at least in print. Darwin, himself had accepted the support of some of Spencer's ideas in formulating a theory of conscience. Spencer's own evolutionary ethics, synthetically constructed in his *Principles of Ethics* in the 1890s, had much in common with Darwin's, especially the effort to ground moral principle on social instinct (see Spencer 1893, 1:234-41; Richards 1987:295-330).

Both Spencer's theory and Darwin's, however, met a formidable obstacle in the argument of another evolutionist and friend of both, Thomas Henry Huxley. In his famous Romanes Lecture of 1893, entitled "Evolution and Ethics," Huxley posed an objection that later would travel under the rubric of the "naturalistic fallacy." Huxley granted that our moral sentiments, just as our other fixed traits, had evolved. In this respect they did not differ from our aggressive and murderous impulses. We can, however, always weigh an aggressive instinct against an altruistic instinct, and ask: Why ought I follow my altruistic instincts? And that's a question, he maintained, that evolutionary theory cannot answer—except through fallacious argument. The factual results of evolution can offer no reasons for concluding that one ought to perform any behavior (Huxley 1893).

In 1903, G. E. Moore, who gave currency to the conception of the naturalistic fallacy, condemned Spencer because he had fallaciously maintained that evolution, "while it shews us the direction in which we are developing, thereby and for that reason shews us the direction in which we ought to develop" (Moore 1903:46). Most philosophers today, reformulating somewhat Huxley's and Moore's ideas—and Moore's notions need a revivifying transplant, lying as they do in the suffocating heat of Bloomsbury—would maintain that it is logically incorrect to argue from empirical facts to imperatives, to slide from statements of what *is* the case to statements of what *ought* to be the case. The naturalistic fallacy has been thought to preclude any justification of a moral system by appeal to evolutionary processes. Since the time of Darwin and Spencer some egregious examples of efforts to fashion an evolutionary ethics—for instance, those of Ernst Haeckel in the 1900s, Julian Huxley in the 1940s, and C. H. Waddington in the 1960s—certainly support the common wisdom about the logical liabilities of attempting to establish an ethics based on evolution.

The biologist who most recently has attempted to vault over the fact-value distinction is George Williams (this volume), who takes his departure from T. H. Huxley. Huxley recognized that the objects of evolutionary theory were the factual, albeit law-governed processes of nature. And nature so understood harbors no moral values: human beings, who are conscious, intentional agents may perform virtuously or may commit the most heinous acts imaginable, but the heavens will neither smile on the former nor open up in revenge over the latter. If a child, crawling in the garden, is bitten by a serpent and dies, we will grieve and surely smash the brains out of the snake. But in a cool hour, we must recognize that those brains had no mind, and could form no intentions; the snake struck the child in the same way as lightning might strike the child. No moral evil will have been committed, though a great physical harm will have been done. Nature, as Huxley correctly portrayed her, is indifferent to moral good or evil. I say Huxley "correctly" argued this to emphasize that I believe Williams commits a very large fallacy when he describes nonhuman nature as positively evil (see also Williams 1989). Nothing is either morally good or bad, but only thinking makes it so; and nature, at least in her viperous manifestations, does not think, and does not form the kinds of intentions necessary to assign ethical responsibility. I will say more about the intentional requirement for moral assessment in a moment.

After this long prolegomena, I wish to argue three propositions and ward off, along the way, some misunderstandings, as I take them, by other contributors to this book. The first proposition is that Darwin's moral theory can be modified to make it conceptually acceptable. Thus, I also want to show, secondly, that there is no general fallacy in arguing from facts to values, from "is"s to "ought"s, though one can, indeed, argue fallaciously in attempting to derive moral propositions from statements of evolutionary facts. And finally, I wish to emphasize what the naturalist fallacy forces us to recognize, namely, the crucial requirement of justification. It is in relation to this last point that I wish quickly to rehearse three recent proposals for an evolutionary ethics before I outline my own—the proposals of Edward Wilson, Richard Alexander, and Michael Ruse.

Ethical Theories of Wilson, Alexander, and Ruse

Renewed interest in considering the possibility of an evolutionary construction of ethics was launched with Edward Wilson's remark in 1975 that "time has come for ethics to be removed temporarily from the hands of the philosophers and biologicized" (Wilson 1975:562). Wilson advanced a theory of reciprocal altruism, according to which human beings, both at the level of their genes—through some vaguely characterized selection process—and at the level of conscious reflection recognized that they could secure the greatest amount of advantage if they cooperated with one another. This is a theory of enlightened selfishness, bearing strong resemblance to older theories of utilitarianism. Wilson skirted the logical and moral force behind the naturalistic fallacy. He did not attempt to justify his position morally, but only empirically.

Let me try to make clear this important distinction between empirical justification and moral justification. To justify empirically a set of rule-governed behaviors is simply to explain them by appeal to empirical science and presumed facts. Thus we might be able empirically to explain dietary rules laid down in the Old Testament—for example, rules forbidding the eating of pork—by appeal to the ease with which early peoples contracted disease from undercooked pork. These rules, within the Jewish tradition, are also low-level moral rules. And if you asked an observant Jew to justify the use of these rules, he or she would undoubtedly turn to higher-level ethical principles, such as the requirement of obedience to God's commands. And this would be a moral justification, in contrast to the empirical justification a biological anthropologist might offer in respect to liability to disease. When T. H. Huxley asked himself why he should follow his altruistic sentiments rather than his aggressive ones, he was demanding a moral justification, not an empirical one.

Wilson, when his time came to stand the philosophical round, sought to stiffen the demand for a moral justification by asserting that "morality has no other demonstrable ultimate function" than "to keep human genetic material intact" (1978:167). His claim, then, amounts to the declaration that rules of behavior can only be given an empirical justification. I should add, parenthetically, there was an unregenerated Michael Ruse, who endorsed this same position. With swagger he bellied up to proclaim that human beings will help a stranger in distress only in anticipation of some return, for "only a fool or a saint (categories often linked) would do something absolutely for nothing" (Ruse 1984:171). I will talk in a moment about the Ruse of the final conversion, a finer, more noble Ruse—a better philosopher, whose position, while it yet expires from lack of philosophic nerve, is carefully considered and exhibits even in its dying breath a thoughtful sensitivity.

Richard Alexander, in his recent book *Biology of Moral Systems* (1987), formulates an evolutionary ethics full of interest because of the many empirical studies and considerations he brings to his task. The theory, though, logically is essentially the same as Wilson's: he interprets "moral systems as systems of indirect reciprocity" (Alexander 1987:93). His theory, then, descends to a conception of morality as enlightened self-interest. In the main part of his argument, Alexander sketches some general evolutionary conditions that likely characterized human groups in the past; with these and the principles of natural selection and kin selection, he derives a set of rules that would likely be learned by such a society, whose members have been induced to acquire them through gentle genetic persuasion. These rules constitute, he maintains, the moral rules governing the society—that is, our society. And these rules are simply those of reciprocity, of enlightened self-interest.

Now there are several simple objections to the proposals of Wilson and Alexander. First, the rules they generate do not constitute what we normally mean by moral rules. They may indeed be rules operative in our society, but they might as well be the rules of addition and subtraction. Wilson and Alexander offer no satisfactory reason, or no plausible justification for taking them as moral rules. Wilson simply denies that any justification other than an empirical one can be given to rules of behavior, which means that all genetically conditioned rule-governed behavior—for example, humans' ability to learn language, do mathematics, etc.—will have exactly the same biological and justificatory status. Alexander, in an epilogic afterthought (1987:259-62), does attempt to identify the rules he has generated from evolutionary theory and social assumptions with standard moral rules. His definitional justification, however, partly assumes what he attempts to prove, and the residual simply fails to meet our ordinary moral intuitions. Let me explain.

Alexander, with the caution of a scientist too often battered by philosophers, mildly suggests (1987:259):

> It is possible to consider an act immoral to the extent that it represents interference with the legitimate or rational expectations of another person, particularly in the service of a perpetrator's interests, and most

particularly if the perpetrator carries out the interference with conscious intent, with knowledge of the legitimacy or rationality of the victim's expectations, and by employing deliberate deception.

Now insofar as "legitimate" means "morally legitimate," then, of course, it follows—by definition—that an immoral act is one that violates the legitimate, that is, moral rights of others. And if the perpetrator does so with "deliberate deception," that is, in a deliberately immoral way, then it follows as the night the day that immoral behavior has been perpetrated. But if this is Alexander's justification, then only dictionaries will be required of moral philosophers. The thrust of Alexander's analysis, however, is to suggest that rational expectations—that is, those declaimed by enlightened self-interest—should be our *moral* guide. But acting for self-interest is not what is ordinarily meant by moral action. We can see the force of this objection by testing the theories of Wilson and Alexander against the evidence of an intuitively clear moral case—for we do test moral theories in the same way as empirical theories: we see whether they can explain the evidence.

Consider Dr. Moreau, a biologist persuaded of the moral theory of enlightened self-interest, and Moreau's son. According to both Alexander and Wilson, Dr. Moreau would be genetically disposed to advance his son's welfare; and the son, of course, will be genetically disposed toward enlightened self-interest. Now to be "enlightened in one's self-interest" means that one will rationally consider all circumstances in order to get the best long-run outcome for oneself. Now suppose Dr. Moreau's son were to come to him and say, on our small island at the sanatorium, there is this ten-year-old girl who is quite out of touch with reality, and I would like to rape her. Suppose both father and son know there is absolutely no possibility of getting caught and that they recognize this. They have made an enlightened calculation. But should the son do it? I believe Alexander's and Wilson's theories would dictate yes. It would be fun for Moreau's son, relieving the tension of being the scion of a famous father, and would not injure him in the short or long run. Why should he not? All theories of enlightened self-interest rupture on such cases.

I will not say too much about Ruse's position, since, in his book *Taking Darwin Seriously*, he himself takes the requirement of moral justification and the problem of the presumed naturalistic fallacy quite seriously. And does justice, in a way that neither Wilson nor Alexander do, to the logic of the moral situation (Ruse 1986:250-72). In the end, though, he sports a Hemingwayesque kind of existentialism—*Credo quia evolutio absurda est*. His position is this: evolution provides an empirical justification of ethical systems, but no moral justification is ultimately possible. However, we are all in the moral system. We have evolved to care for the young and defenseless, to be solicitous for children. Thus we feel, we believe, we experience in our bones that raping a young girl is horribly wrong and shudder at performing a Benthamic calculation to determine whether we should or not. We refrain from the act and do not count the cost.

I differ from Ruse in maintaining that we can morally justify a system founded on evolution—we can coherently and reasonably derive moral values from facts. But consider what happens when Dr. Moreau approaches Dr. Ruse, and asks, should I let my son do it? What does the philosopher say? He can only logically and rationally say: "I would prefer you wouldn't. I don't like the injury of children, nor those responsible for it." But the logic of his remonstrance with Moreau would be no different than if he were to say, "I also don't like pistachio-nut ice cream, and don't associate with people who do." Now Ruse might respond to Moreau by belting him in the nose—but even for a Chicago philosopher that is not a reasoned justification.

The Revised Version of Darwinian Ethics

The theory I wish to argue, which can only be sketched in bare outline here (see Richards 1986a, 1986b, and 1989), derives its inspiration from Darwin's original conception. It might, therefore, be called the "revised version." The revised version has two logically distinct parts. First, there is a speculative theory of human evolution, based on current anthropological and biosocial studies, as well as on the systematic requirements of general evolutionary theory. The second part is a moral theory designed to rest on the presumptively secure foundations of the evolutionary scenario. Wilson and Alexander have spent considerable time constructing a plausible empirical-evolutionary account of the rise of our moral behavior. My own effort in this respect has been exercised from the comfortable vantage of the armchair; for my concern has been to show, not the truth of the just-so story of man's moral rise, but the logic of an ethical theory based on evolution. Thus my empirical foundations might ultimately crack and give way as new scientific research undermines even my small number of assumptions; nonetheless, my design for the moral structure, which rests upon the supposed facts, could still remain sound. I wish to show, in short, that *if* the speculative empirical part is true, it can adequately justify the second part of the revised version, the moral theory. My aim, then, is fundamentally logical and conceptual: to demonstrate that an ethics based on presumed facts of biological evolution need admit no logical flaws and need not collapse because facts cannot support imperatives, but rather that such an ethics can be justified by using those facts and the theory articulating them.

The speculative part of the revised version supposes that a moral sense has evolved in the human group. The moral sense is an innate attitude, a set of inborn inclinations, that disposes the individual to act for the common good of the particular community of which he or she is a member. Understanding of what constitutes the "common good" will alter over the history of a society, but will necessarily include the well-being, safety, health, and life of its members. The altruistic attitude will, according to the revised version, evolve under the guidance of kin selection and, perhaps, group selection on small communities. The revised version supposes that original human societies were based on extended kin groups, that is, on clans. Such clans would be in competition with others in the geographical area, and so natural selection might operate on them to promote a great variety of altruistic impulses, all having the ultimate purpose of serving the community good.

The elements are so mixed in human beings that their natures show no clear divisions between biology and culture. Their biological endowment fits them to live as their forebears did, in an environment of other social beings. Even as they slip from the womb, their immediate responses will reflect selection pressures of past cultural ages. However, as they enter into a society that gyrates to constant changes in habits and knowledge, then their behavior begins to bear the stamp of a particular time and place. Thus, our human understanding of well-being, safety, health, and the means of their procurement; our recognition of family members, neighbors, and friends—all of these are interpreted according to traditions established in the history of particular groups, traditions which if constant enough become etched at various depths into their genetic endowment. Darwin appreciated, however, that innately guided behaviors and perceptions must be molded by immediate experience, by what an organism learns during ontogeny. The revised version similarly insists that the moral attitude will be informed by an evolving intelligence and by cultural traditions. Nature demands that we protect our brothers and sisters, but we must learn who they are. During human history, evolving cultural traditions may translate "community member" as "red Sioux," "black Mau Mau," or "white Englishman," and the "community good" as "sacrificing to the gods," "killing usurping colonials," or "saving prostitutes from a squalid life." But as civilization progresses, superstitions may fade, irrational fears may diminish, and scientific understanding may enlarge; then human beings will, perhaps, see their community as embracing all humanity and will more intelligently and generously seek the good of that community.

It might be objected, as Gewirth does (this volume), that the notion of community prescribed by the revised version is too vague, too indeterminate. Does the
liquidity of the concept allow, for example, moral exculpation of Nazis who treated
with altruistic solicitude only Aryans of appropriate credentials but slaughtered inno-
cents outside this group by the millions? At one level, of course, "community" is no
more vague than the standard concepts populating most ethical theories—concepts of
freedom and well-being, for instance. Biologically, it has fair precision: it is that
group initially tended by selection, but which may grow into a unit in which the members regard each other as potential mates (with sexual discrimination) and as fellows
with whom one can communicate needs and desires, form cooperative alliances, and, in
short, treat as other selves. According to this view, community inclusion depends on
the belief-systems operative in a group at a particular time. One can imagine, with
some anthropological license, that early in human history one primitive tribe might
regard members of another as on all fours with insensate beasts of the forests and
would treat them accordingly. From our perspective those primitive groups would have
defective beliefs, but invincibly so. And most classic ethical systems take invincible
ignorance as excusing. But we certainly cannot generally believe that the Nazis, in the
twentieth century, sincerely exercised comparable ignorance. Those whom the Nazis
savaged obviously bore the traits just enumerated; they had to be recognized by their
persecutors as members of the same community. That easy identification reveals to all
of us the great evil of our century.

This adumbration of the speculative part of the revised version may suffice. Let
us now turn to the moral part, the dimensions of which might more easily unfold in the
face of direct challenge.

Objections to Evolutionary Ethics

Systems of evolutionary ethics have attracted objections of two distinct kinds: those
challenging their adequacy as biological theories and those challenging their adequacy
as moral theories. Critics focusing on the biological part have made various complaints,
a few I have already mentioned (see also Richards 1986b, 1989). These objections are
common enough, but so are the positions objected to. The disputes concerning evolutionary scenarios that depict the biological transformation of protohuman into human
beings cannot at present be resolved. For the moment, I simply ask the reader to accept

as true the spare, speculative story I have spun concerning the likely course of human evolution. This will allow me to develop the subject that can best be handled from the armchair—namely, the moral theory and its conceptual supports. So let me now begin to introduce the distinctively moral and logical objections to an evolutionary ethics, especially the charge that any ethics born of evolutionary facts must quickly succumb to the deadly naturalistic fallacy.

But one common objection must be attended to before we can talk about the naturalistic fallacy—an objection that echoes through Sober's chapter (this volume). My speculative scenario about the evolution of impulses or instincts of altruism may be thought to equivocate over the meaning of "altruism," which I do wish to apply to animals and humans with the same significance. It might be objected that "altruism" when applied to courageous acts of a human soldier means something different from the "altruism" used to describe the actions of a soldier bee that sacrifices its life for the hive. But to avoid this charge, let me here stipulate that when I talk about "altruistic impulses" or "altruistic instincts" I will mean something that is perfectly univocal when applied to animals and man: namely, the motive cause that usually leads to behavior that benefits the recipient and costs the agent some good, without any significant probability of recompense to the agent. At this level of analysis no conscious intentions are involved, so the term "altruism" can be applied unequivocally to animals and humans. What will distinguish animal altruism from human altruism is that humans can act from altruistic motives intentionally; animals, as we know them, act from altruistic motives without conscious intention.

Now let me build on this distinction between acting from motives with intention or without intention by adding another distinction—that between an ethics of consequences and an ethics of intention. Some varieties of ethical utilitarianism, including that of Wilson and Alexander, regard behavior morally good if it has certain consequences. The evolutionary ethics that I am advocating, however, looks to the internal states of the organism; it construes an action good if the action meets three requirements: (a) it flows from a certain kind of motive, the altruistic motive; (b) it is performed intentionally for that motive; and (c) it can, therefore, be justified by appeal to that motive. I will assume as an empirical postulate that the motive has been established by community or kin selection. The altruistic motive encourages the agent to attend to the needs of others, which needs will be defined for the agent by biological disposition or cultural learning (or both). The Aristotelian-Thomistic ethics, as well as the very different Kantian moral philosophy, holds that action from appropriate motives, not action having desirable consequences, is necessary to render an act moral or immoral. The commonsense moral tradition sanctions the same distinction. Consider the student, on her way to a jazz concert, who stops to help a struggling, little old lady across Michigan Avenue. How do we judge the student's behavior? Initially, I believe, we would consider her as having performed a morally good deed. She was motivated by an altruistic sense, and intended to act on the motivation. If we subsequently learned, however, that the student needed funds for the jazz concert and thought the lady would reward her with enough money for tickets, we would likely alter our judgment—regarding her behavior as certainly not morally praiseworthy, though not reprehensible either. The student in this case would not have acted from an altruistic motive, rather from a selfish one; since, however, the receipient received a good, we take the agent's act as morally neutral. But if we learned that the student was taking the lady across the street in order to rob her of money for tickets, we would surely regard the student's apparently altruistic behavior as evil. We evaluate behavior on the basis of the motives and intentions of the agent, since only under some motive and intention do we regard it as a human act at all.

These internalistic features of the revised version blunt one kind of charge that might be brought against an evolutionary ethics (and indeed, a charge that retains its edge when wielded against consequentialist ethics): namely, that identifying the moral sense with social instinct would make animals moral creatures. For certain species of animals might have been impregnated with altruistic motives—consider the labors of love performed by honey bees. We do not, though, believe bees can form conscious intentions to engage in such labors. After all, a moral theory that made African killer-bees into morally virtuous creatures would be damned by all but entomologists.

Some will argue (P. Williams and Gewirth, this volume) that the causal understanding provided by evolutionary theory encumbers any ethical system based on it. Moral acts are deliberate and intentional, not determined and coerced. To say that I "ought" to perform an action implies that I need not. But evolutionary theory supposes that altruistic motives descend from a mechanically fixed process and that these motive causes beat the agent into submission: willy-nilly, the agent must act according to the hardened laws of biological nature. It certainly is true that any moral theory based on evolution must balance along the edge of practical reason on the one side, in which we judge ourselves and others as intentional, free agents, and theoretical reason on the other, in which as scientists we fix behavior with unyielding causes. This difficulty, of course, is not unique to an evolutionary ethics. Every ethical system must assume that behavior is caused, otherwise motives and intentions could not determine action. But if motives and intentions are causes of behavior, they must also be regarded as effects of previous causes, since that is the nature of our concept of the causal relation. Admittedly, the difficulty of squaring our belief in human freedom with our coeval belief in causal determinism remains profound and troubling. It is a difficulty, however, that indiscriminately infects all ethical theories. Any moral theorist who encourages this objection will not escape its toxic consequences. However, the revised version, while not solving this difficulty, tries like all moral theories to keep a momentary balance between two inexorable epistemological forces: on the one hand, appraising behavior as the act of conscious, intentional agents who deliberate over competing urges, and, on the other, analyzing behavior as the causal result of an organism's innate tendencies, its past experiences, and the immediate influences of its environment.

At last, let me now turn to the one kind of objection generally thought to be fatal to any Darwinizing in morals, the naturalistic fallacy. Let me try first to deflect attacks by showing that we commonly derive imperatives from factual propositions, without committing any logical sins.

Consider the relatively unproblematic arguments we make with each other, arguments that depend on a commonly agreed upon set of linguistic and conceptual assumptions. Take the threadbare illustration: "All men are mortal. Socrates is a man. Therefore, Socrates is mortal." We reflexively take the conclusion to be justified by the premises because we have implicitly agreed upon certain rules—not only Aristotle's rules of the syllogism, but also those of grammar and semantics. If our grammatical rules were different—such that, for instance, the second appearance of a term in succeeding sentences meant the negative of its first appearance—then we would not, in the example just cited, regard the premises as justifying the conclusion. Consider another example. Within the community of geneticists this argument would be unexceptional: "Joe's hereditary abnormality is carried on the male chromosome, therefore, it must have been passed on by his father." Given background knowledge of simple genetics and the rules governing the disposition of terms, especially "male" and "father," the conclusion soundly follows from the premise. Or at a meeting of the American Philosophical Society, this argument would be certified as perfectly just: "Hilary knows we are not brains in vats, therefore, we are not brains in vats." This argument is sound, of course, because if the premise is true—that someone does "know" something—then the conclusion stating the proposition known must be true. These one-premise arguments depend on certain rules embedded in our common conceptual and linguistic heritage, but in that they are no different from the canonical arguments that instruct us about Socrates' mortality. Of course, if someone in the genetics society were to walk in on the philosophers, he or she might find the Hilary argument not at all persuasive, since only within the tight little community of the descendants of Plato have the rules governing "know" been absorbed into the blood.

Now consider a community of fundamentalist Christians and two faithful members who have fallen into dispute. The community holds firm to Scripture as the final authority in all matters of proper behavior. Suppose one member, perhaps washed over by the larger waves of Hollywood culture, maintains that premarital sex is permissible. The other member, who keeps his head above water, cries no. The clearer-eyed of the brethren might save the one slipping into the depths with this line of argument: "The Bible says fornication is wrong; but fornication is sex outside of marriage. Therefore, premarital sex ought not be engaged in." Here appeal would be made to nonmoral, nonimperative premises (i.e., those specifying what can be found in the Bible and the definition of terms) to arrive at an ethical conclusion—a perfectly legitimate derivation of an "ought" from an "is." To be sure, the argument depends on the parties accepting a metamoral rule, one that might be formalized something like this: "From 'behavior x is condemned in the Bible' conclude 'behavior x ought not be done.'" All sound arguments, it must be remembered, depend on the parties accepting certain rules—the rules of the syllogism, *modus ponens*, grammatical rules, etc.—that will govern the derivation of conclusions from premises.

We have just seen how normative conclusions may be drawn from factual premises. This would be an internal justification if the contending parties initially agreed about inference principles, such as *modus ponens* or certain metamoral rules. However, they may not agree, and then the problem of justification becomes the framework issue of what justifies the inference rule? Ruse gives up about here. He sees no way out but the tingle in the blood, the feeling in the gut. Yet our intellectual resources have not been exhausted. We can and do meet framework challenges. To do so, one must move outside the system in order to avoid a circularly vicious justification. When philosophers take this step, they typically begin to appeal (and ultimately must) to commonsense moral judgments. They produce test cases to determine whether a given principle will yield the same moral conclusions as would commonly be reached by individuals in their society—just as I have done in producing the test case of Dr. Moreau's son. In short, frameworks, their inference rules, and their principles are usually justified in terms of intuitively clear cases—that is, in terms of matters of fact. Such justifying arguments, then, proceed from what people as a matter of fact believe to conclusions about what principles would yield these matters of fact.

This method of justifying norms is not confined to ethics. It is quite commonly used in all normative disciplines. In aesthetics we justify principles of artistic value by showing that they would yield the conclusion that the Madonna of Leonardo is quite beautiful, and not really to be compared with the Madonna of MTV. In logic, this same strategy has established *modus ponens* as the chief principle of the modern discipline: *modus ponens* (i.e., the schema "If *a*, then *b*; but *a*; therefore *b*," where *a* and *b* stand for propositions) renders the same arguments valid that rational men consider valid. But this strategy for justifying norms utilizes empirical evidence, albeit of a very general sort. Quite simply the strategy recognizes what William James liked to pound home: that no system can validate its own first principles. The first principles of an ethical system can be justified only by appeal to another kind of discourse, an appeal in which factual evidence about common sentiments and beliefs is adduced.

According to this understanding of the concept of justification, the justification of metamoral inference rules must ultimately lead to an appeal to the beliefs and practices of men, which, of course, is an empirical appeal. So moral principles ultimately can be justified only by facts. The rebuttal, then, to the charge that at some level evolutionary ethics must attempt to derive its norms from facts is simply that every ethical system must.

The Justification of the Revised Version as an Ethical System

The revised version stipulates that the community welfare is the highest moral good. It supposes that evolution has equipped humans with a number of social instincts, such as the need to protect offspring, to provide for the general well-being of members of the community (including oneself), to defend the helpless against aggression, and for other dispositions that constitute a moral creature. These constitutionally embedded directives are instances of the supreme principle of heeding the community welfare. Particular moral maxims, which translate these injunctions into the language and values of a given society, would be justified by an individual's showing that, all things considered, following such maxims would contribute to the community welfare.

To justify the supreme principle, and thus the system, requires a different kind of argument, however. I want to remind you that I will attempt to justify the revised version as a moral system *under the supposition that it correctly accounts for all the relevant biological facts.* If I had time enough and the reader patience, I would provide three justifying arguments. But I will offer only one (for others, see Richards 1986a). Alan Gewirth will recognize a family resemblance with an argument he mounts (Gewirth 1982:100-128), though I'm sure he thinks I've gotten on this steed backwards.

This argument makes use of the commonly accepted rule that governs the disposition of the concept "ought" in our language. I will use this rule, just as that fundamentalist community did theirs, to derive a moral conclusion from evolutionary facts. First, consider the rule governing the use of the word "ought."

Take the simple argument "Carbon dioxide is building up in the atmosphere; carbon dioxide molecules reflect back heat to the surface; therefore, world temperatures ought to rise." The argument has two premises and a conclusion that includes the term "ought." Several rules are involved in the operation of this argument, for instance, those of grammar, those governing the semantic relations of "heat" and "temperature," and so on. One involves the semantic disposition of the "ought." In the above argument, the rule of "ought" allows us to move from premises stating a causally structured context to a conclusion which asserts that a less-than-certain causal result ought to occur. So, when a student comes to me and asks, "How can I get an A on your exam?" I will reply: "Look, you're a bright kid, the material is not difficult. If you study hard, you ought to get an A." That is, given the factual situations stated in the premises, we may conclude: Mary ought to get an A (i.e., she must get an A, except that some unforeseen event intervenes).

Or consider this likely scene: An elderly woman is attempting to cross Michigan Avenue at 5:00 p.m. Joe comes up next to her. I say to a companion: "Joe is extremely altruistic. He sees the lady in distress. Therefore, he ought to act altruistically and help her across." Here the ought-conclusion has been derived from facts by a rule. The rule operates like *modus ponens*. It joins premises to a conclusion because of the characteristics of the premises. The rule for the use of ought might be formulated in this fashion: "From 'y is enmeshed in causal matrix x' conclude 'y ought to act in x fashion.'" That is, Joe is enmeshed in the causal matrix of evolution, which instilled in him altruistic motives; therefore, he ought to act in an altruistic fashion, which our society translates as helping little old ladies across Michigan Avenue.

Now according to the speculative theory of evolution that I've spun out, and which I've asked the reader to accept, evolution provides the structured context of moral action: it has constituted human beings not only to be moved to act for the community good, but also to approve, endorse, and encourage others to do so as well. The constructive forces of evolution impose a practical necessity on each person to promote the community good. In our practical reasoning, we must, we are obliged to heed this imperative. We might attempt to ignore the demand of our nature by refusing to act altruistically, but this does not diminish its reality. Freud notwithstanding, feelings of guilt often stem from the unheeded but unstilled motive to act for the welfare of other members of the community. Hence, just as the context of physical nature allows us to argue "Since carbon dioxide has built up, atmospheric temperature ought to increase," so the structured context of human evolution allows us to argue *"Since each person has evolved to promote the community good, each ought to act altruistically."* And here I've gone from a factual premise about evolution to an ought proposition, without, I believe, any fallacy. The rule that allows me to join the premise with the conclusion is one that governs the usage of the term "ought." In this situation it is no different from the rule employed in the fundamentalist community I earlier referred to or no different from the rule of *modus ponens* in logic, which allows me to go from premises of a certain kind to conclusions of a certain kind.

Now what does "ought" mean in this derivation? That is, what is the rule governing the use of "ought"? In reference to structured contexts, "ought to occur," "ought to be," "ought to act," etc., typically means "must occur," "must be," "must act, *provided there is no interference."* Structured contexts involve causal processes. Typically "ought" adds to "must" the idea that perchance some other cause might disrupt the process (e.g., "Carbon dioxide has built up, so the earth's atmosphere ought to get hotter; that is, it must get hotter, provided that the sun keeps radiating the same amount of energy, the oceans are not absorbing carbon dioxide as fast as it is increased, etc."). In the context of the evolutionary constitution of human behavior, "ought" means that the person must act altruistically, provide he or she has assessed the situation correctly and a surge of jealously, hatred, greed, etc., does not interfere. The "must" here is a causal "must"; it means that in ideal conditions—that is, perfectly formed attitudes resulting from evolutionary processes, complete knowledge of situations, absolute control of the passions, etc.—altruistic behavior would necessarily occur in the appropriate conditions. In moral discourse, "ought" has the additional function of encouraging the agent to avoid or reject anything that might interfere with the act.

Some patient readers at this point will hesitate, and wish to object: Is the word "ought" used any differently here than in the proposition about the greenhouse effect? The answer is yes and no. The "ought" of the greenhouse example is not a moral ought. What makes the conclusion a moral-ought conclusion is that the structured context from which it is derived is that of the evolution of altruism. The "ought" derived from the structured context of human evolutionary formation, then, will be a moral ought precisely because the activities of promoting the community good and of approving altruistic behavior constitute what we mean by being moral. And here my conclusion arches back to Kant. According to Kant, the moral value of action stems from the good will that performed it; and so we judge the moral character of the action from the structured complex that gives rise to it. The Kantian good will was one that operated in a certain fashion—that is, according to duty, which under one interpretation of his categorical imperative was acting altruistically (i.e., treating each individual as a member of a community of ends). Now if any neo-Huxleyan were to reflect and ask himself whether his altruistic impulses should be followed, he would have to judge that they should—for if we have evolved according to the empirical scenario I have asked the reader to accept, then the reflective critic could do no other than hold as special, prize, and endorse—that is, regard as moral—the altruistic motive in his breast. He would have to conclude that the altruistic motive was the one he "ought" to follow.

References

Alexander, R. 1987. *The Biology of Moral Systems*. New York: Aldine De Gruyter.

Darwin, C. 1859. *On the Origin of Species*. London: Murray.

Darwin, C. 1871. *The Descent of Man and Selection in Relation to Sex*. 2 vols. London: Murray.

Gewirth, A. 1982. *Human Rights: Essays on Justification and Applications*. Chicago: University of Chicago Press.

Haeckel, E. 1904. *Die Lebenswunder: Gemeinverständliche Studien öder Biologische Philosophie*. Stuttgart: Kröner.

Huxley, J. 1947. *Touchstone for Ethics, 1893-1943*. New York: Harper.

Huxley, T. H. [1893] 1989. "Evolution and Ethics." Reprinted in *Evolution and Ethics, with New Essays on Its Victorian and Sociobiological Context*. Essays by J. Paradis and G. Williams. Princeton, NJ: Princeton University Press.

Mivart, St. G. J. 1871. *On the Genesis of Species*. New York: D. Appleton.

Moore, G. E. [1903] 1929. *Principia Ethica*. 2d ed. Cambridge: Cambridge University Press.

Richards, R. 1986a. A defense of evolutionary ethics. *Biology & Philosophy* 1:265-93.

Richards, R. 1986b. Justification through biological faith: A rejoinder. *Biology & Philosophy* 1:337-54.

Richards, R. 1987. *Darwin and the Emergence of Evolutionary Theories of Mind and Behavior*. Chicago: University of Chicago Press.

Richards, R. 1989. Dutch objections to evolutionary ethics. *Biology & Philosophy* 4:331-43.

Ruse, M. 1984. The morality of the gene. *The Monist* 67:167-99.

Ruse, M. 1986. *Taking Darwin Seriously*. Oxford: Blackwell.

Spencer, H. [1893] 1978. *The Principles of Ethics*. 2 vols. Indianapolis: Liberty Classics.

Waddington, C. H. 1961. *The Ethical Animal*. New York: Athenaeum.

Williams, G. 1989. A sociobiological expansion of *Evolution and Ethics*. In *Evolution and Ethics, with New Essays on Its Victorian and Sociobiological Context*. Essays by J. Paradis and G. Williams. Princeton, NJ: Princeton University Press.

Wilson, E. O. 1975. *Sociobiology*. Cambridge, MA: Harvard University Press.

Wilson, E. O. 1978. *On Human Nature*. Cambridge, MA: Harvard University Press.

The New Evolutionary Ethics

Michael Ruse

Evolutionary ethics is a subject with a deservedly bad reputation. As every scholar knows, there are some subjects that are not merely false but with a bad smell around them. One knows that their enthusiasts probably have unspoken but unfortunate quasi-mystical or religious yearnings. Parapsychology falls into this camp. So also, on the biological front, does so-called Lamarckism or the inheritance of acquired characters. The evidence against this in any genuine sense is so overwhelming that those who would open the subject again are rightly considered with extreme distrust by conventional biologists (Dawkins 1986). A third topic is evolutionary ethics, the project which argues that for a full understanding of the nature and grounds of morality one must turn to the process and theories of the evolutionist.

Or so it was thought almost generally until about ten years ago. Now a few biologists and philosophers are starting to think that perhaps the question of evolution and ethics has not been answered quite so definitively as we all had thought (Mackie 1978, 1979; Murphy 1982; Alexander 1987). There might be more to be said on the subject than any of us had imagined. There is by no means a stampede to the new position, but now we are starting the initial shift from "false and not worth discussing" to "false but interesting in a way and perhaps worth putting in readers for our introductory students." (In thus characterizing people's attitudes toward evolutionary ethics I am, in fact, being rather unfair to biologists. As I shall show in a moment, there have almost always been some biologists, including leaders in the field, who have felt that the question of evolutionary ethics is by no means as cut and dried as the average philosopher supposes.)

I was, myself, a disbeliever until recently, but have now come round drastically (anti, Ruse 1979; pro, Ruse 1986). Neither I nor anyone else would claim that our current understanding of evolutionary biology answers all the questions of the ethicist nor, indeed, would we think that such a claim could ever be made soundly. But, as I shall argue here, it does seem to matter that we are the products of a long slow undirected process of organic change rather than the special creation of a good god some six thousand years ago. Being modified monkeys counts, and nowhere more so than in the realm of social and moral behavior and thought.

I intend to deal first with traditional evolutionary ethics, often called, somewhat inaccurately, "Social Darwinism." For reasons that I shall explain (certainly not reasons original with me) I do not think it succeeds. However, I do hope to show that this program is perhaps somewhat more interesting and more varied than critics usually allow. Then I shall discuss the form of evolutionary ethics which has in recent years started to gain favor-able attention, particularly from philosophers. As I shall argue, it depends crucially on new moves being made by evolutionary biologists but, at the same time, I hope to show that it has roots deep in conventional philosophy. One should be wary always of any philosophy that claims to be entirely new. Those parts which are good are probably not original, and those parts which are original are probably not that good.

Before turning to biology, however, it will be useful to remind ourselves of an elementary distinction made by moral philosophers between so-called "substantive" or "normative" ethics and so-called "metaethics" (Taylor 1978). The former speaks of the kinds of moral rules that people should follow, the latter of foundations. Thus, in a paradigmatic moral system such as Christianity, with respect to substantive ethics the Christian is supposed to follow the Golden Rule or some such thing ("Love your neighbor as yourself"). With respect to foundations, there is some dispute among Christians, but undoubtedly many accept morality because they believe in some divine command theory, namely, one ought to do what one ought to do because this is the will of God. (This is so despite the fact that some four centuries before Christ, Plato in the *Euthyphro* had pointed to difficulties with the divine command theory, namely, does God want one to do that which is good because God wants one to do it or does God want one to do that which is good because it is good?)

I recognize that sophisticated moral philosophers see many difficulties with the separation of ethics into substantive ethics and metaethics (Williams 1985), but for the level of approximation we need here the distinction will stand us in good stead. So let us turn now to traditional thinking on evolution and ethics.

Social Darwinism

The idea of evolution, that all organisms living and dead, including ourselves, are the products of a long gradual natural process of development from primitive forms, even from inorganic matter, has its beginning in the eighteenth century. Some two hundred years behind the great revolution in the physical sciences, in the Age of the Enlightenment, a number of thinkers began to suspect that perhaps the story of creation in Genesis might not be literally true. Rather, a regular law-bound process of change was responsible for the diversity we see around us today and (as is being increasingly revealed) in the fossil record (Greene 1959; Bowler 1984).

However, in the early years no one really thought of turning to evolutionism for moral guidance or support. Rather, evolution's processes and results were thought to be the harmonious subjects of otherwise-grounded moral norms, no less than any other part of the world around or within us. Typical in this respect was Erasmus Darwin, the grandfather of Charles Darwin—in his own right, one of the most articulate and enthusiastic of the early evolutionists (King Hele 1977). A firmly committed utilitarian, Erasmus Darwin saw moral obligations as centering on the promotion of human happiness, and he thought that in some way the Unmoved Mover lying behind all creation is the support of this dictate. Evolution, for Erasmus Darwin, was simply God's way of promoting a maximum amount of happiness inasmuch as it led to the production of higher animals capable of enjoying God's bounty (McNeil 1987).

However, as evolutionary thought matured in the middle of the nineteenth century, people's confidence in traditional morality and its supports began to fall away. Interestingly, this seems to have been less a function of the rise and negative implications of science and more one of other social and intellectual factors, not the least of which was the critique levelled against conventional Christianity by scholars who turned on traditional beliefs, skills which had been developed and honed on secular writings and thoughts (Ruse 1979). I refer, of course, to the practitioners of so-called "Higher Criticism," who showed that the Bible is a very fallible, humanly produced document. Somehow, the commands of God—and His Son—seemed suddenly less authoritative.

Whatever the causes, in the middle of the nineteenth century, in the industrial world we found ourselves with traditional supports and norms falling away. Yet, newly developed industrial societies called for fresh and vigorous answers to social and economic questions. It was at this point that many thinkers started to turn to biology for insights into ethical understanding and behavior (Hofstadter 1959; Russett 1976; Jones 1980). Obviously, a major spur was Charles Darwin's great work on evolutionary theory *On the Origin of Species by Means of Natural Selection* in 1859. In this work he argued not merely for evolution, but also for his own particular mechanism, the natural selection of organisms (otherwise known as the survival of the fittest) brought on by a struggle for existence, which in turn is a function of the ever-present population pressures. Paradoxically, however, although Darwin's promotion of evolutionism undoubtedly made the way for evolutionary ethics much easier—and it was he whose name was adopted in the term "Social Darwinism"—it was not he who was chiefly responsible for articulating and promoting a transmutationist approach to moral behavior. Rather, chief credit must go to Darwin's fellow evolutionist and fellow Englishman, Herbert Spencer. Around 1850 (some ten years before the *Origin* appeared) Spencer had begun arguing that the key to ethical understanding must lie in the evolutionary process. This was a theme he kept pressing in many writings for the next half-century (Spencer 1850, 1857, 1892).

Spencer was what one might describe euphemistically as a somewhat loose thinker, which means that he was not always totally consistent in what he claimed. But, it seems not unfair to say that Spencer was attracted both morally and socially to a fairly extreme form of *laissez-faire* individualism. He believed that liberty is a moral good because it will promote happiness and, therefore, one has an obligation to maximize liberty inasmuch as one can. Living as he did in industrialized Victorian Britain, Spencer thought that morality demands a minimum of state interference with the way in which people run their lives, be this at the level of business or of personal behavior. This is not to say that Spencer preached a doctrine of unrelieved selfishness. Indeed, he very much thought the fortunate in society have personal obligations to the less fortunate, but he was strongly opposed to state-imposed systems for the amelioration of society's ills (Richards 1988).

Moreover, perhaps even more important than what Spencer himself thought, this doctrine of libertarianism was taken up and promoted in his name or in the name of Charles Darwin who, incidentally, generally sat uneasily on the sidelines of all attempts to draw world philosophies from evolutionary biology. Thus, for instance, the sociologist William Graham Sumner, who like many of Spencer's Social Darwinian supporters was American, ardently denied the possibility of any effectively socialist state.

> What we mean by liberty is civil liberty, or liberty under law; and this means the guarantees of law that a man shall not be interfered with while using his own powers for his own welfare. It is, therefore, a civil and political status; and that nation has the freest institutions in which the guarantees of peace for the laborer and security for the capitalist are the highest. (Sumner 1914:293)

How did Spencer and his followers justify their exultation of human freedom and how, in particular, did they tie this into the evolutionary process? Their moves were simple and direct. First, they drew attention to the main processes of evolutionary change that presuppose an ongoing struggle for existence, which in turn leads to natural selection. (Spencer had spotted the idea of natural selection before the *Origin* was published, although as a matter of historical fact, several years after Darwin himself had hit upon the idea [Spencer 1852].) Next they claimed that one's moral obligations are to promote the forces of change or at least not to stand in the way of their full execution. Thirdly, they concluded that one's moral obligations are to support struggle and selection in the social realm, which they translated as implying fairly extreme libertarianism. Thus, Sumner again:

> The struggle for existence is aimed against nature. It is from her niggardly hand that we have to wrest the satisfactions for our needs, but our fellow-men are our competitors for the meager supply. Competition, therefore, is a law of nature. Nature is entirely neutral; she submits to him who most energetically and resolutely assails her. She grants her rewards to the fittest, therefore, without regard to other considerations of any kind. If, then, there be liberty, men get from her just in proportion to their works, and their having and enjoying are just in proportion to their being and their doing. Such is the system of nature. If we do not like it, and if we try to amend it, there is only one way in which we can do it. We can take from the better and give to the worse. We can deflect the penalties of those who have done ill and throw them on those who have done better. We can take the rewards from those who have done better and given them to those who have done worse. We shall thus lessen the inequalities. We shall favor the survival of the unfittest, and we shall accomplish this by destroying liberty. Let it be understood that we cannot go outside of this alternative: liberty, inequality, survival of the fittest; not-liberty, equality, survival of the unfittest. The former carries society forward and favors all its best members; the latter carries society downwards and favors all its worst members. (1914:293)

Any successful and widespread moral system harbors within its boundaries differences of opinion. During the First World War, while the armies of the two sides clashed secure in the knowledge that they were following God's will, there lay at home rotting in the prisons Christians who were equally convinced that the God of the New Testament bars them absolutely from the use of arms. So it is with Social Darwinians. Whether because of genuine differences in the interpretation of evolution's processes, or for other extra-scientific reasons, for every ardent Spencerian like the industrialist John D. Rockefeller, who supposedly assured a Sunday School class that the law of God is the law of big business and, therefore, it is good and right that Standard Oil (his company!) should have pushed its competitors to the wall, there was some other evolutionarily inspired thinker who took an altogether different tack as to the moral norms one should support and follow (Russett 1976).

One interesting alternative, at the time of Sumner, was the Scottish-American steel

magnate Andrew Carnegie. As is well known, Carnegie turned in midlife to philan-
thropy, which he expressed by sponsoring and supporting the founding of public libraries. This was no whim on Carnegie's part, but grew directly out of his belief that the
best way to promote the evolutionary process is to concentrate on the survival and
success of the fit rather than on the nonsurvival and nonsuccess of the unfit. In founding public libraries, Carnegie hoped thereby to provide a place where the poor but tal-
ented child could go and raise himself or herself in society. This was indeed practical
Darwinism with a very different cast from that of Sumner.

Then, again, there were those like the Russian anarchist thinker Prince Peter Kropotkin (1902), who thought that the way in which natural selection acts is through the
promotion of group characteristics and sentiments. The survival of the fittest refers not
to the success of the individual but rather to the success and survival of the group,
specifically the species. Thus, in his major work, *Mutual Aid*, Kropotkin argued that we
have a natural evolutionary sentiment to help each other and that this translates into a
quasi-Christian directive to support one's neighbor. Not surprisingly, this sentiment
found favor with many evolutionists. In this century one of the most articulate was
Julian Huxley (1947), the grandson of Charles Darwin's great supporter, Thomas Henry
Huxley. For all of his life Julian Huxley argued that it is within the evolutionary
process that we find the clues to moral behavior and these clues lead us in turn to the
need to promote some kind of idealized human welfare. One should add that Julian
Huxley, like Carnegie before him, took his evolutionism seriously and devoted much of
his later life to the cause of world happiness and peace, particularly through his leader-
ship of the newly formed UNESCO after World War II.

In our own time, are also evolutionary ethicists of different stripes. In the traditional mold, promoting stringent *laissez-faire* policies, are many representatives. Today,
they exist particularly in positions of power in Washington and Whitehall. Mrs. Margaret Thatcher, for instance, was much given to exhortations to recognize the reality of
life's struggles and the need to respond, not through idealized socialistic measures, but
through very nineteenth-century-sounding solutions of thrift, work, and individualism.
Because of this, she was much more radical than previous British Conservative leaders,
like Harold Macmillan and Edward Heath, who stood much more in the benevolent
paternalistic tradition of Benjamin Disraeli. They wanted to preserve traditional institutions, whereas she wanted to break them down. Like Spencer, Thatcher came from
lower-middle class, nonconformist, Midland stock.

Conversely, on the soft side as it were, is the Harvard biologist, Edward O. Wilson,
who in many respects has been the person most responsible for the resurgence of

interest in evolutionary ethics in our time, arguing that humans can and must live with rest of the living world. Therefore, we have a moral obligation to preserve and protect nonhuman species. For Wilson, this translates into a need to take environmentalism seriously (Wilson 1984). He is at this moment much involved in projects such as the preservation of the Brazilian rain forests.

I have thus far been dealing with what has been characterized as the substantive or normative aspects of traditional evolutionary ethics, and looking at what Spencer and others would have us do in the name of evolution. This is the part of their moral theory which corresponds to the Christian's love command. What of foundations? Why should one promote *laissez-faire* individualism? Why should one found public libraries? Why should one care about the trees in South America? Here one must be careful not to generalize uncritically, but it does seem that traditional evolutionary ethicists do have, explicitly or implicitly, a metaethical move behind them and this is one which is shared by all. In particular, the traditional evolutionary ethicist argues that the process of evolution is not meaningless. It is not an endlessly oscillating stream, going nowhere, and rather slowly at that, but with direction, in particular leading onwards and upwards. Value and meaning come through evolution because the change which leads to organisms, especially to higher organisms, is *progressive*. In the eyes of Social Darwinians, therefore, one ought to cherish and aid the evolutionary process, otherwise one will degenerate and decay.

Spencer (1857) certainly was an ardent progressionist. He believed that, in the animal world, there is a limited amount of basic creative fluid available to any organism at any time and that this can go to the production of thinking power or of offspring. Consequently, what Spencer saw as a result of life's struggles was a gradual rise in the ability of organisms to think, with a consequent falling away of reproductive abilities. It is for this reason that we find mammals, for instance, have evolved to a far higher state than the fish. Within the mammals, we get a like ordering. Indeed, Spencer was sufficiently Victorian to suggest that within the human species we get evidence of progress, and he was not beyond drawing attention to the large families of the Irish and their consequent inabilities to better themselves as opposed to the far more successful achievements of the much more temperate Scottish and English families with fewer children (Spencer 1852). This, incidentally, was a point noted and endorsed by Charles Darwin in the *Descent* (1871), although he did not take his biologizing to the extreme taken by Spencer, who remained a lifelong childless bachelor.

Sumner and other nineteenth-century biological ethicizers were also progressionists, as have been their counterparts in the twentieth century. Julian Huxley (1942), for instance, devoted major parts of his most detailed evolutionary theorizings to claims about the existence and significance of progress and similar moves are made today within and without the biological community. Wilson (1975) makes little secret of his beliefs in upward improvement and he is explicit in seeing humans as sitting on the top of the pyramid. As one whose major biological achievements have been in our understanding of the social insects, it is perhaps no surprise to find that it is sociality that Wilson prizes most highly. It is in this respect that he finds humans having greater abundance and hence more worth than any other animal (Wilson 1978).

These, then, are the ways of the traditional evolutionary ethicist or Social Darwinian. The processes of evolution are taken as substantive guides to conduct and the upward progress of the evolutionary process is taken as the metaethical underpinning. To the traditionalist, progress is a good thing and unless one allows, if not actively promotes, the process of evolution, one will get a falling away and consequent degeneration. One's moral obligations, therefore, are to see that evolution succeeds.

Critique

Almost from its first appearance, traditional evolutionary ethics has had its critics and such critics continue their complaints unabated today. The objections occur both at the substantive and at the metaethical levels. First, at the substantive level, we find objections of many kinds. Most naturally, of course, we find that the hardline Spencerian types come in for much negative attention. It is argued that no moral theory could be so counter to common decency—to intuition—as to conclude that the state has no moral obligations at all to its weak and poor. It is argued that it is our task, here on earth, to combat the struggle rather than to go mindlessly on with it. It is argued, moreover, that only the self-serving capitalist could think that there are positive moral virtues in the success of Standard Oil and similar large concerns (Huxley 1894).

Appeals to one's own personal moral intuitions are easy and satisfying. Regretfully, they do not always carry the authority needed to refute opposing views. More successful criticisms of the traditional evolutionary ethical claims have come from those who have pointed to the frequent inconsistencies made at the substantive level by evolutionary ethicists of the Spencerian world. Thus, for instance, although Sumner is ardent in his support of unrestricted capitalism, curiously—and critics would argue inconsistently—he pulls back sharply when it comes to personal property and sexual propriety. One might think that an unrestrained *laissez-faire* philosophy would allow the strongest simply to seize the goods of the weakest as well as opening the way for unrestrained sexual license. However, Sumner denies this absolutely. Yet, it is hard to see his denial is based on anything other than his own personal inclinations or prejudices. The argument is not that Sumner is wrong in valuing personal property or sexual restraint, but rather that he makes no argument for his position.

The moral sentiments of the soft side to evolutionary ethics usually arouse no immediate hostility. After all, who could be opposed to urgings toward world peace and today there is a positive stampede in favor of environmental and ecological improvements. Yet, here also, critics have made their bite felt. In particular, the scientific basis on which the substantive claims are made have come in for severe discussion. Against people like Prince Kropotkin and Julian Huxley, it is argued that there is no warrant at all for rather mushy readings of the evolutionary process which cherish the promotion of the ends of species. It is argued, to the contrary, that the struggle for existence exists between conspecifics no less severely than between members of different species. Consequently, selection works just as strongly between same types as between different types (Williams 1966, 1988).

Likewise, critics argue that Wilson's argument about the biological needs of human beings to preserve other species is tenuous, at the very least. Whilst, to survive successfully, we may need some of the organisms in our immediate vicinity, claims about those more distant or remote seem much looser. It is hard not to see that Wilson has simply decided on the ecological moves that he thinks should be made, and that he has then given a cloak of evolutionary biological respectability to precisely these moves (Singer 1986).

The metaethical foundations of traditional evolutionary ethics have also come under fire. Here, in particular, philosophers as well as biologists have joined in the cry. Most famous or perhaps most notorious is the critique of G. E. Moore at the beginning of this century in his *Principia Ethica* (1903). As is well known, Moore argued that one cannot go in ethics from claims about matters of fact to claims about matters of obligation, without committing what he labelled the "naturalistic fallacy." As many consequent commentators have noted, Moore's naturalistic fallacy is but part of the broader charge about the illicit nature of moves from "is" to "ought," first made by David Hume in his *Treatise of Human Nature* (Hudson 1970).

Moore wrote, specifically about evolutionary ethics, that it is illicit to go from the nature and process of the evolutionary world, to claims about the ways in which we ought to behave. It may, indeed, be true that we have come about through a struggle for existence leading to a consequent natural selection but this in itself says nothing of obligations to help the struggle or selection along. Even more specifically, about a theory like Spencer's, Moore says:

> The survival of the fittest does not mean, as one might suppose, the survival of what is fittest to fulfil a good purpose—best adapted to a good end: at the last, it means merely the survival of the fittest to survive; and the value of the scientific theory, and it is a theory of great value, just consists in shewing what are the causes which produce certain biological effects. Whether these effects are good or bad, it cannot pretend to judge. (1903:48)

Philosophers generally find this objection satisfyingly definitive. It is only fair to report, therefore, that by and large biologists do not find it particularly effective at all (Waddington 1962; Wilson 1978). They feel that it is a paradigmatic example of verbal chicanery by philosophers, who are determined not to take a naturalistic approach in the first place. When challenged, biologists will sometimes even allow some force to Moore's objection; but, in the case of evolutionary ethics, they simply declare that the point is not well taken. Although value does not generally come from the material world, in the unique case of the upward progressive improvements of organic evolution it does. That is what makes evolutionary ethics so special and so effective.

However, as more persistent critics have pointed out, matters cannot be left quite here (Singer 1981; Kitcher 1985). Among the more persistent critics I would include Moore himself, who certainly in *Principia Ethica* thinks that more is needed towards the refutation of Spencer than simply an invocation of the naturalistic fallacy. These critics point out that, at the general level all of the evolutionary ethicists' claims about organic progress are, to say the very least, dubious. There is little warrant in a theory of evolution through natural selection for suggesting that improvement must necessarily or even occasionally emerge. The one who spotted this point, immediately, was one of the first and most effective critics of Spencer himself, namely Julian Huxley's grandfather T. H. Huxley! Flatly against Spencer he argued that we have no reason to think that the evolutionary process will necessarily lead to improvement.

> "Fittest" has a connotation of "best"; and about "best" there hangs a moral flavour. In cosmic nature, however, what is "fittest" depends upon the conditions. Long since, I ventured to point out that if our hemisphere were to cool again, the survival of the fittest might bring about, in the vegetable kingdom, a population of more and more stunted and humbler and humbler organisms, until the "fittest" that survived might be nothing but lichens, diatoms, and such

microscopic organisms as those which give red snow its colour; while, if it became hotter, the pleasant valleys of the Thames and Isis might be uninhabitable by any animated beings save those that flourish in a tropical jungle. They, as the fittest, the best adapted to the changed conditions, would survive. (Huxley and Huxley 1947:298-99)

At the more specific level one can also see problems which arise out of notions of progress. Is one, for instance, to say today that the AIDS virus—which is clearly doing very successfully from a biological perspective—is necessarily superior to the great apes—which certainly in their natural habitat are unsuccessful almost to the point of extinction? Surely, we would not want to argue this. And the reason is that the value that we put in the products of evolution comes, not from their success in the evolutionary process, but from the external criteria by which we evaluate them. As Moore pointed out in the case of Spencer, the trouble with evolutionary ethicists is that they keep slipping into their premises notions like happiness and improvement and value, and then pretending that they are simply reading these notions out of the evolutionary process.

If the metaethical foundations collapse, then the whole traditional Social Darwinian program has gone under. It is interesting to note, that in our age, probably the most successful traditional evolutionary ethicist of all was one who was not really trying to use evolution to justify his position, but rather to illustrate a position in which he believed on other grounds. I refer, of course, to the Jesuit paleontologist Father Pierre Teilhard de Chardin (1957). He argued that the whole of evolution is a progressive move upwards, which culminates in something he identified as the Omega point, a place which in some way is bound up with the Christ. Despite the occasional claims otherwise, it is clear that Teilhard was not offering a scientific theory at all, but rather his own interpretation of Christianity infused by his deep feeling for evolutionism (Oldroyd 1980). As it happens, at the time of his writing he received little support either from his fellow Catholics, who responded by suppressing his work, or from most of his fellow scientists who were scornful in the extreme about his aims (Medawar 1972; although see Huxley 1957 and Dobzhansky 1967, 1973). But in the opinion of many today, time has perhaps shown that as long as one is not trying to get everything out of evolution unaided, then if one's aim is to bring evolutionism to bear on prior held religious or metaphysical beliefs, the kind of synthesis that Teilhard aimed to produce has much to commend it (Haselden and Hefner 1968).

Sociobiology: From "Altruism" to Altruism

Have we said all there is to be said about evolution and ethics? As noted earlier this was certainly the opinion of many until about ten years ago and is, indeed, probably the opinion of the majority still today. However, although philosophers are loath to admit it, advances in science often lead to new avenues in philosophy. It is certainly the case that in the past twenty years or so in evolutionary biology there have been major moves—moves which in the opinion of some open up whole new prospects for a fruitful unification of evolution and ethics. In this section I will talk about the science and then in the next section I will go on to discuss the possible philosophical juice which might be extracted. I appreciate that any adequate new approach to evolutionary ethics must, as before, give answers both at the substantive and at the foundational level.

The scientific claims are as simple as this. We now know that despite an evolutionary process, centering on a struggle for existence, organisms are not necessarily perpetually at conflict with weapons of attack and defence. In particular, cooperation can be a good biological strategy. We know also that humans are organisms which have preeminently taken this route of cooperation and working together. Further, there is good reason to think that a major way in which humans cooperate together is by having an ethical sense. Humans believe that they *should* work together, and so—with obvious qualifications—they do so. I emphasize, in connection with this last point, that the claim is not that humans are hypocritically consciously scheming to get as much out of each other as they possibly can while perhaps pretending to be nice, but rather that humans do have a genuinely moral sense and awareness of right and wrong. It is this which motivates them.

Now, let us unpack the science. We begin with the general claims about cooperation, or as today's evolutionists dealing with social behavior (the so-called "sociobiologists") like to call it, altruism (Wilson 1975; Dawkins 1976). I should emphasize at this point that nothing is being said about disinterested giving to others because it is right—that is to say, literal altruism, or what one might call Mother Teresa altruism. Rather, the talk is of cooperating for one's biological ends, which today translates into cooperation to maximize one's units of heredity (the genes) in the next generation (Maynard Smith 1978). In this sense, therefore, evolutionary altruism is a metaphorical sense of the term and perhaps is best thus marked in quotes: "altruism." I point out that there is absolutely nothing wrong with evolutionists appropriating such a term metaphorically. This is what all scientists do. Where else do terms like "workforce" and "attraction" come from? The danger is not in the borrowing of terms, but in the thinking that such terms are, thereby, necessarily being used literally. Midgley (1985) disagrees at this point about the very legitimacy of any biological metaphors.

Both the theory and the empirical evidence that biological "altruism" is widespread and promoted by natural selection is very secure and well documented. The simple fact of the matter is that, although winning in the struggle for existence is the best of all possible results, such success is often not possible—especially given that every other organism is likewise trying to win. Consequently, one is frequently much better off if one decides to accept a cake shared rather than gambling on the possibility of a whole cake but one which might be lost entirely.

There are various mechanisms which are believed to promote this kind of cooperation. The most striking examples occur in the social insects, where some females devote their whole lives to the well-being of the offspring of their mother, having none of their own (Hamilton 1964a, 1964b). But in organisms closer to us one likewise sees much evolutionary "altruism" (Trivers 1971). The dog family, for instance, relies very heavily on cooperative hunting, with the concern of the whole pack being devoted to the well-being of pregnant or lactating females and their offspring. I emphasize, however, that there is no question that at this point cooperating animals are necessarily in any sense ethical. There is little reason to think that, for instance, the hyenas heed the call of the Categorical Imperative. And, if anything is certain in this life, it is that social insects are blissfully ignorant of the Greatest Happiness Principle. The cooperative "altruism" occurs simply because there are good biological reasons for it. I emphasize also that today's evolutionists are not endorsing notions of "group selection," for which we have seen Kropotkin and Julian Huxley criticized. Today's mechanisms for "altruism" all show how cooperation benefits the cooperator, even if it is just a simple "I'll scratch your back, if you scratch mine" transaction.

The next point is that humans are obviously animals that need biological "altruism" and are, moreover, animals very skilled at employing it. They are not particularly good as hunters or fighters or even as escapers from danger; but, they are good at working together (Isaac 1983). (Not all of the time, of course, although it is interesting to note that modern ethological surveys suggest that, even after world wars are considered, humans as a species are significantly more peaceful than most other mammalian species.) Of course, our ability to cooperate and our need to cooperate did not just come about by chance. There was a feedback process in evolution, as so frequently occurs. It is now believed by paleoanthropologists that a very important part of human evolution involved scavenging together in bands. Clearly, if one is to be successful at this, one must have the ability to locate dead or dying animals and to warn or frighten off possible competitors—which competitors may or may not have been our fellow humans. By working together humans succeeded, and those that worked together more success-fully tended to have more offspring than those who did not. Hence, down through the ages until the present we evolved as highly successful "altruists."

Now come the more speculative moves—although they are still intended as claims of empirical fact and, indeed, are being increasingly supported by a flood of empirical information. The question arises as to how humans have evolved to put their "altruism" into place? How is it that we work so well together? There are at least three options that we might have taken in the course of evolution. Indeed, it is possible or probable that in respects we have taken all three, although today's students of evolution suspect some are more probable or prevalent than others.

The first way in which human evolution might have promoted "altruism" is through what has been characterized as "genetic determinism" (Lewontin, Rose and Kamin 1984). The ants, for instance, clearly do not think about what they are doing when they work together in their nests. Rather, they are programmed by their genes to do what they do. They are, if you like, puppets of their DNA, no less than, for example, a clock is a puppet of the clockmaker. Just as the clock's hands have no choice about where they will point, so the ants have no choice about what they will do.

What of humans? No doubt in respects humans are genetically determined in their actions and behaviors. It is hard, for instance, to suspect that all of the parent-child interactions are learned rather than preprogrammed. But, apart from the obvious phe-nomenological reasons for not thinking that we are determined like the ants, there are very good biological reasons why we should not have been thus determined. The simple fact is that genetic determinism is a good biological strategy when one can afford to take losses. A queen ant can afford to loose three or four hundred offspring through failure to respond when the environment changes, because she is turning out literally millions of offspring. Humans, however, have gone the route of heavy parental investment, that is to say, they raise but a few offspring but put a lot of effort into this. They cannot afford to lose offspring whenever the environment fluctuates which, of course, is the danger with genetic determinism. Hence, as a general rule, this option was not a viable evolutionary strategy.

The second option that humans might have taken, and obviously did take, is that of supercomputers who reason rationally whenever a need for cooperation or "altruism" arises. They do nothing without thought nor do they do anything which cannot be seen to pay immediate returns to the performer. From a biological point of view, this is a viable option in theory and again, as I have just said, it is clearly a route that humans have taken to a certain extent. We are great bargainers and dealers with each other. However, we seem not to be calculating in every action that we take and there are good evolutionary reasons why we should not be totally rational. The problem with always making the right decision is that it has heavy costs, in brain power and even more in time. To make a rational decision about self-interests on every occasion would require an inordinate deal of calculating. In life, what one often needs is not so much the perfect solution but the quick and dirty solution where the dirtiness is offset by the quickness. To make humans good "altruists," therefore, what evolution needed to do was to make us into cooperators, who could just get on with the job as it were.

And this leads us to the third option, that humans should be preprogrammed to think in certain broad patterns of cooperation, where this preprogramming would not be sufficiently stringent as to restrict their actions completely in any particular situation. The claim, therefore, is that to make us cooperators, nature has filled us full of thoughts about the need to cooperate. We may not always follow these thoughts, but they are there. We are somewhat in the same situation as today's computers which have been programmed to play chess. The early chess-playing computers were rather like the second option, where they thought through every option rationally before making a move. Unfortunately, as in the second option they were virtually useless because, within a move or two, there were so many alternatives to be calculated they could never make up their minds. Today's computers can, in fact, be beaten by the very top masters but normally they win because, when a particular configuration comes up on the board, they have been preprogrammed in certain strategies that are best in those circumstances. Likewise, we humans may sometimes act against our own best interests, but overall we do fairly well because we have thoughts about the need to cooperate.

What is the nature of these thoughts about the need to cooperate? The final move of today's evolutionary biologists is to suggest that these thoughts are none other than beliefs about obligations to help! In other words, to make us "altruists" nature has made us altruists. At once, I emphasize a point made above, that there is no question that we are scheming to do what is in our own interests and yet pretending to be nice. As any evolutionist will point out, often we perform better if we are deceived by our biology—and this seems to be the general case with respect to cooperation (Trivers 1976). We think that we ought to help, that we have obligations to others, because it is in our biological interests to have these thoughts. But, from an evolutionary perspective they exist because and simply because those of our would-be ancestors who had such thoughts survived and reproduced better than those that did not. In other words, altruism is a human adaptation, just as our hands and eyes and teeth and arms and feet. We are moral because our genes, as fashioned by natural selection, fill us full of thoughts about being moral.

There is more that one could say, but I will end this empirical section simply by reemphasizing that although much of what has just been presented is speculative it is intended seriously as empirically true. As noted also, evidence is starting to come in supporting this. For instance, detailed studies have been and are being done on some of our closest relatives, like the gorillas and chimpanzees (de Waal 1982; Goodall 1986). These suggest that such animals rely heavily on altruistic acts (or if you prefer, since they do not have articulate language, *proto* altruistic acts). Likewise, there is evidence from human studies pointing to uniformities of moral beliefs beneath all the cultural variations and that these uniformities are innate rather than learned (van den Berghe 1979). Without putting too great an emphasis on the analogy between language and morality, just as the evidence seems hardening that some form of Chomsky's beliefs about the innate nature of language are well-taken (Lieberman 1984), so also cross-cultural and developmental studies suggest that human moral beliefs are rooted in biology as well as in the environment of culture.

Philosophical Implications

Let us suppose now, if only for the sake of argument, that the empirical scenario sketched in the last section is well taken. We now must return again to philosophical discussion and ask about implications. In particular, following our earlier pattern, we must ask about implications at the substantival level and then about the metaethics of the evolution of altruism.

In fact, at the substantival level, the answers come fairly readily. Moreover, if the biology be accepted, even if only for the sake of discussion, then they are probably not all that controversial. The kinds of animals whose evolution has just been sketched will be animals which work together, certainly for their own ultimate biological gain, but not necessarily for their own conscious immediate gain. They will rather be animals which, as it were, throw their efforts into the general pool and then draw upon them as needed or as necessary. In respects, this sounds remarkably like animals that have made some sort of social contract. And, indeed, if one thinks of some of the versions of social contract theory, particularly some of the modern versions, then the above evolutionary scenario seems to mesh very nicely.

Take John Rawls's views in his *Theory of Justice* (1971), without necessarily endorsing every last aspect that Rawls himself proposes. As is well known, he suggests that one should promote justice, and this he equates with fairness. But, to Rawls fairness does not mean simply giving everybody an equal amount. Rather we are, as it were, to put ourselves in a position of ignorance where we do not know what our status in society might be. If we did then presumably we would maximally reward what we actually are. But, not knowing what we might be, we are inclined to suggest a society where everyone benefits the maximum amount that it is possible that each individual should benefit. Thus, for instance, if we would all benefit by paying doctors twice as much as anyone else, then this is compatible with, if not demanded by, the principles of justice.

It seems plausible to suggest that Rawls's "original position," which he himself admits is hypothetical, might well have been simulated by natural selection working on our genes. In other words, we have a social contract, but it is not one which involved our ancestors deciding literally to cooperate. Rather, it is one which was put in place by evolutionary biology. It is interesting to note, incidentally, that Rawls himself is not unsympathetic to this idea. Indeed, in defending the workability or stability of his views on justice Rawls writes as follows:

> In arguing for the greater stability of the principles of justice I have assumed that certain psychological laws are true, or approximately so. I shall not pursue the question of stability beyond this point. We may note however that one might ask how it is that human beings have acquired a nature described by these psychological principles. The theory of evolution would suggest that it is the outcome of natural selection; the capacity for a sense of justice and the moral feelings is an adaption of mankind to its place in nature. As ethologists maintain, the behavior patterns of a species, and the psychological mechanisms of their acquisition, are just as much its characteristics as are the distinctive features of its bodily structures; and these patterns of behavior have an evolution exactly as organs and bones do. It seems clear that for members of a species which lives in stable social groups, the ability to comply with fair cooperative arrangements and to develop the sentiments necessary to support them is highly advantageous, especially when individuals have a long life and are dependent on one another. These conditions guarantee innumerable occasions when mutual justice consistently adhered to is beneficial to all parties. (1971: 502-3)

To this, Rawls adds the following highly interesting footnote:

> Biologists do not always distinguish between altruism and other kinds of

moral conduct. Frequently behavior is classified as either altruistic or egoistic. Not so, however, R.B. Trivers in "Evolution of Reciprocal Altruism," Quarterly Review of Biology, vol. 46 (1971). He draws a distinction betweeen altruism and reciprocal altruism (or what I should prefer to call simply reciprocity). The latter is the biological analogue of the cooperative virtues of fairness and good faith. Trivers discusses the natural conditions and selective advantages of reciprocity and the capacities that sustain it. See also G. C. Williams, *Adaptation and Natural Selection*, (Princeton, Princeton University Press, 1966:93-96, 113, 195-97, 247). For a discussion of mutualism between species, see Irenaus Eibl-Eibesfeldt, Ethology, trans. Erich Klinghammer (New York, Holt, Rinehart and Winston, 1970:146F, 292-302).

I note in passing that, in finding a coincidence between the results of Darwinian evolutionary theory and social contract theory, one is hardly finding something remarkable. Historically, obviously, both have their roots in a common soil, namely, the British socioeconomic political theorizing of the eighteenth century or earlier. However, I suspect here that what we have is not a vicious circle but a self-reinforcing relationship. Note that there is no claim being made now that people are outrightly selfish or hostile or whatever to each other. We cooperate from genuinely moral sentiments. Note also, however, that in line with points made earlier, there is no need to rely on fuzzy and inadequate views about selection promoting the good of the group. The selective forces of evolution which are presupposed are simply and utterly those which promote the good of the individual. It is just that there is often more to be gotten out of life by cooperating than by fighting.

Of course, even if the substantival points be granted, none of this speaks to the subsequent questions about metaethical justification. What can one say here? One suspects that it is at this point that many traditional philosophers will fall away. However, much empathy might be felt for the kind of position which has been articulated thus far, the traditional thinker will argue that to think that a genetic account of the evolution of morality says anything about justification is to leave an unfilled gap. At best one's position is incomplete and at worst one smashes into the is/ought barrier. In the end, Rawls says, therefore, one is still no further along than is the traditional evolutionary ethicist.

Perhaps so! But in the opinion of a number of today's thinkers, there might be a third option. This is the option which suggests that there is no foundation to ethics at all! This is not to say that substantival ethics does not exist, but, it is to say that the supposed underpinning is chimerical in some sense or another (Murphy 1982; Mackie 1977; Ruse 1986). What these thinkers argue is that sometimes, when one has given a causal explanation of certain beliefs, one can see that the beliefs, themselves, neither have foundation nor could ever have such a foundation. The claim of this kind of evolutionary ethicist, therefore, is that once we see that our moral beliefs are simply an adaptation put in place by natural selection, in order to further our reproductive ends, that is an end to it. Morality is no more than a collective illusion fobbed off on us by our genes for reproductive ends.

It must be noted that the qualification collective is very important here. For this reason, one can certainly distinguish between sensible ethical beliefs like "Don't hurt old ladies" and crazy ethical beliefs like "Be kind to cabbages on Fridays." The whole point about ethics is that we are all in it together. If we are not, then some can cheat and the rest of us lose out in the evolutionary game. For this reason ethics has its own standards and rules, just as do baseball or cricket. Yet, contrary to the beliefs of some devotees, just as baseball and cricket tell us nothing about the real world, in the sense of the world "out there," neither does ethics.

The position that I am articulating has been well stated by the moral philosopher Jeffrey Murphy.

In his valuable article "Hopes, Fears, and Sociobiology" (forthcoming in *Queen's Quarterly*), my colleague John Beatty suggests that sociobiologists sometimes ignore two important distinctions that all of us in philosophy know how to make: (1) a distinction between reasons and causes, and (2) a related distinction between explaining why a belief is in fact held and justifying a belief that one ought to act in a certain way. There are standard distinctions we always draw for our students in introductory courses. But there is a very important sense in which these are the very distinctions that sociobiology seeks to challenge! Thus if one rejects sociobiology because it fails to draw these distinctions, then one is simply begging the question against it, and if one tries to "save" sociobiology by showing that its practitioners sometimes embrace those distinctions, then one is rendering sociobiology inane by failing to see the genuinely profound, exciting, and troubling issues it raises. The sociobiologist may well agree with the point (made by Beatty) that value judgments are properly defended in terms of other value judgments until we reach some that are fundamental. All of this, in a sense, is the giving of reasons. However, suppose we seriously raise the question of why these fundamental judgments are regarded as fundamental. There may be only a causal explanation for this! We reject simplistic utilitarianism because it entails consequences that are morally counterintuitive, or we embrace a Rawlsian theory of justice because it systematizes (places in "reflective equilibrium") our pretheoretical convictions. But what is the status of those intuitions or convictions? Perhaps there is nothing more to be said for them than that they involve deep preferences (or patterns of preference) built into our biological nature. If this is so, then at a very fundamental point the reasons/ causes (and the belief we ought/really ought) distinction breaks down, or the one transforms into the other. This may all be wrong, of course, but it is at least

interesting at a rather profound level, and it requires something more by way
of a response than attacking it with very distinctions it seeks to undermine.
(1982:112-13)

The position which is being articulated here is known technically as "ethical skepticism." It is important to reemphasize that the skepticism is not about the substantival
claims of ethics. No one, least of all the evolutionary ethicist, denies the existence of
these. The skepticism is about the foundations which supposedly lie behind substantival
ethics. To make the case a little clearer, perhaps more plausible, consider the analogy
of spiritualism, something much relied on in World War I. Many people turned to
spiritualists for solace and comfort after their loved ones were killed. Moreover, they
did not come away disappointed. Through the ouija board or other channels would
come the comforting messages: "It's all right, Mom! I'm happy now! I'm just waiting
for you and Dad!"

Of course, we see that there was no justified foundation for a claim such as this.
Excluding obvious cases of fraud, and I suspect that these were a lot fewer than cynics
maintain, we know full well that the successes of the seance were due exclusively to
the capacity of people under stress to deceive themselves. They wanted to hear (or if
you like "hear") the comforting messages—and so they did. Once the causal analysis
is given, we see that there is no place or rational justification. Likewise, in ethics once
we see that moral claims are simply adaptations, there is neither place for nor need of
rational justification.

One final point and then the positive case is made. Why does such a thesis as is
being argued for here seem to be intuitively implausible? Why does it seem—or so it
appears to many people—so ridiculous to argue that morality is no more than an illusion of the genes? Why does it seem so silly to suggest moral claims are on a par with
the rule in cricket that there should be six balls to an over? (Actually, it is not quite on
a par with such a rule, since a moral claim is imposed on us by our genes, whereas a
cricket law is imposed on us by posterity and could, in principle, be changed. Witness
the great changes that have occurred in cricket in the last thirty years.) There is a
simple answer and, when seen, adds to the evolutionist's case rather than detracts from
it. The simple fact is that if we recognized morality to be no more than an epiphenomenon of our biology, we would cease to believe in it and stop acting upon it. At once,
therefore, the very powerful forces which make us cooperators would collapse. Unfortunately, from a biological point of view, although some of us might get an immediate gain, most of us would be losers.

It is important, therefore, that biology not simply put moral beliefs in place but also put in place a way of keeping them up. It must make us believe in them. What this means is, that even though morality may not be objective, in the sense of referring to something "out there," it is an important part of the experience of morality that we think it is. Its phenomenology, if you like, is that we believe it to be objective. In the words of John Mackie (1979), we are led to "objectify" morality, thinking that morality is something imposed on us rather than a matter of free choice. Hence, we are led to obey it and thus it works. If, when I interact with you, I realize that I could simply pull out of the deal if I so wish, then very shortly that is precisely what I will be doing. But, if as is the case I think that morality is truly binding on me—and even the fact that I can recognize its base does not alter the psychological feelings that I have—I am led to continue in moral ways. Obviously, no one is claiming that we are always moral. The whole point is that we do have the choice to be moral or not to be moral. Where we have no choice is in the beliefs that we have. I can decide whether or not to steal. What I cannot decide is whether stealing is right or wrong.

In short, the claim is being made that when people like G. E. Moore argued that morality is a nonnatural property or some such thing, they were correctly identifying an important aspect of our experience of morality. It is not simply something which we choose or decide on, like the clothes we put on. Yet, at the same time the evolutionist argues that Moore was wrong in his analysis of the objectivity of morality. It is rather something subjective or noncognitive. Where it differs from other subjective feelings is in having an aura of objectivity about it. Just as the Freudian argues that those who deny his explanation thereby confirm it, so the evolutionist argues that those who find his or her explanation implausible support the very point to which is being made!

Clarifications and Consequences

The positive case for the new form of evolutionary ethics is now made. I want in this final section to offer three points by way of clarification and development. The first takes us back to questions of substantive ethics. The evolutionary ethics expounded in the last two sections argues that, substantivally, the sort of ethics which emerges from the evolutionary process—or rather the sort of ethics that *Homo sapiens*, as a product of the evolutionary process accepts—is something altogether familiar. In particular, I have argued that there will be strong family resemblance, if not identity, with some sort of social contract-type ethics. But, it is surely appropriate at this point to do a little personal introspection. We have out own sense of right and wrong. Does the sociobiological analysis of ethics, in fact, yield sentiments that we as ethical beings would want to endorse? Is a biological social contract style (substantive) ethics in tune with what we, as ordinary beings, really feel?

There is one major possible point of conflict. For the evolutionist, sentiments must track biological consequences, and this point must apply equally to moral sentiments, even though they may be distinctive. But if one thing is certain to the evolutionist it is the following: not all social interactions are going to have the same payoff. All other things being equal, your best reproductive investments are going to be in helping close kin. Then, probably, more distant kin and those nonrelatives who offer the most likelihood of reciprocation. Biologically, it makes more sense to cooperate with those in a position to cooperate and with a common interest in cooperation (Wilson 1978). Finally, one reaches an outer limit, where one is dealing with strangers and, indeed, where the possibilities of danger from the unknown may well exceed any virtues or possible reciprocation.

What all of this seems to mean, from a biological perspective, is that not only will one's feeling of affection fall away as one moves beyond one's immediate family but so also will one's sense of moral obligation. It is virtually a truism that one loves one's children more than one loves some unknown stranger; but, the evolutionist's position seems to imply also that one will feel a greater sense of moral obligation towards one's own children than towards some unrelated child. Even with nonrelatives there will be a moral differential, with a stronger sense of obligation within one's own society than towards those without.

But this seems to go flatly against what has been argued by many moralists, for instance, Peter Singer. He like others argues that our obligations to the unknown starving child in Africa is no less than our obligation to one of our own children (Singer 1972). Of course, he loves his own children more than he loves the children of others, but this is not quite the point. He feels he has identical obligations to all. Or, at least, this is what he claims—for himself and for the rest of us. Yet, if this is so, then at the substantival level, not only do we have a clash but we have a clear refutation of the evolutionist's case. No amount of careful talk or verbal juggling can save the day.

I am not sure how one can resolve a clash like this other than by appealing to people's feelings and asking them to examine themselves deeply and carefully. At the same time, one can look at the ways in which people behave. It is indeed true that we often feel one way but act in another. However, if someone persistently behaves in a certain way then we might be forgiven if we start to disregard the contrary claims that they are forever making. Free will is important. So also is sincerity.

All that the evolutionary ethicist can say at this point, therefore, is that people do seem to have this differential sense of moral obligation, naysayers like Peter Singer notwithstanding. Moreover, and here I believe the evolutionary ethicist does have a strong point, people's actions show that this is precisely how they feel. Of course, we do feel that we have obligations to others, but given the care and attention that we lavish first on our own children and then on those within our neighborhood, it seems pushing a philosophical thesis to the point of extremity to suggest that all of the time we think that we are behaving in a grossly immoral way.

Moreover, argues the evolutionist, from the way that people think and behave it is clear that, although we may sometimes pay lip service to our equal obligations to unknowns in the third world, we do not really feel such an obligation. Were you to learn of me that I give 90% of my income to some charity like OXFAM, while my children have to eat at the Salvation Army soup kitchen, it is unlikely that you would think me a candidate for sainthood. You would rather be indignant at my failure to discharge my proper obligations. In this context, it is worth remembering the stark moral message of Dickens's great novel *Bleak House*. Mrs. Jellyby spends all her time concerned with the welfare of the natives of some far away African country. Dickens responds savagely that her first obligations are to her own family which she neglects, then to the unfortunates in her own society, like Jo the crossing boy, and then and only then to those beyond one's societal boundaries.

Do note that the evolutionary ethicist is *not* arguing that one has no obligations whatsoever to people in other parts of the world. Thanks to modern technology we are all brought much more closely together. But the evolutionary ethicist does argue that it is foolish to pretend that we feel an equal sense of obligation. Indeed, he would argue that once we recognize the limited nature of our moral sentiments, we will probably all be much better off recognizing that in dealing with other people proper attitudes are often those of enlightened self-interest rather than mystical and unfounded feelings of affection. As it happens, nations—which have to take seriously international relations—are much less inclined to the pretence that they are dealing with each other on grounds other than self-interest. The evolutionary ethicist takes this as confirmation of the position.

The second question looks again at the matter of metaethical foundations, or rather of nonfoundations. To the claim of ethical skepticism, there is an obvious objection which runs somewhat like this: The fact that our ethical sense is a product of evolutionary processes in no way denies the reality of its referent. Take an analogy from the world of the epistemologist. If a speeding train is bearing down on me, I am inclined to jump out of its way. How is it that I am aware of this train? Obviously through my evolved capacities of sight and hearing and so forth. My awareness of the train comes to me through and only through adaptations which selection has put in place. Yet, no one would want to claim that the train does not have a reality in its own right. Why, therefore, should one feel able to deny that ethics or morality likewise has a reality in its own right? The fact that awareness of morality comes through adaptations is quite irrelevant to matters of ontology. There is, therefore, a blatant fallacy, right in the middle of the evolutionary ethical position (Nozick 1981).

To counter this objection, the evolutionary ethicist must show that the analogy is not a true one. How can this be done? Start with the fact that the argument about the train goes through because and only because the existence of the train is assumed independently. Suppose, for instance, one had two worlds identical except that one has a speeding train and the other does not. There would be no reason to think the evolutionist is committed to a belief in speeding trains in both worlds. One is aware of the speeding train only because there is such a train. Now consider two worlds, one of which has an objective morality, whatever that might mean (God's will? Nonnatural properties?), and the other world has no such morality. If the evolutionist's case is well taken, the people in *both* worlds are going to have identical beliefs—subject to normal laws of causation and so forth. The existence of the objective ethics is in no way necessary for a derivation of our belief in an objective ethics from an evolutionary perspective. So, at the very least, what we can say is that an objective ethics is redundant to the evolutionist's case.

Of course, one might still say that this does not deny that objective ethics, in some sense, does not exist. But, in fact the evolutionist thinks the arguments somewhat stronger than this. If what has been said earlier about the nonprogressionist nature of evolution is well taken, then there was absolutely no guarantee that evolution would have led us to the point that it has. Perhaps, to make us cooperators, evolution might have filled us with other sentiments entirely opposite from those about the worth of altruism and so on and so forth. Perhaps, for instance, we might have been led to some kind of reverse morality, where we feel an obligation to hate each other. But, we know that others feel the same way about us and so consequently social interactions are kept in place in this way. This is not so implausible, when one thinks of the emotions operative in the 1950s during the Cold War. The situation, therefore, seems to be that not only is objective morality redundant but it might be something entirely different from that which we think that it is!

This surely is a paradox quite unacceptable on just about any normal notion of what one might mean by objective morality. Certainly, it is unacceptable on traditional notions, for instance that morality is endorsed by God's will or a function of nonnatural properties or some such thing. There is something distinctly peculiar about saying that God wants certain things of us, but that not only is our behavior in no way predicated on God's wishes but that what we do might be something quite different because our biology has led us thuswise (Ruse 1989). In short, because of the disanalogy between epistemology and ethics, the evolutionary ethicist feels one can continue to endorse ethical skepticism.

I come to the third point. Rather than objecting to what has just been said, the next critical move is to complain that we have heard it all before! The argument now will be that in denying that there is an objective morality, the evolutionary ethicist is simply postulating and then knocking down straw men. No sensible moral philosopher has believed in objective morality as it has been characterized, at least not since before the eighteenth century. Kant (1959), for instance, argues that morality refers not to something "out there," but rather comes about through the necessary conditions of rational beings interacting socially. Surely, therefore, the evolutionary ethicist is simply telling something which we knew all along.

In response, the evolutionist begins with a denial that objective moralities are quite as unfashionable as all that. G. E. Moore (1903), for instance, postulated the existence of non-natural properties of which we become aware intuitively. Certainly for him morality had some disinterested objectivity, beyond our sensing it. Again, while it may not be particularly popular in philosophical circles, it is probably true to say that for most lay people morality also has some objective referent, be this located in Platonic forms or God's will or whatever. Of course, most lay people, not being philosophers, do not inquire too deeply into the foundations of their moral beliefs. They simply know that there must surely be such foundations.

But having said this, the evolutionary ethicist freely agrees that many thinkers have denied any ultimate foundations. Kant was one instance, and in this century the emotivists have been others. Although, parenthetically, mention of the emotivists at once shows how the evolutionary ethicist is more honest to the phenomenology of morality than many predecessors. To the evolutionary ethicist, as to the objectivist, there is something absurd tinged with the immoral in the claim that morality is no more than emotion heightened with feeling or whatever. To say "Killing is wrong!" means much more than "I don't like killing! Boo Hoo! Don't you do it either because it upsets me dreadfully!" or some such thing. To the evolutionary ethicist the meaning of "Killing is wrong!" is simply that, just as it is to the traditional objectivist.

But, generally, one must agree that the evolutionary ethicist is hardly unique—or first—in denying a moral foundation existing "out there." This now raises the question of where the true predecessors should be located. Mention has been made of Kant and one might naturally think that his philosophy is the obvious forerunner. Although it is true that Kant himself was no evolutionist, he certainly stood on the edge of such ideas (Lenoir 1982). More importantly, influenced by social contract theory he does rather derive morality out of the conditions of sociality in a way not unlike the evolutionary ethicist.

Nevertheless, with all due respect to Kant, the evolutionary ethicist feels some unease about being linked too closely to the great German philosopher. For Kant, in ethics as in epistemology, the way that we think is a necessary condition of the way of thinking of *any* rational being. Contingency or subjectivity is ruled out at this level, on Andromeda as on earth. The mathematics will be the same and so will be morality. Rawls (1980), a neo-Kantian, endorses this argument. But to the evolutionary ethicist, whose initial premise is the nondirectedness of evolution, there is something distinctly and dissatisfyingly paradoxical about arguing to the necessity of the way that we think, especially in the moral realm. Although ethics here on earth may not be relative (in fact the evolutionary ethicist strongly denies relativity because then the universality of cooperating would break down), across galaxies other evolutionary paths may have been followed. For these other worlds, the evolutionist is loath to argue to one universely shared pattern of belief. There is no reason to think evolution is goal directed in this sort of way.

This then points one to the other great philosopher of the eighteenth century, David Hume (1978), which pointing does, of course, link one with the emotivists and their noncognitivism, inasmuch as they, too, look back to Hume. Hume, like the evolutionary ethicist, denied the ultimate objectivity of ethics, considering it rather in some general sentiment possessed by humans. And for Hume, unlike Kant, but like the evolutionary ethicist, this sentiment seems very much to be a contingent facet of human nature rather than a necessary emergent of rationality. Hume is always ready to assert our oneness with the brutes and he is always ready to see morality in some way as emerging from our brute nature. This is not to say that morality is any less genuine for the Humean than it is for the Kantian; but, morality is certainly not something beyond and divorced from the sorts of beings that we are.

In short, therefore, the evolutionary ethicist of the kind that I have been articulating and defending in the second part of this essay looks upon his position as one very much in the tradition of the author of the *Treatise of Human Nature*. It is Humeanism brought up to date by Darwinian evolution. I might add, incidentally, that this conceptual analysis fits well with history. It is clear that Darwin who is much more the inspiration for this approach to ethics than he is for so-called "Social Darwinism." He himself stood in an intellectual line which goes back to the world of David Hume and his contemporaries. Apart from anything else, there is growing evidence of the importance of Erasmus Darwin's influence on Charles Darwin's intellectual development— and Erasmus Darwin, we know full well, was much influenced by Humean notions (Richards 1988).

Conclusion

Fortunately, nothing stands still in philosophy. Ideas at one time unfashionable, come again into their own right. Sometimes the changes are fueled by developments internal to philosophy, sometimes, most frequently, by changes external to philosophy, particularly by those occurring in the natural sciences. The latter, I believe, is the case with evolutionary ethics. For many years now it has been almost a laughingstock of professional philosophy—something that one mentions sneeringly in introductory classes and then dismisses as one passes on. If the arguments of this essay are well-taken, then dismissal is probably the proper fate of the traditional evolutionary approach to ethics, although I hope I have shown that it is not necessarily as silly or offensive as many have claimed. More importantly, thanks to new developments in evolutionary biology itself, the traditional approach does not exhaust the subject. Other, more promising avenues, remain open.

It is true that there are still many moves to make and many gaps to be filled. A naturalistic approach such as this rests crucially on developments in science itself, and certainly no one would yet claim that we have a fully articulated and confirmed theory of the development of human moral nature. Nor would anyone claim that all the ramifications of the application of modern biology to moral thought have as yet been explored, but perhaps now the reader will agree that some progress has been made. As suggested at the beginning of this chapter, even though a convincing and definitive case cannot yet be offered, we may at least have moved to the point where evolutionary ethics can be judged interesting. Remember also that time is on the side of the evolutionist. It took a hundred years for Copernicus's ideas to be accepted fully. The same seems true of Darwinian views on evolution, especially as applied to *Homo sapiens*.

Perhaps now and only now are we ready to grapple fully with our animal nature. If we are, we shall soon find that this demands an evolutionary approach to ethics.

References

Alexander, R. D. 1987. *The Biology of Moral Systems.* New York: Aldine de Gruyter.

Bowler, P. J. 1984. *Evolution: The History of an Idea.* Berkeley: University of California Press.

Dawkins, R. 1976. *The Selfish Gene.* Oxford: Oxford University Press.

Dawkins, R. 1986. *The Blind Watchmaker.* London: Longman.

Dobzhansky, T. 1967. *The Biology of Ultimate Concern.* New York: New American Library.

Dobzhansky, T. 1973. Ethics and values in biological and cultural evolution. *Zygon* 8:261-81.

Goodall, J. 1986. *The Chimpanzees of Gombe.* Cambridge, MA: Harvard University Press.

Greene, J. 1959. *The Death of Adam.* Ames: University of Iowa Press.

Hamilton, W. D. 1964a. The genetical evolution of social behaviour. I. *Journal of Theoretical Biology* 7:1-16.

Hamilton, W. D. 1964b. The genetical evolution of social behaviour. II. *Journal of Theoretical Biology* 7:17-32.

Haselden, K., and P. Hefner. 1968. *Changing Man: The Threat and the Promise.* Garden City, NY: Doubleday.

Hofstadter, R. 1959. *Social Darwinism in American Thought.* New York: Braziller.

Hudson, W. D. 1970. *Modern Moral Philosophy.* New York: Anchor.

Hume, D. 1978. *A Treatise of Human Natures.* Oxford: Clarendon Press.

Huxley, J. S. 1942. *Evolution: The Modern Synthesis.* London: Allen and Unwin.

Huxley, J. S. 1957. Introduction. In *The Phenomenon of Man*, P. Teilhard de Chardin. London: Collins.

Huxley, J. S., and T. H. Huxley. 1947. *Evolution and Ethics.* London: Pilot Press.

Huxley, T. H. 1894. *Evolution & Ethics and Other Essays.* London: Macmillan.

Isaac, G. L. 1983. Aspects of human evolution, 509-43. In *Evolution from Molecules to Men*, ed. D. S. Bendall. Cambridge: Cambridge University Press.

Jones, G. 1980. *Social Darwinism and English Thought.* Brighton, Sussex: Harvester.

Kant, I. 1959. *Foundations of the Metaphysics of Morals.* Trans. L. W. Beck. Indianapolis: Bobbs-Merrill.

King Hele, D. 1977. *Doctor of Revolution.* London: Faber.

Kitcher, P. 1985. *Vaulting Ambition*. Cambridge, MA: MIT Press.

Kropotkin, P. 1902. *Mutual Aid: A Factor of Evolution*. London: Heinemann.

Lenoir, T. 1982. *The Strategy of Life*. Dordrecht: Reidel.

Lieberman, P. 1984. *The Biology of Language*. Cambridge, MA: Harvard University Press.

Lewontin, R., S. Rose and L. Kamin. 1984. *Not in Our Genes*. New York: Pantheon.

Mackie, J. L. 1977. *Ethics: Inventing Right and Wrong*. Harmondsworth, England: Penguin.

Mackie, J. L. 1978. The law of the jungle. *Philosophy* 53:553-73.

Mackie, J. L. 1979. *Hume's Moral Theory*. London: Routledge and Kegan Paul.

Maynard Smith, J. 1978. The evolution of behaviour. *Scientific American* 239(3):176-93.

McNeil, M. 1987. *Under the Banner of Science*. Manchester: Manchester University Press.

Medawar, P. 1972. *The Hope of Progress*. London: Methuen.

Midgley, M. 1985. *Evolution as Religion: Strange Hopes and Stranger Fears*. London: Methuen.

Moore, G. E. 1903. *Principia Ethica*. Cambridge: Cambridge University Press.

Murphy, J. 1982. *Evolution, Morality, and the Meaning of Life*. Totowa, NJ: Rowman and Littlefield.

Nozick, R. 1981. *Philosophical Explanations*. Cambridge, MA: Harvard University Press.

Oldroyd, D. 1980. *Darwinian Impacts*. Kensington, NSW: New South Wales University Press.

Rawls, J. 1971. *A Theory of Justice*. Cambridge, MA: Harvard University Press.

Rawls, J. 1980. Kantian constructivism in moral theory. *Journal of Philosophy* 77:515-72.

Richards, R. 1988. *Darwinism and the Evolutionary Development of Mind*. Chicago: University of Chicago Press.

Ruse, M. 1979. *The Darwinian Revolution: Science Red in Tooth & Claw*. Chicago: University of Chicago Press.

Ruse, M. 1986. *Taking Darwin Seriously*. Oxford: Blackwell.

Ruse, M. 1989. *The Darwinian Paradigm*. London: Routledge.

Russett, C. E. 1976. *Darwin in America*. San Francisco: W. H. Freeman.

Singer, P. 1972. Famine, affluence, and morality. *Philosophy and Public Affairs* 1:229-43.

Singer, P. 1981. *The Expanding Circle: Ethics and Sociobiology*. New York: Farrar, Straus and Giroux.

Singer, P. 1986. Life, the universe & ethics: A review of Edward O. Wilson, *Biophilia*. *Biology & Philosophy* 1:367-72.

Spencer, H. 1850. *Social Statics*. London.

Spencer, H. 1852. A theory of population, deduced from the general law of animal fertility. *Westminster Review* 1:468-501.

Spencer, H. 1857. Progress: Its law and cause. *Westminster Review*.

Spencer, H. 1892. *Principles of Ethics*. London: Williams and Norgate.

Sumner, W. G. 1914. *The Challenge of Facts and Other Essays*, ed. A. S. Kelle. New Haven: Yale University Press.

Taylor, P. W. 1978. *Problems of Moral Philosophy*. Belmont, CA: Wadsworth.

Teilhard de Chardin, P. [1957] 1989. *The Phenomenon of Man*. London: Collins. Reprinted in *Philosophy of Biology*, M. Ruse, 289-96. New York: Macmillan.

Trivers, R. 1971. The evolution of reciptrocal altruism. *Quarterly Review of Biology* 46:35-57.

Trivers, R. 1976. Foreword to *The Selfish Gene*, R. Dawkins. Oxford: Oxford University Press.

van den Berghe, P. 1979. *Human Family Systems: An Evolutionary View*. New York: Elsevier.

Waal, F., de. 1982. *Chimpanzee Politics*. London: Jonathan Cape.

Waddington, C. H. 1960. *The Ethical Animal*. London: Allen & Unwin.

Williams, B. 1985. *Ethics and the Limits of Philosophy*. Cambridge, MA: Harvard University Press.

Williams, G. C. 1966. *Adaptation and Natural Selection: A Critique of Some Current Evolutionary Thought*. Princeton, NJ: Princeton University Press.

Williams, G. C. 1988. Huxley's *Evolution and Ethics* in sociobiological perspective. *Zygon: Journal of Religion and Science* 23:383-407.

Wilson, E. O. 1975. *Sociobiology: The New Synthesis*. Cambridge, MA: Harvard University Press.

Wilson, E. O. 1978. *On Human Nature*. Cambridge, MA: Harvard University Press.

Wilson, E. O. 1984. *Biophilia*. Cambridge, MA: Harvard University Press.

Biological Considerations in the Analysis of Morality

Richard D. Alexander

The theory of natural selection identifies the self-interest of every individual organism as the maximal representation of its own genes in future generations. There is no encouragement for any belief that an organism can be designed for any purpose other than the most effective pursuit of this self-interest.

—Williams 1989:196-97

. . . not surprisingly, philosophers and anthropologists have taken sociobiologists to task for their cheerful optimism that the biological reduction of symbolic culture is just around the corner.

—Murphy 1982:93

I will discuss theories and facts from evolutionary biology with which I believe analyses of human activities and tendencies such as moral behavior and thinking must be compatible, and from which to some degree they must eventually derive. I will identify what I see as the most difficult problems or paradoxes for analyses of morality arising out of biological theories and facts, and discuss some possible solutions.

I begin with the assumption, familiar to those who will read this chapter but accepted by only a minuscule proportion of humans in the world, that all organisms, including humans, are evolved through a process guided principally by natural selection, or differential reproduction of genetic alternatives. Directly or indirectly, so necessarily are all of their features, including the ability and tendency of humans to generate, use, and analyze the concepts of ethical and moral and their opposites ("indirectly," here, means that some attributes or behaviors appear as incidental effects of mechanisms or traits evolved in other selective contexts). The arguments need not be repeated; they have been given elsewhere—amply, repeatedly, across decades, and on a wide scale now in even introductory biology courses (Dawkins [1976] 1989; Alexander 1979). The reasons for widespread failure to accept or understand them, among both academics and non-academics, seem not to have received serious consideration. I will suggest that these reasons derive partly from intuitive feelings arising out of human perceptions of motivations of both self and others and the use of intent; for the evolutionary biologist this problem includes the reasons for incomplete control of expression of the emotions and peculiarities of use of conscious and nonconscious "intent" (Alexander 1989). Perhaps as much as the prior existence of alternative explanations (such as divine creation), or more mundane difficulties of understanding, such feelings may ultimately be responsible for failure of knowledge and acceptance of evolution to spread, and for hostility toward it. I imply that the indifference and hostility of academics and other educated people is a crucial barrier to widespread acceptance of evolution by natural selection as an explanatory device for human self-understanding. One consequence of this hostility and indifference is that anyone can secure the highest possible degree or position in any human-oriented discipline except medicine without taking so much as a single course in the biological sciences, and in medicine without taking a course in evolutionary biology.

Within the past quarter of a century, Darwin's (1859) argument that natural selection is the principal guiding force of organic evolution has been progressively refined. Thus, since Williams (1966), arguments have been widely accepted that natural selection is more potent at lower levels, so that when there are conflicts at different levels the lower levels tend to "win." Essentially this means that the interests of individual organisms tend to prevail as the driving force in the evolution of traits. In 1964, Hamilton presented the first thorough and reasonable discussion of inclusive fitness— the concept that reproductive success by the individual can be achieved by helping collateral relatives as well as by producing and helping descendant relatives. Then Trivers (1971) developed the argument that, because of the possibility of reciprocity, under certain social circumstances selection can even favor helping nonrelatives. Reciprocity can be either direct or indirect, in the latter case involving benefits, such as increased social opportunities, accruing as a result of reputation. Prominence of indirect reciprocity in human social interactions and the importance of reputation creates opportunities for, at the extreme, positive effects on reproductive success from even indiscriminate beneficence (Alexander 1987).

These are the fundamental contributions to current understanding of the working of evolution as concerns social behavior, especially that of humans. They have enabled us to be confident about issues that had been debated endlessly within biology and used uncritically and vaguely both inside and outside biology. That certain opinions on these various topics (both biological and nonbiological)—and others relevant to the following discussion—happened to be correct during previous periods of history (while others were not) gives us no leave to cite their authors as having either demonstrated or understood the essentials of evolution by natural selection prior to the above contributions, or as having employed such knowledge in reaching their conclusions. The only individual who expressed an understanding of the "levels of selection" argument prior to Williams (1957, 1966) appears to be Fisher (". . . the principle of Natural Selection

. . . affords no . . . explanation for any properties of animals or plants which, without being individually advantageous, are supposed to be of service to the species to which they belong"—[1930] 1958:49; see also, heroism, p. 264); and only Darwin (1859), Fisher [1930] (1958), Haldane (1955), and Williams and Williams (1957), seem to have shown rudimentary understanding of the significance of reproduction via collateral relatives prior to Hamilton (1964). None of the extensive discussions of reciprocity in the social science or other literature approaches the clarity and perspicacity of Trivers's analysis, or has provided the means for analyzing reciprocity by placing it into an evolutionary context. We can, therefore, reject widespread implications that the above contributions represented nothing particularly new after all. In fact, the effect since 1964 is necessarily revolutionary. [For a compact and easily understood "short course" in modern evolutionary biology—by which I mean ideas and facts developed since 1964, particularly as they bear on social behavior—I recommend Richard Dawkins's three books, *The Selfish Gene* (original 1976, but read the revised edition 1989), *The Extended Phenotype* (1982), and *The Blind Watchmaker* (1986).]

This beginning from biology poses four principal problems for students of morality. First, the potency of selection at lower levels such as the individual questions the usual view of moral behavior as serving the interests of others, or of the group as a whole, and may explain the failure of the seemingly logical extension of beneficent behavior eventually to serve all people equally. Second, there seems to be widespread difficulty in understanding how evolution can produce via differential reproduction of genes a phenotype whose actions are not wholly determined by antecedent ontogenetic events in such fashion as always to yield reproductive advantage. This difficulty seems to many to remove any possibility of an evolved tendency to be moral as a result of choice. Third, given arguments that individuals have evolved to serve their own (genetic) interests and the questions surrounding genetic and ontogenetic determinacy, the problem of understanding conscious intent or motivation versus actual behavior, and its outcomes regardless of conscious intent, is at the very least daunting. Finally, and perhaps most paradoxical of all, if motivation and expressions of the emotions have evolved to serve the interests of the individual, it is difficult to understand why individual control over the emotions and conscious understanding of motivation are so obviously incomplete or imperfect, or even deceptive, to the actor him/herself—that is, why conscious effort or intent in social communication is often superseded or contradicted by seemingly involuntary or nonconsciously produced transmissions of knowledge and intent. The intuitive skepticism arising out of these problems seems to cause real difficulty in understanding evolution, as it applies to human morality. As said earlier I regard this skepticism as largely responsible for evolution not being taken seriously by those who do know about it, and by extension responsible for evolution failing to become widely known and widely applied to understanding human behavior.

Levels of Selection, Heredity, and Ontogeny: The Nature of the Organism

Group selection and ontogeny are two of the topics least well discussed, not only by Dawkins in the above-recommended publications, but by evolutionary biologists in general. These two topics, however, must be related to one another in the effort to understand the most important product of evolution (and, therefore, the most important concept underlying a biological analysis of morality), the individual organism. Our failures here are responsible for our inability to make sense of evolution to those attempting to use it to understand themselves and other humans.

Although Dawkins (following Williams 1966) argues successfully that populations and societies of individual organisms are not group-selected, in the main he fails to discuss living entities that *are* group-selected. As a consequence he does not discuss extensively the results of group selection. The genes in the genomes of asexual organisms (whether primitively or secondarily asexual) are in fact group-selected, and for most practical purposes so are those in sexual organisms (Alexander and Borgia 1978). Dawkins (1989:273), in an argument that the organism itself is not a replicator, acknowledges that "In the case of an asexual stick-insect, the entire genome (the set of all its genes) is a replicator." He does not, however, describe the genes in the genome of an asexual organism as group-selected and discuss the consequences of that fact and how they bear on the hierarchical organization of life and our understanding of the organism.

The evidence that genes in genomes are group-selected is, first, that they have evolved to co-exist in the same group (genome), and to die within the group in which they initially placed themselves, leaving only their dispersed progeny in sexually produced gametes or their descendants as products of asexual mitosis—all of these descendants necessarily living either in other groups or in descendant groups of approximately (with mixis) or precisely (without mixis—or mutation) the same composition. Second, they have also evolved to share equally in the reproductive opportunities afforded in their respective groups (this can be true even if there are rare circumstances when they do not share equally, as in meiotic drive or segregation distortion: for example, Dawkins 1989:235-36). As a consequence, once formed, the genome is (for the most part in sexual organisms and entirely so in asexual ones) an indivisible unit with a unified function; the interests of all the genes in a genome are identical all the time (asexual organisms) or nearly all the time (sexual organisms). It is an aspect or outcome of this evolved identity that the organism has come to be an entity selected according to a singular principle: the maximizing of inclusive fitness via nepotism to either identical or only partially related descendants. Also as a consequence, the organism has acquired a lifetime: an ontogeny, a patterned reproductive period, and senescence. These are the kinds of "emergent" traits that group-selection may (at least in retrospect) be expected to yield. Some social anthropologists used to think that societies or cultures had such attributes, and were group-selected, but societies and cultures do not have ontogenies nor senescence, so to whatever extent they are group-selected, in the sense of their component individuals tending to have identical interests or having identical interests some of the time, the effect has to be extremely weak. Even during the momentary exception of reduction divisions and gamete formation in sexual (recombining) organisms, chromosomes and other subgroups of genes tend to remain intact, thus to be selected as units. Recombination is not differential reproduction; during oogenesis no chromosome or gene gains from ending up in a polar body, yet each allele has essentially an equal chance of appearing in the daughter cell destined to become an egg. A minuscule amount of differential reproduction occurs during this crucial less than one-millionth part of the life span, as a result of meiotic drive. To the extent that Mendelian expectations hold in inheritance, however, differential reproduction of alleles occurs because of the differential success of the groups (entire genomes) in which they find themselves, by virtue of differential success of the gametic and zygotic offspring of the individual organisms deriving from the zygotes containing those genomes (into which alternative genetic elements have roughly—or usually—an equal chance of getting). Despite implications to the contrary, (e.g., Rodseth 1990), inclusive fitness maximizing via nepotism is, therefore, not only a theory of the organism but *the* theory of the organism. It is not that the organism should be expected to have a general mechanism that instructs it to maximize inclusive fitness: the organism itself is that mechanism, and all of its component parts are continually modified and compromised in such fashions as to approximate that accomplishment. To understand fully any activity of groups or societies, we cannot avoid considering such basic facts about organisms as individuals.

The problem of ontogeny (development)—of the underlying mechanisms of inclusive-fitness-maximizing behavior—becomes the problem of precisely how the group-selected genes in the genome have evolved to cooperate in the production of the organism (individual). The break in our understanding between the genes themselves and the organism and its functioning (hence, the interaction of genes and environment in yielding development and producing the organism), Waddington (1956) called "the great gap in biology." The implication is still largely correct (Alexander 1990). Understanding the general nature of evolution—long-term directional changes, and even the components of the evolutionary process and how they interact—may not be particularly difficult. Understanding the interaction of heredity and development well enough to assume an appropriate attitude with regard to the proximate background of behavior, however, is extremely difficult, and here the biological understanding of nonbiologists tends to break down. As a result, with dismayingly few exceptions, nonbiologists tend to become either naive enthusiasts who are wrong or naive skeptics who are wrong.

Having established that humans, as with other organisms, have indeed evolved to maximize inclusive fitness, biologists are now concentrating increasingly on the nature of underlying mechanisms of inclusive fitness maximizing behavior—hence, development, physiology, learning, the nature and consequences of evolved phenotypic plasticity, and particularly the mechanisms of kin recognition and nepotism (Hamilton 1964; Alexander 1977, 1979; Lumsden and Wilson 1981; Flinn and Alexander 1982; Holmes and Sherman 1983; Johnston 1982, 1985; Boyd and Richerson 1985; Tierney 1986; Fletcher and Michener 1987; West-Eberhard 1987; Symons 1987; Waldman et al. 1988; Cosmides and Tooby 1988; Tooby and Cosmides 1988; Barkow et al. 1991; Hepper, in press; for other references, see Alexander 1990, in press). The *existence* of such mechanisms can be established in any particular case merely through convincing evidence of evolved adaptive function. *Characterization* of the mechanism(s), on the other hand, requires knowledge of ontogenies, necessary and sufficient stimulus sequences, differential eases of learning, sensitive periods (Gould 1986; Hinde and Stevenson-Hinde 1973; Cosmides 1989), and ideally even geographic location and functional interdependence within the central nervous system and with respect to the minimal sensorimotor units (see Alexander 1969, for a detailed example from cricket song).

Efforts to focus attention on the proximate mechanisms of behavior in neural, developmental, and hereditary terms are by no means new. For example, it will be unfortunate if "Darwinian psychologists," who assert their mission to be the analysis of psychological mechanisms underlying evolved and adaptive behavior, repeat the futile arguments of the mid-century ethological "instinctivists." A half-century ago, evolved and adaptive behaviors were seen as plastic emanations from underlying innate or inherited instincts. The analysis of instincts was touted as the highest order of business for behaviorists. Controversies were prominent over how instincts might be inherited, the degree to which their effects were genetically determined, how independent they were from one another, whether there was an underlying instinct for each behavior, how unlike learning instincts were, and what they really might be. These controversies culminated in an elaborate and specific definition of the hypothetical construct of "instinct" by a Cambridge Round Table Conference in 1949 (Thorpe 1950, 1951). This effort did not result in any "instinct" being identified or characterized in a way useful enough to last. Eventually the study of behavior and its underlying proximate causes seems to have continued much as it had before the special fuss about instincts.

In my opinion, most of the errors and oversimplifications in applying evolutionary theory, most of the arguments between biologists and nonbiologists on topics such as sociality and morality, and most of the seeming disagreements among investigators over mechanisms result from simplistic views of development, hence, of underlying mechanisms of behavior. A crucial problem in human self-understanding is incomplete knowledge of the nature of motivation, both in general and by individual actors concerning their own lives. It is not satisfactory merely to apply terms indicating ignorance of development, such as "innate." Nor is it helpful to invoke plasticity vaguely, referring to a behavior simply as "learned" and pretending that the problem has been solved. It is not sufficient to say that any behavior is "genetic," or to assume that individual genes determine any behavior whatsoever. Stages and events in the developing organism are inevitably epigenetic—not only influenced by the genome as a whole but controlled by feedback from the developing phenotype as a whole:

> . . . the idea of genes containing 'blueprints' for behaviors is probably false. I will emphasize . . . the concept of nervous system development as an epigenetic phenomenon in which, once set into motion by the entire genome, one event simply leads to another. A functional nervous system depends on the astonishing ability of developing neurons to select among thousands of candidate targets precisely the correct cell with which to establish a connection. But this precision is best viewed as a developmental consequence of the two cells' being in a particular place at a particular time rather than of genes' specifying the formation of neural circuitry . . . specific genes do not control specific events in normal nervous system development. There are not one-to-one correspondences between genes and neural structures, but rather many-to-many relationships, with each developmental stage guided by epigenetic information . . . (Tierney 1986:341-42)

Suppose that there is a gamut from phenotypic attributes that represent many-to-many genetic and ontogenetic relationships to another extreme in which the genome (organism, phenotype) "allows" control of a difference between phenotypes or a change in a phenotype by a single gene's effect such that it appears that "a gene" controls "a" behavioral variation. Nevertheless, any such gene's effect, and its activity or non-activity, is under the control of the organism as a whole, therefore epigenetic, and results from the relationship between the internal and external environment and the genome as a whole, rather than being in any (alternative) sense genetic or particulate. Eventually we must understand how the flexibility (through responses to environmental variations) represented by the overall phenotype itself, and particular kinds of flexibility such as learning, have originated, and how they have been formed, adjusted, biased, and elaborated by natural selection (Johnston 1982, 1985; Tierney 1986; West-Eberhard 1987; Alexander 1979, 1990). We must unravel the ways in which the unitary phenomenon called the organism, with its cooperative collective of genes evolved toward the singular evolutionary function of inclusive fitness maximizing, has been created from what Dobzhansky (1961) called "the particulateness of heredity." We must understand the unity of development in environments rendered modular by the independence and multiplicity of the different "Hostile Forces of Nature" (Darwin 1859). We must develop concepts of different kinds of epigenetic preprogramming to replace notions of inherited, genetic, genetically determined, "innate," or "instinctive" behavior (or templates or substrates). The last two terms are simply vague and useless, but they lead us to the others, which are wrong, and promote erroneous thinking about the interactions of heredity and development and the nature of phenotypic plasticity. The genes may cooperate to produce a singular organism, but natural selection impinges on the organism as a result of reproductive failures and mortality from many different sources: climate, weather, food shortages, parasites, diseases, predators, and mate shortages (all such problems, of course, mediated by conspecific competitors). As a consequence partly of the multiplicity of selective forces, the organism evolves traits (and underlying mechanisms of behavior). But the traits of an individual organism, however separate they may seem, are not independent of one another, as is well understood by any biologist who has tried to interrupt the "stream" of activities (or the continuity of morphological or physiological features) of an organism to itemize its traits in an ethogram or to maximize their numbers to, say, construct the most likely phylogenetic tree. No trait of an organism is maximized in its own particular function because all traits are part of a compromise in which the singular function of inclusive fitness maximizing remains as the perpetual combined effect of natural selection on the organism. Evolutionary compromises within the evolving organism as a result of conflicts among the "idealizing" of different functions are parliaments not so much in the sense of conflicting interests as in the sense of coordinations of extremely complex programs of effort (and possibly of differences in information among agreeing parties—or parts). If this unity is disrupted by any gene behaving other than as group-selected in its genome, the consequence will nearly always be disaster; the exceptions are alleles that show meiotic drive (e.g., reduce their chances of going into a polar body) *without* showing accompanying deleterious effects on the organism's phenotype.

In what sense is plasticity—for example, learning—primitive or derived? The phenotype as such—the original and general manifestation of flexibility—is ancient, so that any of its current features in any organism are likely to represent successive waves of derivation. It does not follow that plasticity *per se* is invariably derived from non-plasticity, or greater plasticity from lesser plasticity. Learning is not always derived from nonlearning, or greater flexibility in learning from less (Johnston 1985; Tierney 1986). For example, plasticity or flexibility *per se* can be seen as either adaptive or as "noise." Consider a communicative signal. At first it may be variable, with the variability resulting from the primitiveness of the signal, perhaps best termed imprecision, and having little reproductive significance because all variants of the signal still work. If, however, some parts of the variability come to cause confusion with, say, signals by other species new to the region, then variability (plasticity) is likely to be reduced accordingly. Different parts of the range of variability in a signal may begin to have different levels of significance in different life circumstances for the species (say, more intense signals are more useful for pair formation because they attract mates from a greater distance, and less intense signals for courtship because they lessen interference by attracted competitors). Now the variability may be compartmentalized, producing "nodes" of functionality within the original range of variation, with the eventual effect of reducing observable "plasticity." One might expect that, for any particular trait, "waves" of different kinds and degrees of plasticity would occur during evolution, with perhaps repeated tendencies to modularize after "rushes" of plasticity or variability had occurred—for example, when a new habitat is entered or a new function appears. Thus, in the earliest stages of song evolution in crickets, a reasonably wide spectrum of frequencies was surely produced. While such frequency spectra might appropriately be described as physically "complex," functionally this complexity would be an aspect of rudimentariness and primitive variability rather than evolved precision. The ability of most modern crickets to produce a narrow range of frequencies (essentially a sine wave) has to be regarded as derived or a specialization. Similarly, the precise rates and rhythms within the songs of modern crickets are surely not primitive but derived from less precise, more variable primitive ancestral efforts. When wings (secondarily used to produce song in crickets) evolved in any organism, they may have passed through early stages in which they were modified as gliding organs (probably after serving some entirely different function at an earlier stage). When actual propelling features appeared, a new wave of selective change would take place in a slightly different direction, probably leading to a new "rush" of variability. As different flying techniques or advantages appeared, further changes would occur in different directions, and in succession, within any genetic line. In modern forms wings have evolved several times and are used for not only flying and signal production (e.g., crickets, katydids, butterflies, birds), but have evolved many other functions such as fighting (e.g., ducks, geese), food and mating lures (katydids, crickets), and grasping and holding devices during mating (scorpion flies). Each time a new effect with reproductive significance appears, selection causes changes in one or more different directions, sometimes seeming to alter the wings in a general overall fashion, sometimes seeming to modularize their structure and function. In many cases plasticity will seem to be reduced following a stage in which multiple uses occurred rudimentarily because of what would be perceived as a phenotypic variability or plasticity.

It seems reasonable to hypothesize that the kinds of behavioral flexibility we call learning have evolved in fashions similar to those of other traits; there is no reason to restrict ourselves to hidden features of the human mind or CNS when trying to understand such general features of the organism as the underlying physiological and psychological mechanisms of behavior. In the above example, wings would be parallel to learning ability, the changes in wings as a result of selection favoring different functions paralleling modularization or multiple biasing of learning to favor its uses in different life circumstances. Despite any "domain-specific" aspect in which wings (or learning) evolved to serve some particular function, the "domain-general" phenomenon (of wings or learning) would remain. "Domain-specificity" is necessarily a relative term, so that to use evidence of it to deny "domain-generality" seems futile. We ought not to let the extreme "blank slate" arguments about learning (Skinner 1965) distract us from this realization. It can also be seen from this example that the question whether plasticity or canalization (learning or some alternative to it) is genetically or developmentally more expensive is not easily settled (Johnston 1985; Tierney 1986).

Some traits of organisms are identifiable, or give the appearance of being partially independent, because of the modularity of the selective environment. All such traits, however, cannot be explained in this way. Consider a gasoline engine. It is designed for a singular function, to create maximum torque at a certain speed on a particular shaft. Nevertheless, it will have different "traits" just as does the organism: cylinders, pistons, valves, spark producers, distributors, timers, cooling devices, intake and exhaust systems, crankshaft, fuel tank, etc. Some of this modularity occurs because of previously perceived efficiency by the designers. Worn-out parts are more easily replaced if they are made separately and fastened together. Some components of an engine are more easily constructed by creating separate parts and fastening them together. Even excepting these examples, "traits" will still exist, just as organisms have separate circulatory, filtering, locomotory, and alimentary devices. Part of the evident particulateness of the organism as well as the engine therefore is due to efficiency of specialization of parts. But a significant part of organismic phenotypic modularity is surely caused by the particulateness of the external environment.

What are the reasons for heredity remaining particulate? Because of the tendency of "genes" to live in variously tight large and small groups (supergenes, chromosomes, and other kinds of "linkages"), yet to remain incompletely "congealed" even in secondarily apomictic (non-recombining) forms, we might speculate that the manner by which the genetic materials are changed is partly responsible. That is, perhaps heredity remains particulate at least partly because radiation and other mutagens tend to influence small regions in the genetic material, resulting in what are called "point" mutations. Collections of such "point" mutations are generally responsible for individual organisms differing genetically in particular amounts and ways, and therefore lead to the differential reproduction that creates the patterns of life. Nevertheless, when "point" mutations occur on chromosomes, except for rare breaks in the chromosome (and the resulting inversions and crossovers) the chromosome as a whole is altered, and gene changes are either saved or lost primarily because whole chromosomes are saved or lost. To this extent the genome has in fact congealed and heredity is not so particulate. Explaining the particulateness of heredity is different from accounting for the retention of sexuality; recombination is facilitated by the particulateness of heredity, but its advantages may not be responsible for the retention of particulateness.

To go beyond avoiding the oversimplifications and mistakes we already recognize, in discussing underlying mechanisms of behavior (thinking of learning as simply a "blank slate" or unbiased, undirected plasticity; referring to behaviors with cryptic ontogenies as "inherited"; conjuring up misleadingly precise definitions of hypothetical underlying mechanisms as "instincts" or "psychological mechanisms," visualizing the central nervous system as a single-layered conglomerate of innate, specialized, separate, and independent mechanisms for particular behaviors), is a monumental task in which behaviorists will eventually have to depend heavily on developmental neurophysiologists. In turn, developmental neurophysiologists will have to depend on evolutionary biologists to understand how the various phenomena they analyze can be understood as "mechanisms." Part of the analysis cannot be completed without knowing what each mechanism is evolved to accomplish—therefore, knowing the evolved life functions or adaptations of the organism as a whole. Social scientists and philosophers will have to keep up with at least the bare bones of the arguments.

Extrapolating from the best-studied phenotypic attributes in the most familiar organisms, mechanisms evolve which tend to yield particular behaviors in particular environments. To understand them behavior must be studied first and the mechanisms only later. Nothing requires (or allows!) that underlying mechanisms of behavior be identified prior to understanding what they have evolved to do, and nothing requires that any particular mechanisms—"epigenetic rules"—be unchangeable.

As for virtually all aspects of all phenotypes in all organisms, nothing about the human phenotype involving morality either has been identified or need be identified as innate, instinctive, inherited, or unchangeable. It is a fundamental misunderstanding of inheritance and development to believe that such a requirement is necessary for a biological discussion, or that it is assumed in every discussion by a biologist about the evolution of behavioral tendencies and abilities such as those involved in morality. Both genes and environment contribute to every aspect of the phenotype, and the evolutionary significance of the concept of phenotype in all its ontogenetic or life stages is plasticity, in the interests of maximizing inclusive fitness in the environments of history. Genomes, which are by definition nonplastic and unchangeable (except by mutation and recombination), do not occur (any longer?) naked in the environment (that is, without phenotypes). Presumably naked genes have been universally less capable than organisms of adjusting appropriately to environmental contingencies, and on this account less persistent. Ontogenies are increasingly complex systems of feedbacks involving the the entire genome and the internal and external environment of the organism, turning genes on and off and modifying their actual effects. It may be possible to conceive of ways that certain phenotypic effects do not represent plasticity, but in general phenotypes evolve as cushions of plasticity interposed by selection between the genome and the environment. Even when a phenotype consists of what seems to the observer an entirely rigid structure or unalterable activity, the evolutionary (and onto-genetic) production of that expression represented a change in the previous "organism," thus flexibility in that sense, and as well in the sense of susceptibility to further change when selective forces change again. Once phenotypes evolve, gene frequencies change because of the particular structures genes produce in particular environments, and the significance of the structures (phenotypes) is that they alter the way selection acts on gene differences. The different kinds of plasticity that represent the phenotype, including learning, are ways of providing reproductively appropriate responses to varying forces of natural selection but not ways of escaping them entirely.

It seems fallacious to argue that we are evolved beings whose every attribute has been produced by an evolution guided primarily by differential reproduction, and then to follow that argument with the assertion that nevertheless we have somehow magically and more or less suddenly escaped the underlying mechanisms that have resulted from this continual, inexorable process of natural selection that is our heritage (regardless whether or not the evolved mechanisms happen to be maximizing reproduction in current environments). This is not the way, for example, that long-term effects of culture would be expected to have changed us. If the underlying mechanisms of our behavior do not persist unchanged, they surely have been changing so as to render our behavior in the cultural situations of recent history more reproductive, not less. The challenge is to describe how the underlying mechanisms of reproductive maximization are working in modern society, not to interpret all of modern human behavior as if the mechanisms had somehow disappeared. Culture is ancient, and the learning capacities on which it is based are even more ancient. As culture developed through the ages, human learning either served individual reproduction or it did not; we can be sure the parts that did not have been damped by natural selection. Regardless of the speed of cultural change, there has been ample time for much alteration of learning tendencies and capacities since culture began. I am not aware of evidence that learning capacities have been diminished, in any general sense or measurable degree, since the origins of human culture. They may, however, have been altered dramatically in the service of individual reproduction. In this there is no suggestion of escape from the evolved mechanisms of our behavior. Any semblance of "escape" is most likely as a result of the particular kind of dramatic, rapid, and potentially progressive (sequential) learning represented by new understanding of the evolutionary, reproductive backgrounds of our behavior.

Particular examples of misunderstanding of the relationship between evolved ontogenies and the nature of human motivation, decision-making, and choice may be instructive. Thus, some authors (e.g., Slobodkin, this volume) suggest that if organisms show nepotism to relatives solely as a result of having been reared with them (rather than, say, through having evolved mechanisms for identifying strangers who are kin), this means that cumulative genetic change through natural selection is not responsible for the effect. Such a view implies that social learning is not a consequence of evolution and is not designed to cause reproductive behavior in organisms living in the environments of history; that learning particular things from association at particular times and in particular circumstances cannot comprise a mechanism of inclusive fitness maximizing. We know this view is false, since learning about helping relatives and avoiding inbreeding is patterned in the ways denied by it, and they are patterned differently in group living and solitary forms precisely in ways predicted by evolutionary considerations (Alexander 1979, 1990, in press). Moreover, the inadequacy of such views is not merely academic: knowledge of sensitive periods and learning biases have implications of great significance in resolving human suffering resulting, for example, from homicide, incest, and child abuse (Daly and Wilson 1981, 1988; see also, Alexander 1987, 1989). Knowledge of learning experiences that are not conscious, hence not remembered, may have remained trivial in terms of conscious reflection (that is, failed during evolution to become conscious, and as a result failed to *seem* important) because in the environments of history they did not typically go awry without the intervention of consciousness. Current social environments, however, may cause such experiences to go offtrack considerably more frequently than is necessary or desirable, making their conscious understanding exceedingly valuable. It is not trivial that associative learning, as a mechanism of kin recognition, serves the interests of all the genes in the genome equally, therefore accords with the earlier description of the organism as evolved by group selection of genes; some other proposed (but not demonstrated) evolved mechanisms of kin recognition do not (Alexander 1990, in press).

Patricia Williams (this volume) argues that theories of prescriptive evolved ethics are internally contradictory because, to be ethical, organisms require freedom from external and internal coercion. She seems to mean that an organism evolved to maximize its inclusive fitness is coerced by this aspect of its makeup, so that either ethical behavior is independent of evolution or evolved beings cannot be ethical—as she puts it they cannot legitimately be blamed, praised, and held responsible for their actions. For this argument, however, she must also assume that the existence of rules, and of threats about the consequences of breaking them, is independent of the existence of moral and ethical behavior. It seems to me that her view also requires that many decisions of humans (all of those in the realm of ethics and morality) are made in the absence of potential costs or independent of potential costs that could, in a broad view of the concept, be viewed as "coercive"—or at least in the absence of any kind of knowledge (conscious or nonconscious) of such costs. I would argue, to the contrary, that every act of every organism involves potential costs and potential benefits, and some kind of cost-benefit analysis, so that in this sense every human decision is "coerced"—including the formation of conscience itself. To take this position one need not argue (and I never have argued) that any particular ethical or moral rules will ever be discovered to follow naturally or inevitably or at all from evolutionary facts. Rather, I would argue that acts *considered* moral or ethical are typically acts that result in a perceived temporary net cost, or risk, to the actor, in the process of giving benefits to others, particularly when there is evidence that the actor did not consciously calculate the cost or risk and determine that the likelihood of eventual overcompensating return actually made the investment worthwhile (Alexander 1987). To me, the interesting or difficult question is *why* humans tend to regard only acts of this nature moral or ethical, and what are the consequences of this tendency not only for the active investigation of motivation in social behavior but for the prospects of eventual widespread acceptance and understanding of organic evolution as the causal sequence giving rise to humanity and its traits and tendencies? Returning to Patricia Williams's comments about praise and blame, I think we praise people for following the rules of society even if they do it as a result of recognizing that it will be even more expensive to break them, and that we tend to blame them for failing to follow the rules in nearly all cases except when they are incapable of comprehending them. In any case, the existence of rules, and of admonitions concerning them, alters people's behavior; this must be a consequence of evolution and certainly is in no way contrary to it.

Even if I have not erred, and Patricia Williams really is using the term "coercion" to mean essentially any potential costs that might modify actions, I nevertheless would not wish to imply that in the everyday sense of the word any and all costs represent coercion. It seems that, as with any rule-based system, to give the concept of coercion a useful meaning one has to be willing to specify degrees of restraint, hindrance, or compulsion that are appropriately termed "force" and others that are not, and more specifically kinds or degrees of force that are considered legitimate and illegitimate. Thus, morality is not usually seen as requiring that everyone entirely cease serving his or her own interests and serve only those of others. Rather, what is required is that the effort to serve one's own interests not exceed certain limits in directions that interfere with others serving their own interests. The appropriate limits, I think, tend to be set according to some kind of opinion—of a majority or a power structure—and such opinion tends to become highly dependent on precedents. What constitutes unacceptable coercion (or imposed costs) of particular acts also tends to depend upon precedents. Precedents lead to expectations, and the parading of precedents reinforces this tendency. We often speak of interfering with legitimate expectations, and I would suppose that such considerations often enter into people's notions of moral and ethical behavior. Some degrees and kinds of "coercion," in the form of restraints or hindrances or costs, thus seem to exist for essentially all courses of action.

George C. Williams (1989, this volume), author of the bleak statement quoted at the outset, attempts to solve the problem of evolution and morality by following Thomas Huxley (1896, reprinted in 1909) in declaring that natural selection is evil and morality combats it. According to this view, actually resembling that of Patricia Williams, to serve the interests of morality we presumably act intentionally counter to our evolutionary interests. Unfortunately, this view does not explain what possible impetus we might have to pursue such a course—or to be moral. It provides no explanation for the striking human tendency to generate moral systems, discuss morality endlessly, and adhere to moral rules in particular circumstances. It does not explain why humans tend widely to identify as immoral actions within their groups that they nevertheless regard as highly moral between groups. Ultimately, George Williams's view would have humans no less amoral than any other form of life. He seems to refer only to the fact that evolution tends to serve individual interests and to pass over the question of how individual interests may be served by serving the interests of the individual's group, however composed for particular and different questions pertinent to that proposition. His analysis ignores that cooperation, which to many seems antithetical to the service of individual interests, is actually consistent with natural selection, and it seems to deny that cooperative behavior which facilitates reproduction can ever be moral. In this ignoring and denying, it also thwarts any likelihood of understanding how tendencies to cooperate, and indeed to generate and espouse the kind of view Huxley and Williams put forth, could have come about.

The Evolutionary View of Morality as Contractarian

Because selection is primarily effective at and below the individual level, it is reasonable to expect concepts and practices pertaining to morality—as with all other aspects of the phenotypes of living forms—to be designed so as to yield reproductive (genetic) gains to the individuals exhibiting them, at least in the environments of history. To put such an approach into practice it is necessary to understand the life interests—therefore the life patterns—of humans as outcomes of an evolution guided principally by natural selection. This also means understanding theoretical arguments from the science of biology about such things as somatic effort (and ontogenies), reproductive effort, and senescence (Williams 1957, 1966; Hamilton 1966; Alexander 1987).

As with most organisms, humans serve their interests as individuals by interacting with others of their species, even if they interact in some ways unique to the human species. Their interactions are not merely competitive but also cooperative. They give and receive benefits from one another. Sometimes they compete by cooperating. Both their cooperation and their competition can be extremely complex. We all know these things, although it often seems that there is an undue emphasis on cooperation in a way that refuses to acknowledge its competitive aspects, speaking of cooperation as a replacement for competition and talking only of the "brighter side" of human nature. If humans had evolved to cooperate only to avoid nonhuman hostile forces, there might be no reasonable argument that self-deception is involved in efforts to argue for cooperation *as an alternative to* competition (rather than as a form of it). Since Darwin, however, we have known that this is not likely to be the case; current arguments that the human intellect evolved as a social tool, moreover, seem to lend potent fuel to the opposite argument, that human social cooperation may literally have evolved as a method of intraspecific competition (Humphrey 1976; Alexander 1989, 1991).

In humans, uniquely, intraspecific competition has become dominated by intergroup competition facilitated by cooperation in large numbers of coalitions that overlap in indefinitely large and complex patterns, both vertically (between generations) and horizontally (within generations). Nepotism to both descendant and collateral relatives, and reciprocity involving both relatives and nonrelatives are the means of dispensing and withholding benefits in patterns appropriate to the serving of evolved interests. Such beneficence in the contexts of evolved nepotism and reciprocity—whether in evolutionary terms appropriately or inappropriately directed today—is actually what has been termed the altruism of morality; selfishness, in the sense of egoistic behavior, is expected to be designed in the interests of creating a phenotype maximally capable of the beneficence of nepotism. In the service of inclusive fitness maximizing, the organism may thus be described as evolved to be the most effective possible nepotist (Alexander 1979).

Through indirect reciprocity, even beneficence to nonrelatives unable or unlikely to reciprocate may be favored because it can lead to the establishment of reputation that benefits the beneficent individual with respect to later choices of partners in reciprocity (Trivers 1971; Alexander 1979, 1987). Centrality of indirect reciprocity in modern human social systems creates situations in which reputation depends significantly on (1) evidence of general acceptance of, and adherence to, sets of rules and (2) the presence of conscience as a vehicle to such behavior, as opposed to simpler forms of indirect reciprocity depending on beneficent individuals simply repeating the same kinds of altruism in the same kinds of situations in which they have previously been observed.

Under this model reputation may become so important that for some people in some circumstances indiscriminately dispensed beneficence can be favored (Alexander 1987).

Thus, along with others, I have argued for a contractarian view of morality, thoroughly understandable only through knowing, at the outset, the life goals or interests likely to be produced by organic evolution, but relative in the sense of being modifiable to fit particular social situations and including enormously complex patterns of cooperative and competitive interactions. I argued that intragroup cooperativeness is designed evolutionarily to serve intergroup competitiveness. The universality of intergroup competitiveness and the seeming altruism of within-group morality, I maintained, are together responsible for morality seeming erroneously to be a group phenomenon that serves the interests of the group contrary to the interests of the individual; they represent the vehicle to understanding (1) the correlation between the existence and the intensity of within-group amity and the existence and intensity of between-group enmity and (2) the failure of humanity to accomplish the cultural derivation of a single cooperative group encompassing all of humanity with a common set of moral rules—a goal otherwise seeming to many philosophers and moralists as the logical but perplexingly unachieved extension of within-group amity. I have also argued that the significance of indirect reciprocity has to do not only with rules but with intent, that systems of indirect reciprocity lead to avoidance of selfishness as well as positive acts of (at least temporary) altruism, that we are evolved to appear to be honest and altruistic, and that "We use motivation and honesty in one circumstance to predict actions in others." (Alexander 1987:96, and Table 2.5). I have argued consistently that, even though evolution and natural selection directly or indirectly underlie all our actions and motivations, conscious understanding of our evolutionary background does not provide easy ways either to interpret or to justify opinions about right and wrong in particular situations. One reason is that right and wrong are group decisions, sometimes by majority opinion, sometimes by a power structure that may represent a minority, and sometimes only by unanimity. With regard to human behavior selection has not worked at such levels; as a result individual opinions, however learned, are unlikely to represent group compromises, and, when they reflect conflicts of interest, may even conflict ludicrously with them.

Among the many publications about morality in the last five years or so, a contractarian view seems to have gained ground. Moral behavior is evidently a result of some kind(s) of contractual agreements among participants in sociality. Moral contracts are somehow less formal than the more familiar legal contracts—maybe even less explicit—but they are there, as contracts, all the same. Rawls (1971), Gautier

(1990), and Gibbard (1990) are examples of moral philosophers who view moral behavior as a result of contractual behavior (see also Axelrod 1984, 1986; Frank 1988). Legal contracts might have arisen out of the history of moral, and perhaps other kinds of verbal or somehow understood and accepted, contracts by which society operated, and that written language was one reason legal contracts in their present forms became possible. Written language necessarily enhanced the possibility of unequivocal precedence, and the concept of precedence enhances the basis for rules. Unlike moral contracts, however, legal contracts are always *consciously* entered into and developed, and they are not always regarded as moral.

Contracts are made between people who have real or potential conflicts of interest. There is no other reason for making them. There is no reason for a contract between people whose interests are identical and will remain so. Among sexually reproducing organisms, in which every generational link halves the likelihood of any particular gene being present in any two related individuals, the (evolutionary) interests of individuals will rarely, and then only temporarily, overlap completely (Hamilton 1964; Alexander 1979, 1987). The implication is that through understanding the evolutionary significance of the human organism, and the nature and individuality of its evolved interests, we may derive useful insights into human concerns about morality.

Moral behavior refers explicitly to the *rights* of others. It represents how far anyone can go without being judged unfair, unjust, wrong—without being judged immoral. How far anyone can go means, presumably, how far one can go in serving his own interests. In other words, the rules of society—whatever they may be or whatever kind they may be—are designed to control the tendencies of individuals to serve their own interests in various ways, presumably in ways that have minimally deleterious effects on those who make and maintain the rules (sometimes virtually all of society), and sometimes have downright positive effects on those other than the individuals being inhibited.

In my experience people do not regard themselves as serving only their own interests—not even as serving only the interests of themselves and their own family. How people think about motivation, and that how they think about how motivation is likely to be altered by statements about motivation, represents a principal difficulty in securing widespread acceptance of evolution and natural selection, and an evolutionary approach to human behavior. That sophisticated writers such as Frank (1988) and Gibbard (1990), who attempt evolutionary analyses of aspects of human behavior, can nevertheless (in my view) underplay human activities and tendencies prominent in the daily news (that is, selfish and exploitative behaviors: see below) illustrates the potency of this difficulty. I believe that it also accounts in part for the curious tendencies of authors such as Hayles (1990) to attempt to relate science and human nature by skipping from the physical sciences to moral philosophy or literary criticism without significant mention of the science of biology or the facts of evolution.

The Problem of Intent

Earlier I suggested that the most paradoxical problem in applying evolution to human behavior—of analyzing the evolution of concepts and activities related to morality—is that of understanding motivation. People do not see themselves as designed to maximize inclusive fitness. They do not think of their activities as serving only reproduction. They tend to be hostile to any concept or discipline that seems to rely upon this kind of reduction. This intuitive rejection, moreover, is only part of the paradox. Consider expression of the emotions, much of which is tied to intent and the communication or expression of intent to others. From an evolutionist's viewpoint it is reasonable to hypothesize that initially expressions of physiological changes that incidentally but accurately signaled intent—or imminent action—were used by other individuals to their own benefit. To the extent that this occurred, organisms surely began to evolve so as to alter externally perceptible evidences of intent to serve their own interests rather than those of observers, at least when the two sets of interests conflicted. Assuming that this is a reasonable view of the evolutionary background of current expressions of intent through the emotions (Alexander 1989), it is extremely perplexing that humans are to a large extent imperfectly or incompletely in control of expression of the emotions. Everyone blushes sometimes when not wanting to. Everyone has lost his or her temper and regretted it. Everyone has suffered embarrassment because some indication of sexual excitement was not concealed. Probably no one regards him or her self as always in complete control of the emotions (that is, in complete *conscious* control).

I doubt that many evolutionarily oriented behaviorists would accept that lapses of the sorts I have just described are simply evidence of failures of natural selection. Why should such things happen if expressions of the emotions—as indicators of desires or intent—should exist to serve the interests of the individuals expressing their emotions? Why should humans have evolved so as not to understand their own motivations, and not to be able to control even the evidence of the motivations that they believe they do understand? It is difficult to imagine that we are here dealing merely with inevitable concomitant costs of other tendencies.

Biologists typically do not ask about the intent of nonhumans, the most obvious exceptions being our closest relatives such as chimpanzees, bonobos, orangutans, and gorillas. Nonbiologists concerned with establishing the connections between natural selection and human behavior not only lack the biologist's background in examining endless evolved features without being concerned with intent, but rather are more likely to be preoccupied with intent from the beginning. This preoccupation does not derive solely from the fact that anyone who studies or thinks about humans must constantly consider intent. It also arises out of the difference between scientific investigations and the pursuits of the humanities. Science is a process of accumulating knowledge, with the aim of approaching irrefutability or undeniability—of discovering factual information of general and uniform applicability. Work in the humanities—with some of the most complex and difficult-to-understand human activities—seems, in contrast, primarily a search for meaning (Alexander 1989, 1991). The inevitable and perpetual individuality of interests among humans (itself a product of evolution through sexual recombination, leading to genetic individuality—see Alexander 1987, and Williams's quote above) indicates that meanings will tend to be different for different individuals. That generalities of meaning also exist does not alter the fact that the emphasis of the humanities is on human endeavors in which meanings will always tend to be diverse, and often individual. Thus, when I state my personal intent in a given matter, to the extent that I am being honest I am describing some aspect of the individuality of meaning in that matter. This distinction is surely responsible for some controversies currently prominent about the nature of reality and the importance of individual viewpoints, extending even into the difficulties of discussing cultural and other human variations and judging the outcomes of social interactions, the meaning of which is seen differently by different participants.

Expressions of intent, and other uses of intent, as with other traits, have presumably been shaped by natural selection. As already suggested, many aspects of communication, such as expression of the emotions, probably evolved originally not because they transmitted any honest information at all but rather because they were useful coverups for honest information originally produced only incidentally and as such detrimental to the interests of those producing it because of its use by others (Alexander 1989). The notion of communication as simply a system of transmitting honest information to social associates has long been dead (Otte 1974; Lloyd 1977; Dawkins and Krebs 1978; Alexander 1987). Whether or not it includes honest information, communication is also likely to involve deception and misinformation. It will have to be analyzed in terms of the degrees and kinds of overlaps of interests among communicators, and such analysis will depend upon understanding histories of genetic relatedness and the means available to humans of recognizing and responding to patterns of common and differing reproductive interests.

Frank (1988), an economist, dealt extensively with the problem of intent in *Passions within Reason*. His initial thesis seemed to be that a self-interest model of human behavior will not account for morality—for some easily observed instances of beneficence or altruism such as the leaving of tips at restaurants visited but once, following one's conscience, or returning found money. His arguments about costs and benefits depend on whether or not there is any possibility of being found out (that is, chances of imprisonment or effects on reputation), and although he declares that detection is impossible in some of his examples, it is doubtful that one can ever be sure of this. I would guess that the prisons are filled with individuals who at one point or another were certain they would not be caught.

Frank attempts to show that many acts of beneficence are indeed unmitigated altruism—net-cost acts for the actor. Then he argues that the reason such acts are undertaken is that the actor gains sufficient benefit from having previously committed himself to such acts that, should the occasion for them arise, he will actually to reap a net social benefit overall. This benefit comes both from the responses of social interactants to the evidence of the existence of the commitment, and to the readiness of the actor to act in ways seemingly contrary to his own interests without having to ponder the question (Alexander 1987). In other words, just as it pays not to dwell consciously on the rhythm of the heartbeat or how fast to breathe, it sometimes pays to conduct social acts without prior conscious calculation, even if as a result of foregoing conscious reflection occasional mistakes occur.

Only at the very end of his book does Frank acknowledge what the reader has long before begun to suspect: that, after all, his arguments do indeed fit a self-interest model—just not a *conscious* pursuit of self-interest. *Commitment* actually becomes his term for nonconscious pursuit of self-interest, which pays both because of the effect of commitment on other social interactants and because most of the time commitment leads to net-benefit acts. Frank believes he has explained why *some* acts caused by commitment may be a net cost to the actor. When what he had originally described as altruistic acts are evolutionary accidents, they are not explainable directly from natural selection. Such acts are often explainable, however, in the same way that, say, senescence is explainable from natural selection—indirectly—in the case of senescence as inevitable concomitants (or pleiotropic effects) of otherwise beneficial genes (Williams

1957). It is appropriate and useful to point out the inevitable concomitant costs of evolutionary designs, and that there are always such costs; it is not the case, however, that biologists have been operating as if such costs did not exist, or that they deny a self-interest model of human behavior.

In the end Frank's analysis, although extremely enlightening from its ease of reading and wealth of examples, seems not to differ substantively from others previously generated around the concept of indirect reciprocity (Trivers 1971; Alexander 1987). Self-interest as inclusive fitness maximizing remains the central evolved goal of the human organism, and the concept of commitment simply represents a particular kind of contract with society, or some part of it. The difference between Frank's self-interest and commitment models is not whose interests are being favored but whether or not costs and benefits are being calculated consciously.

Similarly, Simon (1990) argues that there is much net-cost altruism among humans and that it is induced by social learning that has a net benefit but entails costs because it sometimes leads to mistakes. He points out that it is often to the advantage of others (or to "society") to induce such mistakes, which he calls a "tax" imposed by society "on the gross benefits gained by individuals" from what he calls "docility," which translates as "the human tendency to learn from others." (p. 1665; also, Alexander 1987). He also notes that what he calls "docile" acceptance of others as authorities for phenomena of great significance in our lives takes place because in complex human society it is often prohibitively expensive to seek the answers for ourselves. Costs resulting from the wrong things being learned have long been understood as an inevitable concomitant of learning. That there are social benefits from being committed to social beneficence, that even indiscriminate altruism can be beneficial to the actor, and that people exert effort to get others to behave in ways beneficial to others and deleterious to themselves has also been argued extensively (e.g., Alexander 1987, especially pp. 96-126). Simon, as with Frank, seems primarily to have rediscovered indirect reciprocity and perhaps not to be aware that all acts of all organisms involve costs.

"Docility" and "commitment" are thus aspects of indirect reciprocity, with the costs to foregoing immediate benefits for long-term benefits on average overcompensated by those long-term benefits. In other words, both Frank (1988) and Simon (1990) are suggesting that you cannot accept learning and following the rules, and develop your tendencies to their fullest in regard to returns from this procedure, without incurring costs from occasional mistakes of beneficence that would not otherwise have been necessary in the particular circumstances in which they occurred.

Neither Frank nor Simon provides an answer to the next question: Why are we not in complete control of the use of the expression of our emotions to manipulate others? Earlier, though, Frank says, "A blush may reveal a lie and cause great embarrassment at the moment, but in circumstances that require trust, there can be great advantage in being known as a blusher."

Blushing is not restricted to situations involving lies. Sometimes it occurs when we simply are thinking thoughts we do not wish revealed. Are we evolved to give the impression (sometimes true, sometimes not) that in certain situations we cannot control our emotions therefore cannot accurately convey our intent or regulate it? Or else that we have incomplete intent (are undecided) but do not wish to convey (reveal) that fact, though we are indeed revealing it (against our wishes) and presumably are thereby benefiting (at least in the long run)? Are we designed to convey incompleteness or imperfection of intent (or motivation)?

I have argued (Alexander 1989) that we may have evolved incomplete control of the emotions to dispel the notion that we are in complete control of our emotions in particular situations. This hypothesis implies that incomplete control of the emotions— or unwanted expression of them such as blushing, uncontrollable anger, or uncontrollable sexual excitement—occurs in interactions with others of great importance to us, especially when we are establishing, cementing, or furthering the relationship, and much less or not at all in casual or brief interactions. Without such lapses we appear as "cold fish" who have our emotions entirely under control, or as uncommitting individuals who are not undergoing the changes and indecisions involved in establishing an expensive social investment, therefore that the current involvement is not particularly important to us. The costs of occasional mistakes from not employing our conscious abilities in all social encounters may sometimes be high, but the cost of being discovered to be insincere is usually enormous.

The vast majority of expensive human social interactions across history have probably been nepotistic, and involved extensive commitment or investment to either relatives or spouses. From this it could also be argued that some social interactions used extensively by Frank, such as tipping in a strange restaurant—in other words actions involving the question of beneficence toward strangers that will not again be encountered—are to a large extent novel or actually apply to (or are incompletely associated with) intergroup interactions, in which (sometimes) short-changing and other versions of what Sahlins (1965) called "negative reciprocity" are not only expected but admired.

Incompleteness of control of expression of the emotions is not part of the general public's problem with evolution: only the serious student of human behavior in relation to evolution is likely to expose it and worry about it. If critics of evolutionary approaches to human evolution had been aware of it, they surely would have exploited it as a major part of the reason that an evolutionary view of human behavior does not seem to "make sense" and has not spread to include a much larger portion of the world population of educated humans.

Consider this set of arguments:

> *Human society cannot operate without rules* because too many people— acting as both individuals and groups—will go "too far" in serving their own interests; that is, individuals acting without restraint will often infringe the rights of others in ways widely enough deemed unacceptable as to result in rules.
>
> *Rules cannot be enforced without threat of punishment.*
>
> *Threats are not effective unless real.*
>
> *When threats must be carried out, punishment will be resisted.*
>
> *When punishment is resisted force becomes necessary.*

These arguments, which seem (perhaps unfortunately), to describe the operational background of everyday law and order in modern societies, obviously assume that individuals and groups tend to seek to serve their own interests, and that, therefore, peace at least *usually* results from the use (or threat) of force (it obviously does not follow that *all* uses of force lead to peace). This is more an argument from empiricism than from deterministic theory.

So it appears that, if morality is actually an evolved phenomenon—a way people have worked out to serve their own interests in ways that tread on the toes of others only in acceptable fashions—then anyone who analyzes morality, who attempts to bring its cost-benefit decisions into his own and others' consciousnesses, is likely to be judged immoral both for doing it in his own mind and for trying to cause it, or risking it happening, in others' minds. He will be seen as reducing the likelihood of Frank's version of "self interest" turning into, being perceived as, or remaining as "commitment" through indoctrination and practice that produces a "suitable" social conscience. Recall Ambrose Bierce's (1911) definition of a cynic as "a blackguard whose faulty vision sees things as they are, not as they ought to be." The requirement that social motivation be nonconscious may turn out to be the most remarkable and restrictive of all moral rules, enforced by the extreme cleverness of humans at ferreting out what is in an associate's conscious mind, as opposed to his unconscious mind, and by the maintenance of heavy penalties for deliberate deception because deliberate deception implies the greatest danger to the deceived, and repetition when opportunities arise. In other words, this situation is in many ways the most important one involving reputation. Gibbard writes as follows:

> Singer (1981) discusses systems of unpaid blood donation as working refutations of the contention that altruism can only exist among kin, within small groups, or where it pays off by encouraging reciprocal altruism. Alexander (1987) offers an explanation in terms of indirect reciprocity: the blood donor shows himself altruistic, and so "he may receive his 'payment' from the members of society who accept him in social interactions or treat him deferentially." This raises a number of questions. Why will others specially accept the unconditional altruist or defer to him? In hope of gain? An unconditional altruist would be one who showered goods irrespective of whether other accepted him or deferred to him. Blood donation must signal something other than this, but how? Then too, there are puzzles about signals in general. Why not signal the usefulness of accepting me or deferring to me, and then save myself the trouble of delivering the expected reward? And if everybody does that, why should anyone take blood donation as a sign it will pay to cultivate me? (1990:260, footnote)

Actually, my discussion was designed to show, not that a blood donor is an unconditional altruist, but that he explicitly is a conditional altruist. It is difficult to know whether Gibbard realized this or not. By my argument, blood is given only when potential, possible, likely rewards exist, whether or not they are consciously understood by anyone. The main reward is reputation, and all the benefits that high moral reputation may yield. Reputation as an altruist pays: everyone gains by the presence of beneficent people and the possibility of interacting with them, and so we tend to cultivate and reward them. In his text, Gibbard goes on to explain precisely this (p. 261): "A sense of fair dealing prompts one to cooperate, and that elicits cooperation from others. Gratitude prompts the kinds of actions that will draw more favors. Retaliation deters. These sentiments pay . . ." He then argues that judgments about fairness have to mesh among social cooperators, and that they tend to be established by discussion and interaction. He wishes to establish that our social behavior cannot be preset by the interaction of genes and parts of the environment other than our actual sociality. I expect that we all agree with him. Would that this could end the debates about determinism.

Returning to Gibbard's footnote, the reason it won't work for me just to tell you how good I am as a reciprocator, and you me, and for all of us then to act on this information, is that we are all too clever for that. We do not always mean what we say. And we also deny that we deceive—both to others and to ourselves. If Gibbard really believed what he wrote in his footnote, then one would have to expect that he would always lose in a horse trade or when buying a used car. Horse traders and used car salesmen invariably tell us what good reciprocators they are, but we had better form our own opinions or stay home.

Horse traders and used-car salesmen also tend to be notorious as examples of unscrupulous people—people who are not moral. Why? Because we imagine that they are not only out to serve their own interests but that they do what they do from entirely conscious motivations. They know what they're doing, and they do it "on purpose." This is apparently, in part, the implication that causes Frank (1988) to substitute "self interest" for "conscious self interest."

Then do the rest of us—all of us moral folk—not know what we are doing? Is that what makes us moral? Are we moral when we serve our own interests if we actually think we are serving the interests of others? Is that all it takes? In the eyes of others, pretty much so, I would say (Alexander 1987, Table 2.5, pp. 98-99), and if that is true, it means that we had better keep it that way if we wish ourselves to be judged moral.

I have now come around to the idea, expressed at the outset, that evolution is denied (one way or another) by many who know about it because of intuitive feelings about human motivation. I believe that evolutionary biologists who attempt to explicate human behavior are ignored or maligned, in many instances, because of a widespread belief that if their analyses are correct or become public the effects will be contrary to whatever people in general believe would be beneficial. We are returned to the exclamation of the wife of the Bishop Wilberforce, upon hearing of Darwin's view of evolution, that we should pray that it not be true and if it be true pray that it not become generally known.

What is the situation, then, in which the concept—the idea, practice, or realization—of morality arises? First, social reciprocity of the direct sort must be an integral part of sociality. That may not be the case in any species except our own. What is required are indefinitely continuing interactions between intelligent beings in which each can benefit from cooperating with the other, and interactions in which defection or failing to give the share that will cause the other also to benefit are possible but will in the long run represent net losses to the defector. All of this requires a great deal of social learning. Social reciprocity depends on social learning because participants in a socially reciprocal interaction change continually and only the quick and capable learner—probably only the competent and clever scenario-builder who knows and understands his interactants—can continue to cause the interaction actually to be reciprocal. So sometimes we know that we attempted a selfish act through a seemingly beneficent one and failed—failed, that is, to receive a return benefit fitting for the occasion. And we all know that even this kind of consciousness about kindnesses tends to be viewed with suspicion or skepticism. It borders closely enough on being immoral as to require great tact and care in its expression.

The second requirement for the concept of morality to arise and permeate social interactions is for *multiple* parties to be cooperative in the way that *two* parties can be, so that multiple cooperative associations are possible and reputation becomes crucial. To say that reputation becomes crucial means that those who become known as defectors lose—they are less able to locate and engage in the cooperativeness that benefits nondefectors. It means that there are multiple possible cooperators available for all so that changing associations can occur and the defectors—the immoral—can be shunned and left out, and as a result lose. When, and if, we are able to create a permanent situation like this among the nations of the world as well as within nations and smaller groups, then, I suggest, we will have reduced the problem of arms races and international competition to a manageable state.

Finally, I will attempt to state more precisely the paradox inherent in the nature of human intent and its relationship to consciousness. First, we relegate to the nonconscious cost-benefit decisions about particular social acts, perhaps in a fashion similar to our relegation to the nonconscious relatively simple acts such as typing or the playing of a musical instrument. This we can understand as part of a system for becoming able to respond quickly and certainly in ways that tell others we are likely to be good reciprocators—good social interactants. In other words we demonstrate that we are prepared to be beneficent without thinking about it, without a cold calculation of costs and benefits (Alexander 1987; Frank 1988): we develop a social conscience. Second, our nonconscious is evidently designed to expose to our social interactants at least some evidences of our honesty or lack of guile: thus we blush "inadvertently" in situations and fashions that also indicate to others that we are programmed to behave honestly or fairly or innocently. Perhaps this is a system for suggesting to others that we have acquired the already described tendencies to behave quickly and certainly as good reciprocators. Third, and considerably more problematic, our nonconscious also seems designed to expose at least some of its evidences of our *dishonesties*! We blush and shift our eyes and smile and do other things that reveal to others when we are lying or failing to tell something that we know. We do such things while we seem (to ourselves) to be striving as hard as possible not to. This is more difficult to explain, but it may represent a window into our mental activities that also implies programming for honest, guileless behavior. Knowledge of the particular situations and behaviors involved in such inadvertent expressions of intent is needed to test this question; should such behaviors appear only when a strong likelihood of being discovered in a deception exists, or when the cost of being discovered is greatest (perhaps at that moment when the conscious self is otherwise about to make a costly mistake), they could indeed have an effect beneficial to the inadvertent revealer of emotions. Fourth, and most problematic, we use the conscious and nonconscious aspects of our mentality in the particular fashions I have just described, even though consciousness itself, and the building of mental scenarios, is increasingly regarded as having evolved as social machinery; that is, as having been favored because it enabled us to manipulate others in the service of our own interests by projecting alternative behaviors that interpret and manipulate social sequences as they unfold. How does it happen that we gain from removing crucial aspects of social communication from the conscious, or perhaps never actually gaining control over nonconscious social communication, especially if consciousness evolved as a tool of social communication and a predictor of the actions of others? Is it primarily a question of timing of revealing responses? I believe that when such questions are answered, human behavior can begin to make sense in terms of an inclusive-fitness-maximizing goal for the human organism, and a significant barrier to human self-understanding will be removed.

Conclusions

The evolutionary approach to human behavior has serious problems. The most obvious is that evolution is accepted by only a minuscule proportion of the world's population. More importantly, and probably contributory, even within that minuscule proportion, many academicians and others among the intelligentsia tend to wall evolutionists off like a malignant tumor. This happens partly because a minority of thoughtful people are educated in biology, and this in turn is partly because the interaction of heredity and development is so poorly understood within biology. Also involved is the convoluted nature of human efforts to self-understand, owing not only to the fact that we must use the properties we wish to understand to carry out the analysis, but also to the nature of the evolutionary (selective) history that no one wants to hear about. It is not easy for anyone to believe, from his own thoughts about his personal motivation and that of other humans, that humans are designed by natural selection to seek their own interests,

let alone maximize their own genetic reproduction. If natural selection is being interpreted accurately by modern biologists, then it appears to have designed human motivation in social matters as to cause its understanding to be resisted powerfully.

We lose, in analyzing such problems, if we restrict ourselves to discussing only
the brighter side of human nature or pretend that the topic is cooperation *not* competition. Moral philosophers and other academicians for the most part live in pleasant
worlds, with little opaque clouds that tend to admit only the delightful aspects of human
intentionality floating above their heads as they move along the sidewalks of urbania
between their offices and their homes. But the misery in the world is not all there
because of pathologies easy to understand or proximate causes easy to remedy; nor is
it all owing to those "other" kinds of people whose motivations, unlike our own, are
pernicious and self-serving. Moreover, civilization and technology have created circumstances in which virtually all human striving, designed as it is to better the "current"
quality of life, threatens increasingly the (more distant) future of humans, or even of life
itself.

Analysts of morality must retreat from their subject far enough to examine the
reasons for its convolutedness. We must know the ways in which kindness, beneficence, and good fellowship can be selfish, and we must also understand why this idea
is repugnant and what if anything to do about that. Most important, to solve the problems human evolutionists have glimpsed so far, we must enlist a far greater proportion
of the world's thinkers. If, as knowledgeable people increasingly suggest, massive
altruism by our generations will be required to ensure the survival of later generations,
then, unless we don't care, we have to know how to modify the relevant aspects of the
striving we have evolved to accomplish. We have to know how to escape our history.
No part of biological theory has ever legitimately implied that humans cannot employ
their evolution-given traits to set and accomplish goals that are purely incidental—even
contrary—to their history of natural selection. My arguments suggest that these things
will happen only when evolution-minded people have overcome resistance to evolutionary analysis of behavior by explaining, much better than they have so far, the nature of
human motivation and the reasons for its partial concealment and seeming convolutedness.

Acknowledgments

I thank Robert Smuts and Kyle Summers for their help with ideas and concepts across
the past several years, and especially for their careful reviews and suggestions regarding

the manuscript. I also thank M. H. Nitecki for astute editorial comments.

References

Alexander, R. D. 1969. Arthropods, 167-219. In *Animal Communication,* ed. T. A. Sebeok. Bloomington, IN: University of Indiana Press.

Alexander, R. D. 1977. Evolution, human behavior, and determinism. *Proceedings of the Biennial Meeting of the Philosophy of Science Association* (1976)2:3-21.

Alexander, R. D. 1979. *Darwinism and Human Affairs.* Seattle, WA: University of Washington Press.

Alexander, R. D. 1987. *The Biology of Moral Systems.* Hawthorne, NY: Aldine de Gruyter.

Alexander, R. D. 1989. The evolution of the human psyche, 455-513. In *The Human Revolution. Behavioural and Biological Perspectives on the Origins of Modern Humans,* ed. P. Mellars and C. Stringer. Edinburgh: University of Edinburgh Press.

Alexander, R. D. 1990. Epigenetic rules and Darwinian algorithms: The adaptive study of learning and development. *Ethology and Sociobiology* 11:1-63.

Alexander, R. D. 1991. How Did Humans Evolve? Reflections on the Uniquely Unique Species. Ann Arbor, MI: *University of Michigan Museum of Zoology Special Publication* 1:iii + 38 pp.

Alexander, R. D. In press. Social learning and kin recognition: An addendum. *Ethology and Sociobiology.*

Alexander, R. D., and G. Borgia. 1978. Group selection, altruism, and the levels of organization of life. *Annual Review of Ecology and Systematics* 9:449-74.

Axelrod, R. 1984. *The Evolution of Cooperation.* New York: Basic Books.

Axelrod, R. 1986. An evolutionary approach to norms. *American Political Science Review* 80:1095-1111.

Barkow, J., L. Cosmides, and J. Tooby, eds. 1991. *The Adapted Mind: Evolutionary Psychology and the Generation of Culture.* New York: Oxford University Press.

Bierce, A. 1911. *The Devil's Dictionary.* New York: Crowell.

Boyd, R., and P. J. Richerson. 1985. *Culture and the Evolutionary Process.* Chicago: University of Chicago Press.

Cosmides, L. 1989. The logic of social exchange: Has natural selection shaped how humans reason? Studies with the Wason selection task. *Cognition* 31:187-276.

Cosmides, L., and J. Tooby. 1988. Evolutionary psychology and the generation of culture. Part II. Case study: A computational theory of social exchange. *Ethology and Sociobiology* 10:51-97.

Daly, M., and M. Wilson. 1981. Abuse and neglect of children in evolutionary perspective, 405-16. In *Natural Selection and Social Behavior. Recent Research and New Theory,* ed. R. D. Alexander and D. W. Tinkle. New York: Chiron Press.

Daly, M., and M. Wilson. 1988. *Homicide.* Hawthorne, NY: Aldine de Gruyter.

Darwin, C. R. [1859] 1967. *On the Origin of Species.* A facsimile of the first edition with an introduction by Ernst Mayr. Cambridge, MA: Harvard University Press.

Dawkins, R. 1982. *The Extended Phenotype.* San Francisco: W. H. Freeman.

Dawkins, R. 1986. *The Blind Watchmaker.* New York: Norton.

Dawkins, R. 1989. *The Selfish Gene.* New Edition. Oxford: Oxford University Press.

Dawkins, R., and J. R. Krebs. 1978. Animal signals: Information or manipulation? 282-309. In *Behavioural Ecology,* ed. J. R. Krebs and N. B. Davies. Oxford: Blackwell Scientific Publications.

Dobzhansky, T. 1961. Discussion, 111. In *Insect Polymorphism,* ed. J. S. Kennedy. London: Symposium of the Royal Entomological Society of London 1.

Fisher, R. A. [1930] 1958. *The Genetical Theory of Natural Selection.* 2d ed. New York: Dover.

Fletcher, D. J. C., and C. D. Michener, eds. 1987. *Kin Recognition in Animals.* New York: John Wiley and Sons.

Flinn, M., and R. D. Alexander. 1982. Culture theory: The developing synthesis from biology. *Human Ecology* 10:383-400.

Frank, R. H. 1988. *Passions within Reason: The Strategic Role of the Emotions.* New York: W. W. Norton.

Gautier, D. 1990. *Moral Dealing: Contract, Ethics, and Reason.* Ithaca, NY: Cornell University Press.

Gibbard, A. 1990. *Wise Choices, Apt Feelings. A Theory of Normative Judgment.* Cambridge, MA: Harvard University Press.

Gould, J. L. 1986. The biology of learning. *Annual Review of Psychology* 37:163-92.

Haldane, J. B. S. 1955. Population genetics. *New Biology* 18:34-51.

Hamilton, W. D. 1964. The genetical evolution of social behaviour. I, II. *Journal of Theoretical Biology* 7:1-52.

Hamilton, W. D. 1966. The moulding of senescence by natural selection. *Journal of Theoretical Biology* 12:12-45.

Hayles, N. K. 1990. *Chaos Bound: Orderly Disorder in Contemporary Literature and Science.* Ithaca, NY: Cornell University Press.

Hepper, P. G., ed. In press. *Kin Recognition.* Cambridge: Cambridge University Press.

Hinde, R. A., and J. Stevenson-Hinde, eds. 1973. *Constraints on Learning: Limitations and Predispositions.* New York: Academic Press.

Holmes, W., and P. W. Sherman. 1983. Kin recognition in animals. *American Scientist* 71:46-55.

Humphrey, N. K. 1976. The social function of intellect, 303-18. In *Growing Points in Ethology,* ed. P. P. G. Bateson and R. A. Hinde. London: Cambridge University Press.

Huxley, T. H. [1896] 1909. *Autobiography and Selected Essays.* New York: Houghton Mifflin.

Johnston, T. D. 1982. Selective costs and benefits in the evolution of learning. *Advances in the Study of Behavior* 12:65-106.

Johnston, T. D. 1985. Learning and evolution. *Scientific Progress* (Oxford) 69:443-60.

Lloyd, J. E. 1977. Bioluminescence and communication, 164-83. In *How Animals Communicate,* ed. T. A. Sebeok. Bloomington, IN: Indiana University Press.

Lumsden, C. J., and E. O. Wilson. 1981. *Genes, Mind, and Culture: The Co-Evolutionary Process.* Cambridge, MA: Harvard University Press.

Murphy, J. G. 1982. *Evolution, Morality, and the Meaning of Life.* Totowa, NJ: Rowman and Littlefield.

Otte, D. 1974. Effects and functions in the evolution of signaling systems. *Annual Review of Ecology and Systematics* 5:385-417.

Rawls, J. 1971. *A Theory of Justice.* Cambridge, MA: Harvard University Press.

Rodseth, L. 1990. Prestige, hunger, and love: Plumbing the psychology of sexual meanings. *Michigan Discussions in Anthropology* 9:1-21.

Sahlins, M. 1965. On the sociology of primitive exchange, 139-236. In *The Relevance of Models for Social Anthropology,* ed. M. Banton. London: Tavistock.

Simon, H. A. 1990. A mechanism for social selection and successful altruism. *Science* 250:1665-68.

Skinner, B. F. 1965. *Science and Human Behavior.* New York: The Free Press.

Symons, D. 1987. If we're all Darwinians, what's the fuss about? 121-46. In *Sociobiology and Psychology,* ed. C. Crawford, M. Smith, and D. Krebs. Hillsdale, NJ: Erlbaum Publishers.

Thorpe, W. H. 1950. The modern concept of instinctive behaviour. *Bulletin of Animal Behaviour* 1(7):2-12.

Thorpe, W. H. 1951. The definition of terms used in animal behaviour studies. *Bulletin of Animal Behaviour* 1(9):34-40.

Tierney, A. J. 1986. The evolution of learned and innate behavior: Contributions from genetics and neurobiology to a theory of behavioral evolution. *Animal Learning and Behavior* 14:339-48.

Tooby, J., and L. Cosmides. 1988. Evolutionary psychology and the generation of culture. Part I. The oretical Considerations. *Ethology and Sociobiology* 10:529-49.

Trivers, R. L. 1971. The evolution of reciprocal altruism. *Quarterly Review of Biology* 46:35-57.

Waddington, C. H. 1956. *Principles of Embryology.* New York: Macmillan.

Waldman, B., P. C. Frumhoff, and P. W. Sherman. 1988. Problems of kin recognition. *Trends in Ecology and Evolution* 3:8-13.

West-Eberhard, M. J. 1987. Flexible strategy and social evolution, 35-51. In *Animal Societies: Theories and Facts,* ed. Y. Ito, J. L. Brown, and J. Kikkawa. Tokyo: Japan Scientific Society Press 1.

Williams, G. C. 1957. Pleiotropy, natural selection, and the evolution of senescence. *Evolution* 11:398-411.

Williams, G. C. 1966. *Adaptation and Natural Selection*. Princeton, NJ: Princeton University Press.

Williams, G. C. 1989. A sociobiological expansion of *Evolution and Ethics,* 179-214. In *Evolution and Ethics*, ed. J. Paradis and G. C. Williams. Princeton, NJ: Princeton University Press.

Williams, G. C., and D. C. Williams. 1957. Natural selection of individually harmful social adaptations among sibs with special reference to social insects. *Evolution* 11:32-39.

Philosophical Skepticism

Evolutionary Altruism, Psychological Egoism, and Morality: Disentangling the Phenotypes

Elliott Sober

What Is in a Word?

During the opening round of the sociobiology debate, critics complained that socio-biologists applied human characteristics to the nonhuman world, invented evolutionary explanations of those characteristics for the nonhuman cases, and then read those stories back into the human species. Terms such as "rape" and "slave-making" are ordinarily understood to apply to human beings. Sociobiologists broadened the terms' applications to include nonhuman examples. They then invented evolutionary explanations of rape and slave-making that were said to apply to other species. Finally, these stories were claimed to explain rape and slave-making in our species. The double accusation was that this strategy anthropomorphizes nonhuman organisms and, so to speak, animalizes human beings (Allen et al. 1978).

Defenders of sociobiology replied that there is nothing wrong with extending vocabulary in this way. Concepts like "parental care" and "altruism" were originally used to describe human beings, but there is nothing wrong with extending the terms to nonhuman organisms. Indeed, this is just what happened to the term "selection." The term was first used to imply conscious human sorting, but Darwin proposed that it be used in a "wider and metaphorical sense." It is undeniable that this extension of the term's domain of application turned out to be enormously fruitful. Prohibiting such novel use of language would tie science into a terminological straitjacket.

What general lessons can we extract from this exchange? Were critics of socio-biology simply indulging in a kind of linguistic puritanism? I think not. Although we often dismiss questions about terminology as "merely semantic," the use of language can carry substantive theoretical presuppositions. True, there can be no *general* prohi-bition against redefining terms first introduced for human beings so that they apply to the rest of the living world. But this does not mean that each and every such extension is unproblematic. The legitimacy of such extensions must be examined on a case-by-case basis.

The familiar biological distinction of *homology* and *homoplasy* allows us to see what is at issue here. When two species have a trait in common because each inherited it from a common ancestor, the similarity is said to be homologous. When the two traits are consequences of separate origination events, the similarity is a homoplasy.

Within the category of homoplasy, I want to distinguish two subcases. When a trait originates independently in two lineages, this may be because similar processes were at work in the two lineages, or because quite dissimilar processes happened to yield the same endproduct. The distinction I have in mind can be understood by considering two simple examples.

Birds have wings and so do bats. Although they did not derive this trait from a common ancestor,[1] the same kind of causal process (suppose, for the sake of argument) drove the evolution of wings in the two lineages. Wings evolved in both cases because wings facilitate flight and natural selection favored the ability to fly. For want of a better term, I will call similarities of this sort *functional similarities*.

In contrast, consider the fact that lizards are green and so are ferns. Not only is this similarity not a homology; in addition, the causal processes responsible for the evolution of greenness in the two lineages were entirely different in kind. This sort of similarity I will call an *accidental similarity*.

My contrast between functional and accidental similarities is not the same as the more familiar distinction between parallelism and convergence. A homoplasy is a parallelism when the descendants are about as similar as the ancestors were; it is a convergence when the descendants are more similar than the ancestors. If two descendant species independently evolved limbs that have four digits, the similarity will be a parallelism if their ancestors both had two digits, but a convergence if one ancestor had three and the other five. Notice that parallelism and convergence are defined by comparing ancestors and descendants, not by comparing the kinds of processes that mediate the evolution of descendants from ancestors. Whether the similarity in digit number in the descendants is a parallelism or a convergence, the question is open whether the causal processes that produced the end result were similar or different. The concepts of homology, functional similarity, and accidental similarity are depicted in figure 1.

When an existing term is redefined in science, there should be a reason for doing so. For example, if the term "rape" is to be applied to nonhuman organisms, this implies that those nonhuman cases have something significant in common with the human cases to which the term is ordinarily applied. Of course, sociobiologists have not suggested that human rape and rape in ducks are homologs. But they do argue that the traits exhibit a functional similarity. The evolutionary explanation of rape in ducks is

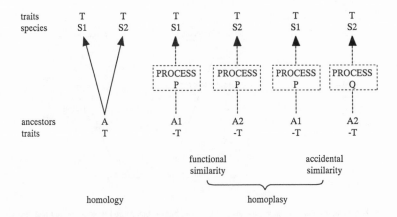

Figure 1. A similarity between two species is *homologous* if it was obtained unmodified from a common ancestor. If the similarity independently evolved in the two lineages, it is termed a *homoplasy*. Within the category of homoplasy, a similarity is said to be *functional* when it resulted from the same processes operating on the two lineages; when entirely different kinds of process produced a common end result, the similarity is said to be *accidental*.

said to have much in common with the evolutionary explanation of rape among human beings (Barash 1979).

Critics of this sociobiological position attack the extension of the term to the nonhuman case because they believe that the human and the nonhuman cases have nothing very significant in common. Even if forced copulation has a reproductive explanation in ducks, it has been suggested that the variety of acts we term *rape* in human beings are to be understood as acts of violence, not as having a reproductive function at all. The similarity is only superficial; it is, in my terminology, accidental.

So the dispute about terminology reflects a deeper and substantive disagreement about the way the world is. The sociobiological use of the term "rape" reflects a conjecture—that the explanation of rape in humans and of "rape" in other species has something significant in common. And critics of this usage are thereby expressing a conjecture of their own—that human rape and forced copulation among ducks are not similar in their evolutionary origins. The issue is not linguistic invention versus linguistic conservatism; the issue is functional similarity on the one hand versus accidental similarity on the other (Sober 1985).

It is important to realize that this dispute is not about the psychological motives that rapists have. Sociobiologists are not claiming that rapists consciously seek to maximize their reproductive success. What goes on in the rapist's mind constitutes the

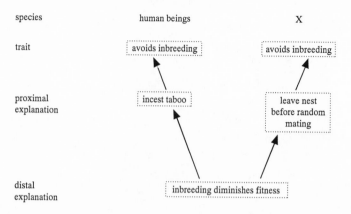

Figure 2. A behavior (such as incest avoidance) found in human beings and in some nonhuman species may have the same distal explanation, although the behavior may have different modes of proximal implementation in the two species.

proximal mechanism behind the rape. Sociobiologists are interested in identifying the more distal explanation of the behavior, not its proximal cause.

This distinction—between proximal and distal explanation—has been set forth by Ernst Mayr (1961).[2] Let me illustrate this idea by turning to another standard sociobiological example. Modern human beings engage in incest avoidance. To a large extent, they outbreed; they rarely have children with close relatives. The same is true for a variety of other species. It has been suggested that there is an evolutionary explanation of this behavior; outbreeding diminishes the chance that one's offspring will possess deleterious recessives in double dose.

This is the distal explanation of the behavior. But what is the proximal cause? In human beings, the behavior is frequently mediated by a *system of beliefs*—by an incest *taboo*. In another species (call it species *X*), the behavior's proximate cause may be entirely nonmental. Perhaps individuals in species *X* leave the nest before mating at random. The effect is that individuals rarely mate with close relatives. The pattern of explanation at work here is illustrated in figure 2.

I do not mention this explanation to endorse it, but to set forth its logic.[3] The strategy of explanation is entirely typical in sociobiology. A distal evolutionary explanation is offered for some behavior. When the behavior occurs among human beings, it is suggested that the mind provides a proximal mechanism for implementing the behavioral regularity. The fact that we have minds does not complicate or confound the evolutionary explanation; rather the mind is a convenient addendum to the evolutionary account.

There is another role that the mind can play, however, one that I think sociobiologists have underestimated. A characteristic may evolve for a given evolutionary reason, but then have consequences that would not be at all foreseeable if only the evolutionary explanation were taken into account.

Consider the connection between copulation and pleasure that exists in our species and arguably in others.[4] There obviously is an evolutionary explanation for why organisms mate. But for natural selection to make this happen, the organisms must be equipped with a proximal mechanism that gets them to do the right things. Many human societies failed to grasp the connection between copulation and reproduction; the same is doubtless true of our primate relatives. True belief is not needed as a proximal mechanism; pleasure seems to have worked just fine.

My point is to ask you to consider the consequences that genital pleasure have had in our own species. Pleasure is a powerful motivator, and we have been clever enough to figure out ways of securing it that have nothing much to do with reproduction. I won't bother to cite chapter and verse from the *Kama Sutra*. But it is a remarkable fact that so much of the activities we label "sexual" do not contribute to reproduction. Some may even diminish reproductive success.

Another, perhaps parallel, example is *eating*. Food is needed for survival, so there is an obvious evolutionary explanation for why we eat. But this distal explanation needs to be supplemented with a proximal one. *Hunger* is an important, though not exclusive, proximal cause. I say that it is not exclusive, because *pleasure* also seems to have found its way into the machinery. The results have been explosive. There is no need to cite chapter and verse from Brillat-Savarin for you to see the point. Think of the vast arenas of culinary activity that are disconnected from the biological need for sustenance.

Sex and food are categories of human endeavor. Both categories include some behaviors that are unique to human beings and others that we share with other species. Sociobiologists typically use broad definitions of behavior, so that the behavior thus defined is not uniquely human. Much of what we include under the heading of sex and food in common parlance is thereby pushed into the shadows, as not part of the "real" phenomenon at all. By broadening the definitions of the behaviors, we perhaps can obtain an *explanandum* that is tractable from an evolutionary point of view. The danger is that we may confuse this part with the whole from which it was extracted. There is much to food and sex that goes beyond the evolutionary explanation of why we eat and copulate.

This general preamble about sociobiology is intended to set the stage for a discussion of the relevance of evolutionary considerations for morality. Sociobiologists tend to use a rather "thin" definition of morality, one which allows them to see a continuity between "morality" in our own species and "morality" in other species. I do not wish to argue that this is necessarily a mistake. Perhaps abstracting away from various details of what we commonly call "morality" will lead to some scientific insights. My worry is that we forget what we have left behind. We relegate what is peculiarly human to the shadows, claim that we have an evolutionary explanation of "morality" (so defined), and think that what is unexplained is of peripheral importance.

One way to thin the concept of morality is to equate morality and altruism. Put in its starkest form, the argument I want to consider is this:

Morality involves altruism.

Evolutionary theory explains the evolution of altruism.

———————

Hence, evolutionary theory explains morality.

There is an analogy between this argument and similar ones pertaining to sex or food. Sex, in its vernacular sense, includes reproduction. And food provides nutrition. But it is a long jump from these truisms to the conclusion that evolutionary theory can help us understand the *Kama Sutra* or Brillat-Savarin.

I now want to explain some of the gaps I see between the concepts of morality and altruism. Indeed, there are three concepts here that need to be disentangled, not just two. Evolutionists use the terms "altruism" and "selfishness" in a way that differs from the usage found in ordinary parlance. So my goal is to separate evolutionary altruism, psychological altruism, and morality. The point is not to claim that they have no bearing on each other. Rather, there are a variety of empirical issues concerning how they are connected. These empirical issues will become clear only if the concepts are not elided.

Evolutionary Altruism

Evolutionists speak of altruism and selfishness. The terms also occur in ordinary language and in the theories of social psychologists. One difference between the evolutionary and the psychological concepts is straightforward. You don't have to have a mind to be altruistic or selfish in the evolutionary sense. Evolutionary altruists confer fitness benefits on others at their own expense. Consider a plant that leaches an insecticide into the soil. Suppose the insecticide benefits neighbors as much as it benefits the plant that produces it. This means that a free-rider plant can enjoy the benefits of protection from insects without incurring the energetic costs of producing the chemical. In this case, the plant that produces the insecticide is altruistic and the free-rider plant is selfish, even though neither plant has a mind.

In contrast, the psychological concepts of altruism and selfishness describe the motives that people have—whether and how much they care about the welfare of others. The evolutionary concepts are purely behavioral—what matters is the fitness consequences of the action. The proximal cause of the action—whether it is driven by benevolent motives, selfish motives, or by no motives at all—does not matter to the evolutionary concepts.

Evolutionists have described a number of possible mechanisms that allow "helping behavior" to evolve by natural selection. If you help your own children, or, by extension, your own kin, it is hardly puzzling how natural selection can favor this sort of donation. Similarly, if you help individuals who reciprocate and you punish individuals who do not, it is not hard to see how there can be a net fitness advantage in this pattern of behavior. And even when the recipients are nonrelatives and there is no mechanism to ensure reciprocation, there are possible evolutionary scenarios that allow the trait to evolve. Regardless of which of these processes occurs, it is quite clear that helping behavior—even helping deleterious to self—is something that evolutionists have learned to explain.

There is considerable disagreement among biologists about how evolutionary altruism should be defined. I will not enter into this dispute, but will explore some consequences of the definition I prefer. The nuances of the definitional issue will not affect the main conclusions I want to draw.

A trait is altruistic in the evolutionary sense if two conditions are satisfied. First, bearers of the trait are less fit than nonbearers of the trait within the same group. Second, groups of altruists have a higher average fitness than groups of selfish individuals (Sober 1984, 1989). These two ideas are summarized in figure 3.

It follows from this definition that not all helping behavior counts as evolutionarily altruistic. Helping one's own offspring is to the selfish advantage of parents, since a parent's fitness depends on its reproductive success. Similarly, helping others and punishing those who fail to reciprocate may fail to be an example of evolutionary altruism, if this trait is fitter than the alternative behavior of not helping or of not punishing cheaters. As Trivers (1971) remarked, reciprocal altruism takes the altruism

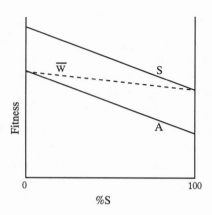

Figure 3. Trait *A* is altruistic and *S* is selfish, according to the evolutionary meanings of those terms, when two conditions are satisfied. Within any group, selfish individuals are on average fitter than altruists; groups of altruists have a higher average fitness (represented by *W*) than groups of selfish individuals.

out of altruism.

More fundamentally, evolutionary altruism cannot evolve by a process of Darwinian selection that occurs within the confines of a single persisting population. Altruism requires group selection. Groups must compete against other groups; they must experience unequal rates of extinction (death) and of founding colonies (reproduction). Only then can the disadvantage that altruists suffer within groups be offset by the advantage that a group of altruists has over a group of selfish individuals.

So to ask whether human beings are evolutionary altruists is to ask a question about the kind of selection processes that occurred in the human lineage. If human beings evolved by group selection, we may have various altruistic traits. If we evolved by purely Darwinian individual selection, then we are selfish in the evolutionary sense of that term.

To say that people are altruistic or selfish in the evolutionary sense is to describe the consequences of their behavior for their own and for others' fitness. It is to say nothing about the proximal mechanisms that produce the behavior. As noted before, a plant can be altruistic or selfish in the evolutionary sense, even though a plant does not have a mind. And human beings, who act on the basis of motives, can produce behaviors that have altruistic or selfish fitness consequences by way of a variety of motivational structures.

We now need to see that the psychological concepts of altruism and selfishness are quite independent of the evolutionary concepts that go by the same names. There is no simple relation between the distal evolutionary explanation of a behavior and the proximal explanation of why the behavior occurs. A given distal end can be achieved by a variety of proximal devices. If we are evolutionary altruists, we may be psychological altruists *or* psychological egoists. And if we are evolutionarily selfish, the question is also left open as to whether we are psychological altruists *or* psychological egoists. To make good this claim, I now must describe how these psychological categories should be understood.

Psychological Egoism

The thesis that we are psychological egoists is a claim about the motives we have; it concerns the proximal causes of behavior, not the evolutionary origins of those proximal mechanisms. In particular, the thesis of psychological egoism asserts that the benefits we sometimes provide for others are merely instrumental; our ultimate motive in all our actions is to secure some benefit for ourselves.

These benefits to self may take a variety of forms. There is money, status, and power. In addition, there is the attainment of pleasure and the avoidance of pain or discomfort. Often we help others at some cost to ourselves. But, according to the thesis of psychological egoism, when we look more carefully, we can discern a psychical reward. Behaviors that apparently are altruistic in fact allow people to avoid feeling guilty and to think well of themselves. The benefit that someone else receives from the help is a mere by-product, not a goal.

I believe that this thesis is empirically false as a generality about human motivation. People often have noninstrumental preferences about the welfare of others. True, we do care about our own welfare. What I deny is that this is the only thing we care about.

I will describe briefly a format for thinking about this issue (see Sober 1989 for fuller discussion). First, I need to distinguish *self-directed* from *other-directed* preferences. A self-directed preference describes what one wants for one's self, but does not say anything about the welfare of others. An example would be my wanting to have more money rather than less. An other-directed preference describes what one wants for others, but does not say anything about what one wants for one's self. An example would be my desire that some other person have more money rather than less. Of course, this division is not exhaustive. In addition to self-directed and other-directed preferences, some preferences are *mixed*. An example would be my preferring that you and I be equally well-off.

Consider a model of behavior according to which agents perform that action, among the ones thought to be available, that most satisfies their preferences. I want to describe four possible relationships that might obtain among a person's self-directed and other-directed preferences. These are depicted in figure 4. The numbers in each case represent a preference ranking; their absolute values have no significance.

Extreme Altruists, as I will use the term, do not care at all about their own well-being. The only thing that matters is the welfare of the other person. Symmetrically, Extreme Egoists do not care at all about whether the other person is better off or worse; the only thing that matters to Extreme Egoists is their own well-being.

I doubt very much that people are very often well described by either of these constructs. Flesh and blood people typically have both self-directed and other-directed preferences. They care about themselves *and* about others. The Extreme Altruist and the Extreme Egoist have in common the fact that each cares about only one thing. Such single-factor theories of human motivation are rather unrealistic.

Of greater interest are the preference structures that I label Moderate Altruism and Moderate Egoism. Both these individuals have both self-directed and other-directed preferences. They would rather be better off than worse off; they also prefer that other people be better off rather than worse.

Moderate Altruists and Moderate Egoists differ as to whether self-interest is more important than the welfare of others. This is most clearly seen when an agent confronts an *antidiagonal choice situation* (i.e., when the choice is between upper-right and lower-left). Suppose you find yourself in a zero sum game. There is a cookie that would be good for you to have and also would be good for the other person to have. If you obtain the benefit, the other person goes without. In such circumstances, egoists place themselves first. Altruists, in contrast, sacrifice their own welfare so that the other person can have the benefit.[5]

There are two characteristics that are common to all four preferences structures. In each case, agents choose the action that maximizes their preferences. This is a feature of the model that is not specific to egoism. In other words, the fact that people do what they most want to do does not establish that people are egoists.

The second feature of the model is more interesting. Suppose you face a choice between the two options on the main diagonal (i.e., the choice is between upper-left and lower-right). You can help someone else and receive a benefit to self; or you can deny the other person a benefit and also deny yourself. The point to notice is that the four preference structures predict the very same choice. All say that the agent will prefer

EXTREME ALTRUISM		
	Other-directed preference	
	+	-
Self-directed preference +	4	1
Self-directed preference -	4	1

MODERATE ALTRUISM		
	Other-directed preference	
	+	-
Self-directed preference +	4	2
Self-directed preference -	3	1

MODERATE EGOISM		
	Other-directed preference	
	+	-
Self-directed preference +	4	3
Self-directed preference -	2	1

EXTREME EGOISM		
	Other-directed preference	
	+	-
Self-directed preference +	4	4
Self-directed preference -	1	1

Figure 4. Psychological altruism and selfishness are defined in terms of the weight given to self-interest and the welfare of others in a person's motivational structure. A person decides which action to perform by seeing which of the actions that are available most satisfies the person's preferences.

upper-left over lower-right.

Let us consider a concrete situation. Suppose you are thumbing through a magazine and come across an advertisement that asks you to contribute to a charity that helps starving children. The picture in the ad is quite pathetic. You write a check and send some money to the charity.

Why did you do this? Was it purely because you cared that the situation of the children be improved? Was it purely because you wanted to feel good about yourself and avoid feeling guilty? Or was it a mixture of the two? In this last case, in which your motives were mixed, which one was more important? Although additional possibilities might be considered, let's limit ourselves to these alternatives.

None of these questions are answered by the simple fact that you mailed the check. I leave it to the scientific imagination to design an experiment that would provide data that would help decide whether you were an Extreme Altruist, an Extreme Egoist, a Moderate Altruist, or a Moderate Egoist in this circumstance.

Clearly people are not altruists in all choice situations. Few of us would die to make someone smile. And few of us are selfish in all choice situations. These four motivational structures do not describe enduring personality types. Rather, they describe the ways an individual might be motivated in a given choice situation. Change the choices and the motivations may change.

What does welfare mean in the format I have suggested? Agents want things for themselves; they also believe that some things will benefit others. These self-directed and other-directed preferences need have nothing to do with what will actually benefit self or other. Still less do they have to correlate with evolutionary fitness. I may regard a package of contraceptives as something that would be good for you to have and also as good for me to have. If we face a zero sum game, and if I give the contraceptives to you, I may have behaved altruistically. The fact that I may have reduced your reproductive success by my donation is irrelevant. Again, recall that these psychological concepts concern motives, not the actual consequences of the actions produced by the motives.

How Are the Psychological and the Evolutionary
Concepts Related?

Psychological altruism and psychological egoism are different sorts of preference structure. Evolutionary altruism and evolutionary egoism are behaviors that are distinguished by their different fitness consequences. How, then, are the psychological and the evolutionary concepts related? The main point to grasp is that the two levels of description are logically independent of each other.

Suppose for the sake of argument that we have evolved by group selection and that many of our behaviors exist because they are beneficial for the group to which we belong. How might Mother Nature have wired us up to get us to behave in this way? That is, which proximal mechanisms could produce behaviors that have this sort of distal explanation?

One possibility is that we should be psychological altruists. We might have preferences concerning the welfare of others and we might in various circumstances accord those preferences stronger weight than the preferences we have about our own welfare.

But there is another way to get us to sacrifice our own fitness for the sake of the group. Suppose we have a psychology in which we act only to maximize our own pleasure and minimize our own pain, but we happen to take pleasure when others are well-off and feel pain when they are not. Under this scenario, we would be psychological egoists through and through, while all the time being evolutionary altruists.

A similar set of options is available for the motivational structures we might have if we were selfish in the evolutionary sense. Let us suppose for the sake of argument that we have evolved by a process of individual selection; the behaviors that evolved in this process are ones that maximize the fitness of their bearers. What sort of motivational structure might serve as the proximal cause of such behaviors?

One possibility is that people care only about gaining pleasure and avoiding pain. Psychological egoism of this sort might lead to behaviors that maximize an individual's fitness.

But there is another motivational structure that also would serve. Suppose we genuinely care about some other people. These others may include one's children and spouse. The preferences we have about these others may be psychologically irreducible; at no level do we think of these people as mere instruments for advancing our own self-interest. It is possible that such preferences should lead to behaviors that maximize individual fitness. Caring irreducibly for one's offspring and for one's spouse may have been advantageous in evolution. In this case, we would be psychological altruists though we would be selfish in the evolutionary sense.

I do not think it is plausible to view the mind as a mere passive implementation of evolutionary imperatives. Perhaps we have evolved by exclusively individual selection or by group selection, but neither of these possibilities entails that each and every behavior can be explained by that evolution. My point is that even if we adopt an unrealistically strong picture of the mind as a proximal cause of behaviors shaped by natural selection, there still will be considerable slack between the evolutionary and the psychological levels.

Morality

Having separated evolutionary altruism and egoism from psychological altruism and egoism, I now want to consider how each is related to morality. Evolutionists, from Darwin (1871) to the present, have noted that morality often leads to individual self-sacrifice. Darwin came as close as he ever came to a group-selection hypothesis when he proposed to explain how such self-sacrificial behavior evolved. More recent theorists have tried to avoid group-selection hypotheses and so have tried to demonstrate a selfish payoff for apparently self-sacrificial behaviors (Alexander 1987). Although the evolutionary explanations differ, the basic strategy is the same. The evolutionist's problem of "explaining morality" is the problem of showing how the self-sacrificing behavior that morality sometimes requires could have evolved. Belief in a moral system is simply the proximal mechanism that natural selection has favored as a device for producing behaviors that have an evolutionary rationale.

Let us suppose for the moment that some such explanation is true. What I wish to emphasize is what the explanation omits. Belief in morality may promote self-sacrifice, but so may many other proximal mechanisms. The evolutionary story just described does not explain why morality evolved *rather than some other proximal mechanism* that could have achieved the same end. Whatever is specific to morality within this class is not illuminated by the explanation.

This omission is characteristic of many functional explanations deployed in evolutionary theory. When evolutionists explain why an ivy plant grows towards the light, they focus on the selective advantages of phototropism. A plant physiologist, on the other hand, will describe the mechanisms inside the plant that allow it to grow along a light gradient. The plant physiologist thereby fails to address the evolutionary question. But symmetrically, it also is true that the evolutionist has failed to address an important question about the proximal mechanism. Even if it is true that phototropism is selectively advantageous, this fails to explain why the plant possesses one proximal mechanism for achieving this end *rather than any other.*[6] It also fails to illuminate how the physiology of the plant manages to generate the behavior.

A second incompleteness in the evolutionary account is that viewing morality as a proximal mechanism for producing self-sacrifice does not explain features of morality beyond the fact that it sometimes leads to self-sacrifice. To the degree that "morality" is a complex phenotype encompassing a multiplicity of characteristics, we run the risk of thinking we have explained the whole when we have explained only a part.

To illustrate what is at stake here, I want to conclude by highlighting one aspect of morality that strikes me as very important, which is glossed over when one equates morality and altruism. This is the *impersonality* of moral rules. By this I mean that people generally recognize that what is right for them to do is right for anyone else to do who is similarly situated. This recognition does not mean that people automatically treat others as they would wish to be treated themselves. Rather, the principle is a fulcrum; it can lead either to a conclusion of equal entitlement or to a conclusion of relevant difference. That is, people constrained by this idea of impersonality feel obliged to find some relevant difference between self and other, if they do not wish to grant another individual the same entitlements they see themselves as enjoying. The impersonality of moral rules leads to rationalization just as much as it leads to reciprocity.

It isn't just modern "universalistic moralities" that have this feature; the idea can be found in "tribal moralities" as well. A tribe may circumscribe the moral universe so that members of the tribe are treated as important, whereas nonmembers are not. The rules governing behavior will still be impersonal, if individuals believe that nonmembers of the tribe would have had moral standing if they had been members. Indeed, even a contemporary morality that views all human beings as having equal standing may still draw the line at nonhuman animals. Again, the constraint of impersonality requires people who take this position to produce some relevant difference that shows why humans and nonhumans are to be treated differently.

It is important to see how this idea of morality is and is not connected to the concepts of altruism and selfishness discussed above. Evolutionists have emphasized the part of morality that requires us to behave altruistically. But no morality requires limitless altruism. Almost all require that an individual sometimes place self ahead of other.

Let me describe an example that is easily recognizable within our own common morality. Suppose you possess a drug that is in short supply. For you, the drug is a matter of life or death. However, there is another person who will be mildly benefitted by having the drug, but who will get along quite well without it. Suppose the circumstances are such that one of you, but not the other, will get to take the drug. What action does morality require here?

Most of us would conclude that morality dictates that you are entitled to keep the drug for yourself. Here you are placing yourself ahead of the other person. You are declining to act altruistically.

Morality is not the same as altruism. Morality is not something that stands in opposition to selfishness. Rather, altruism and selfishness are on one level, whereas psychological altruism and psychological egoism described above concerns whether self-directed or other-directed preferences receive the greater weight. Individuals may be altruistic or selfish without moral considerations playing any role at all. Morality comes into the picture as a possible guide to the preferences we should have. Morality says *whether* and *why* we should place others ahead of ourselves or ourselves ahead of others.

Morality sometimes tell us to act altruistically; at other times, it tells us to give pride of place to self-interest. But if morality is impersonal, it connects selfishness and altruism in a very special way. If morality tells us that we should give first priority to our own interests in a given situation, it also tells us that if we were to switch roles with the other person involved, we then would be required to be altruistic (Nagel 1970). Morality does not rule out selfishness. What it rules out is *selfishness come what may.* It rules out a kind of selfishness that is totally insensitive to the situations of self and other. Symmetrically, I also would suggest that morality rules out a kind of willful and unconditional *altruism.* Always putting yourself last, no matter what the circumstances happen to be, seems to violate the constraint of impersonality.

I am not claiming that this aspect of morality cannot have an evolutionary explanation. What I am trying to emphasize is that morality and altruism are not the same. The idea that morality evolved as a device for insuring altruism (or apparent altruism), therefore, does not explain this property of the phenotype under consideration.

It might be useful if we stopped talking altogether about "explaining morality." By this I do not mean that evolutionary and social scientific inquiries should stop. Rather, my point is that "explaining morality" is too crude a specification of the problem. Morality includes a variety of characteristics. We need to say which of these is the object of our inquiries. Evolutionary considerations may have more pertinence to some of these traits than to others. Just as there is more to sex than reproduction and more to food than nutrition, so there is more to morality than altruism. If we can avoid the mistake of thinking we have explained the whole when we have explained only the part, we may yet be able to advance our understanding of what morality is and where it came from.

Notes

1. Of course, there are some elements in the wings in the the lineages that are homologies. But the property of having wings—roughly of having a surface stretched over forelimbs—was not present in the most recent common ancestor of bats and birds.

2. Mayr contrasts "proximal" and "ultimate" explanation, but I use the more neutral term "distal" to characterize evolutionary explanations. I wish to avoid the suggestion that evolutionary explanations of human behavior are always deeper or more important than explanations in psychology.

3. A few questions about this explanation bear mentioning: Lots of incest occurs among human beings. Why is the appropriate problem to explain why incest is so rare rather than to explain why it is so common? And even if the evolutionary explanation of incest *avoidance* were correct, the question would remain why this behavior is regulated by an incest *taboo*. A third problem concerns the empirical support for the claim that incest avoidance and incest taboos are universal. See Hartung's (1985) critique of Shepher's (1983) argument.

4. See de Waal (1984) for discussion of sexual behavior in chimps.

5. It may be asked why those I call Moderate Egoists should be termed Egoists, since such individuals have preferences about the welfare of others. The reason is that these individuals refuse to sacrifice their own welfare for the sake of another's, when the two come into conflict. Since they are incapable of altruistic action, I think it apposite to call them Egoists.

6. My point here is not that evolutionary theory cannot address this question, but just that the simple functional explanation of why phototropism evolved does not do so. Presumably, historical constraints account for which of the possible mechanisms for achieving phototropism evolved.

References

Allen, E., et al. 1978. Sociobiology—Another biological determinism, 280-90. Reprinted in *The Sociobiology Debate*, ed. A. Caplan. New York: Harper and Row.

Alexander, R. 1987. *The Biology of Moral Systems*. New York: Aldine de Gruyter.

Barash, D. 1979. *The Whisperings Within*. London: Penguin.

Darwin, C. [1871] 1981. *The Descent of Man, and Selection in Relation to Sex*. Reprint. Princeton, NJ: Princeton University Press.

Hartung, J. 1985. Review of Shepher's *Incest: A Biosocial View*. *American Journal of Physical Anthropology* 67:169-71.

Mayr, E. [1961] 1988. Cause and effect in biology. *Science* 134:1501-6. Reprinted in *Towards a New Philosophy of Biology*, ed. E. Mayr. Cambridge, MA: Harvard University Press.

Nagel, T. 1970. *The Possibility of Altruism*. Oxford: Oxford University Press.

Shepher, J. 1983. *Incest: A Biosocial View*. New York: Academic Press.

Sober, E. 1984. *The Nature of Selection*. Cambridge, MA: MIT Press.

Sober, E. 1985. Methodological behaviorism, evolution, and game theory, 181-200. In *Sociobiology and Epistemology*, ed. J. Fetzer. Dordrecht, North Holland: Reidel Publishing Co.

Sober, E. 1988. What is evolutionary altruism? 75-99. In *New Essays on Philosophy and Biology*, ed. B. Linsky and M. Matthen. *Canadian Journal of Philosophy*. Suppl. Vol. 14.

Sober, E. 1989. What is psychological egoism? *Behaviorism* 17:89-102.

Trivers, R. 1971. The evolution of reciprocal altruism. *Quarterly Review of Biology* 46:35-57.

Waal, F. B. M. de. 1984. *Chimpanzee Politics*. New York: Harper.

Mother Nature Is a Wicked Old Witch

George C. Williams

> Let us understand, once for all, that the ethical progress of society depends, not on imitating
> the cosmic process, still less in running away from it, but in combating it.
> — Thomas H. Huxley 1894:83

I agree with Huxley's statement, but others do not. Romantic traditions persist in finding practical lessons and moral directives in natural phenomena and, at least by implication, in urging back-to-nature sentiments or in somehow imitating the cosmic process. Others prefer to run away, or at least turn their backs on nature's hostility and pretend it is not there. Their main method is to use the verbal camouflage of nice names for adverse conditions or ethically unacceptable actions. This chapter attempts to support Huxley's position, that the universe is hostile to human life and values, and to counter prevalent romanticism and what Lillie (1913) called the "biocentric" view of the universe.

The idea that the universe is expressly designed to be a suitable abode for life in general and especially for human life is, of course, an old one. It had to be abandoned in its early forms with the triumph of Copernican astronomy in the Renaissance, but some scholars still find it possible to argue that the Earth, at least, could be regarded as especially suited for human life. This idea found eloquent expression in Henderson's (1913) *The Fitness of the Environment*. Its main modern manifestation is in the Gaia concept of Lovelock (1979, 1988; Lovelock and Margulis 1974).

The Unfitness of the Cosmic Environment

I will be concerned mainly with the Earth and with material properties shown under physical conditions found on the surface of this planet, but it may foster a balanced perspective to begin at a more macroscopic level. A clear message may be read in the fact that our galaxy is an infinitesimal part of the universe, the solar system a minuscule part of the galaxy, the Earth only about a hundred-thousandth part of the solar system, and the biologically relevant part of the earth only a thin film on its surface. There is nothing in this deployment of materials to suggest that there is anything of cosmic importance about what happens on Earth. It is also important to note that what we regard as normal environmental conditions, conducive to animal and plant life as we know it, have prevailed for only about a quarter of the history of our planet.

Consider just one detail of traditional cosmology, that the sun was put there to heat and illuminate the surface of the Earth. The sun is about 150,000,000 km away and the Earth's diameter about 13,000 km. A bit of geometry with these figures shows that the Earth intercepts about a billionth of the solar output, the rest radiating out into space. Obviously no considerations of energy efficiency went into the designing of the Earth's power system.

With a more parochial concentration on our current and immediate environment, it may appear that conditions are eminently suitable for ourselves and other organisms. This impression stems from failure to appreciate how completely one-sided adaptation is, and what it can be expected to accomplish. Living organisms are elaborately adapted to their particular ways of life in the environments in which they evolved. There is no evidence for any other kind of adaptation.

Our Physical Environment

Life, at least on this planet, takes place in an aqueous medium, and it is closely dependent in many ways on the special properties of water. This led Henderson (1913) to argue that water was designed as a medium ideally suitable for life. His argument was not a traditionally theological one, but on my reading he was a vitalist and a teleologist in his belief in a predetermined course of evolution. Not only was organic evolution proceeding towards a goal but, prior to organic evolution, the properties of matter were formed by a process that adapted it to its biological role. This "biocentric" cosmology was quickly criticized by Lillie (1913), and other aspects of Henderson's work have been criticized by others, most recently and cogently by Craik (1989). Here I will merely deal with a few additional criticisms, related mainly to the properties of water, which formed an essential part of Henderson's argument.

In a list of the attributes of common substances, water is found to have extremely high values for specific heat and for heats of fusion and vaporization. As Henderson and many others have argued, these properties undoubtedly make a planet largely covered by a deep ocean much less variable in temperature than it would be if these values were lower. A planet with a more variable temperature might be considered a less suitable abode for life, but this is gratuitous. The biosphere of the Earth in fact has a range of commonly encountered temperatures, and organisms are observed to adapt to them (more on the thermal adaptability of organisms in the discussion of Gaia below). I presume that if a broader temperature range were experienced over long periods of geologic time, organisms would adapt to that too.

The thermal inertia of water not only makes the environment difficult to heat or cool, it has the same effect on organisms themselves, and Henderson cites this stability as an adaptive aspect of water. If it were not for its high specific heat, we would be heated by a given exertion more than we are. This, as Henderson points out, would be maladaptive for a mammal in hot weather. The greater heating, for the same mammal, would be adaptive in cold weather. The high specific heat of water is clearly disadvantageous for any reptile or insect or other animal that depends on basking to reach a favorable temperature on a cold day.

I suspect that, with moderate effort, additional adverse effects from the properties of water and other common substances could be found and emphasized for the thesis that our physical environment is diabolically perverse. Many such arguments could be based on the same features that Henderson cites as especially favorable to life, such as the expansion of water when it freezes. This means that ice floats and that a body of water in contact with sufficiently cold air freezes at the surface. It is thereby insulated against further thermal exchanges with the air, so that the moderation of climate by the ocean is largely frustrated when it is most needed.

An additional problem, if thermal stability is thought to be biologically desirable, is that snow has the ideally wrong color. It greatly exacerbates winter chill by reflecting solar radiation into space, an effect recently emphasized in the white-earth models of climatologists (Wetherald and Manabe 1975:2057). If ever an ice age advances beyond a critical threshold, it must continue advancing with no possibility of retreat, and the Earth will stay frozen forever. There would be no such threat if snow had a darker color.

There is a more directly biological effect of the expansion of water on forming ice. Any freezing organism will be killed by the mechanically disruptive effects of expanding ice crystals, unless it has special adaptations to prevent such effects. I imagine that an extraterrestrial observer, from a planet that either lacks water or never experiences freezing temperatures, would conclude that terrestrial life of middle or high latitudes must be destroyed every winter with the first freeze. The observer would probably confine the search for perennial organisms to the tropics or deep water.

Or perhaps only deep water. Surfaces exposed to the air or with only a shallow covering of water would be vulnerable to sunlight, which an educated visitor might well assume to rule out all vital activity. The rapidly lethal nature of both the ultraviolet and visible wave lengths can be convincingly shown by earthworms and trout embryos and any other organisms that lack elaborate defenses against this environmental threat (Perlmutter 1961). The extraordinary transparency of water makes it extraordinarily ineffective as a shield against radiation.

An even greater discouragement to an extraterrestrial visitor's search for life would be the high concentration of oxygen in the Earth's atmosphere, which might plausibly be attributed to the photolysis of water. It is most unlikely that the visitor would speculate that this process might be used by illuminated organisms to power the recovery of carbon from the minute trace of CO_2 in the atmosphere. The abundance of oxygen would force the conclusion that all materials at the Earth's surface must be oxidized, in other words, dead. Only in locally anoxic aquatic environments would there be any hope of finding living organisms, but the capacity of water to dissolve oxygen would be another of its unfortunate attributes.

The Gaia Concept

The modern form of the idea that adaptation is symmetrical, with organisms adapted to their environments and the environments adapted to organisms, is the Gaia concept (Lovelock 1979, 1988; Lovelock and Margulis 1974). *Gaia* was an Earth goddess of the ancient Greeks. It is an appropriate name for the collective biota of the Earth, if that collective is, as the advocates claim, a superorganism devoted to the management of the environment in her own collective interest. Overt mysticism is not an essential element of the Gaia concept. I am not sure that I really understand its logical structure, but it seems to be rather similar to the *invisible hand* model in economics: if each organism freely pursues its own interests, the average result over the ecosystem will be favorable to organisms.

Discussions in support of Gaia are often unclear as to what sort of interests organisms are supposed to be pursuing. The advocates claim that the idea is fully in accord with mainstream opinion in evolutionary biology, but examples are often overtly group-selectionist (e.g., Lovelock 1988:39, 143-49). The characters that a species evolves, according to Lovelock, are those that benefit the species, rather than those that enable its members to compete better with each other. There is no illogic or inconsistency in Gaia advocates seeking support in group selection theory (e.g., from Van Valen 1975, or Wilson 1980), because no one doubts the reality of group selection. What currently prevails in biology is a great doubt of its strength relative to individual selection (Futuyma 1986:258-66; Krebs and Davies 1987:14-21). If the Gaia concept depends heavily on group selection, it should not be represented as in harmony with modern Darwinism.

Its conflict with current evolutionary theory forms the basis of much recent criticism of Gaia (e.g., Dawkins 1982:234-37). I think the criticisms valid but not decisive. If Gaia is real and has the properties claimed, the proper reaction is to modify the evolutionary theory, not deny the facts. My criticism will focus on two complaints. The first is that there is no evidence that the metaphorical invisible hand really manipulates the evolutionary process so as to produce results favorable to organisms. The second is that, even if this invisible-hand effect were valid, it would not justify the claim that Gaia is "a total planetary being," which practices "homeostasis" (Lovelock 1988:19). It would not even justify Kerr's (1988) weaker claim for planetary homeostasis.

What Does Gaia Do?

I do not know whether Adam Smith's invisible hand manipulates economies the way he proposed. I do know that the biological equivalent often manipulates ecologies in seriously maladaptive ways, and I will give two of many possible examples. The first is the widespread habit of trees of producing, in the pursuit of their individual interests, conditions that favor forest fires. Conceivably this need not have been so. On a uniformly arid Earth, the vegetation might nowhere be more abundant than widely spaced clumps of shrubs. If so, I would expect the Gaia advocates to seize upon this circumstance for a favorable argument: the vegetation is careful not to produce continuous high-density concentrations of combustible materials, which could be ruinous to the whole community.

Any recent visitor to Yellowstone Park will see dramatic evidence that this is not so. Each individual tree tries to grow out of the shade of its neighbors so as to intercept enough light to produce an abundance of pollen and seeds. This can be done only by supporting its photosynthetic tissues on a massive infrastructure of cellulose. The collective result, over enormous regions, is the accumulation of a high concentration of combustible material. Sooner or later there will be disastrous forest fires, like those that recently struck Yellowstone.

My second example affects a far larger part of the Earth's biota, the marine epipelagic and all dependent communities. Some marine productivity is contributed by benthic plants, such as the grasses and seaweeds of rocky shallows, but this is globally trivial compared to the phytoplankton contribution over about seven-tenths of the surface of the planet. Planktonic algae, like the plants of a forest or corn field, use sunlight to convert CO_2 and dissolved minerals into organic matter. This matter forms the base of the food chain on which almost all animal life depends.

Phytoplankton productivity depends on the strength of illumination and the concentration of dissolved nutrients, of which nitrates and related compounds are most critical. Unfortunately for the marine ecosystem, the efforts of planktonic organisms to survive and reproduce give rise to a severe depression of collective productivity. The invisible hand imposes a perverse dilemma: where there is light enough for abundant photosynthesis there is a severe shortage of nutrients; where nutrients are abundant the light is grossly inadequate (fig. 1).

The sparse algal community is confined to near-surface layers where (at certain latitudes and times of day) there is light to power its growth and maintenance. Growth depends on the necessarily slow capture of nutrients from water already severely depleted. Any success in this effort further depresses nutrient levels and productivity. Nutrients are returned to the water when the cells die, but dead cells sink to lower levels, and other biological processes also conspire to rob the surface layers of nutrients. Dead animals and animal products such as feces and molted exoskeletons sink to lower levels as they decompose and release nutrients. Many animals feed on the plankton near the surface at night, but then descend and do much of their metabolizing and release of plant nutrients in poorly illuminated depths by day.

Replenishment of surface nutrients depends on the nonbiological processes of turbulent mixing by wind or on seasonally or geographically restricted upwelling. Gaia's destructive influence is more pervasive and influential than these inorganic processes. She depresses marine productivity to levels far below what would prevail if there were some countervailing biological process that would transport plant nutrients from their gigantic accumulation in deep water up to where they can do some good.

This argument is valid, of course, only if I have properly identified the sort of good that Gaia is supposed to accomplish. Is it really Gaia's role to maximize marine productivity? Unfortunately there are no adequately explicit Gaia-theory axioms from which one might deduce such a proposition, although I should think it intuitively acceptable that more productive is preferable to less productive. This is Lovelock's (1988: 135) position when he proposes that "the health of Gaia is measured by the abundance of life." If so, Gaia must be sick indeed over most of the Earth, where the

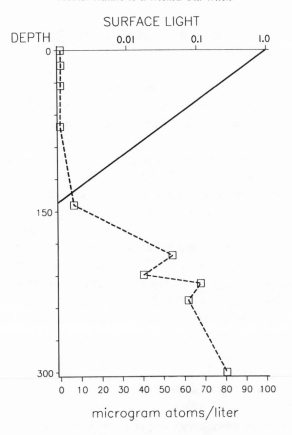

Figure 1. Intensity of blue light (most penetrating wave length) as a proportion of surface illumination is shown by the continuous line. Nitrate concentration is shown by the dashed line. Values for light are hypothetical, but realistic for extremely clear water. Nitrate values were measured in the western Gulf of Mexico in June 1951 (from Collier 1958). The conditions shown can be considered typical for most of the ocean most of the time. The highest nitrate values shown would be rather low for terrestrial soils. Light of less than a thousandth of full sunlight is inadequate for phytoplankton maintenance.

biological community is a desert and life's abundance at a paltry level.

Mere competition would be bad enough. The success of one organism will often mean failure for another, but the real mischief in the pelagic ecosystem is in the relentless downward transport of nitrogen and phosphorus and other nutrients. Other communities may be poisoned by waste products. The accumulation of combustibles causing a much later catastrophe, for successes and failures alike, is a more remote and indirect effect, but surely a real one. One can also, with the Gaia advocates, identify ways in which one organism may have a directly or indirectly beneficial effect on some other organism or on a widely scattered group of organisms. Should the question of the reality and importance of Gaia be decided on the basis of which side can muster the more impressive list of examples?

I think not, because it will often be too difficult to distinguish Gaia's benefits from Gaia's harm to which organisms have adapted. An effect of Lovelock's (1988:19) *total planetary being* since the late Precambrian has been to keep a high concentration of oxygen in the atmosphere. This free oxygen is now a vital necessity to most of the organisms we think of as important, but this could not have been true originally. In the early stages of oxygen accumulation, at least some organisms evolved ways to avoid getting oxidized. From some of them modern obligate aerobes such as ourselves evolved. To organisms with aerobic metabolism, oxygen is a resource that allows much higher rates of energy use than is possible for any anaerobe. This does not mean that the first appearance of free oxygen was the production of a beneficial substance. It means that some organisms were able to evolve a beneficial usage. The problem was clearly recognized by Lillie (1913), who proposed that "this world may be the best possible environment for the organisms that have come to exist in it, but it might not be so for the living beings of another and quite different cosmos." Very much the same sentiment was independently expressed by Craik (1989).

The Claim for Planetary Homeostasis

No matter how many general benefits may arise from the activities of organisms, they can never provide a basis for an analogy between such a collective effect and an organism with homeostatic controls. The analogy confuses mass-action equilibria or input-output balances with homeostasis. Homeostasis requires a feedback loop from a sensor of the controlled variable to the machinery by which the control is achieved. The thermostatic control of house temperature is an excellent, if trite, example of homeostasis, which is found only in living organisms or, like that persistently comfortable house, in the products of living organisms.

Homeostasis should be recognized only if special sensory and control machinery can be shown. Stability of some condition, even if the condition is rapidly restored after disturbance, should not be uncritically attributed to homeostatic machinery. For instance, if I could magically cause all atmospheric moisture to condense and fall to the surface, the resulting zero humidity everywhere on Earth would be an extremely temporary condition. Evaporation from the oceans and other wet surfaces would, perhaps in a few days, restore the atmospheric humidity to something in the normal range. This would not be homeostasis. The long-term maintenance of the normal range of total atmospheric moisture is a direct result of a balance between evaporation and condensation. There is no sensor that monitors the humidity and no control machinery is activated by abnormality.

The regularity of periodic geyser eruptions is Falk's well-chosen example of stability without homeostasis (1981). A nearly constant inflow of shallow subterranean water with nearly constant heating far below the surface sooner or later results in an explosive release of superheated water. The only operative factors are the hole and the heat and the water and its eruptions, which Falk calls the "main effects." No feedback loop activates the eruption machinery as a result of monitoring temperature or pressure or the passage of time. Falk concludes that Old Faithful is not an organism because it is not homeostatic. I would say the same about Gaia for the same reason.

What Would a Really Fit Environment Be Like?

Adaptation is always asymmetrical; organisms adapt to their environments, never vice versa. If the environments at the surface of the Earth seem well suited to living organisms, it is simply because those are the environments to which organisms have adapted. It is certainly likely that life, however broadly conceived, can exist only within a certain range of physical conditions. Terrestrial environments fall within that otherwise unknown range. Lunar and Martian ones apparently do not.

I have trouble imagining any kind of life that is not based on chemical reactions between surfaces and diffusible substrates in a fluid medium. Perhaps the medium must be liquid, with no adequately controlled metabolism possible in a gas. It may even be, as Henderson (1913) argued, that all other candidates (e.g., hydrocarbons, liquid ammonia) can be ruled out, and that only liquid water is a suitable medium. If so, the cosmos is indeed hostile to life, because liquid water can exist only under special conditions.

But perhaps they are not as special as we might imagine. The boiling point is not a property of water, but rather a relationship between water and pressure. Liquid water can exist in a household pressure cooker more than 20° C hotter than in the open air. The freezing point of pure water is also a function of pressure, so that subterranean waters can stay liquid under permafrost at many degrees below zero Celsius. Equally important is the fact that both boiling and freezing points are sensitive to solute concentrations. Seawater freezes at about −2° C, and boils at about 103° at one atmosphere pressure.

Lovelock (1988) believes that Gaia keeps most habitats between 0° and 30° C because that is the most favorable range for organisms. He also believes that aquatic organisms are favored by moderate solute concentrations, and that the salt content of seawater is near the upper end of the favorable range. It is certainly true that the greatest diversity of organisms lives in these ranges of temperature and salinity, and that life is less abundant and diverse outside this range.

My explanation (and that of Craik 1989) of these observations is that organisms will be most abundant under the most common and persistent conditions, where they will have had the greatest opportunity to adapt. Diversity decreases with increasing latitude, not because low temperature is biologically unfavorable, but because the far north and far south have included seasonally liquid water for only a few thousand years. Diversity is likewise low in hot springs and hypersaline desert sumps, not because the conditions in such places are extreme, but because they are local and new on an evolutionary time scale. Coral reef and rain forest communities are more diverse because they have been there for many millions of years, perhaps 70 million for the southeast Asiatic rain forest (Thorhallsdottir 1989).

Salinity gives a good test of extremity-vs-brevity interpretations. Oceans and fresh waters have been present as large continuous habitats throughout the Phanerozoic. Medium-salinity intermediates have been local and ephemeral. Today's brackish estuaries, such as the Chesapeake and the lower Shannon, are products of Recent sea-level changes and are only a few thousand years old. Biotic diversity in these new and scattered habitats is severely depressed compared to nearby fully marine or fully fresh-water habitats (Giere 1968). Suppose it were the intermediate salinities, like intermediate temperatures, that were most common and had the most diverse communities. I would expect Gaia proponents to argue that brackish water is most favorable to organisms and that this is the reason that Gaia maintains mostly intermediate salinities.

Craik (1989) and Pool (1990) have provided handy summaries of what is known of some organisms' tolerance of extreme conditions. Some bacteria thrive in deep-sea hydrothermal vents at temperatures at least up to 110° C and perhaps considerably higher. Other bacteria thrive in pH ranges from 1.0 to 11.5. Most processes studied by biochemists are severely disturbed by pressures of 100 atmospheres, but deep-sea bacteria and members of all major animal phyla including vertebrates may live out their lives at pressures around a thousand atmospheres.

Some marine algae show a tolerance of extreme conditions not considered by Craik or Pool. They are trapped in sea ice as the surface freezes and must spend the winter there. The return of springtime light enables them to photosynthesize, and then the summer sun melts the ice and disperses them (Palmisano and Sullivan 1983; McConnville and Wetherbee 1983). The formation of sea ice separates the ice crystals from trapped water, which must, therefore, reach ever higher salinities as temperatures fall and more ice forms. Measurement of physical conditions in the microscopic channels of ice-bound water is difficult, but the resident algal cells obviously experience salinities far above that of normal seawater, and temperatures far below the seawater freezing point of $-2°$. It is possible that they live in saturated brine near Fahrenheit's theoretical minimum of $-18°$ C. Not only do they survive this imprisonment in sea ice, they can photosynthesize and grow at an appreciable rate under those extreme conditions.

It would seem that evolution has been capable of producing organisms that can be active and thrive at temperatures from perhaps as low as $-18°$ to at least $110°$ C, in the entire range of naturally occurring salinities, at pressures from a fraction of an atmosphere to more than a thousand, and over most of the possible pH spectrum. Preoccupation by Lovelock (1988) and other Gaia proponents with the maintenance of the narrow range of conditions normally experienced by human life seems a bit parochial. Until some real exobiological data are available, we can only speculate about what physical and chemical conditions are most favorable for the origin and evolution of life. Perhaps such data will come from exploring the dense hydroatmospheres of the major planets, where chemically complex conditions are stable for immense periods of time.

Evolution and Ethics

Huxley (1894) was concerned with several issues of central importance for this volume: the hostility of the cosmos to human life and aspirations, a moral evaluation of the evolutionary process and its products, and the evolutionary origin of the human moral impulse. My discussions above dealt with the first of these topics. I have already had much to say about the second and third (Williams 1988, 1989), and will venture only a brief summary here.

That natural selection is a morally unacceptable process has been clear to honest thinkers since it was first proposed. It was clear to Huxley (1894), who urged that we must "refuse any longer to be the instruments of the evolutionary process" (p. 63) and that morality must be "directed, not so much to the survival of the fittest, as to the fitting of as many as possible to survive" (p. 82). George Bernard Shaw (1921:33-34) thought natural selection so evil an idea that no theory of evolution that made use of it could possibly be valid.

If Huxley and Shaw could have been informed of later conceptual developments in evolutionary biology it could only have strengthened their convictions. Today more than ever, natural selection can be regarded as a process that maximizes shortsighted selfishness. If one organism ever does something that benefits another it must result from either (1) an accident or malfunction, (2) kin selection, with the benefit going to a relative and partial genetic surrogate for the provider of the benefit, (3) exploitative manipulation of the giver by the receiver, or (4) reciprocity that sooner or later is profitable to the giver. The practice of charity, with net cost to the practitioner, will always be disfavored by natural selection.

This conclusion follows from the usual model of selection operating within a population of organisms. A somewhat different result may be expected from group selection. A population of more charitable individuals might well supplant one with a lower level of charity. As noted above, most evolutionary biologists today believe that selection at the level of groups is a weak process that cannot effectively counter selection among individuals within groups. Even if they are wrong in this, I doubt that the group selection idea would have had much appeal to Huxley or Shaw. Success of one group in group selection theory is always achieved at the expense of another. Arguing the moral superiority of group selection over individual selection is like arguing the superiority of genocide over random murder. Alexander (1987) explicitly recognized that selfishness among groups is more to be feared than selfishness within them, and that there is an acute "problem of within-group amity serving between-group enmity" (p. 195).

Apparent amity and the related ideas of kin selection and reciprocity are really just a minor aspect of biology. Most of the phenomena found in the biological world are clearly those of selfishness and often of gross destructiveness. Organisms constantly engage in activities that violate the dicta of human ethical systems and moral sensitivities. That which is natural is far more often deserving of condemnation than of imitation. As Huxley (1894: 73-74) recognized, there has been "immeasurable mischief" done by "the moralizing of sentimentalists" who look to Nature for "an exemplar for human conduct."

The "moralizing of sentimentalists" continues to work its mischief in the use of biological material in literature intended for the lay public. There is a steady production of works that lead one to believe that only our own species, and perhaps only its modern representatives, regularly indulge in conspecific killing, rape and other sex crimes, or wasteful use of resources. In fact the opposite is true. Our own species is extraordinarily benign in all these respects compared to many others. I document these points in detail in earlier works (Williams 1988, 1989).

It is undoubtedly true that many of the ethical systems that are preached, and sometimes practiced, are thoroughly unselfish and genuinely altruistic. This means that the benign motivations that underlie them can not have been directly favored by natural selection. They must have been produced indirectly by some sort of accident, the sort of thing that happens routinely in evolution. On an evolutionary time scale natural selection is immensely powerful, but it is also abysmally stupid. It is utterly indifferent to the long-term consequences of current action. It produced a human organism that would reliably practice unfair nepotism and self-seeking conspiracies in a tribal microcosm. In so doing it also produced one that, in the abnormal modern macrocosm, could advocate compassion towards strangers and even animals. These motivations must arise from biologically normal attitudes favored by kin selection and reciprocity, but have biologically abnormal manifestations in our abnormal modern environment.

It is on this abnormality that human ethics depends. It led Dillard (1974:177) to exclaim "I came from the world, I crawled out of a sea of amino acids, and now I must whirl around and shake my fist at that sea and cry shame!" It led Dawkins (1976:215) to urge that we must "rebel against the tyranny of the selfish replicators." It led Lopreato (1981:124) to propose that the essence of moral striving is the "ultimate negation of the commandment of natural selection." They all eloquently endorse Huxley's (1894) call for volunteers in his combat against the cosmic process.

Summary

A century of progress in biology confirms Huxley's thesis: the universe is hostile to life in general and human life in particular; the evolutionary process and its products are contrary to human ethical standards; human survival and ethical advance can be achieved only in opposition to the cosmic process. The hostility of the universe is abundantly shown by its general physical properties. What seem like benign conditions on the Earth's surface result from the adaptation of organisms to those conditions, not from any accommodation by the conditions. Contrary to the recently formulated *Gaia* concept, normal biological activities often aggravate the environmental hostility. Gaia's supposed homeostatic regulation of physical factors is a fallacy that arises from confusing the general concept of stability with the special biological phenomenon of homeostasis. Recent theoretical works on natural selection and studies of organisms in nature emphasize the moral perversity of natural selection. Inquiries into human evolution and the origin of human ethical motivations vindicate Huxley's call for combat against the cosmic process.

References

Alexander, R. D. 1987. *The Biology of Moral Systems*. New York: Aldine de Gruyter.

Collier, A. 1958. Gulf of Mexico physical and chemical data from *Alaska* cruises. U.S. Fish and Wildlife Service, Special Scientific Report—Fisheries 249:1-417.

Craik, J. C. A. 1989. The Gaia hypothesis—Fact or fancy. *Journal of the Marine Biological Association of the United Kingdom* 69:759-68.

Dawkins, R. 1976. *The Selfish Gene*. Oxford: Oxford University Press.

Dawkins, R. 1982. *The Extended Phenotype*. Oxford: W. H. Freeman.

Dillard, A. 1974. *Pilgrim at Tinker Creek*. New York: Harper's Magazine Press.

Falk, A. E. 1981. Purpose, feedback, and evolution. *Philosophy of Science* 48:198-217.

Futuyma, D. J. 1986. *Evolutionary Biology*. 2d ed. Sunderland, MA: Sinauer Associates.

Giere, O. 1968. Die Fluctuationen des marinen Zooplankton im Elbe-Aestuar. *Archiv fur Hydrobiologie* 31 (Suppl.):379-546.

Henderson, L. J. [1913] 1958. *The Fitness of the Environment*. Reprint. Boston: Beacon Press.

Huxley, T. H. [1894] 1989. *Evolution and Ethics*. Reprint, ed. J. Paradis and G. C. Williams. Princeton, NJ: Princeton University Press.

Kerr, R. A. 1988. No longer willful, Gaia becomes respectable. *Science* 240:393-95.

Krebs, J. R., and N. B. Davies. 1987. *An Introduction to Behavioural Ecology*. 2d ed. Oxford: Blackwell.

Lillie, R. S. 1913. The fitness of the environment. *Science* 38:337-42.

Lopreato, J. 1981. Towards a theory of genuine altruism in *Homo sapiens*. *Ethology and Sociobiology* 2:113-26.

Lovelock, J. 1979. *Gaia. A New Look at Life on Earth*. Oxford: Oxford University Press.

Lovelock, J. 1988. *The Ages of Gaia*. New York, London: W. W. Norton & Co.

Lovelock, J., and L. Margulis. 1974. Biological modulation of the Earth's atmosphere. *Icarus* 21:471-89.

McConnville, M. J., and R. Wetherbee. 1983. The bottom-ice microalgal community from annual ice in the inshore waters of east Antarctica. *Journal of Phycology* 19:431-39.

Palmisano, A. C., and C. W. Sullivan. 1983. Sea-ice microbial communities (SIMCO). 1. Distribution, abundance, and primary production of ice microalgae in McMurdo Sound, Antarctica, in 1980. *Polar Biology* 2:171-77.

Perlmutter, A. 1961. Possible effect of lethal visible light on year-class fluctuations of aquatic animals. *Science* 133:1081-82.

Pool, R. 1990. Pushing the envelope of life. *Science* 247:158-60.

Shaw, G. B. [1921] 1965. *Back to Methuselah.* Reprint. Baltimore: Penguin Books.

Thorhallsdottir, T. E. 1989. Regnskogar hitabeltisins [Rainforests of the tropical zone]. *Natturufraedingurinn (Reykjavik)* 59:9-37.

Van Valen, L. M. 1975. Group selection, sex, and fossils. *Evolution* 29:87-94.

Wetherald, R. T., and S. Manabe. 1975. The effects of changing the solar constant on the climate of a general circulation model. *Journal of the Atmospheric Sciences* 32:2044-59.

Williams, G. C. 1988. Huxley's *Evolution and Ethics* in sociobiological perspective. *Zygon* 23:383-407.

Williams, G. C. 1989. A sociobiological expansion of *Evolution and Ethics*, 179-214, 228-36. In reprint of *Evolution and Ethics*, T. H. Huxley (1894). Princeton, NJ: Princeton University Press.

Wilson, D. S. 1980. *The Natural Selection of Populations and Communities.* Menlo Park, CA: Benjamin/Cummings.

Can Beings Whose Ethics Evolved Be Ethical Beings?

Patricia A. Williams

In this volume we are not discussing the old, and rightly discredited, evolutionary ethics, but rather, a new kind of ethics, what Neil Tennant (1983) has called "evolved ethics," in order to distinguish it from its older cousin. The old, evolutionary ethics asked whether we could look at the course, or the theory, of evolution and learn how we should behave. The new, evolved ethics asks whether our ethical dispositions are the products of evolution, and, if they are, whether we ought to follow them.

The old, evolutionary ethics had two main problems. One was that while it depended either on the process or the product of evolution being good, evolution seems morally neutral. The other was that it committed the logical fallacy of deriving an "ought" statement from a series of "is" statements. As long as the new, evolved ethics is merely used descriptively, it does not face these difficulties. However, there have been recent attempts to turn it into a prescriptive theory, that is, not only to describe what sort of ethical dispositions may have evolved in us, but also, exclusively from this information, to prescribe what we ought to do. Foremost in this attempt have been Robert J. Richards (1986a, 1986b, 1989), and Michael Ruse and E. O. Wilson (Wilson 1978; Ruse 1984, 1985, 1986a, 1986b, 1988; Ruse and Wilson 1986).

I will focus on these new theories of prescriptive evolved ethics, addressing the central philosophical problem of any attempt to derive a normative theory exclusively from scientific facts, namely, whether any such theory can succeed logically. The conclusion I reach is that every theory of prescriptive evolved ethics will fail due to internal contradiction. The source of the internal contradiction is this: in order for any beings to be ethical beings, they must have a certain kind of freedom, namely, freedom from external and internal coercion, a freedom which theologians and philosophers who believe that the human will is a special faculty refer to as "free will." Yet, as I explain below, in order to escape the logical fallacy of deriving an "is" from an "ought," pre-scriptive evolved ethics requires coercion. The stronger the beings' coercion, the better prescriptive evolved ethics works; but the stronger the beings' coercion, the less they are ethical beings. Thus the question I have asked in the title of my paper, "Can beings whose ethics evolved be ethical beings?" is actually restricted here to the question of whether any ethical theories falling under the category of prescriptive evolved ethics can be developed without internal logical contradiction.

This chapter is divided into two parts. In the first, I adumbrate the requirements for any being to be an ethical being. In the second, I locate the is/ought gap in prescriptive evolved ethics and discuss the problems inherent in bridging it.

The Requirements for Ethical Beings

Almost all moral philosophers, no matter what their particular school of moral philosophy, agree that for any beings to be ethical beings they must have freedom from external and internal coercion. Without such freedom, they cannot reasonably be blamed, praised, or held responsible for their actions, yet the minimum requirement for beings to be ethical is that they can legitimately be blamed, praised, and held responsible for their actions. (Nearly all cultures and legal systems assume that most people have such freedom most of the time.) Almost all moral philosophers would also agree that, in order to deserve praise or blame or to be held responsible for their actions, beings must meet at least three criteria. First, they must be able to self-reflect, whether or not they actually do so, and to ask themselves, "Why am I doing this?" That is, they must be able to generate problems. This requirement, of course, presupposes that they have some sense of self. Secondly, they must be able to weigh and deliberate among various options and to decide what to do. That is, they must be able not only to generate problems, but to solve them. Thirdly, they must be able to act on the conclusion of their deliberations, and, having decided what to do, to do it. That is, they must be beings whose deliberations make a difference to their behavior. Because this sounds rather abstract, an example may help.

Mary awakes one morning to find herself quite accountably hung over. She does not recall exactly how many beers she had the night before. What she does remember is that her head has felt like this many, many mornings during the last six months. But this morning is different. This morning, she self-reflects, asking herself, "Why am I drinking so much beer?" If she had not paused to self-reflect, there would be no possibility of her freely changing her habit. Immediately, she realizes that there are other options, and she deliberates among them. "I could switch to rum," she thinks to herself. "I might not get hangovers if I drank rum." She also considers abstinence. "I'd lose a lot of pleasure," she maintains to herself, "but I'd also lose a lot of weight." She decides, finally, to switch to Haig and Haig because, she reasons, "I'll drink less of it because I don't like the taste of Scotch and because it's too expensive for me to afford to drink for half the night, as I have been used to doing." If she had not realized that at least one other option existed, she would not have been free to change. That evening when she goes by the bar, she adheres to her resolution: she orders Haig and Haig and leaves earlier and soberer than usual. Had she not been able to adhere to her resolution, she would not have been free, but a slave to drink.

This example, I hope, demonstrates that all three criteria, self-reflection, deliberation, and the ability to act on the conclusions of those deliberations, are required for any being to have full freedom. It is the sort of freedom necessary for beings to be praised or blamed, for beings to be held responsible for their actions, that is, for any being to be an ethical being.

Is/Ought and Prescriptive Evolved Ethics

Theoretically, descriptive evolved ethics tells us what ethical dispositions may have evolved in any evolved beings. It tells us what is. Prescriptive evolved ethics, on the other hand, tells us what ought to be, that is, what beings ought, ethically, to do. It is generally considered to be the case that there is a logical gap between "is" and "ought," such that one cannot have a valid argument with only "is" standing in the premises, yet "ought" emerging in the conclusion. This logical gap cannot be bridged except in special situations. In such situations what beings ought to do is attached to their respective functions so that "is" and "ought" are intertwined contextually. For example, the function of a king is to rule, and, therefore, someone who is a king ought to rule, teachers ought to prepare classes adequately, the police ought to fight crime. Because prescriptive evolved ethics does not involve this sort of special case, but, rather, applies to evolved beings regardless of their function, the logical gap cannot be closed by this method. The problem for prescriptive evolved ethics, then, is how else the gap might be closed.

Two options are available. One is to develop an ethical theory without reference to evolution, then to demonstrate how the particular beings in question evolved to follow the prescriptions of that ethical theory. Ruse and Wilson disallow this because they think there is no valid source of ethical prescriptions except evolved ethical dispositions (1986:186-87). Richards rejects it in favor of solely employing scientific facts (1986a:272). It appears from this that theories of prescriptive evolved ethics must derive a prescriptive ethical theory solely from evolutionary facts (Ruse and Wilson 1986:174; Ruse 1986a:99; Richards 1986a:272).

The other option is exclusively to use our knowledge of what has evolved, that is, to derive a prescriptive ethical theory solely from evolutionary facts. Given that option, the problem for theories of prescriptive evolved ethics becomes why beings with evolved ethical dispositions should do what their evolved ethical dispositions tell them. If the answer is that their evolved ethical dispositions are good simply because they evolved, then prescriptive evolved ethics must show that the products of evolution are necessarily good. However, as Ruse himself argues, this cannot be proven. Indeed, Ruse demonstrates that it is equally as easy to show that the products of evolution are evil (Ruse 1986b:93), and what seems actually to be the case is that they are ethically neutral (Ruse 1986b:92-93). Therefore, this answer will not work.

Another answer is that evolved beings must do what their ethical dispositions prescribe, because, given the situation, they cannot do otherwise. This strong solution is what Richards suggests (1986a:290). Ruse and Wilson have developed a weaker version of this solution, namely, that beings with evolved ethical dispositions will suffer psychological and social stress if they do not follow them (Ruse 1986b:271).

Richards's strong solution will not work. If beings must do what their ethical dispositions tell them to do, then they are internally coerced. And, if the beings are internally coerced, then, even if they can self-reflect and deliberate, their deliberations will not make a difference to how they behave because their internal coercion will override their reflective conclusions. Such beings do not meet the criteria for ethical beings. And, if they are not ethical beings, then no prescriptive ethical theory applies to them. If all evolved beings are like this, we may as well give up developing pre-scriptive ethical theories for evolved beings.

Ruse and Wilson's proposal is more interesting. Ruse and Wilson suggest that beings whose ethics are the products of evolution ought to follow their evolved ethical dispositions because they will suffer if they do not. Ruse and Wilson's proposal contains elements of both internal coercion, in that the beings will suffer psychological stress, and external coercion, in that they will suffer social disorder. It does not deny their freedom to commit acts which contravene their evolved notions of right and wrong, however (Ruse 1986a:104).

The ability of ethical beings to contravene the dictates of their evolved ethics is Ruse's idea of ethical freedom (1986b:259). He holds that beings have evolved to feel that certain things are right, others wrong. They will never be able to change these feelings, but, nonetheless, they are capable of doing what they feel to be wrong. This is a limited notion of ethical freedom, because it denies the beings' ability to choose ethical first principles (1986b:259). Such beings lead restricted ethical lives.

What I have adumbrated thus far is Ruse's (and Wilson's) descriptive ethical theory. In order to make it prescriptive, Ruse and Wilson must also posit that beings with evolved ethics suffer stress when they contravene their ethical dispositions. If they suffer stress, then Ruse and Wilson can prescribe a remedy: to avoid stress, do what your ethical dispositions tell you to do. However, a small amount of stress will not suffice because the being could ignore it, replying "So what? I don't mind the stress, and doing the act which contravenes this disposition is a lot of fun." Their theory has to posit serious psychological suffering. Then they can prudently prescribe behavior which will avoid it, namely, behavior which coincides with the beings' evolved ethical dispositions.

Ruse's example of ethical suffering is Raskolnikov, Dostoevsky's hero in *Crime and Punishment* who thinks that, without God as a basis for ethics, all things are allowed, and kills an old pawnbroker to prove it. The act results in extreme psychological suffering for Raskolnikov. He nearly goes mad, and, finally, turns himself in to the police.

Raskolnikov does not submit to the police because he has ethical doubts about his behavior, however. He confesses because he is driven by unconscious forces which he does not understand and cannot control. Dostoevsky ends the novel here, but evidently he was dissatisfied with this ending precisely because it does not solve the ethical dilemma, for he adds an epilogue to the novel in order to tell about Raskolnikov's ethical awakening while serving his sentence in a Siberian prison.

Raskolnikov's degree of psychological stress, which does not stem from ethical deliberation but from unconscious forces, constitutes internal coercion. A lesser degree weakens the force of prudent prescriptions based on psychological stress. There seems to be no discernible balance point where internal coercion is so minor that full ethical being is possible while, at the same time, prescriptions based on psychological stress have sufficient force to be considered seriously.

Ethical freedom may also involve the ability of ethical beings to choose ethical first principles and to do what follows logically from them. Unstressed by their evolved ethical dispositions, or lacking evolved ethical dispositions, these beings would be complete ethical beings in that they could self-reflect, freely deliberate, and act on the conclusions of their deliberations. Under a great deal of stress because of their evolved ethical dispositions, they would cease to be ethical beings. In other words, the same ethical pattern applies to them that applies to their more limited cousins described above.

One counterexample will refute the Ruse-Wilson thesis that evolved beings should follow their evolved ethical dispositions because social stress, rather than psychological stress, will result from not following them. Suppose that beings evolved who tend to form strong ingroup/outgroup dichotomies with a set of ethical dispositions toward the ingroup which says, "be friendly," a set toward the outgroup which says, "be hostile," and an ethical disposition toward increasing the welfare of the ingroup. Over time the beings realize that intergroup wars are diminishing all of the groups' welfare, and that their natural groups are too small for the efficient utilization of resources. They conclude that everyone would be better off if the groups united. Rather than following their evolved ethics regarding ingroups and outgroups, they would have to contravene those particular sets of ethical dispositions in order to enhance their own welfare. Deciding not to enhance their own welfare, but, rather, to live in penury and under constant threat of war, produces social stress like, for example, food riots and assassination of group leaders.

Ruse and Wilson's prescriptive theory cannot handle this situation. Whatever these beings do, they have to endure stress. The solution to their situation is to reflect on the situation, to realize that following ingroup/outgroup ethics is harming their welfare, and then to change their evolved ethical dispositions, if they can, through using some of their greater united resources to educate each future generation in the new ethics. If their dispositions are extremely strong, of course, there will be a lot of social stress, but it will be because they have strong, evolved ethical dispositions which limit their freedom to act on their rational deliberations. Their ability to be ethical beings will be reduced.

Conclusion

The problem I have addressed here is whether there can be theories of prescriptive evolved ethics which do not suffer from internal, logical contradictions. I have concluded that such theories cannot be coherently developed. The reason they cannot be coherently developed is that, in order to be ethical, beings require a certain kind of freedom, namely, the freedom to self-reflect, deliberate, and act on the results of their deliberations. But in order to work, theories of prescriptive evolved ethics must restrict precisely this kind of freedom. Thus, the best theories of prescriptive evolved ethics will be those that apply only to nonethical beings, while fully ethical beings need pay little heed to their evolved ethical dispositions.

References

Dostoevsky, F. [1866] 1964. *Crime and Punishment*. Trans. J. Coulson. New York: W.W. Norton & Company, Inc.

Richards, R. J. 1986a. A defense of evolutionary ethics. *Biology & Philosophy* 1:265-93.

Richards, R. J. 1986b. Justification through biological faith: A rejoinder. *Biology & Philosophy* 1:337-54.

Richards, R. J. 1989. Dutch objections to evolutionary ethics. *Biology & Philosophy* 4:331-43.

Ruse, M. 1984. The morality of the gene. *The Monist* 67:167-99.

Ruse, M. 1985. Is rape wrong on Andromeda? An introduction to extraterrestrial evolution, science, and morality, 43-78. In *Extraterrestrials*, ed. E. Regis, Jr. Cambridge: Cambridge University Press.

Ruse, M. 1986a. Evolutionary ethics, a Phoenix arisen. *Zygon* 21:95-112.

Ruse, M. 1986b. *Taking Darwin Seriously*. Oxford: Blackwell.

Ruse, M. 1988. *Philosophy of Biology Today*. Albany: State University of New York Press.

Ruse, M., and E. O. Wilson. 1986. Moral philosophy as applied science. *Philosophy* 61:173-92.

Tennant, N. 1983. Evolutionary v. evolved ethics. *Philosophy* 58:289-302.

Wilson, E. O. 1978. *On Human Nature*. Cambridge, MA: Harvard University Press.

How Ethical Is Evolutionary Ethics?

Alan Gewirth

The general idea underlying evolutionary ethics has an extensive and controversial history. Since long before Darwin, philosophers have been concerned about the ethical implications of biological phenomena; but this concern has led to conflicting conclusions. To go back no further than the thirteenth century, Thomas Aquinas claimed to derive by reason, from the laws of biological nature, such moral precepts as that children ought to be nurtured by their parents and that humans ought to live peacefully together (*Summa Theologica* II.1, ques. 94, ans. 2). Four centuries later, by contrast, Spinoza claimed to prove by reason that the laws of biological nature are completely indifferent to ethical criteria, so that it is entirely in accord with natural laws for the big fish in the sea to eat the little fish and for men to use force and fraud to attain their ends (*Tractatus Theologico-Politicus:* chap. 16, para. 2).

Even allowing for the ambiguity of words like "laws," we find a similar contrast between ethical and nonethical interpretations of biological phenomena in the nineteenth century when Darwin's evolutionary theory exploded on the scene; and it continues to the present day under the influence of sociobiology and related doctrines. Thus one of the main arguments of contemporary evolutionary ethicists appeals to the so-called altruistic behaviors that occur among lower animals, behaviors wherein individual animals risk or even sacrifice their own lives in ways that serve to protect their kin or their groups against attacks by various predators (See Wilson 1979: chap. 7; Maynard Smith 1980; Ruse 1988:32-33). Now even if we hold that such behaviors bear witness to some kind of evolutionary *ethics*, what shall we say about the predators? Are they somehow *outside* the evolutionary process, or do they instead bear witness to a kind of evolutionary *un-ethics* or *im*morality? Thus at the very outset the attempt to derive ethical norms from biological evolution runs into the contrast I have already mentioned, and it raises what I have elsewhere called *the problem of specificity*—the problem of whether the evolutionary process can account for what is specifically ethical as against what is unethical, or how the same process can account for such ethically conflicting results (Gewirth 1986).

Evolutionary Ethics as an Explanatory Theory

I now want to approach this problem in another way, as follows. Evolutionary ethics purports to give an explanation of human morality. One of the main issues raised by such an attempt is whether the explanation provides sufficient conditions or only necessary conditions of the phenomena that are to be explained. No one here denies that we humans are products of biological evolution, in that we have come up through natural selection, the survival of the fittest (or perhaps, as Stephen Jay Gould [1989] has said, the survival of the luckiest). This evolutionary process has surely provided the necessary conditions for all human achievements, just as, more remotely, without the astronomical and geological processes whereby our solar system and our earth came into being, we humans would presumably not have developed, or been able to develop, as we actually have.

The question, however, is whether the biological evolutionary process also provides *sufficient* conditions of the various aspects of human mortal development—that is, whether, given that process, nothing further is needed to explain human morality. To get at this question, let us recur to the kinds of empirical phenomena I mentioned before, the so-called altruistic behaviors that occur among lower animals, behaviors wherein individual animals risk or even sacrifice their own lives in ways that serve to protect their kin or their groups against attacks by various predators. Such so-called ethical behavior is evolutionarily adaptive for the animal's group or kin because it enables their genes to survive and multiply.

The central idea of evolutionary ethics is that human morality, including both moral judgments and moral conduct, is to be explained in similar adaptive terms. According to this theory, human beings have the morality they do because, through the process of evolutionary adaptation, such a morality enables human groups to survive and reproduce.

Now this theory of evolutionary ethics, in its general form, is a very old one. Moral philosophers, going back at least to Plato in the Western tradition, have upheld the thesis that morality arises as a means of enabling the members of various social groups to live together peacefully, and thereby not only to survive but also to flourish.

The distinctive contribution of evolutionary ethics bears on the specific causal mechanism whereby this salutary effectiveness of morality comes into being. The mechanism in question is held by the evolutionary ethicist to consist not, as with other theories, in some kind of rational contrivance, but rather in genetic determination; that is, just as in lower animals so-called altruistic behavior selects out for reproductive survival the genes of the kin group to which the altruistic animal belongs, so, too, is it with human beings. The cause of humans' having the morality they have is that such a morality enables human genes to survive and reproduce.

Much more can, of course, be said to spell out in detail the various contentions of different evolutionary ethicists. But I want to take the above sparse statement as the basis for indicating what I think are two serious discontinuities between evolutionary ethics and human ethics or morality—discontinuities that make it very doubtful whether evolutionary ethics can explain human ethics in the sense of providing its sufficient conditions, as against merely its necessary conditions. These discontinuities bear on two kinds of problems. One is the problem of intentionality; the other is the problem of determinacy.

Before spelling out these problems, let me say something about the word "ethical" as it figures in the title of this paper. "Ethical" can have either a descriptive meaning or an evaluative meaning. In its descriptive meaning, "ethical" signifies a certain general code of behavior or mode of life which is upheld as right or justified in some group or society; but in this meaning the word carries no evaluative judgment on the part of the user or speaker as to whether the behavior or mode of life really is right or justified. Thus we use this descriptive meaning when, for example, we talk of the ethical ideas of the Nazis, the Hottentots, the British, and so forth. The opposite of "ethical" in this descriptive sense is "nonethical," not "unethical." In its evaluative meaning, on the other hand, "ethical" is a normative term; it means what is morally right or good; its opposite is "unethical."

Now when I raise the question, "How ethical is evolutionary ethics?", I shall be referring to "ethical" sometimes in the descriptive sense and sometimes in the evaluative sense. The context will usually make clear in which of these senses the word is being used, and with it what are the relevant criteria for the application of the word.

The Problem of Intentionality

Let us now turn to the problem of intentionality, which I said was the first of the two main problems raised by the discontinuity between evolutionary ethics and human ethics. To get at this problem, we may begin by comparing the phrase "evolutionary ethics" with other phrases using the word "ethics" that have the same grammatical structure. One example is "professional ethics," which has such species as medical ethics, legal ethics, business ethics, journalistic ethics, academic ethics, and so forth.

All these branches of professional ethics set out to provide reasoned precepts for how the respective professional persons ought to act, especially toward their recipients. For example, in medical ethics we have such precepts as that physicians ought to refrain from doing harm to their patients and that they ought to consider primarily the health of their patients, not the cost-benefit balance sheet of their hospitals; in business ethics we have such precepts as that merchants ought not to engage in fraud or in deceptive advertising, and so forth. In other words, the various branches of professional ethics set forth normative moral 'oughts.' And one of the main features of such 'oughts' is that they assume that behaviors of the kind they prescribe are under the voluntary control of the persons addressed by the precepts, in that they can know what kinds of conduct are prescribed by the precepts and can make unforced, reasoned choices to act in the ways prescribed. In this regard, then, the actions prescribed by moral 'ought'-judgments are voluntary or intentional: their agents are required to *intend* to act in the appropriate ways, knowing what these ways are and choosing so to act.

Similar aspects of intentionality are also found in more general normative ethical theories that are also grammatically parallel to evolutionary ethics, such as utilitarian ethics, deontological ethics, and so forth.

Now evolutionary ethics differs from professional ethics, utilitarian ethics, and so forth, in that it is not—or at least not primarily—a normative theory about how persons ought to act toward one another; rather, it is a metaethical theory that purports to give a causal explanation of why moral 'ought'-precepts have the content they do and why humans act toward one another in ways that are deemed to be ethical. The evolutionary ethicist does not, like the professional ethicist or the utilitarian ethicist, say: You ought to act so as to maximize utility; nor does he say that you ought to act in accordance with the evolutionary process of natural selection. Such a normative way of talking on the part of the evolutionary ethicist would be nonsensical, because, according to the causal theory in which evolutionary ethics consists, humans cannot help acting in the kinds of moral, altruistic ways involved in kin selection, and so forth. The process of natural selection to which the evolutionary ethicist appeals make it causally necessary that humans, like other animals, behave in ways that enable their respective gene pools to survive; for otherwise they would not have survived. This causal necessity is at least hypothetical, in that *if* their gene pools are to survive, then certain kinds of behavior *must* occur. And these kinds of behavior are altruistic ones in the sense that the respective animals cooperate for the reproductive survival of their respective kin. Hence, it makes no sense to say to human beings that they *ought* to act in these ways. As Immanuel Kant [1788] (1956:30) and others long ago pointed out, 'ought' implies both 'can' and 'may not.'[1] So if it is not the case that humans can refrain from acting, and in this sense *may not* act, in accordance with the evolutionary process of natural selection, then it makes no sense to say that they *ought* to act in this way.

The general conclusion that emerges from these considerations is that evolutionary ethics, being a causal theory, cannot account for the voluntariness or intentionality of moral 'oughts.' There is a discontinuity between the intentionality of such 'oughts' and the causal necessity that the evolutionary theory attributes to what it depicts as ethical behavior. Thus, even if the theory sets forth a necessary condition of the emergence of human ethical behavior—namely, that it in some way involves cooperation that preserves human genes—it does not set forth a sufficient condition of ethical 'oughts.'

The fuller understanding of this point requires some further consideration of just what kind of explanation is purportedly provided by evolutionary ethics. Some theorists construe it as a mechanical explanation, ultimately on a par with physicochemical explanations. On this view, of course, the criticism I have just presented about the discontinuity with intentional 'oughts' would be reinforced. Other theorists construe evolutionary ethics as giving a kind of teleological explanation, i.e., an explanation in terms of the biological function that is subserved by cooperative or altruistic behavior. Such behavior is held to occur and persist because it enables the kin or other relevant group to survive and reproduce.

Now, as Aristotle pointed out, teleological processes may be either conscious and intentional or unconscious and unintentional (*Physics* II. 5,8). Biological explanations adduce teleologies of the latter sort. So, even if we construe the explanations given by the evolutionary ethicists as teleological ones, this still leaves a sharp discontinuity between the kinds of deterministic, unconcious behaviors to which these ethicists appeal and the kinds of voluntary, conscious behaviors that are invoked in human ethical precepts.

This discontinuity, then, is one of the main grounds for raising the question: How ethical is evolutionary ethics? If to be ethical involves intending to act in certain ways that not only benefit other persons besides or in addition to oneself, but also are subject to knowledge, voluntary control, and reasoned choice on the part of the agent, then what evolutionary ethics presents as the content of what it calls ethical behavior is not, in fact, ethical. It is closer to a tropism than to a human action.

In reply to this criticism, it may be contended that voluntariness or intentionality may itself be an effect of the evolutionary process. To have the power of reasoned choice, of voluntary control over one's actions, could have been singled out by the evolutionary process as being more adaptive, more effective for individual and group survival than having only simple automatic reflex responses.

Even if we accept this, however, we still have to distinguish between two different interpretations of the relation between the power of choice and the evolutionary process. On one interpretation, we have evolved so as to have the power of choice, but the object of our choice, what we choose, is itself left indeterminate. So on this view, we can choose what is evolutionarily nonadaptive as well as adaptive—for example, we can choose to smoke and engage in other self-harming ways, and to entice other persons to behave in these ways—and we can also choose what is immoral or unethical as well as what is moral or ethically right. On this interpretation, then, the evolutionary process would not provide any specific support for evolutionary ethics, since it would have given us the power to choose unethical as well as ethical behavior. And when we do choose ethical behavior, this choice cannot itself be attributed to or explained by the evolutionary process because, as far as concerns what that process has given us, we may choose either ethical or unethical kinds of conduct.

In making this point, there is no need to give an exaggeratedly indeterministic interpretation of the power of choice. Our choices may indeed be influenced by various aspects of our background, religious, national, economic, sexual, and so forth. But influence is not the same as exclusive causal determinism. It is also true that we are not free to choose between just about anything. Choice, to be genuine, must be effective, and to be effective, the alternatives between which it chooses must be actually available for attainment by the chooser. The alternatives need not be equally available; when some person is able to choose between two alternatives X and Y, he may choose X even though its attainment may be much more difficult than Y. Think, for example, of the choice, for an inveterate smoker, between smoking and not smoking. If, because of addiction, he is really incapable of refraining from smoking, then he has no effective choice in the matter, and he has in effect programmed himself to continue smoking. Even here, however, the incapacity is not so great that it can in no way be overcome. In any case, most of the behaviors which are the objects of ethical precepts are not like that; the ethical 'oughts' that figure therein prescribe behaviors that are indeed open to voluntary choice on the part of agents. Hence, the conclusion remains that evolutionary ethics is not ethical because the kinds of behaviors it upholds as ethical derive not from voluntary choice or intentionality but rather from a process of causal determination.

On a second interpretation of the relation between the power of choice and the evolutionary process, the object of choice, what we choose, is itself causally determined by the evolutionary process. On this view, through natural selection we have evolved so as to choose what is ethical or altruistic over what is unethical. Just as in the lower animals, their engaging in so-called altruistic or even self-sacrificing behavior is evolutionarily adaptive for the kin or the group, so that survival of the group's genes is promoted by such behavior; so, on the second interpretation now under consideration, human beings are causally determined by the forces making for group survival to choose ethical behavior, behavior that is evolutionarily adaptive.

But this second interpretation of the relation between the evolutionary process and the power of choice is self-contradictory. For to have the power to choose is to have the power to select freely between at least two alternatives X and Y, and this excludes being determined to go for X as against Y, or vice versa. Thus the power of choice that figures in ethical behavior is quite different from the kind of causal determination that figures in natural selection. Voluntary choice excludes natural selection, where the latter is viewed as involving the causally determined selection or one alternative as against another. So, even if we grant that our having the power of choice has resulted from the evolutionary process, as in the first interpretion, this does nothing to refute the conclusion that evolutionary ethics is nonethical because its causal explanation of so-called ethical behavior leaves no place for the intentionality or voluntariness of choice that figures crucially in genuinely ethical behavior. Thus, while the evolutionary process does provide the necessary conditions for the operation of human choice or intentionality, in that without that process we would not have developed as choosing or intending beings, it does not provide the sufficient conditions that enter into the voluntary actions that are addressed by moral 'oughts': it is not the case that the evolutionary process can fully account for the voluntariness and intentionality of such 'oughts.'

The more plausible theory of ethical choice is the one first developed by Aristotle. According to this, so far as concerns ethical conduct, biological nature gives us bare, undifferentiatcd and undeveloped powers or potentialities which can be turned in different directions—for example, we can smoke or not smoke, help or harm, and so forth. But which of such alternatives we come to actually choose as matters of stable states of character, and, therefore, which moral 'oughts' we follow, depends first on habituation, how we are brought up in families and societies, and then on our ability to use reason.[2] But both of these—habituation and reasoning—are as such matters not of biological nature or of evolution but rather of cultural influences that supervene in different ways on the initial biological foundation. And these cultural influences allow for considerable contingency and variability. The intentionality of ethical 'oughts' is thus to be explained not by biological evolution but rather by this more complex cultural matrix.

Alan Gewirth

The Problem of Determinacy: The Distributive Question

I turn now to a second discontinuity that sets serious difficulties for evolutionary ethics. This bears on the problem of determinacy. To get at this problem, we must first note that philosophical ethics deals with three central normative questions about human action (See Gewirth 1978:3-5). First, there is the *authoritative* question: why *ought* one to be moral, in the sense of promoting or giving favorable consideration to the important interests of other persons even when this conflicts with one's self-interest? I have already indicated, in connection with the problem of intentionality, how the 'ought' of this question excludes the kind of causal determination that figures in evolutionary ethics. But there are also two other central normative questions of philosophical ethics. One is the *distributive* question: *whose* interests ought to be promoted or given favorable consideration in action? And the other is the *substantive* question: *which* interests ought to be promoted or favorably considered in action?

Now the problem of determinacy that besets the theory of evolutionary ethics is that the theory leaves open the possibility of many different and mutually opposed answers to each of these questions. The result is, again, that while the theory of evolutionary ethics provides necessary conditions for answering the two questions, it does not provide sufficient conditions.

Let us first consider the distributive question: *whose* interests ought to be promoted or given favorable consideration in action? Different normative ethical systems have provided widely diverse answers to this question. Thus, for example, the Nazis said that only the interests of Aryans should be promoted; the Marxist says that only the interests of the proletariat should be promoted; still others say that only the interests of some favored nation, race, religion, or sex should be promoted, or the interests of some class defined by intellectual, aesthetic, economic, or other criteria, and so forth. And in addition to all these particularistic moralities there are universalist moralities which say that what ought to be promoted is the interests of all human beings equally. This principle is set forth in a long series of human rights documents extending at least from the Declaration of Independence to the United Nations Universal Declaration of Human Rights.

Which of these alternative answers to the distributive question an ethical theory upholds, and what kinds of arguments it gives for its answer, obviously make a very great difference for the understanding and evaluation of the theory. Such different ethical theories as those of Bentham, Kant, Hegel, Kierkegaard, Marx, Spencer, Nietzsche, and so forth are largely defined by the different answers they give to the distributive question and the different arguments they give for their respective answers.

Where does evolutionary ethics stand on this question? Even though it is not directly a normative ethical theory but rather a metaethical one, it suggests an answer to the distributive question through the kinds of behaviors it singles out as ethical. We may distinguish two different aspects of its answer.

One aspect is very general. In this aspect, the evolutionary ethicist answers the distributive question by a kind of undifferentiated reference to other organisms which are the beneficiaries of possible cooperation and support. The distributive thesis of evolutionary ethics in this general aspect is that when organisms cooperate with one another and thereby promote one another's interests, such behavior is evolutionarily adaptive and thus more conductive to survival so that moral behavior is explained in this way. Thus one writer says, "success in life's struggles is often achieved more through cooperation and morality than through aggression . . . working together with other organisms can frequently pay far greater dividends than trying to fight all comers . . . We succeed biologically only inasmuch as we work together" (Ruse 1988:31-33). Thus it is the interests of *cooperators* that provide a general answer to the distributive question. This is a version of the thesis, whose critical examination goes back at least to Plato, that being moral pays off, that to be just toward others contributes more to self-interest than to be unjust, so that this provides an explanation of why animals, including humans, are moral beings.

But one can only wonder here at the excessive optimism of such writers. When the big fish in the sea eat the little fish, is the former's success in life's struggles "achieved through cooperation"? Was it through cooperation and morality that Hitler and Stalin achieved their successes? For that matter, how about the robber barons of nineteenth-century America, or the Mafia chieftains of the twentieth century, or the long-ruling tyrants throughout most of human history? Such examples make it clear that competitiveness and immorality have often contributed far more to "success in life's struggles" than have cooperation and morality. Hence, the general answer to the distributive question that the evolutionary ethicist tries to draw from evolutionary success in life's struggles through general moral cooperativeness seems quite unsound.

It is indeed true, as Thomas Hobbes and others have pointed out, that when animals, including humans, are roughly equal in power and ability, cooperation often pays off for each animal more than does competitiveness. But this involves a strong limitation on the answer to the distributive question. As is shown by much not only of natural history but also of human history, animals are not often equal in power and ability—and this emphatically applies to human beings; for otherwise the long eras of slavery and tyranny in human history would not have any explanation. Hence, taking human beings as they are, we cannot in general explain the existence or contents of human morality by adducing its supposed contribution to evolutionary success or adaptation. The fact that evolutionary adaptation, or "success in life's struggles," often comes through immorality and competitiveness rather than morality and cooperativeness casts serious doubt on the evolutionary ethicist's general answer to the distributive question.

Let us now turn to a second, more specific answer that the evolutionary ethicist gives to the distributive question. This answer focuses on groups as against individuals. A main variant of this answer is "kin selection," where "relatives aid each other because they thereby increase the prospects of their own reproductive ends," (Ruse 1988:32) or, in another version "a gene Alpha causes an individual that carries it to perform an act Alpha Prime, with the effect of reducing the fitness of the individual but increasing the fitness of some of its relatives. The result of performing the act Alpha Prime may be to increse the frequency of the gene Alpha in the future, because relatives of the individual may also carry copies of the gene Alpha"[3] (Maynard Smith 1980:23).

On this view, the answer to the distributive question—whose interests are promoted in ethical behavior—would be the kin or relatives of the original individual agent. Now if we extrapolate literally from the so-called altruistic behavior of lower animals to human beings, then the humans whose interests are promoted in ethical behavior as a result of the evolutionary process of kin selection would be one's close relatives. But while such an answer to the distributive question has indeed been upheld in the history of ethical theory, it hardly serves the purposes of those evolutionary ethicists who want to explain, let alone uphold, an answer that is more in keeping with our modern egalitarian universalist view of morality. Such a restrictive answer would give no support, either explanatory or justificatory, to those principles of morality which hold that we have moral obligations to help people who are not our blood relatives and who indeed belong to quite different races, communities, or ethnic groups.

Similar considerations apply to evolutionary ethicists who go in for what they call "group selection," or, even more extensively, to the thesis that, as one evolutionary ethicist puts it, "we have evolved under the aegis of kin and group selection . . . to heed the community welfare . . . to act in specific ways for the good of the community" (Richards 1986:337, 272), so that, on this view, "the community welfare is the highest good" (Richards 1986:286). For such evolutionary ethicists the answer to the distributive question of whose interests are to be promoted is: the community's.

This answer, however, suffers from all the vaguenesses that attach to contemporary moral and political theories of communitarianism. *Which* community are they referring to? The Nazis, for example, went in heavily for *Gemeinschaft*, which is the German word for "community"; so, too, do the South African Afrikaners. The trouble is that ideas of community, including who are authentic members of communities, can be very restrictive; they need by no means provide for the equal human rights of all the individual persons who live within the geographic confines of what they consider the community.

Now when the ideas of "kin selection," "group selection," and even "community welfare" are incautiously extrapolated from the animal sphere to the human sphere by the evolutionary ethicists, they seem too uncritically unaware of how sinister and adverse their evolutionary theses are for the egalitarian and universalist moralities they implicitly want to uphold as well as to explain. This, then, is another aspect of their failure to deal adequately with the problem of determinacy in its bearing on the distributive question of *whose* interests are to be promoted by the system of morality whose causal development they are trying to explain.

An evolutionary ethicist may seek to avoid this conclusion by assimilating biological causal factors to cultural influences. Thus one author writes:

> Men are cultural animals. Their perceptions of the meaning of behaviors, their recognition of "brothers," their judgments of what acts would be beneficial in a situation—all these are interpreted according to the history of particular groups. Hence, it is no objection to an evolutionary ethics that in certain tribes—whose kin systems only loosely recapitulate biological relations— the natives may treat with extreme altruism those who are only cultural but not biological kin. In a biological sense, this may be a mistake; but on average the cultural depiction of kin will serve nature's ends. (Richards 1986:273)

This view concedes that biological evolution alone does not provide a sufficient condition or explanation for the ethical behavior that goes beyond kin selection as far as concerns the distributive question of whose interests are promoted. Thus this author seems to acknowledge that if the necessary conditions provided by evolutionary ethics are to be expanded so as to become sufficient conditions, explanations based on culture, history, and tradition must be invoked. But to assimilate cultural explanations to biological ones is to blur their basic conceptual and empirical discontinuities. Moreover, if the position upheld is that biological evolution gives the initial, general shove toward altruism, and cultural development simply fills in the details, this would still leave an enormous amount of indeterminacy so far as concerns the answer to the distributive question. So, in whichever way we construe the attempt to add cultural influences to biological ones, it still leaves serious inadequacies for evolutionary ethics as an explanatory theory for the distributive question of human morality.

The Problem of Determinacy: The Substantive Question

Let us now turn to the other main part of the problem of determinacy—the substantive question of *which* interests are to be promoted by ethical action. The direct answer of evolutionary ethics is *reproductive success*, the survival of one's gene pool; it is this interest that is furthered by the kind of social cooperation that figures in kin selection.

Now this is indeed an important goal of moral conduct. But the problem it raises for evolutionary ethics is the following. The goal of reproductive success is presumably common to many or all other animals in addition to human beings. How, then, is this goal or interest related to the many other, specifically human interests that should be furthered by morally right action?

There are many ways of classifying these human interests; I shall here present just one which I have worked out in detail elsewhere (See Gewirth 1978:31-42, 52-61). The general idea is that human beings are not only living animals; they are also, characteristically, agents who act for ends or purposes they want to achieve. We may, therefore, distinguish two broad kinds of general interests that all human beings have qua agents—interests that may also be called *necessary goods* because they must be fulfilled if people are to be able to act, either at all or with general chances of success in achieving their purposes. One kind of necessary good is *freedom*, which consists in controlling one's behavior by one's unforced choice while having knowledge of relevant circumstances. The other kind of necessary good is *well-being*, which consists in having the general abilities and conditions that are needed for achieving one's purposes. Freedom and well-being are, respectively, the procedural and the substantive conditions of action and of generally successful action. Well-being, moreover, falls into a hierarchy of three kinds of goods that are progressively less needed for action. First, there is *basic well-being*, which consists in having the essential preconditions of action, such as life, physical integrity, mental equilibrium. Second, there is *nonsubtractive well-being*, which consists in having the general abilities and conditions that are needed for retaining undiminished one's general level of purpose-fulfillment and one's capabilities for particular actions; examples are not being lied to, insulted, stolen from, threatened with violence, and so forth. Third, there is *additive well-being*, which consists in having the general abilities and conditions that are needed for increasing one's level of purpose-fulfillment and one's capabilities for particular actions; examples are education, opportunities for earning wealth and income, and a sense of one's own worth or dignity.

Now the central principle of morality is the principle of human rights, which says that all human beings have rights to freedom and to well-being in its three dimensions. Because each human being has these rights, all other human beings have at least the correlative negative duty to respect these rights by not interfering with all other humans' having freedom and well-being. And, in appropriate circumstances, all humans, aided where needed by the appropriate institutions, also have the correlative positive duty to respect these rights by helping persons to have freedom and well-being where they cannot attain them by their own efforts.

The spelling out of the contents of these central moral rights and duties involves many specifications and qualifications into which I cannot enter here.

Given this complex web of central human interests in the rights of agency, how is it related to the reproductive fitness that we have seen to be the goal upheld by evolutionary ethics? Taken at face value, this seems like a very sparse though basic goal. One way to put the difference is to say that the reproductive goal is solely biological, whereas the goals of freedom and well-being, especially in its nonsubtractive and additive phases, are cultural; they consist in or require various cultural artifacts, including language, property, education, wealth and income, self-respect, honor, dignity, and so forth. And even if the evolutionary process is the necessary condition of the attainment of these artifacts, it is hardly their sufficient condition.

Some theorists have, nevertheless, tried to reduce the complex culturally circumscribed goals of freedom and well-being to the reproductive goal maintained in evolutionary ethics. One apparent attempt of this sort goes as follows:

> The human animal has been selected to provide for the welfare of its own offspring (e.g., by specific acts of nurture and protection); to defend the weak; to aid others in distress; and generally to respond to the needs of community members. The individual must learn to recognize, for instance, what constitutes more subtle forms of need and what specific responses might alleviate distress. But . . . once different needs are recognized, feelings of sympathy and urges to remedial action will naturally follow. These specific sympathetic responses and prods to action together constitute the core of the altruistic attitude. The mechanism of the initial evolution of this attitude I take to be kin selection, aided, perhaps, by group selection on small communities. (Richards 1986:272)

In this passage the evolutionary ethicist moves from the distributive criteria involved in kin selection and group selection to a vast array of behaviors that seem to have little or nothing to do either with one's own kin or with one's membership in some small group. Can one go from either of these particularist selections to the author's statement that "the human animal has been selected . . . to defend the weak; to aid others in distress"—even when the "weak" and the "others" are not part of one's kin group, such as when Poles aided Jews who were being hunted by the Nazis, or when white abolitionists hid black slaves who were being sought by their masters? Can biological kin or group selection really explain all this? Similarly, on the substantive question, can it be in biological evolutionary terms alone that the author can explain how, as he puts it, "The individual must learn to recognize . . . what constitutes more subtle forms of need"? Is such "learning" a biological phenomenon or a cultural one?

One way to try to answer these questions would invoke the same relation between biological causality and cultural influence that I mentioned earlier: biological factors give the initial shove—or, as this author puts it, kin or group selection provides "the mechanism of the initial evolution of this [altruistic] attitude"—and then cultural factors enter to fill in the specific details. But such a view would still leave a vast area of indeterminacy in the answers to both the distributive and the substantive questions.

These considerations lead me to the conclusion that when the evolutionary ethicist tries to account for the vast scope of the interests that must be subserved by moral conduct, he can do so only by stretching, beyond plausibility or empirical evidence, the reach of what he regards as biological causality. At a minimum, he here confuses necessary with sufficient conditions. The biological, evolutionary background is indeed the necessary condition of moral, and for that matter intellectual, aesthetic, and other cultural development. But it is also the necessary condition of immoral development; and it is not the sufficient condition of any of these modes of cultural development. And in trying to give an evolutionary explanation of moral judgments and moral conduct the evolutionary theorist lays himself open to the charge that he confuses the biological background without which morality cannot occur and the constitutive conditions which are the direct components of morality.

Summary

Evolutionary ethics takes its start from the important, and imaginatively gripping, biological phenomena that it calls altruistic behavior in lower animals. But in trying to move from such behavior to human morality, it provides at most necessary conditions, not sufficient conditions. Its explanations fail to accommodate the intentionality that is characteristic of moral "oughts" and the kinds of answers to the distributive and substantive questions that figure centrally in human morality.

All of this can be admitted without our being driven to the conclusion that, as one writer put it, morality is "some kind of transcendental phenomenon, with laws and dynamics beyond the reach of scientific analysis, independent of the biological structures of the human (and humanoid) organisms that originated and perpetuated it" (Stent 1980:6). In contrast to this antinaturalist extreme, we can accept that human morality does indeed have as its *necessary* condition "the biological structure of the human organisms," so that it is in this sense not "independent of" those structures. But at the same time human morality has further, sufficient conditions that must be explained and justified in ways that go beyond evolutionary ethics.

So, to the question posed by the title of this paper—how ethical is evolutionary ethics?—the answer, I fear, must be: only slightly.

Notes

1. This point can be traced back to Aristotle, *Nicomachean Ethics* III. 1.

2. See Aristotle, *Nicomachean Ethics*. II. 1; VI. 3-7; *Metaphysics* E. 1. 1025b 19ff. For a fuller discussion of this point, see Gewirth 1984:104-8.

3. I have altered the letters as given in Maynard Smith's essay.

References

Aquinas, T. *Summa Theologica.*

Aristotle. *Metaphysics.*

Aristotle. *Nicomachean Ethics.*

Aristotle. *Physics.*

Gewirth, A. 1978. *Reason and Morality.* Chicago: University of Chicago Press.

Gewirth, A. 1984. The ontological basis of natural law: A critique and an alternative. *American Journal of Jurisprudence* 29:95-121.

Gewirth, A. 1986. The problem of specificity in evolutionary ethics. *Biology & Philosophy* 1:297-305.

Gould, S. J. 1989. *Wonderful Life: The Burgess Shale and the Nature of History.* New York: Norton.

Kant, I. [1788] 1956. *Critique of Practical Reason.* Trans. L. W. Beck. Indianapolis: Bobbs-Merrill.

Alan Gewirth

Maynard Smith, J. 1980. The concepts of sociobiology, 23-30. In *Morality as a Biological Phenomenon*, ed. G. S. Stent. Berkeley: Univ. of California Press.

Richards, R. J. 1986. A defense of evolutionary ethics. *Biology & Philosophy* 1 (3):265-93.

Ruse, M. 1988. Evolutionary ethics: Healthy prospect or infirmity? *Canadian Journal of Philosophy*. Supp. Vol. 14: *Philosophy and Biology*.

Spinoza, B. de. *Tractatus Theologico-Politicus*.

Stent, G. S. 1980. *Morality as a Biological Phenomenon*. Berkeley: Univ. of California Press.

Wilson, E. O. 1979. *On Human Nature*. New York: Bantam Books.

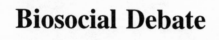

Biosocial Debate

The Moral Career of Vertebrate Values

Andrzej Elzanowski

As in many other questions, the solutions of which depend on knowledge rather than formal analysis, philosophy has produced a number of incompatible schools of thought on human values and has proved essentially helpless on the issue of justification of basic, nonderivative value judgments (Frankena 1967). A common conclusion of those contemporary philosophers who use a stock-taking approach instead of defending their preconceptions is well characterized by the concept of fragmentation of value (Nagel 1979), which refers to the existence of a number of disparate "types" of value without a common denominator. As a result, philosophy has been unable to provide guidance for the rational prioritizing of values which seems to be a necessary condition for the solution to the world's most urgent problems (Sperry 1972; Pugh 1977). In addition, the lack of a consistent theory of human values leaves them freely accessible to religious and political demagoguery.

Although, with only a handful of attempts at any sort of theoretical synthesis, the science of human values is still at the embryonic stage, the scientific approach seems to be much more promising than pure philosophizing. Drawing primarily on the decision theory, George Pugh (1977) provided a logical starting point for the conceptualization of human values. The most fundamental distinction for the understanding of human or any other system of values is the distinction between values that are built into a system and those derived from the inbuilt values by an intelligent system (such as an individual or a computer). Pugh calls them primary and secondary, respectively. The inbuilt values are experienced with such sensations as, for example, pain or hunger, which are generated by the brain. The secondary values are deduced from the primary values by a logical operation ("valuative deduction"). I shall refer to the values that are perceived and experienced as *perceived* values and to those derived by reasoning using value concepts as *conceived* values. The idea of linking the source of human values with brain automatisms is correct. The ultimate source of human value is value experience, not reasoning (Herrick 1961). For anything to be of value it has to be either experienced as good or bad or thought to be a factor of good or bad experience. Only those objects, situations or ideas are of value that are either capable of activating the appropriate brain reward and punishment mechanisms or are conceived of as being instrumental in causing good or bad experiences. Reward and punishment centers have been precisely located in the limbic system, while reward alone has been obtained from extensive extralimbic areas of the forebrain whereas pain control seems to be diffuse.

The derivation of conceived from perceived values in the human brain seems to be very different and logically much more complex when compared to artificial decision systems using numerical value assignments. The process involves two discontinuities, one of which is beyond and the other on the borderline of the grasp of today's science. The first discontinuity is just one more aspect of the formidable brain-mind problem and concerns the generation of positive or negative subjective (affective) states from percepts or ideas. The second discontinuity concerns the interface of affective experience and propositional thought, as affective experience cannot *directly* lead to any logical operation such as the deduction of values. Although the second discontinuity seems much more accessible to common sense than the first one, the interface of value experience and reasoning continues to be a stumbling block in both science and philosophy.

Seymour Epstein (1989) developed the Cognitive-Experiential Self-Theory that permits an accurate conceptualization of the relationship between a rational value judgment and affective value experience. This theory distinguishes two domains of consciousness: the experiential conceptual system (ECS), which employs affective experience and preconscious thought of self-evident validity, and the rational conceptual system (RCS) of propositional thought requiring logical validation. The conceptualization presented in figure 1 attempts to synthesize Epstein's model and the present knowledge of the biological basis of affective experience. Value perception is a name for the entire process of activation of the brain reward and punishment mechanisms which generate positive or negative affective states in the ECS (discussed in more detail below). These states carry information on the value of incentive objects and events, which is extracted and conveyed to the RCS in the process called here apperception. Apperception leads to the formation of value concepts, that is, cognitive, propositional proxies of affective value experience. Value concepts correspond to Young's (1967:38) "affective meanings," that is, "cognitive meanings of pleasantness and unpleasantness apart from, and independently of, affective arousal." Many of Rokeach's (1973) terminal values, such as happiness or wisdom, are more or less generalized positive value concepts (apparently, value may only be positive by its definition in the social sciences). There are, of course, generalized negative value concepts as well, for example, the concept of suffering. The value concepts are formally definable and accessible to logical operations of causal, propositional thinking, resulting in the *deductive attribution*

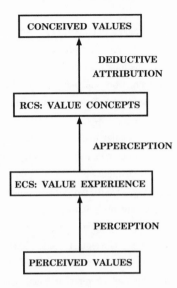

Figure 1. A conceptualization of value processing in humans. The brain mechanisms perceive values that have been assigned to things, processes or patterns by genetic transmission or by internalization. It is proposed that values are experienced by mammals, birds, and possibly some other vertebrates, but apperceived only by humans and possibly their closest relatives. RCS and ECS refer to the rational conceptual system and the experiential conceptual system (Epstein 1989), respectively.

of values to objects, behaviors or ideas thought to be useful in the pursuit of positive and avoidance of negative value experience.

Both ordinary people and philosophers tend to concentrate on conceived values which are inferred, substantiated and verbally taught, whereas perceived values are just experienced by everyone as subjectively evident but objectively difficult to articulate. "Because the secondary [= conceived] values are in one way or another the product of rational thought, people tend to be consciously aware of the secondary values . . . Conversely, because the primary [= perceived] values are innate, and subjectively seem absolute, they tend to be ignored in our ordinary discussion of values" (Pugh 1977:33). In a similar vein, Epstein (1989:16) observed about perceived values: "One does not normally think of these implicit values as values because values have been treated as self-reported, socially oriented beliefs . . ." As Daniel Batson (1989:223) put it, value has to be *demythologized* in order to be scientifically understood.

A major complication of the human value system in general and of morals in particular is that conceived values are, to various degrees, turned into perceived values by one of many value-learning processes subsumed under the heading of internalization (Hoffman 1988). For this reason, the distinction between perceived and conceived values does not coincide, as asserted by Pugh (1977) and apparently assumed by Mandler (1984), with the distinction between the primary, innate and secondary, learned (Mandler's predicated) values. As important as the difference between the innate and learned value experience may be, from the point of view of an individual and his decisions it may not matter when and how values were assigned as long as they are experienced.

At first glance, the conceptualizations of the various sources of human value experience proposed so far seem to be rather disparate, but upon scrutiny reveal essential commonalities. Pugh (1977) distinguished "*selfish*" values which "are functionally related to survival and well-being," *intellectual values* which manifest themselves in curiosity, humor and preferences for truth and beauty, and *social values*, almost certainly a heteregenous category including in part the rewarding experience of socializing and in part the self-values. Pugh's concept of social values is partly based on the obsolete concept of the selection acting for the benefit of species. George Mandler (1984) distinguished *innate* values which refer to phenomenological experiences of goodness and badness accompanying the approach and avoidance behavior, *predicated* values encompassing all values assigned by cultural transmission, and *structural* values deriving from the cognitive processes of assimilation and accommodation. According to Epstein (1989), there are four sources of human basic (= perceived) values: (1) *pain and pleasure*, (2) *assimilating the data of reality*, (3) *belonging and relatedness*, and (4) *self-evaluation*. This wording invites an objection that any of the remaining sources may provide pleasure (unless pleasure is defined very restrictively, which is difficult to do in a nonarbitrary way). The three consensus sources of human value experience include *external incentives, intellectual activities*, and *social contacts*. All three are demonstrably shared with other higher vertebrates. External incentives and intellectual activities as sources of value experience are addressed below. The social preferences based on individual acquaintance and recognition are well evidenced in mammals and birds (Hinde 1987), which, in keeping with other evidence, suggests derivation of some reward from this source as well. Another higher vertebrate source of value experience, discussed below, is an individual's *own activities per se*, independently of the goals and effects.

Higher vertebrates employ at least some elements of the ECS including affective experience, preconscious thought and imagery associated with past emotional experience. There can now be little doubt that mammals and birds use mental representations (Walker 1983, 1987; Mackintosh 1987; Terrace 1987), which are preconscious in terms of human information processing. Whether empathy or vicarious value experience, as discussed below in connection with morality, is limited to humans and their closest relatives, remains to be determined. What clearly distinguishes humans from most animals is the RCS. Only chimpanzees and orangutans, who have the conscious self concept and the capability of causal thinking and prediction (Gallup 1983; Goodall 1986), seem to employ an inchoative RCS. The self as a major source of value experience, that may project into, or blend with, other kinds of value experience, seems to be almost exclusively human.

Direct Value Experience

Value experience is the outcome of various forms of automatic, subconscious information processing and/or intentional appraisal of an incentive object or situation (Bargh 1988; Smith and Lazarus 1990). When both intentional and automatic pathways are involved, the outcomes may disagree, as in the case of fear of certain objects that are known to be harmless (Griffiths 1990). Identification of an actual incentive or invocation of its mental representation triggers the process of value perception which is in part dependent on, and shows parallels to, sensory perception, for example, in being opaque to introspection. The conscious (or preconscious) value experience is the end result of the unconscious process of value perception.

A good insight into the nature of both value perception and experience in humans and other vertebrates has been obtained with the technique of electrical brain stimulation (ESB) (Kalat 1981). There are two kinds of behaviors elicited by ESB (Delgado 1968; Doty 1969; Vowles and Beasley 1974). ESB-*imposed* behaviors are automatic reactions limited in duration to the time of stimulation and *per se* do not have affective concomitants, for example, reactions elicited by stimulation of motor centers in the mammalian neocortex. In contrast, the ESB-*motivated* behaviors that include intracranial self-stimulation and its opposite, the learned avoidance of stimulation, are accompanied by affective expressions and extend beyond the period of stimulation itself, which acts as a reinforcer. When subjects are able to turn the stimulation on and off, some sites are self-stimulated while stimulation of other sites is avoided. ESB-motivated behaviors are elicited by stimulation of various sites in the limbic system and extralimbic parts of the brain reward system. The differences between ESB-imposed and ESB-motivated behaviors demonstrate a fundamental significance of the distinction between instinctive and motivated behaviors as proposed by Alan Epstein (1982). In being stereotyped and automatic, the ESB-imposed behaviors are manifestations of instinct, whereas the ESB-motivated behaviors are unequivocal manifestations of intervening affective states.

ESB-motivated behaviors are well known in mammals and birds. Depending on the location of electrodes, stimulation of the human reward system elicits a variety of pleasant feelings. Some of them, such as orgasm, are well defined, others are general good feelings of joy or satisfaction, that can lead to an integrated change in attitude, for example, when an unannounced stimulation is turned on during a neutral conversation, the subject starts talking about how much he or she enjoys the treatment at that hospital, etc. People may spontaneously self-stimulate, for example, for sexual gratification (Delgado 1976). Also fear and anxiety have been elicited in human patients in the absence of any external threat (Delgado 1968), resulting in hallucinating behavior similar to that evoked in animals, including birds (Vowles and Beasley 1974).

ESB-motivated behaviors demonstrate that positive and negative value experiences arise automatically from neuronal impulses in certain sites of the higher vertebrate brain. Whether an impulse is translated into a good or a bad experience depends on its destination site rather than on its origin or nature, which may be either sensory or inferential. This explains why affective states can be generated independently of propositional thinking (Griffiths 1989). At least insofar as the incentive is natural, there is a good correlation within the limbic system between self-stimulation or the avoidance of stimulation and, respectively, the positive or negative fitness impact of an incentive that naturally activates a site. The positive or negative value experience is generated automatically in concert with the biological meaning of the input resulting in the motivation of appetitive and avoidance behavior.

Good-bad polarization of external incentives. Since positive and negative affective states are directly or indirectly (e.g., via learning) involved in the motivation of evidently adaptive approach and avoidance behavior, the origin of good and bad feelings seems to be obvious in terms of ultimate, evolutionary causes: the negative experience or punishment has been associated with the exposure to factors that decrease fitness and the positive experience or reward has been associated with situations that enhance fitness. The value component of sensations such as pain or taste is well demonstrated experimentally (Young 1961; Cabanac 1979; Stellar 1982), and the evaluation component of such emotions as fear, anxiety, disgust or joy, is now broadly recognized as well (Piaget 1981; Mandler 1984; Scherer 1984; Stein and Levine 1987; Smith and Lazarus 1990). What these affective states have in common is a combination of the stimulus- or incentive-specific components with the positive or negative, rewarding or punishing, value experience. It is value experience that conveys the directional, aversive or appetitive component to the ensuing behavior. The motivational function of such emotions as fear or joy is undeniable (Scherer 1984; Smith and Lazarus 1990) and some controversy over this point, as discussed by Scherer (1984), is due to a rather unrealistic notion of all affective states called emotions being functionally uniform. Some of them (e.g., surprise) may not be associated with a definite, if any, value experience and may not perform a motivational function.

Motivation by perceived value of the external incentives appears early in human development, from the ages of approximately two and a half to seven or eight months, when the infant comes to associate joy with the attainment of a goal and distress with failure (Piaget 1981; Stein and Levine 1987). The early development of motivation by incentive value in infant humans is in keeping with the presence of this type of motivation in mammals, birds, and possibly also in some other vertebrates (Epstein 1982; Walker 1983; Elzanowski 1991). In higher vertebrates at least, value experience is just as important as cognitive processes in the individual's commerce with the environment. The ability to experience value is implicit in the current views on associative learning in higher vertebrates, which recognize the leading role of mental expectancy in both instrumental and classic (Pavlovian) conditioning (Mackintosh 1983, 1987; Walker 1987). Expectancy involves the concentration of attention on a mental representation of something absent. While occurrent events may be neutral and still attract attention, the only reason for animals and humans alike to concentrate on something absent is its being either attractive or aversive. Clearly, in mammals and birds, a value component of the expectancy is necessary to launch the pursuit or avoidance of remote incentive objects.

In addition to the ESB-motivated behavior, there are other phenomena, such as value-dependent interaction of incentives, affective categorization, and affective contrast, that testify to the value polarization of motivational states in higher vertebrates. *Value-dependent interaction of incentives* occurs when two positive or two negative incentives tend to enhance while the incentives with opposite value assignments tend to inhibit their motivational effects (Toates 1986, 1988). In conditioned suppression, a signal for an aversive event interferes with bar pressing for food and a signal for food inhibits bar pressing to avoid shock even though, in each case, the food and an aversive event are delivered independently of each other. Since affective experience is preconscious rather than unconscious, some interference or synergism is to be expected between two affective states of the opposite or same valence, respectively.

Hoffman (1986:250) called attention to *affective categorization* in humans.

"Items that differ in physical appearance may nevertheless satisfy a need or interfere with its satisfaction; consequently, these items evoke the same affect despite their physical differences." In animals, affective categorization is revealed by similarities in learned reactions to either appetitive or aversive but otherwise dissimilar incentives. For example, rats tend to bury such disparate aversive objects as shock electrodes and poisoned food (see Walker 1987 for references and discussion). Since the only commonality of the incentives is their value sign, it is similar value experience that motivates similar behaviors. A spectacular example of affective categorization has become known through behavioral research (Mackintosh 1983): animals tend to react in a similar way to a punishment and an omission of the reward in fixed schedule conditioning. This observation provides unequivocal evidence for the awareness of want/have states in higher vertebrates, which is essential to the experience of emotion (Stein and Levine 1987): in the former case an animal does not want to attain something but attains it, whereas in the latter case an animal wants to attain something and does not attain it.

The aversive reaction to the omission of reward also illustrates the phenomenon of *affective contrast*, which is known in humans, other mammals and birds (Solomon and Corbit 1974; Solomon 1982). In the experimental paradigm, the removal of a stimulus that elicits a primary positive or negative affective state leads to a secondary affective state of opposite valence, rather than to the reinstatement of the initial state or neutrality. The perceived absence *per se* of a stimulus is experienced as negative and thus becomes a stimulus itself. Affective contrast also occurs when an item initially appears to match a value-charged cognitive schema and thus evokes an anticipatory positive or negative value experience but upon closer examination turns into a mismatch, which leads to an affect of opposite valence (Hoffman 1986). Similarly, the expectancy of reward evokes a positive anticipatory affect and the following omission of reward leads to a negative affect.

Activity reward. Good evidence is now available that nonhuman mammals, as well as birds, may derive gratification from their own activities *per se* (Dawkins 1990), in addition to the external stimulation during consummatory acts. For example, both mammals and birds may prefer earned to free food. Play probably derives from such functional, gratifying activities (Elzanowski 1991). As a behavior rewarding for its own sake, play demonstrates at least the channelling potential of individual value experience on the evolution of behavior or, possibly, a manifestation of its autonomy with respect to selective constraints if Martin and Caro (1985) are right that play is of minor adaptive importance. The emergence of activity-derived reward is a result of value transfer from ends to means, whereby the activity is "ontified, changed from a mere means into an end, a value in itself" (Maslow 1963:125). The "ontification" or upgrading of means to ends seems to be an omnipresent driving force in the lives of humans and other higher vertebrates alike.

Intellectual reward. Pugh (1977) considers intellectual (including aesthetic) values to be one of the main categories of his primary (= innate perceived) values and curiosity to be a symptom of intellectual reward. Epstein (1989) views "assimilating the data of reality" as one of four sources of human basic values. Mandler (1984) expounded the cognitive processes of Piagetian assimilation and accommodation as a source of "structural" values (the structure being thought of in the structuralist meaning of a relational system). According to Mandler, the sign and intensity of value experience resulting from the cognitive effort depend on the congruity vs. incongruity of the perceived pattern with an expectation schema and the ensuing course of the processes (assimilation, choosing an alternate schema, or accommodation). As appealing as it is, this model does not seem to be supported by strong evidence if applied to "cold" or affectively neutral schemata. Hoffman (1986:249-50) concludes his discussion of this subject by stating that "a mismatch between a stimulus and an affectively neutral schema may produce a feeling of perturbation, surprise, or relief from boredom" but admits that the preference for novelty presumably involves positive feelings.

Mammals and birds are known to examine and manipulate new objects, which is generally seen as a manifestation of curiosity (McFarland 1987). Since this kind of exploratory behavior is demonstrably voluntary and higher vertebrates are known, on independent evidence, to be motivated by reward and punishment, it is more than likely that exploration of novelty is accompanied by rewarding experience. The exploratory behavior of primates goes far beyond this, for example, rhesus macaques may spontaneously learn a puzzle game without ever receiving an external reward. Intellectual reward could possibly be looked upon as a form of the activity reward, although they differ in the importance of the end state, which does not matter in typical forms of rewarded activities such as play.

Summary of direct value experience. The motivational effects of brain stimulation whether electrical or chemical (the latter resulting in drug dependence, which is known in both mammals and birds), the evidence for good-bad polarization of the motivational states, the activity reward, as well as motivational requirements of the associative and insight learning are some of the many lines of evidence that demonstrate broad employ-ment of value experience in the motivation of mammals as well as birds (Elzanowski 1991). The same evidence demonstrates that humans inherited the capability of value experience as well as biologically important value assignments from their mammalian ancestors, which amounts to the homology of value perception of basic biological incentives in humans and other mammals. This is in keeping with the now well estab-lished existence of pancultural, psychoevolved emotions (Ekman 1984; Griffiths 1990).

Due to their great importance for survival, value assignments have been subject to selective control and incentive objects obviously vary between species. What re-mains conserved, however, is the capability of binary subjective distinction between good and bad and a number of biologically meaningful value assignments to universal, invariably appetitive or aversive vertebrate incentives such as food, injury, threat, etc. These assignments are the heritage of our mammalian ancestry and play an important role in today's morals as yardsticks for the evaluation of our impact on the others' welfare. For example, it is by virtue of the inherited negative value experience of starvation that we do not consider the latter to be a morally appropriate method of population control.

Reward and punishment evolved far back in the phylogeny of nonsocial mam-mals or their ancestors to motivate appetitive and avoidance behavior. Both value experience and the oldest value assignments reflected in today's morals evolved in the service of individual survival, rather than social interactions. Consequently, value experience conveys intrinsic value to the *individual* life. This has not only ethical but also biological consequences. Motivation by reward and punishment sets the limits to the level an individual can be manipulated into self-sacrifice, meaning that value experi-ence imposes specific constraints on the ways inclusive fitness is maximized. Even the most social of nonhuman higher vertebrates, such as naked mole rats (Bathyergidae), do not, and, I believe, cannot reach the level of individual sacrifice known in social insects, such as termites. Once value experience has been developed to motivate individual survival, it apparently cannot be temporarily turned off even if this would bring gains in inclusive fitness. This limitation may be overcome only in humans through the *superposition* of other values.

On the other hand, it is the motivation power of value experience which makes higher vertebrates as inventive as they are and thus opens up new adaptive avenues. Firstly, the phenomenal perception of goal value, which is mediated by a mental rep-resentation of the goal, permits decoupling of the reaction from the stimulus (Scherer

1984) and thus a flexible, cross-situational pursuit. Secondly, the employment of the reward mechanism opens up unlimited possibilities of motivating various intelligent, flexible activities without any external goal and thus doing things of prospective significance such as play and exploration out of curiosity. Whatever their adaptive significance, from the subjective point of view of an individual their rewarding performance enriches individual life. Mammals and birds enjoy not only consumption but also working for it.

The totality of value experience determines the individual well-being. An individual can, to the extent of his or her abilities, control the exposure in time and space to the incentive objects, situations or ideas that release negative or positive experience but can do very little about value assignments and the properties of experience itself (such as intensity), and certainly cannot voluntarily change the valence of releasing factors. Whereas the experience of the internalized, or perhaps not completely internalized, values may possibly be volitionally suppressed or extinguished, the experience of biologically assigned values is only marginally subject to volitional control. Experience of innate vertebrate values constitutes a substantial part of human well-being. Vertebrate values motivating humans may be only counterbalanced but not superseded by the human-specific values including the self-values and the vast array of internalized and conceived values. In some persons the counterbalance is heavier than in others and reaches an extreme among heroes and martyrs. In fact, those extreme cases provide the best proof of the moral relevance of core vertebrate values such as those experienced with pain, fear, hunger and thirst: if they were morally unimportant, as the advocates of speciesism often maintain, martyrdom would be a fiction. Some people are apparently capable of incurring the "peak experiences" which are the best, grandiose moments of their lives, even at the price of pain and torture (Maslow 1963), but this is clearly a high price to pay. Suffering *per se* is pure badness even if some people are ready to incur it for compensation in another currency. The ambivalent status of suffering in Western cultures stems, I believe, from religion. In Christianity and other monotheistic religions, the value experience is given the status of a conceived value, originally conceived of as a means to some sort of compensation, such as salvation, damnation, or whatever, depending on the sign. Aside from the past suppression of pleasure and joy, this doctrinal detour has two opposite effects. On the light side, the conceived value of suffering helps people to cope with it. On the dark side, it diminishes or denies the negative value experienced by those currently seen as having no access to compensation.

Vicarious Value Experience and Morality

The function of moral principles, such as honesty, is to control the deeds and intentions known to be good or bad. Such moral principles obviously cannot say what is good or bad. They are meaningful only if there are some good and bad things out there, for example, honesty is a value only insofar as there is something meaningful to be honest about. Whether honesty evolved by natural selection and/or was once conceived and is internalized ever since, it originated only after the impact of one's behavior on another's well-being could be assessed.

If the function of morality is to control the impact of one's action (or inaction) on another's well-being, then the assessment of this impact is an essential element of any moral evaluation, be it affective or rational. Starting from the age of about two, humans are in possession of a psychological automatic or semi-automatic mechanism that performs the assessment of the individual well-being of others by means of a shared affective response (Strayer 1987) and may, depending on a not yet clarified process of responsibility attribution, motivate a reaction directed at alleviating the perceived suffering (Hoffman 1988; Eisenberg 1988). This mechanism is known as *empathy* and defined as "an affective state that stems from the apprehension of another's emotional state or condition" and "includes emotional matching and the vicarious experiencing of a range of emotions consistent with those of others" (Eisenberg and Miller 1987:91). Insofar as another's affective state has both an incentive-specific and a value component, the vicarious experiencing of this state involves the vicarious experiencing of value; in fact it is the consistency of valence that is a necessary, if not a sufficient, condition for direct and vicarious affective experience to be mutually consistent. As a mechanism by which one individual can participate in another's value experience, empathy belongs to the major determinants of prosocial (mostly helping) behavior (Eisenberg 1988; Hoffman 1988). Since a substantial part of human experience stems from values shared with other vertebrates, *it is through empathy that the ancient mammalian or vertebrate value experience gained moral significance,* that is, the potential to motivate an action directed at another's well-being.

The research on empathy over the last two decades has brought insights into its function and moral significance as well as some controversy over the relationships between empathy and its cognitive antecedents or components, which reflects the more general problems of contemporary psychology in dealing with the interface of affect and cognition. By rigorous conceptual analysis, Janet Strayer (1987) could reaffirm the distinction between empathy as an affective phenomenon and its antecedents that include various cognitive forms of perspective taking (role taking). The moral role of empathy can be best understood by casting the processes of moral evaluation into the already mentioned conceptual framework proposed by Epstein (1989). The evaluative processes that may lead to moral action run either in the experiential conceptual system (ECS) or in the rational conceptual system (RCS). Empathizing (Eisenberg 1988) and "empathic anger" elicited by the experience of an actor's intention (Hoffman 1988) arise in the ECS. The preconscious nature of empathy has been recognized by clinicians (Goldstein and Michaels 1985). Rational moral judgment, which has been in the focus of most moral philosophy and the developmental studies it engendered (Kohlberg 1976; Rest 1983), arises in the RCS. The rational moral judgment is certainly human-specific as it necessitates propositional thinking, whereas affective moral evaluation is clearly present, at least in chimpanzees, as revealed, for example, by their comforting behavior (Goodall 1986).

The rational moral judgment is both developmentally and phylogenetically pre-ceded by, and, as no value can be created out of pure reasoning, functionally dependent on, affective value experience. Therefore, value experience must be *somehow* reflected in the moral judgment. The word "somehow" stands here for a serious problem on the borderline of psychology and logic. Value experience as such is not directly amenable to logical operations in the RCS. The RCS has to rely on a cognitive proxy or the awareness of the positive or negative value experience associated with certain types of situations. We know what is good or bad insofar as we have relevant good or bad experiences that we remember and/or extrapolate on imagined or reported events. We can understand other people's reports of good or bad feelings, even in totally unknown situations, only because we can invoke the awareness of our previous negative or positive value experiences. As is true for other kinds of knowledge, the awareness of value experience can be stored in the memory and *instantaneously* (microgenetically) used for the moral judgment independently of affective evaluation, a point recently featured by Reykowski (1989). However, the moral judgment would not be possible without the prior formation of the value concept through a conscious reflection of one's own preconscious experience. Value experience is the ultimate source of motivation for all voluntary actions, both selfish and moral.

Harold Kelley (1971) envisioned moral evaluation as drawing in part on "the process of reality evaluation." I believe that the empathic vicarious value experience fulfills this vision in being doubly rooted in reality by relying on cognitive perspective taking and direct value experience. The functional dependence of empathy on some form of perspective taking seems to be generally accepted (Underwood and Moore

1982; Batson 1987; Strayer 1987; Hoffman 1988). Affective perspective taking, which has the most direct bearing on empathy (Strayer 1987), clearly depends on the empathizer's own direct experience, for example, persons incapable of feeling pain (which is a real but rare genetic aberration) would empathize less, if at all, with others in pain. Both perspective taking and direct value experience (the motivating sensations and emotions) perform functions that are essential for survival in the physical and social environment, independently of their being antecedents to empathy and its moral consequences. The veracity of perspective taking, as well as of one's own direct experience, due to their survival functions, cannot be corrupted at the risk of the subject's losing contact with his social and biological basis of individual existence. Once activated, empathy seems to have at least a potential for providing reasonably reliable information on another's value experience and thus to prompt a morally well justified action. However, the activation and, thus, the exercise of empathy is controlled by preemptive evaluation, in particular by the devaluation of others, leading to their discrimination and mistreatment (Staub 1989). This is possibly the most consequential natural flaw of human morality, the discussion of which is beyond the scope of this paper.

Conclusions

Morals are based on shared values and must, therefore, rely on the ability to experience any values at all. This capability evolved far back in vertebrate phylogeny. The reward and punishment motivation system, the primary evolutionary source of all good and bad value experience on the Earth, seems to be a vertebrate specialty. Humans inherited from their mammalian ancestors both the capacity for value experience and value assignments to universal biological incentives. Through empathy, which involves vicarious value experience and thus permits feeling good or bad for someone else, the individual value experience came to shape our behavior towards others after motivating mammals ever since their Mesozoic appearance.

Once we comprehend where our values come from and how they work, we will be in a position to manage them in order to get the best for everyone out of our biological and cultural heritage. A synthesis of psychology, neurobiology and evolutionary biology has a potential to provide an objective reference for such consistent value management. The understanding of value experience will provide a rational perspective on moral conflicts and the objective criteria to solve them. However, in order to be understood, value experience has first to be accepted as a natural phenomenon, as an objective source of subjectivity. Meanwhile, science appears to be having problems with this acceptance due in part to the difficulty in handling the discontinuities on the way from value perception to the rational value judgment, and in part to the reluctance to recognize the moral significance of value experience beyond the limits of our species (Rollin 1989).

Acknowledgments

A preliminary version of this paper was presented at the 1991 Biannual Meeting of the International Society of History, Philosophy and Social Studies of Biology (IS/HPSSB) at Evanston, IL. I thank David Shaner (Furman University) for the encouragement to turn my talk into a paper, and Lynne Hromek (Max-Planck-Institut für Biochemie) for the editorial help.

References

Bargh, J. A. 1988. Automatic information processing: Implication for communication and affect, 9-32. In *Communication, Social Cognition and Affect*, ed. L. Donohew, H. E. Sypher, and E. T. Higgins. Hillsdale, NJ: Lawrence Erlbaum.

Batson, C. D. 1987. Prosocial motivation: Is it ever truly altruistic? *Advances in Experimental Social Psychology* 20:65-122.

Batson, C. D. 1989. Personal values, moral principles, and a three-path model of prosocial motivation, 213-28. In *Social and Moral Values*, ed. N. Eisenberg, J. Reykowski, and E. Staub. Hillsdale, NJ: Lawrence Erlbaum.

Cabanac, M. 1979. Sensory pleasure. *The Quarterly Review of Biology* 54:1-29.

Dawkins, M. S. 1990. From animal's point of view: Motivation, fitness, and animal welfare. *Behavioral and Brain Sciences* 13:1-61.

Delgado, J. M. R. 1968. Emotional behavior in animals and humans, 309-17. In *The Nature of Emotion*, ed. M. B. Arnold. Baltimore: Penguin Books.

Delgado, J. M. R. 1976. New orientations in brain stimulation in man, 481-503. In *Brain-Stimulation Reward*, ed. A. Wauquier and E. T. Rolls. Amsterdam: North Holland.

Doty, R. W. 1969. Electrical stimulation of the brain in behavioral context. *Annual Review of Psychology* 20:289-320.

Eisenberg, N. 1988. The development of prosocial and aggressive behavior, 461-95. In *Developmental Psychology: An Advanced Textbook*, ed. M. H. Bornstein and M. E. Lamb. Hillsdale, NJ: Lawrence Erlbaum.

Eisenberg, N., and P. A. Miller. 1987. The relation of empathy to prosocial and related behaviors. *Psychological Bulletin* 101:91-119.

Ekman, P. 1984. Expression and the nature of emotion, 319-43. In *Approaches to Emotion*, ed. K. R. Scherer and P. Ekman. Hillsdale, NJ: Lawrence Erlbaum.

Elzanowski, A. 1991. Motivation and subjective experience in birds. *Acta XX Congressus Internationalis Ornithologici*: 1921-29.

Epstein, A. N. 1982. Instinct and motivation as explanations for complex behavior, 25-58. In *The Physiological Mechanisms of Motivation*, ed. D. W. Pfaff. New York: Springer.

Epstein, S. 1989. Values from the perspective of cognitive-experiential self-theory, 3-22. In *Social and Moral Values*, ed. N. Eisenberg, J. Reykowski, and E. Staub. Hillsdale, NJ: Lawrence Erlbaum.

Frankena, W. K. 1967. Value and valuation, 229-32. In *The Encyclopedia of Philosophy*, vol. 7, ed. P. Edwards. New York: Macmillan and The Free Press.

Gallup, G. G., Jr. 1983. Toward comparative psychology of mind, 473-510. In *Animal Cognition and Behavior*, ed. R. L. Mellgren. Amsterdam: North Holland.

Goldstein, A. P., and Michaels, G. Y. 1985. *Empathy: Development, Training, and Consequences.* Hillsdale, NJ: Lawrence Erlbaum.

Goodall, J. 1986. *The Chimpanzees of Gombe: Patterns of Behavior.* Cambridge, MA: Harvard University Press.

Griffiths, P. E. 1989. The degeneration of the cognitive theory of emotions. *Philosophical Psychology* 2:297-313.

Griffiths, P. E. 1990. Modularity, and the psychoevolutionary theory of emotion. *Biology & Philosophy* 5:175-96.

Herrick, C. J. 1961. *The Evolution of Human Nature.* New York: Harper & Brothers.

Hinde, R. A. 1987. Social relationships, 521-27. In *The Oxford Companion to Animal Behavior*, ed. D. McFarland. Oxford: Oxford University Press.

Hoffman, M. L. 1986. Affect, cognition, and motivation, 244-80. In *Handbook of Motivation and Cognition*, ed. R. M. Sorrentino and E. T. Higgins. New York: The Guilford Press.

Hoffman, M. L. 1988. Moral development, 497-598. In *Developmental Psychology: An Advanced Textbook*, ed. M. H. Bornstein and M. E. Lamb. Hillsdale, NJ: Lawrence Erlbaum.

Kalat, J. W. 1981. *Biological Psychology.* Belmont, CA: Wadsworth.

Kelley, H. H. 1971. Moral evaluation. *American Psychologist* 26:293-300.

Kohlberg, L. 1976. Moral stage and moralization: The cognitive-developmental approach, 31-53. In *Moral Development and Behavior: Theory, Research, and Social Issues*, ed. T. Lickona. New York: Holt, Rinehart & Winston.

Mackintosh, N. J. 1983. *Conditioning and Associative Learning.* Oxford: Clarendon Press.

Mackintosh, N. J. 1987. Animal minds, 111-20. In *Mindwaves*, ed. C. Blakemore and S. Greenfield. Oxford: Basil Blackwell.

Mandler, G. 1984. *Mind and Body: Psychology of Emotion and Stress.* New York: W. W. Norton.

Martin, P., and T. M. Caro. 1985. On the functions of play and its role in behavioral development. *Advances in the Study of Behavior* 15:59-103.

Maslow, A. H. 1963. Fusions of facts and values. *American Journal of Psychoanalysis* 23:117-31.

McFarland, D. 1987. Curiosity, 114. In *The Oxford Companion to Animal Behavior*, ed. D. McFarland. Oxford: Oxford University Press.

Nagel, T. 1979. *Mortal Questions.* Cambridge: Cambridge University Press.

Piaget, J. 1981. *Intelligence and Affectivity.* Palo Alto, CA: Annual Reviews Monographs.

Pugh, G. E. 1977. *The Biological Origin of Human Values.* New York: Basic Books.

Rest, J. R. 1983. Morality, 556-629. In *Handbook of Child Psychology*, vol. 3, ed. J. H. Flavell and E. M. Markman. New York: John Wiley & Sons.

Reykowski, J. 1989. Dimensions of development in moral values, 23-44. In *Social and Moral Values*, ed. N. Eisenberg, J. Reykowski, and E. Staub. Hillsdale, NJ: Lawrence Erlbaum.

Rokeach, M. 1973. *The Nature of Human Values.* New York: The Free Press.

Rollin, B. E. 1989. *The Unheeded Cry: Animal Consciousness, Animal Pain and Science.* Oxford: Oxford University Press.

Scherer, K. R. 1984. On the nature and function of emotion: A component process approach, 293-318. In *Approaches to Emotion*, ed. K. R. Scherer and P. Ekman. Hillsdale, NJ: Lawrence Erlbaum.

Smith, C. A., and R. S. Lazarus. 1990. Emotion and adaptation, 609-37. In *Handbook of Personality: Theory and Research*, ed. L. A. Perwin. New York: The Guilford Press.

Solomon, R. L. 1982. The opponent process theory of acquired motivation, 321-36. In *The Physiological Mechanisms of Motivation*, ed. D.W. Pfaff. New York: Springer.

Solomon, R. L., and J. D. Corbit. 1974. An opponent process theory of motivation: I. Temporal dynamics of affect. *Psychological Review* 81:119-45.

Sperry, R. W. 1972. Science and the problem of values. *Perspectives in Biology and Medicine* 16:115-30.

Staub, E. 1989. Individual and societal (group) values in a motivational perspective and their role in benevolence and harmdoing, 45-61. In *Social and Moral Values*, ed. N. Eisenberg, J. Reykowski, and E. Staub. Hillsdale, NJ: Lawrence Erlbaum.

Stein, N. L., and L. J. Levine. 1987. Thinking about feelings: The development and organization of emotional knowledge, 165-98. In *Aptitude, Learning, and Instruction.* Vol. 3: *Conative and Affective Process Analyses*, ed. R. E. Snow and M. J. Farr. Hillsdale, NJ: Lawrence Erlbaum.

Stellar, E. 1982. Brain mechanisms in hedonic processes, 377-407. In *The Physiological Mechanisms of Motivation*, ed. D. W. Pfaff. New York: Springer.

Strayer, J. 1987. Affective and cognitive perspectives on empathy, 218-44. In *Empathy and Its Development*, ed. N. Eisenberg and J. Strayer. Cambridge: Cambridge University Press.

Terrace, H. 1987. Thoughts without words, 123-37. In *Mindwaves*, ed. C. Blakemore and S. Greenfield. Oxford: Basil Blackwell.

Toates, F. M. 1986. *Motivational Systems*. Cambridge: Cambridge University Press.

Toates, F. M. 1988. Motivation and emotion from a biological perspective, 3-35. In *Cognitive Perspectives on Emotion and Motivation*, ed. V. Hamilton, G. H. Bower, and N. H. Frijda. Dordrecht: Kluwer Academic Publishers.

Underwood, B., and B. Moore. 1982. Perspective-taking and altruism. *Psychological Bulletin* 91:143-73.

Vowles, D. M., and L. D. Beasley. 1974. The neural substrate of emotional behavior in birds, 221-58. In *Birds Brain and Behavior*, ed. I. J. Goodman and M. W. Schein. New York: Academic Press.

Walker, S. 1983. *Animal Thought*. London: Routledge & Kegan Paul.

Walker, S. 1987. *Animal Learning*. London: Routledge & Kegan Paul.

Young, P. T. 1961. *Motivation and Emotion*. New York: John Wiley & Sons.

Young, P. T. 1967. Affective arousal: Some implications. *American Psychologist* 22:32-40.

The Chimpanzee's Mind:
How Noble in Reason? How Absent of Ethics?

Daniel J. Povinelli and Laurie R. Godfrey

Morality and ethics in humans are generally understood by sociobiologists in the same terms as altruism in other animals. According to this perspective, altruism exists because it confers a net reproductive advantage, either through kin selection or reciprocity, on those genes that support it. Thus, the theory of inclusive fitness allows sociobiologists to describe altruistic and ethical behaviors as genetically selfish even if they are individually generous. The position of sociobiologists is clear: When individuals behave in ways that put their own survival and reproduction at risk for the benefit of others, those costs must be genetically recouped.

A Cognitive Gap

In this paper, we examine the evolution of ethics in humans from an entirely different perspective. We ask what characteristics support the expression of altruism and ethics in humans, and how they are distributed among humans and their closest relatives. We seek to understand the unique ways in which altruism and ethics are expressed in humans, including their motivational complexity and cultural plasticity. We recognize that ethical systems can be described as a set of specific behaviors (Alexander 1987). But, instead of concentrating on cataloguing those behaviors and assessing their presumed ultimate causes, we focus on their cognitive underpinnings—the proximate mechanisms that support and motivate them. We believe that these capacities can help account for the fact that ethical belief systems are culturally plastic.

Based on recent research on chimpanzee cognition, it seems likely that some of the cognitive capacities that underlie the expression of ethics in humans were also present in the common ancestor of humans and chimpanzees. In particular, some subset of the abilities to project emotions, intentions, and states of belief onto others appear to have evolved long before the emergence of *Homo sapiens*. It is our contention that the evolution of human ethical systems depended on the appearance of these ancestral cognitive capabilities, in addition to others that are unique to humans. It is an important corollary of our argument, then, that humanity's closest living relatives share some of the cognitive capacities that were necessary, but not sufficient, for the emergence of ethics. Thus, we intend to show how the evolution of specific cognitive features ultimately led to the development of ethical systems in humans.

In order to develop this argument, we must review data on social cognition in nonhuman primates. Admittedly, such data are meager and sometimes contradictory. There is a rich anecdotal database, but it lends itself easily to myriad alternative interpretations, each often lacking in experimental confirmation (Cheney and Seyfarth 1990; Premack 1988a). In this chapter, we limit our comparisons to chimpanzees and humans for two reasons. First, the relevant cognitive capacities of chimpanzees are better understood than are those of other primates. Second, chimpanzees are closely related to humans (perhaps more than any other living ape) and, therefore, shared characteristics of humans and chimpanzees may reveal characters of the most recent human-ape ancestor. This rather restricted comparison in no way implies that we believe comparisons with other primate species are unnecessary. To the contrary, part of our conclusion is that such broader comparisons are critical.

Our interest in the chimpanzee's mind derives directly from our conviction that ethics are the result of complex psychological processes that were, in turn, a consequence of the evolution of the human brain. The first step in reconstructing the evolution of human ethics, is to determine which relevant psychological capacities were present in the common ancestor of humans and their closest living relatives. By determining the shared cognitive capacities of chimpanzees and humans, we may draw conclusions about the likely capacities of their common ancestor. In addition, chimpanzees may also be a fairly good model for the psychological capacities of the human-chimpanzee common ancestor. Due to the rapid, recent, and well-documented changes in both the size and organization of the human brain (Tobias 1971; Holloway 1975; Falk 1987; Godfrey and Jacobs 1981), it is highly probable that the cognitive capacities of living chimpanzees are closer to those of the common ancestor than are those of living humans. The second step in this reconstruction is to determine which cognitive capacities, essential for the emergence of human ethical systems, evolved *after* the divergence of humans and chimpanzees.

In sum, we seek to understand how social caring and cultural networks of shared social values depend on the evolution of cognitive capacities. This means explicitly addressing the cognitive gap left by analyses that focus on ultimate causation.

Attribution and Ethics

Proximate causes of behavior can be studied at many levels, some of which may be more illuminating for our purposes than others. B. F. Skinner's school of radical behaviorism, for example, argued that all behaviors are acquired through positive or negative feedback—i.e., through associations of specific environmental conditions with specific organismal responses. From this perspective, even the most complex human behavior is seen as mere conditioned physical movement that has no underlying basis apart from operant and instrumental learning (Epstein, Lanza, and Skinner 1981).

Another approach to studying proximate causation has been heralded by cognitive psychologists. Dissatisfied with the radical behaviorist's restrictive framework, cognitive psychologists (building upon the work of learning theorists such as Stence and Hull) have argued that mental processes are open to inferential investigation through careful experimental procedures. The emerging view of cognitive psychology is that the presence of mental structures and processes can be experimentally confirmed or refuted. Jean Piaget, for example, used this approach even in the heyday of radical behaviorism and studied the mental representations of young children in order to develop a theory of epistemology.

A third approach to understanding behavior at a proximate level has been adopted by many attribution theorists in the field of social psychology. Social psychologists have developed a "commonsense" psychology based on Heider's (1944, 1958) understanding of the mental processes that people use to account for their own behaviors and the behaviors of others. An entire field of psychology is now devoted to describing and predicting human behavior in terms of attributional processes (Harvey and Weary 1981). Social attribution theory refers to "how one person thinks and feels about another person, how one person perceives another, what one expects another person to do or think, how one person reacts to the actions of another" (Harvey and Weary 1981:5). Self-attribution theory investigates parallel processes concerning how people view themselves.

Thus, some researchers advocate an approach to studying behavior which makes reference to cognition, representation, and meaning, while others believe that behavior is best studied without reference to such mentalistic terminology. This contrast is embodied in Weber's (1947) differentiation of "behavior" from "action." Behavior describes the mechanics of what people (or animals) do—their physical movements. Action, on the other hand, describes the same movements, but addresses them within the context of the meaning which governs them. For example, the statement that "the monkey's head turned in the direction of the leopard" describes behavior, whereas the statement "the monkey turned to look at the leopard" describes action. Burke (1966) made a similar distinction, arguing that action is an inherently human concept—not shared by other animals. Harré and Secord (1972) and Asquith (1984) have discussed this distinction in greater detail.

The distinction between action and behavior can provide an important point of departure for understanding the evolution of human altruism and ethics. It can help us to see that there are potentially two very different types of altruistic behaviors—those that are governed by an organism's awareness of mental states in themselves and others, and those that are not. This distinction is critical, because we believe that it was the emergence of certain forms of *social attribution* (that is, projection of mental states onto others) that made human altruism possible, and that facilitated the development of the diversity of human ethical systems. This is not to say that other levels of analysis are useless or unimportant. Rather, we argue that evolutionary explanations of human altruism, based on either kin selection or on cultural transmission through learning, have lacked a theme that is both unifying and plausible.

What is attribution?   Social attribution is the ability to project mental states onto others. There are many kinds of attributional processes, some of which appear earlier in human ontogeny than others. We can distinguish, for example, intention attribution from belief attribution. Consider a mother watching her 3-year-old child trying to force a large ball inside a cup that is too small for it. How does the mother explain her child's behavior? Of course, explanations and interpretations of the causes of behavior may vary according to context and cultural background. But regardless of cultural background, the mother may attribute to her child the *desire, goal* or *intention* of placing the ball inside the cup. But now let us suppose that the child recognizes the futility of the task and moves over to another cup large enough to contain the ball, but with a lid on it. The child pulls off the lid and peers inside. The mother is now likely to make another attribution, but in this case a *belief* attribution about the knowledge state of her child. The mother reasons, "My child *looked* inside the cup and therefore *knows* what is inside."

In attributing intention the mother is making an inference about a motivational state such as want or desire, but in attributing belief she is making an inference about a knowledge state of her child based upon her understanding of the causal relationship between seeing (perception) and knowing (informational state). This is important because the attribution of intention is a capacity that 3-year-old children share with adults (see Miller and Aloise 1989). Yet the latter skill (understanding the causal relationship between seeing and knowing) is one that 3-year-olds apparently do not share with adults (Hogrefe, Wimmer, and Perner 1986; Wimmer, Hogrefe, and Perner 1988; Perner and Ogden 1988; Povinelli and DeBlois, n.d.; but see Pillow 1989; Pratt and Bryant 1990). It is not that 3-year-old children are unable to understand that other individuals possess states of knowledge, but rather they have not yet developed an understanding of how these mental states arise. Regardless of the specifics of this particular issue, the broader point is that attributional capacities are not present at birth, but rather they are manifestations of normal developmental processes, and certain aspects of their developmental timing or sequence can be predicted.

Self-attribution—the ability to draw inferences about one's own intentions, values, personality, and competencies (Harvey and Weary 1981)—plays an important role in attribution theory as well. The importance of the concept of self was highlighted by the influential work of George Herbert Mead (1934). Mead believed that the concept of self develops in humans through early (and largely unconscious) interactions with others. Indeed, pursuing the ideas of his mentor, Cooley (1912), Mead (1934) offered the then surprising view that the self is not the starting point for human interactions, but rather emerges from them. Thus, Mead believed that interactions with other humans precede and are responsible for the development of "mind," which he defined as "the ability to reflect upon one's actions and those of others" (Ashworth 1979:8). For Mead, "mind" was a process rather than an entity. He placed special emphasis on the importance of role-playing in the development of the mind. Piaget also believed that symbolic thought develops first through action, although his work is less centered on the importance of social interactions. Both Mead and Piaget believed that young children are unable to take on the perspective of other individuals, but that they later develop this ability through complex interactions with others. The importance that both Mead and Piaget placed on role-taking and perspective-taking firmly links their work with modern attribution theory. More recently, interactionists (like Mead) have further explored the ways in which the process of mind functions in daily interpersonal relationships (for example, Goffman 1959).

Is attribution a human universal? We assume that self- and social attributional capacities exist in all humans (in the sense that they are manifestations of normal developmental processes), and that while their expression may be affected by culture, their existence is not. This assumption may seem naive to some cultural anthropologists on the grounds that it appears to ignore the wealth of anthropological inquiries into the unique ways in which concepts such as self, intention, and meaning are construed in different societies (Geertz 1973; Mauss 1984; La Fontaine 1984; Lienhardt 1984; Duranti 1988). An anthropological critic may see our use of evidence derived from Western cultures as at odds with the cultural construction of the meaning of "self" and "other." However, we side with those cultural anthropologists who have consistently emphasized the universal aspects of self, intention and other attributional processes, while simultaneously exploring the ways in which these constructs are shaped by cultural frames of reference (Hallowell 1960, 1971; White 1980; Heelas 1981; Hollis 1984; Lock 1981; Lutz 1985; Ekman 1973). It seems obvious to us that humans, in all cultural contexts, have attributional tendencies. However, it also seems clear that the specific behaviors that emerge from these universal psychological processes may be radically different, and some authors have developed models to explain how such differentiation occurs (Heelas 1981). To clarify our position, let us explore some universal human behaviors that would be impossible without attribution.

Expressions of social attribution in human behavior. Consider storytelling. All cultures have oral traditions that exist in the form of storytelling or myth creation. One of the interesting features of storytelling (and, indeed, of language in general) is that it presupposes the presence of attributional skills. Language is inherently a discussion about belief-desire psychology (Grice 1975; Searle 1983; White 1980; Bennett 1976; Dennett 1971). This is true regardless of whether we focus exclusively on the intentions of the speakers, or take a more interactionist approach which emphasizes the role of the listener in creating meaning (Rosaldo 1982). Language is a means of directing attention and interest, a way of discussing goals and plans, a medium for both imparting and jointly creating personal knowledge, as well as hopes, fears and values. Even the most intelligent creature, if it harbored no suspicion that its fellow beings possessed mental states akin to its own, would have no reason to talk to anyone other than itself. Viewed in this light, stories and myths are quite literally intentional excursions in belief formation.[1]

If storytelling in general is evidence of attribution, then consider what a related universal feature of human language—animal folklore—reveals about human attributional processes. One of the most curious features about human descriptions of animals (even scientific ones) is that they are inherently anthropomorphic (Asquith 1984). Animals are described in human terms, as possessing desires, wants, needs, beliefs and they are often replete with specific personality traits. They are freely characterized as both noble and deceitful, evil and innocent, at once capable of the most selfish greed and the most genuine altruism. Gallup (1982) has argued explicitly that any organism capable of anthropomorphism exhibits prima facie evidence of social attribution. We contend that any being capable of storytelling, and certainly storytelling about anthropomorphic animals, possesses social attributional skills. Perhaps, in this light, our claim that social attributional capacities are universal mental attributes of humans is less controversial. It is the translation of these capacities into particular behavioral (and ultimately, as we shall show shortly, ethical) systems that are peculiarly culture-bound.

As an example of the type of research that demonstrates that attributional processes are universal in humans, consider the widespread use of projective psychological tests by cultural anthropologists in the 1940s and 1950s (see Bock 1988:chap. 4). The assumption behind projective tests (such as the Rorschach test) is that a subject's interpretations of intentionally ambiguous test materials will indirectly reveal important aspects about individuals' views of themselves. The validity of such tests, especially when used cross-culturally, is highly controversial (Bock 1988), and we are not endorsing specific interpretations that have been made of them. However, the mere fact that such tests make sense to people in different cultures provides clear support for a universal ability to project mental states and emotions onto others. The Thematic Apperception Test (TAT), for example, has been used widely by cultural anthropologists. In this test, subjects are shown a series of cards showing ambiguous sketches of one or more human figures. The subjects are then required to tell a story about each card. In every culture investigated, people respond enthusiastically to such requests, creating elaborate stories which involve complex self- and social attributions (see, for example, Wallace 1952, on the Iroquois of New York; Gladwin and Sarason 1953, on the Truk of Micronesia; Hallowell 1971, on a variety of cultures).

We have thus far considered simple explanations of attributional processes and how they relate to human perceptions of self and others. But are such attributions important in determining human behavior? Or are they merely collective grand illusions, which have emerged as a means of cloaking the true (genetically selfish) motivations for our behavior (Alexander 1974)? Social interactionists have long taken the position that attribution can provide a valid, explanative framework for human behavior. As we have seen, G. H. Mead (1934) advanced an influential view of the relationship between attribution and action, although he used different terminology. From this standpoint, interpretations of the intentions and perspectives of others clearly direct our behavior by forcing us to organize our actions into a single, meaningful framework. Social interactionists such as Mead argue that, in humans, behavior is not merely "a matter of responding directly to the activities of others. Rather it involves responding to the inferred future intentions of others" (Ashworth 1979:10). Mead's view that social attribution allows individuals to obtain information about themselves and, inferentially, about others, led him to believe that much human behavior is founded on inferentially obtained information. Analogously, White (1980), proposed that it is essentially this ability that allows humans to make "inferences about the interrelation of actors' goals, intentions, and abilities" and then later to use this knowledge to "formulate probable courses of social action" (cited in Lutz 1985).

An unlimited range of human social behavior can be viewed in this light: from simple acts of deceit to the most duplicitous form of double cross, from simple linguistic exchanges about very recent or near future events to heated discussions about abstract philosophical concepts that have never been, and can never be, seen or touched. In each of these behaviors, one element remains constant—the use of social attribution to make inferences about the minds of others (see Gallup 1985).

The study of attributional processes is far more sophisticated today than when Mead (1934) developed his ideas, but the essential framework remains unchanged. Humans are not bound to respond automatically or directly to objects and events. Rather, they assign meaning to actions of others in an effort to explain those actions within the construct of an intentional theory of behavior. Consider how different humans would be if we lacked such skills. Imagine what we would be like if we remained developmentally arrested at the mental age of a 3-year-old, caught in a social universe where we were unable to understand how knowledge states are formed. We would be constantly misjudging others, assigning knowledge to them that they could not possibly possess, and we would be mystified by their ardent denials, like the child who angrily insists that his mother knows about something that occurred when she was not present. And to anticipate part of a later argument of this chapter, imagine how different our understanding of social behavior would be if we were unable to appreciate the distinction between intentional and unintentional actions. This is not simply a hypothetical enterprise. Each day, developmental psychologists are forced to cope with these issues in the process of constructing theories of the development of mind in young children.

We add a cautionary note. We are not arguing that attribution provides a complete and immediate understanding of why people behave as they do. Indeed, we fully agree with those who have warned against believing that attribution can account for all human behavior (e.g., Gallup 1985). Additional psychological, cultural, and biological factors play a major role in shaping behavior. Nonetheless, most of these influences operate within the larger world of attribution that humans, as intentional systems, continually assign to them. This intentional framework may not have precedence in terms of evolutionary history, but it definitely now colors the way humans interpret even their most basic desires, and it influences the expression of altruism and ethics in humans.

Attribution and altruism. Let us now examine the relationship between attribution and altruism in humans. Careful, controlled experimentation (primarily in Western cultures) has revealed that humans are far more likely to help each other when they experience emotional responses rooted in social attribution, such as sympathy or compassion, than when they do not (Krebs 1975; Coke, Batson, and McDavis 1978; Eisenberg and Miller 1987). Of course, the existence of a correlation between caring about others (social attribution) and helping others (altruism) is far less controversial than are competing explanations for why this correlation exists. Batson (1990) classified these explanations into two broad categories: those that assume humans are social egoists who care about others only insofar as that caring directly or indirectly benefits themselves; and those that assume humans are capable of genuine altruistic caring—i.e., that individuals may care for others for their sake alone and that any benefits helpers might receive are incidental by-products of that concern for others. After nearly a decade of research aimed specifically at testing these competing explanations, Batson and his colleagues have ruled out nearly every egoistic account (Batson 1990). Their experimental results suggest that when people experience strong emotional concern for others, helping behavior is motivated solely by that concern.

This does not mean people always help others for selfless reasons. When people feel little sympathy for others, their pattern of helping reveals underlying egoistic motives (Batson 1990). They may help, but their helping is motivated by a variety of self-concerns. Furthermore, sympathy alone is not a sufficient condition for helping behaviors to emerge. People also care about themselves, and when the costs imposed by helping are too high, altruistic helping disappears (Batson 1990; Staub 1980). The human capacity for caring is thus "a fragile flower, easily crushed by self-concern" (Batson et al. 1983:718).

In any case, it appears that people have a genuine capacity for caring, and that this capacity may be expressed overtly as altruism. We suspect that this is true even in societies which seem to emphasize egoistic selfishness over selfless altruism (Cohen 1972). The capacity to care, to feel compassion for others, appears to be the result of a causal sequence of events which begins with attributional processes (for example, assuming the perspective of others) that in turn elicit emotional responses (Feshbach 1975; Coke, Batson, and McDavis 1978; Stiff et al. 1988). Of course, humans (like other animals) may also experience emotional responses that do not result from attributional processes (Bavelas et al. 1986, 1987; Bavelas et al. 1988; Panksepp 1986). These responses may result directly from what has been termed emotional contagion.

Emotional contagion occurs when one individual's emotional reaction automatically elicits the same response in another (Stiff et al. 1988; Coke, Batson, and McDavis 1978; Davis 1980; Feshbach 1975; Hoffman 1977). The second individual's response is generated through emotional contagion. In contrast, empathic concern, while also an emotional response, does not parallel the emotional response of the individual in need, and is generally characterized by a regard for the welfare of that individual. A variety of terms have been used to describe empathic concern, including "sympathy" (Wispé 1986; Hoffman 1982), "altruistic motivation" (Coke, Batson, and McDavis 1978; Staub 1989; Batson 1989), "sympathetic arousal" (Hoffman 1977), and "empathy" (Batson 1990). Empathic concern is sometimes aroused in people when they see others in need. An individual hearing a neighbor scream may respond initially (through emotional contagion) with fear—the very emotion expressed in the neighbor's scream. But the scream may also elicit a strong emotional concern for the safety and welfare of the neighbor, an intense desire to do something to help, or at least a clear recognition of the fact that the neighbor is in need. Such empathic concern may emerge relatively late in a child's ontogeny and may require a fairly elaborate attributional understanding of self and other (Hoffman 1982). We believe that the distinction between empathic concern and emotional contagion is critical for understanding the emergence of human ethical systems, and we will return to it later.

Finally, it would be a mistake to think that, in humans, egoistic helping behaviors—that is, acts of helping others that are performed solely for the benefit of the self—are somehow completely cognitively distinct from altruistic helping behaviors. Egoistic and altruistic helping operate in the same social universe, only the attributional processes that motivate egoistic helping are complex combinations of self- and social attributions. In other words, many of the factors that result in egoistic helping are judgments that individuals make about the acceptable balance between their own needs, desires and wants, and the social standards of behavior that may be expected of them (Staub 1980). In summary, it seems clear that human helping behavior is complex; it may be motivated by self-concern or by genuine concern for the welfare of others. It may arise through emotional reactions minimally influenced by attribution, or it may be virtually completely determined by attribution.

Attribution and the development of values. If helping behavior in humans is strongly influenced by attribution, so is the development of individual and culturally shared values. In turn, the development of values, or desired states of existence, directly influence helping behavior. We now wish to examine a specific model which attempts to explain variations in human helping behavior to personal and cultural values.

Staub (1980, 1986) has proposed a model which helps to explain the relationship between attribution and variation in prosocial behavior. His model assumes that people are intentional organisms that in the course of their cognitive growth and interactions with others, develop values or personal goals. Given variation in the situational and experiential factors that influence value formation, some individuals will develop, to a greater degree than others, prosocial goals, which are characterized by a general concern for others, and which are gratified through empathically motivated actions. Other individuals will develop stronger approval goals, which are rewarded when their actions are socially approved by others. Still others will develop stronger achievement goals, which are rewarded through the use or demonstration of their skills. Each individual, throughout his or her lifetime, will attempt to satisfy a variety of complementary and competing goals. Different situations may activate different personal goals, and single expressed behaviors may satisfy different goals. Thus, the specific motives for the very same act of helping may not necessarily be identical for different individuals, or even for the same individual at different times.

At any instant, whether an individual helps another in need, and how an individual evaluates the needs of others, depends on a complex set of situational factors and prior experiences. Behavior may be largely determined by how clearly any situation triggers particular (conflicting or complementary) suites of personal goals (Staub 1980, 1989):

> In a particular situation, varied motives or personal goals may be aroused in a person. Sometimes when a person is faced with another's need for help, that is the only force acting on him or her [and] given some degree of motivation that person will act. At other times, a person may be faced with a situation which potentially activates a variety of [personal goals]; to be helpful, to achieve well on some task, to affiliate with other people, to pursue adventure, or to behave in proper social ways. Whether such goals are activated will depend on the nature of the situation and on its activating potential, as well as on the characteristics of the person and the degree to which the person possesses the personal goals that might be activated by the situation. For example, someone might be working on a task, or might simply be sitting in a room waiting. Somebody in another room seems to be in distress. If it is important for this person to both do well on tasks and to help other people, he

> will experience conflict when he is working on the task. His two goals
> may conflict with each other. This will not happen when he is simply
> waiting, because then his goal of achievement will not be activated.
> Neither will this happen if doing well on tasks is unimportant to him.
> . . . If we are to understand how prosocial behavior in particular and
> social behavior in general are determined, we have to consider the joint
> influences of varied motives . . . (Staub 1980:257).

Staub's model is far more intricate and ingenious than we have described it here, but we present it to make two points. First, it provides a framework for understanding the proximate causes of human helping behavior. Staub's (1980) insight that values can be conceived as potentials, which may be activated by a combination of internal and external factors, helps to explain the plasticity and unpredictability of human helping behavior. Instead of viewing humans as fitness maximizing machines who respond to environments based on some universal, unconscious cost-benefit calculation (e.g., Trivers 1971), Staub's model helps to identify specific internal and external variables that may, under any particular set of conditions, determine helping behavior.

Secondly, Staub's model provides a framework for understanding the foundations of ethical systems—that is, cultural networks of shared social values. According to Staub (1980), personal goals exist cross culturally, but the form they take may vary greatly. Furthermore, shared cultural experiences may generate a cultural commonality of personal values. This does not mean that all members of a culture will automatically hold a set of similar values. Indeed, there may be political, economic and social tensions between different segments of heterogeneous societies that help to create different sets of personal goals as manifestations, in part, of the different degrees to which their members are empowered or disempowered. Competing values will generate conflict, not merely at the level of the individual, but also at the level of different segments of society. Furthermore, group needs may shift as social alliances shift, and social alliances may shift radically in different cultural contexts. Nevertheless, central cultural influences should create a system, or systems, of shared values.

Cultural anthropologists have also examined how developmental factors contribute to the production of shared cultural values. In the early 1900s, anthropologists attempted to characterize cultures by generating lists of traits (for example, totemic beliefs) that were either present or absent in individual societies (see review in Boas [1940] 1966). Later, this approach was criticized on the grounds that the cultural meaning of any trait depends upon the suite of other traits that are present in the society. These criticisms led to the belief that cultures are particular configurations of elements which interact with one another. Ruth Benedict founded the school of configurationalist anthropology which attempted to move beyond a mere static under-standing of cultural traits "toward a more just psychological understanding of the data" (1923:7). Thus, societies were characterized as having distinct personalities (such as the "paranoid Dobuans" or the "megalomaniac Kwakiutl") (Benedict [1934] 1946). Another founder of the configurationalist school, Margaret Mead, further developed the school of culture and personality with her detailed studies of growth and development and crosscultural processes of socialization (Mead [1928] 1949, [1930] 1953, [1935] 1963). Kardiner and Linton (1939) developed a theory of basic personality structure, which postulates that common experiences of individuals tend to produce common types of personalities.   Other anthropologists were uncomfortable with this deterministic approach, and attempted to characterize cultures in terms of their variation around modal personality types (DuBois [1944] 1961).   Since then, a number of different approaches have emerged (see Bock 1988 for a review).

Understanding how values are created and shared through attributional processes has important implications for understanding the cognitive underpinnings of ethical behavior. Values are clearly influenced by cultural norms and expectations, and they develop and become established (and change) through a complex feedback loop be-tween self- and social attribution. Ethical systems depend on the ability to attribute values, emotions, knowledge, intentions, and motives to others. Based on these attribu-tions and on an understanding of what are appropriate behaviors in particular social contexts, humans are able to identify specific actions as appropriate or inappropriate. While individuals universally interpret actions within a social context, there is no absolute, universal standard whereby actions are evaluated as "good" or "bad," or situationally "appropriate" or "inappropriate."   But, however specific actions are cul-turally evaluated, human morality depends on having a cognitive appreciation of oneself and of others as conscious beings with specific needs and values, carrying out specific actions with a certain degree (or lack) of control, and with a certain degree (or lack) of awareness of group expectations. In this sense, ethics involve the concept of conscious choice, which is alien to organisms that do not possess attribution (cf. Burke 1966:324).

It is also clear that cultures, groups within cultures, and individuals all contribute to the production of ethical systems. It is the sharing of values across these levels of society that create culturally codified standards of "right" and "wrong." Yet, given the many factors that influence the construction of ethical systems, it is not surprising that ethical codes should be, at times, inherently contradictory. Even within fixed cultural contexts, the situational and attributional factors that motivate behavior will vary, as will the standards by which behaviors are judged to be "moral" or "immoral." Nonetheless, culturally shared values will generate a degree of common understanding, and that understanding will tend to generate culture-specific evaluations of certain behaviors.

In summary, researchers in many academic fields have grappled with the same issue: the production of culturally shared norms, values, and meaning. They have developed different vocabularies ("cultural meaning," "symbolic interaction," "social attribution," "theory of mind") to refer to some of the same underlying cognitive processes. Self- and social attribution underlie those behaviors that, taken together, comprise "ethical systems." Ethical systems emerge at the intersection between socially imposed standards of behavior and individual decisions concerning values. These individual decisions depend upon how people perceive the intentions, beliefs, and motives of themselves and others. Understanding human ethics and altruism demands that we consider how such individual attributional processes develop within a cultural framework to produce shared cultural values. Understanding the evolution of ethics and altruism, as they are manifested in humans, demands that we address the extent to which these same processes exist in our closest relatives.

Thus, having established a link between attribution and ethics in humans, we now ask, is attribution unique to humans?

Chimpanzees and Children: Mind from a Comparative Perspective

In this section, we establish a framework for viewing attribution from an evolutionary perspective. In particular, we seek to identify characteristics of the cognitive-emotional systems of modern apes and humans that will help us to reconstruct the cognitive-emotional system of their common ancestor. As noted above, we believe that certain features of human cognition underlie, or allow for, the expression of the multitude of ethical belief systems (and hence the behaviors associated with such systems) found cross culturally. Recent research with chimpanzees suggests that some (but not all) of these abilities were present in the common ancestor of humans and apes. Some attributional capabilities—i.e., the ability to project emotions, intentions and states of beliefs to others—may have evolved long before humans did. We review the experimental evidence for the presence of such abilities in adult chimpanzees. It is our contention that human ethical systems are emergent features of a cognitive system which elaborated and refined ancestral attributional capacities common to humans and chimpanzees.

In developing this framework, we should make several underlying assumptions explicit. First, we assume that organisms that lack language can nevertheless possess self- and social attribution. Some linguists may object on the grounds that mind cannot exist without language. Indeed, this "mind-language" hypothesis has a long tradition in the social sciences (Wittgenstein 1953; Burke 1966; Langer 1942; Schwartz 1980; Bickerton 1987; Harré and Secord 1972). Second, we believe that the attributional capacities of chimpanzees can be objectively investigated. Some behavioral scientists may object to such a claim on the grounds that human interpretations of the attributional capacities of nonhumans are bound to be anthropomorphic. Third, we believe that the ontogeny of social attribution in human children can assist us in understanding social attribution in chimpanzees. Some may interpret such a comparison to mean that we believe chimpanzees are developmentally arrested children.

Let us consider the mind-language hypothesis. Language, in this view, provides the critical support necessary for the development of the intentional capacities of the human mind. This hypothesis predicts that it is language that provides humans with the cognitive capacities necessary for symbolic interaction, and hence attribution. But this is only a hypothesis, and one that has been challenged (Premack 1988a, 1988b; Gallup 1985; Morin and DeBlois 1989). We adopt a comparative approach to testing the central prediction of the mind-language hypothesis by examining the empirical evidence which suggests that chimpanzees share certain self- and social attributional processes with humans. In our view, the mind-language hypothesis is only as good as the empirical evidence which supports it.

Next, one might question anyone's ability to ascertain what is in the minds of other species on the grounds that any characterization that a human might make of the mind of a nonhuman will necessarily be influenced by the way humans think, i.e., it will be anthropomorphic. In other words, since chimpanzees cannot share their private experiences through language, humans can have no objective way of studying their mental perceptions of the intentions, desires, and emotions of other species. Any inferences we might draw about the subjective experiences of chimpanzees are bound to be mere projections of our own way of knowing. It is important to consider this objection because complicated patterns of animal behavior need not depend on complicated mental processes involving attribution. Patterns of behavior that appear to be the result of attributional processes may have actually been produced through some combination of learning and innate hard-wiring (Dennett 1983; Premack 1986). This is precisely why we cannot rely solely on anecdotal accounts of primate behavior. If we were to draw our inferences about mental processes from the largely anecdotal data currently available for many species of nonhuman primates, our inferences might be highly suspect.

Experiments, however, offer a compelling way out of this impasse. Although chimpanzees do not naturally possess a language sufficiently well developed to enable us to question them about their appreciation of the mental experiences of others, language is not the only mechanism that allows us to make inferences about what other individuals know. During the past twenty years, child psychologists have considerably increased their understanding of the development of attributional abilities in young children. In principle, we should be able to modify their approaches in order to study nonhuman psychology. Of course, we cannot simply ask chimpanzees what they think about a particular event (as we can with children), but experiments that allow the subjects to express what they do or do not know through their behavior can be carefully designed to pose equivalent questions (Premack 1986:102-8, 1988a; Povinelli, Nelson, and Boysen 1990). Thus, the validity of anthropomorphic descriptions becomes an empirical issue, open to refutation through hypothesis testing. The cognitive developmental pathways of both chimpanzees and humans, as well as other primates, are empirical issues that should be empirically explored.

Finally, comparing chimpanzees to children may seem evolutionarily naive. Of course, chimpanzees are not human children. Chimpanzees have evolved a unique set of behavioral patterns and social systems, and perhaps cognitive processes, that are alien to humans. Likewise, humans have evolved behaviors (and undoubtedly cognitive capacities as well) that are strikingly different from those of chimpanzees. But the recognition of this diversity must not obscure an obvious fact: due to their close common ancestry, chimpanzees and humans may well share some aspects of their cognition, and in particular social attribution. In human children, intention and belief attribution probably emerges in the second and third year of life. Developmental psychologists have devised tests for determining the onset of these attributional capacities. Such tests can serve as a point of departure for identifying social attribution in chimpanzees (Povinelli and DeBlois, in press; Premack and Dasser, in press).

We caution that the empirical evidence for and against the presence of specific social attributional capacities in chimpanzees is preliminary and not easy to interpret. It is particularly difficult to ascertain that specific cognitive capacities are lacking in chimpanzees, since negative inferences must depend on negative evidence. Interpreting negative evidence has always plagued comparative psychology, and it is laden with inferential pitfalls (Hodos and Campbell 1969; Cole and Means 1981; McPhail 1987). In light of this, we proceed cautiously, fully understanding that our conclusions may turn out to be a spurious result of contextual variables or the failure to investigate the phenomenon thoroughly. Nonetheless, at some point, a convergence of positive or negative evidence does become convincing, and begins to suggest specific cognitive similarities or differences between species (Bitterman 1987; Goldman-Rakic and Preuss 1987). Our goal, then, is to review the current literature on social attributional development in humans and in chimpanzees in order to determine what capacities they share in common, and what capacities appear uniquely human. Later, we will show how these similarities and differences can help to explain the emergence of ethics in humans.

Do chimpanzees have a concept of self? The development of self-attribution in children has been approached in a number of ways, one of which involves determining the onset of the infant's capacity for self-recognition. Self-recognition has been defined as the ability of the child to determine that the image it sees in a mirror is of itself. This ability emerges around 18 to 24 months of age, and appears to signal the explosion of a variety of selfconscious emotions and behaviors (Lewis and Brooks-Gunn 1979; Lewis et al. 1989). Indeed, the onset of self-recognition in infants demarcates the beginning of what some developmental psychologists have referred to as the year of self-awareness (Kagan 1981).

Prior to Gallup's (1970) investigation of how chimpanzees react to mirrors, it was commonly believed that all nonhuman primates, including chimpanzees, treated mirror images as if they were fellow beings (Yerkes and Yerkes 1929). Gallup, however, observed that after only a few days of mirror exposure, his subadult chimpanzees dramatically changed their behavior toward their images. Instead of continuing to react socially, they began to use the mirror to gain otherwise unavailable information about themselves (for example, to explore the insides of their mouths). During the first two days of exposure to mirrors, the chimpanzees had apparently learned that the images they saw were not those of other chimpanzees, but reflections of their own appearances.

To provide more compelling evidence that chimpanzees understand the special significance of their own mirror images, Gallup devised an objective test for self-recognition. He anesthetized the mirror-wise chimpanzees and applied an odorless, bright red dye to the upper portion of their ears and eyebrows. These were locations which the chimpanzees could not see without access to a mirror. Upon recovery from the anesthesia, none of the subjects made any attempt to touch or inspect the marked areas. However, as soon as the mirrors were placed back in front of their cages, the chimpanzees faced their respective mirrors and displayed considerable interest in the marked areas, inspecting them with their fingers while carefully studying the reflections. Several of them even inspected their fingers after they had made contact with the marked areas.

Perhaps even more striking than the chimpanzees' success at self-recognition is the failure of over a dozen species of monkeys, lesser apes, and gorillas to recognize themselves in mirrors. Even after years of experience and a variety of techniques designed to aid them, these animals continue to respond to their mirror images as if confronted by another individual (reviews by Povinelli 1987, 1991). Gallup (1979) has interpreted self-recognition as an indicator of self-awareness. In other words, he argued that recognition of oneself in a mirror is impossible without a concept of the self, and he defined self-awareness as the ability of an organism to become the object of its own attention. In the context of recognizing oneself in a mirror, an individual must realize that it exists before it can learn to recognize its own physical appearance.

In light of these data, Gallup (1982, 1983) proposed that humans, chimpanzees, and orangutans alone possess self- and social attributional capacities. In keeping with modern attribution theory, Gallup argues that a wide range of social behaviors (intentional deception, sorrow, grief, sympathy) develop from the use of one's own experiences to draw inferences about the experiences of others. Gallup's unique contribution has been to develop a model which attempts to link the existence of self-recognition (and presumably self-awareness) to the presence of attributionally based social behaviors, and to outline a framework through which such a proposition can be empirically tested. He predicts that chimpanzees and orangutans, both of whom show evidence of self-recognition, ought to be able to use their own selfknowledge to make inferences about the emotions, intentions, and knowledge of others. Thus, chimpanzees ought to be capable of a variety of introspectively based social behaviors, such as intentional deception, empathy, sorrow, and grudging. On the other hand, he believes that animals which fail to show evidence of self-recognition do not possess a sufficiently well developed self-concept to support attributional inferences about the mental states of others. While the validity of Gallup's model remains open to empirical refutation, it encourages the investigation of social attribution from a comparative perspective. Our own inquiry has been strongly influenced by his efforts to develop (or revive) a comparative study of mind from a mentalistic perspective.

Do chimpanzees project intention?   One primary attributional capacity is the attribution of intention. Experimental investigations reveal that, by the age of 3, children have developed an ability to attribute intentions to themselves and to others (Smith 1978; Shultz and Wells 1985; Shultz, Wells, and Sarda 1980; reviews by Keasey 1977, and Miller and Aloise 1989). While their understanding of intention is less well developed than that of adults, human children do begin, at a very young age, to distinguish between the intentional and unintentional actions of others, and thus to evaluate behavior from the standpoint of the minds of others.

Attribution of intention in chimpanzees was studied in a classic series of experiments by Premack and Woodruff (1978) who showed, to an adult chimpanzee named Sarah, videotapes depicting human actors attempting to solve staged problems. Sarah's job, after viewing each videotape, was to pick from several photographs the one that depicted the correct solution to the problem. For example, if a videotape showed an actor struggling to obtain bananas suspended from the ceiling, a correct solution might be stepping onto a box to reach the bananas. An incorrect solution might show the same actor engaging in an unrelated activity in the same setting. Premack and Woodruff interpreted Sarah's virtually flawless performance as evidence of attribution of intention in chimpanzees. In the context of defending his position, Premack (1984) has noted that videotapes, in and of themselves, do not depict problems. Rather, they depict series of events which become problems only after intentions are attributed to the actors. Premack and Woodruff have speculated that chimpanzees appear to have a "theory of mind"—i.e., an ability to impute mental states to others.

Interestingly, Sarah not only appeared able to assess the desires and intentions of others, but was able to use this knowledge in conjunction with her own desires to select different consequences for actors she liked and disliked. She was presented with separate videotapes of liked and disliked actors attempting to solve the same problem, and was then asked to select from alternative photographs depicting (1) relevant, favorable consequences for the actor, (2) relevant, but unfavorable consequences (e.g., an accident occurring while the actor attempted, correctly, to solve the problem) or (3) irrelevant and unfavorable consequences, Sarah consistently selected relevant and favorable consequences for those she liked and relevant but disastrous consequences for actors she disliked (Premack and Woodruff 1978).

Role-taking, visual perspective-taking, and attribution of knowledge in chimpanzees? A central element of Mead's (1934) concept of "mind" was the ability to take the role of the other. In daily interactions with others, humans assume social roles. Mead labeled the ability to evaluate the behavior of others from the standpoint of other individuals' roles or perspectives as "role-taking." He saw this as developing, in early childhood, through social interaction. Recent research has supported Mead's position on the importance of role-taking in social interactions, but has refined our appreciation of the variety of cognitive stages that children pass through (Selman and Byrne 1974; Shantz 1975).

Approaching these same developmental issues from a different direction, Piaget (1929) pioneered experiments to assess the "visual perspective-taking abilities" of children. He asked children to evaluate how complex objects appeared to other individuals who saw them from a different angle. Piaget believed that until about age six, children display a profound ignorance of the visual perspectives of others. Modern research supports the notion that visual perspective-taking and role-taking do develop gradually in children, but that the skills develop far earlier than Piaget believed. Even 2- to 3-year-old human children are capable of limited forms of visual and social perspective-taking (Borke 1971; Shatz and Gelman 1973; Masangkay et al. 1974; Mossler, Marvin, and Greenberg 1976; Sachs and Devin 1976; Lempers, Flavell, and Flavell 1977; Zahn-Waxler, Radke-Yarrow, and Brady-Smith 1977). A rudimentary capacity for visual perspective-taking emerges in children by about 2 years of age (Masangkay et al. 1974; Lempers, Flavell, and Flavell 1977), but this early ability appears to be limited, merely allowing the child to infer whether and what another person can or cannot see (Lempers, Flavell, and Flavell 1977). Only by about age 4 do children begin to appreciate that the visual perspectives of others determine how objects appear to them (Flavell et al. 1981). At roughly the same age, children alter their speech styles to fit the presumed mental capacities of their listeners (for example, using simple forms of speech for children younger than themselves; Shatz and Gelman 1973; Sachs and Devin 1976).

The link between perspective-taking and belief structures is more complicated. Until recently, it seemed quite reasonable to suppose that individuals capable of visual perspectivetaking might automatically have knowledge about the beliefs of others. But recent research has cast doubt on such a simplistic model. For example, Wimmer and his colleagues conducted a series of experiments to examine children's comprehension of access to information as a source of knowledge. They sought to determine at what age children begin to understand that visual perception and communication can serve as a basis of knowledge formation, or a causal theory of knowledge. In one experiment, for example, children were given visual access to the contents of a box in the presence of another child who was not allowed to look into the same box (Wimmer, Hogrefe, and Perner 1988). Not only were most children younger than about 4 years of age unable to understand that the other child was ignorant about the contents of the box, but they displayed a startling resistance to being told so. Interestingly, the development of a causal theory of knowledge coincides with the development of more sophisticated forms of visual perspective-taking (Flavell et al. 1981).

Prior to the fourth year of life, children appear largely unaware of how knowledge states arise, and as a result, are incapable of correct attributions of knowledge and false beliefs (Wimmer, Hogrefe, and Perner 1988; Hogrefe, Wimmer, and Perner 1986; Marvin, Greenberg, and Mossler 1976; Mossler, Marvin, and Greenberg 1976; Taylor 1988; Povinelli and DeBlois, n.d.; but see Chandler, Fritz, and Hala 1989; Pillow 1989; Pratt and Bryant 1990). It is not that they are necessarily unable to project and report beliefs, but rather they do not appear to understand how knowledge states are formed (see Leslie 1987 for a different view). Interestingly, the fourth year of life heralds the onset of certain social interactions, such as hide-and-seek games that would seem to require the ability to differentiate between one's own beliefs and the beliefs of others (DeVries 1970; Gratch 1964; Shultz and Cloghesy 1981). Children younger than four years of age may learn to use visual obstruction in the context of hide-and-seek games, but they appear not to understand fully its cognitive implications. The issue is a controversial one, with some researchers arguing that children do not develop a true "theory of mind" until about 4 years of age, with other researchers seeing a gradual emergence of the attribution of mental states beginning early in the second year of life (Bretherton and Beeghly 1982; Perner, in press; Chandler, Fritz, and Hala 1989; Miller and Aloise 1989).

Recent investigations suggest that adult chimpanzees may be capable of both social role-taking and understanding how knowledge states arise. Povinelli, Nelson, and Boysen (in press, a) designed an experiment to ascertain whether chimpanzees understand complicated cooperative tasks, not only from their own perspective, but from the perspectives of others. Four chimpanzees were individually trained to cooperate with a human partner on a task that allowed both participants to obtain food rewards. In each of these chimpanzee-human dyads, one of the participants (the informant) could see which of four pairs of food trays on a simple apparatus was baited, but had no means of obtaining it. In contrast, the other participant (the operator) could pull one of four handles to bring a pair of the food trays to within reach of both participants, but could not see which choice was correct. After about a week of training, the chimpanzees had learned their assigned roles; they could perform the task of either operator or informant with near perfect accuracy. Then, the experimenters reversed the roles of the chimpanzees, forcing previous informants to become operators, and previous operators to become informants. The goal of this reversal was to see whether the chimpanzees, in learning their initial task, had understood the task from the perspective of their partner. Three of the four chimpanzees assumed their new role immediately with no loss of proficiency. In other words, in learning their original role, they understood the entire cooperative task.

Chimpanzees may also recognize that visual perception leads to knowledge. Premack (1988a) tested four juvenile chimpanzees' understanding of the link between perception and knowledge. Each chimpanzee watched as two trainers appeared in front of their cage. One of the trainers then stepped behind an opaque screen, preventing her from seeing what occurred next. The second trainer watched as a third trainer hid food under one of two cups. The chimpanzees could see that food was being hidden and that one of the trainers was watching, but they could not see which cup was being baited. Next, the trainer behind the screen stepped forth beside the trainer who had witnessed the hiding. Finally, the chimpanzees were allowed to select which trainer they wanted to provide advice about where to look for the food. During the course of two dozen trials, two of the chimpanzees consistently selected the trainer who had witnessed the hiding procedure. In other words, they seem to have immediately understood that the trainer who watched the food being hidden possessed knowledge about its location.

Povinelli, Nelson, and Boysen (1990) found parallel evidence that chimpanzees are capable of attributing knowledge to others. They investigated the visual perspective-taking ability of four chimpanzees. The chimpanzees chose between information provided by two experimenters who randomly alternated between two roles, the guesser and the knower. On each trial, the chimpanzees watched the knower hide food under one of four inverted cups, although they could not see which cup was being baited. Meanwhile, the guesser waited outside the room until the food was hidden. Finally, the guesser returned and pointed to an incorrect cup while the knower pointed to the correct cup. Povinelli, Nelson, and Boysen (1990) found that the chimpanzees tended to follow the advice of the knower, rather than the guesser. They also responded similarly to a novel variation of the task in which the guesser remained inside the room, but covered his head while the knower stood beside him and watched a third experimenter hide the food. Based on these experiments and comparable results in Premack's (1988a) independent investigations, Povinelli, Nelson, and Boysen (1990) adopted the working hypothesis that adult chimpanzees possess an ability to attribute knowledge that is comparable to that which develops in human children between the ages of three and four.

Do chimpanzees attribute responsibility to others? A special case of the attribution of intention concerns the attribution of responsibility. People often make judgments about the personalities of others based more on the perceived purpose of their actions than on the actual consequences of their actions. Numerous psychological investigations have demonstrated that people assign less blame to individuals who have hurt or annoyed them when they believe that those individuals had no control over their actions (for example, Burnstein and Worchel 1962). Piaget (1932), however, believed that young children do not make such discriminations in the same manner as adults. He believed that, prior to age eight or nine, children tend to assign responsibility or blame based on the intensity of the outcome of a particular event, rather than on the intentions of the actors. Recent research has confirmed Piaget's ideas, but has revealed that under certain circumstances children as young as three assign responsibility based on perceived intentions (Imamoğlu 1975; Yuill and Perner 1988; see Miller and Aloise 1989 for a review). Typically, such research is conducted by presenting children with stories about other children behaving in certain ways. The children are then asked to evaluate the "naughtiness" of the different characters (e.g., Yuill and Perner, 1988). Other approaches, using videotaped sequences, have also been used (Chandler, Greenspan, and Barenboim 1973).

There is preliminary evidence that chimpanzees attribute responsibility to others. Povinelli, Boysen, and Berntson (unpublished data, cited in Povinelli 1991) studied the reactions of an eight-year-old chimpanzee, Sheba, to actors who brought her juice whenever she called them on an electronic intercom. These actors would sometimes fail to do so, either because they would accidentally spill the juice (accidental test condition), or because they would deliberately, defiantly throw it onto the floor (intentional test condition). Even though the immediate consequence for Sheba was exactly the same in both cases (that is, she would fail to receive juice), Sheba showed a clear preference for clumsy over malicious actors. This preference was evidenced by the threats she directed toward malicious actors, and by the choices she subsequently made when she used the intercom to pick the next person she wanted to bring her juice.

Follow-up tests revealed a remarkable and surprising phenomenon—Sheba's reluctance to relinquish her first impressions of the actors. During the final three days of testing, the roles of the accidental and intentional actors were reversed. Thus the originally clumsy actor became "aggressive," and the aggressive actor became clumsy and these new roles were retained throughout the last three days of testing. Despite the reversal of the actors' apparent intentions during three consecutive sessions, Sheba maintained her preference for the actor whom she had selected on the first day of trials, although in a weaker form. Her behavioral reactions to the intentional and accidental conditions did not change; Sheba continued to threaten the aggressive, intentional actor. But when given a choice of whom she wanted to bring her juice next, she consistently selected the individual who had been originally clumsy. In other words, not only had Sheba apparently formed strong impressions of individuals based on their initial (perceived) intentions, she also demonstrated that first impressions may play an important role in attribution of responsibility.

Are chimpanzees capable of second-order attribution? Not only do humans attempt to discern what other think or believe, they also draw conclusions about what others believe about the beliefs of others or, indeed, themselves. Such higher-order reasoning has been implicated in language use (Grice 1975), the creation of shared meaning between individuals (Schiffer 1972; Smith 1982), competitive interactions among individuals (Rapoport 1967), as well as children's performances on test questions concerning their knowledge of their own representational states (Perner and Wimmer 1985). Dennett (1983) has demonstrated the importance of distinguishing between these varying levels of intentionality for the behavioral sciences. Do chimpanzees conduct this form of embedded inferential reasoning? Premack and Woodruff (1978) demonstrated that Sarah attributed motivational states to other individuals. But could she also attribute the process of attribution to others? In other words, do chimpanzees realize that other individuals attribute motivations as well?

Premack and Premack (1983) reported that Sarah failed tests designed to determine if she could understand how another chimpanzee, Sadie, would respond to videotapes similar to the ones that Sarah had viewed. The procedure was to have Sarah watch a videotape which depicted Sadie watching the videotapes of humans struggling to solve a variety of problems as described earlier. When asked to select among photographs that depicted Sadie choosing an appropriate or an inappropriate solution to the embedded videotape problem, Sarah did not respond in a manner consistent with what one might expect for an organism capable of second-order attributions. Instead, she responded at random (Premack and Premack 1983).

Second-order attributions are difficult to measure, even in human children. The first attempts to determine at what age children begin to use higher-order beliefs found little evidence before the age of 10 (Flavell et al. 1968; Selman 1980; Shultz and Cloghesy 1981). It was not until new paradigms for examining second-order beliefs were developed by Perner and Wimmer (1985) that such abilities were demonstrated in much younger children. Thus, it is possible that chimpanzees possess this ability, but that the test given by Premack and Premack (1983) was too difficult. Nonetheless, there is no evidence that chimpanzees can attribute second-order beliefs to others, and even in children it represents a sophisticated skill that may not emerge until the sixth year of life (Perner and Wimmer 1985).

Do chimpanzees experience sympathy? Do chimpanzees have a sympathetic under-standing of others? Anecdotal evidence seems to suggest an unequivocal "yes" answer to this question. Chimpanzees have been reported to rescue others in distress (Goodall 1986:378), and to exhibit elaborate patterns of reassurance, which Goodall has described as a "deepseated need for reassurance contact experienced by an emotionally or physi-cally distressed chimpanzee" (Goodall 1986:360; de Waal 1989). Indeed, this represents one of the most striking aspects of chimpanzee behavior. Monkeys also show increases in affiliative behavior after conflicts and these behaviors have been labeled reconcilia-tion (de Waal 1989), but they do not show the elaborate reassurance behaviors typical of chimpanzees as, for example, hugging, embracing, and kissing.

There is evidence that, by the middle of their second year of life, human chil-dren view another's distress as something to be alleviated (Hoffman 1975, 1982; Zahn-Waxler and Radke-Yarrow 1982). However, it is not clear what attributional capacities support this behavior. Young children certainly act in prosocial ways, but it is possible, and perhaps likely, that their behavior does not develop from an understanding of the other individual as possessing a unique self-identity which is valued for its intrinsic worth. Rather, children at this age may have some understanding of the relationship between behavior and mental state, and may be beginning to understand how their own behavior can affect the mental states of others. Older children can develop a clearly sympathetic understanding of others (Staub 1989).

Differentiating between these and related processes in chimpanzees is difficult. Accounts of apes cuddling and "protecting" dogs or cats in captive situations seem to confirm their capacity for empathic social caring. Yet, chimpanzees may cuddle pets in front of humans, who reward such behaviors, and threaten, pinch, or bite them as soon as humans leave. In the wild, chimpanzees (like other primates) will sometimes come to the aid of distressed individuals, usually in social power conflicts where such "help" can tip the balance of power. This is by no means self-sacrificial. It is not clear to what degree, if at all, chimpanzees experience genuine empathic concern, in the sense described earlier. True, if a chimpanzee sees an individual he likes in distress, he may become agitated, pout, and embrace the distressed individual. But is that chimpan-zee offering reassurance because he realizes the individual is suffering, or demanding reassurance because he experiences personal distress through emotional contagion? We can offer no easy answer to this question. It is clear, however, that chimpanzees do ex-hibit behavioral patterns similar to those that develop between the ages of two and three in human, and they may possess a comparable understanding of the emotional experi-ences of others. They may experience a "concern" for others that is comparable to that felt by children who do not have a well-developed sense of the needs and perspectives of others, and who tend to react with fear and personal discomfort rather than with understanding when they see another individual in distress.

However, it is important not to lose sight of the fact that chimpanzees have evolved their own peculiar political systems (de Waal 1982). Because of this, their expressions of reassurance occur in contexts that may seem alien to humans. For example, mutilated and dying chimpanzees have been repeatedly observed clinging to and begging for reassurance from their assailants (Desmond 1979; de Waal 1986a; Goodall 1986).

Do chimpanzees intentionally deceive others? The issue of deception has surfaced in many areas of behavioral biology including studies of morphological mimicry (Brower and Brower 1962), behavioral ecology (Dawkins and Krebs 1984), child development (Hartshorne and May 1928) and especially in recent examinations of primate behavior (Woodruff and Premack 1979; Cheney and Seyfarth 1985; Byrne and Whiten 1985; Whiten and Byrne 1988). Mitchell (1986) reviewed the history of behavioral biology's treatment of deception and traced the emergence of two separate intellectual traditions for examining the phenomenon. One has been sociobiology's use of deception as evidence of natural selection's influence on behavior (Dawkins 1976; Dawkins and Krebs 1984). This tradition focuses on behavioral interactions that result in the exchange of misinformation and the resulting consequences. Thus, because of ethology's primary interest in the adaptive value of behavior it has underemphasized the psychological components of deception. In contrast, another tradition has explored the psychological attributes that underpin different types of deception (Romanes 1884; Hartshorne and May 1928; Griffin 1976; Dennett 1978). It is this latter approach, which focuses on issues of intentionality and awareness of the consequences of a given deceptive act, that interests us here.

In studies of child development, deception has virtually always been defined as an intentional act (Vasek 1986). For example, Hartshorne and May defined deception as "the conscious method of circumventing the will of another by misleading the other as to one's own will" (1928:13). Vasek (1986) has pointed out that most early investigators, despite their interest about the intentional nature of deception, focused on evaluations or descriptions of verbal deception (lying) as opposed to investigations of children's understanding of what constitutes a deceptive statement (Hall 1891; Leonard 1920; Tudor-Hart 1926; Krout 1932). Piaget (1932) tried to determine at what age children develop the concept of deceit described by Hartshorne and May's formal definition. Based on his interviews with children, Piaget believed that until about age 10, children equate unintentionally misleading statements with intentionally misleading ones. Recent research has shown, however, that children, between ages 4 and 6, appear to develop cognitive abilities which allow them to mentally represent the inaccurate beliefs that other individuals possess, and they are able to use these representations in simple deceitful behaviors (Wimmer and Perner 1983). Other investigators believe that the capacity for attributing false belief, and hence deception, arises considerably earlier (Bartsch and Wellman 1989; Chandler, Fritz, and Hala 1989; Hala, Chandler, and Fritz 1991).

In the context of the other attributional abilities described (self-awareness, the attribution of intention, and visual perspective-taking), intentional deception would appear to be more sophisticated, drawing on these more fundamental skills. In Mead's (1934) view, symbolic interaction (in the form of language and symbolic behavior) assists the child's development of a self-concept. Ultimately, these forms of symbolic interaction give rise to the child's conception of the generalized other from which general perspective-taking (cognitive empathic) abilities emerge. Yet intentional deception, whether in the form of verbal or behavioral deceit, is only possible after the child realizes that these symbolic interactions hold the same meaning for others as they do for themselves. Wimmer and Perner's (1983) research suggests that children must also have a causal theory of knowledge acquisition and an ability to simultaneously represent conflicting models of reality.

Although there is evidence that chimpanzees are capable of attributing certain aspects of belief and intention to others, is there any experimental evidence that they are capable of representing conflicting models of reality? The issue of intentional deception has been studied in chimpanzees with somewhat ambiguous results. Woodruff and Premack (1979) reported the successful production and comprehension of deception in young chimpanzees after extended training. In the first part of their experiment, the subject was allowed to watch a human trainer place food under one of two cups, both of which were out of its reach. Next, either a cooperative or a competitive trainer entered the room and tried to determine from the chimpanzee's behavior which cup contained the food. The trainers did not know where the food was hidden, and had to use the chimpanzee's behavior to locate the food. If the cooperative trainers were successful, they gave the food to the chimpanzee; if not, the trial ended and the chimpanzee went unrewarded. But when the competitive trainers located the food, they kept it for themselves; however, when they were unsuccessful, the chimpanzee was allowed to obtain the food under the correct cup. After a number of trials, the roles of the chimpanzees and the trainers were reversed. During each of these new trials, a competitive or cooperative trainer was shown the location of the food. And, when the naive chimpanzee was brought into the room, the cooperative trainers would point to the correct cup and the competitive trainers would attempt to deceive the chimpanzee by pointing to the incorrect cup.

Initially, the chimpanzees provided enough information to both the cooperative and competitive trainers to allow them to find the food on most of the trials. However, by the end of the first phase of the experiment, the competitive trainer was performing with much less accuracy, indicating that three of the four chimpanzees had begun to selectively suppress information about the location of the food when that trainer was present.

During the second phase of the experiment, when the roles were reversed, all of the chimpanzees had difficulty avoiding being fooled by the deceptive pointing and glances of the competitive human trainer. However, after a number of trials, two of the chimpanzees developed parallel deceptive practices. When they became informants, they pointed to the correct location in the presence of the cooperative trainer, but consistently pointed to the incorrect location in the presence of the competitive trainer.

Thus, not only did all of the chimpanzees learn to withhold information selectively from their competitive counterparts, but two of them actively misinformed the competitors. Woodruff and Premack concluded that the performance of the chimpanzees "suggests the development of intentional communication," and, in particular, instances of active deception on the parts of two of the subjects "meet the most stringent behavioral criteria for intentional communication" (1979:336).

Woodruff and Premack's (1979) interpretations have been criticized on the grounds that their subjects may have simply learned conditional discriminations during the extended training procedure. That is, rather than understanding how they were being deceived and themselves attempting to deceive their competitor, the chimpanzees had merely learned alternative routes to obtain food. Since they were rewarded for behavior that provided information to the cooperative trainers and were also rewarded for behavior that prevented the competitive trainers from guessing the location of the food, some commentators have argued that traditional learning theory could account for most of Woodruff and Premack's results (Dennett 1983). Woodruff and Premack (1979) addressed some of these issues in their original report, and Premack (1988a) has recently responded to these criticisms in another context. However, given the young age of the subjects and the large number of trials required to produce the described behaviors, learning accounts will remain more plausible than attributional accounts to many researchers. Indeed, Premack's own position on the intentional nature of the results is unclear. Elsewhere, Premack (1986:153) argued that true deception should require second-order attributions, an ability which he believes chimpanzees do not possess (Premack and Premack 1983).

Of course, the ambiguous nature of evidence for comprehension of deception by chimpanzees does not mean that they are incapable of understanding or producing deception. Indeed, anecdotal evidence shows that they are capable of both (de Waal 1986b; Goodall 1986; Whiten and Byrne 1988). However, a convincing demonstration of their ability to comprehend deception is lacking. Indeed, in the Woodruff and Premack study, only one of the four chimpanzees developed the ability to avoid the competitive trainer's deceptive pointing by overturning the opposite cup, and even that subject did so only after numerous trials. The best the other three could do was to withhold any response at all until the end of the trial when the competitive trainer went away and the chimpanzees were allowed to choose the cup they knew all along was correct (Premack 1986). Part of the difficulty in producing experimental demonstrations of intentional deception in nonhuman primates may be due to the fact that true deception does not lend itself well to repetitious experimental designs (Whiten and Byrne 1988; Quiatt 1984). It remains possible that lower level explanations of deception may account for many anecdotal instances of apparent intentional deception (Mitchell 1986; Premack 1988a).

Do chimpanzees pretend? Do chimpanzees pretend? Here we refer not to deception, which sometimes involves pretense, but to situations in which an individual pretends that an object (or individual) is something (or someone) other than what (or who) it really is. For some, the ability to substitute alternate worlds for our own may seem to be a distinction of human mentation. Indeed, many have argued that the ability to pretend is the very source of human creativity. Yet it is exhibited quite early in human ontogeny. Pretense first appears in children's play behavior between 18 and 24 months of age (Fein 1981; McCune-Nicolich 1981). Eighteen to 24-month-old children are even capable of reciprocal pretend games with other children (Dunn and Dale 1984).

Despite the early appearance of pretense in human development, there is little evidence that chimpanzees engage in pretend play. Occasional examples have been recorded, the most striking of which is Cathy Hayes's (1951) description of the chimpanzee Viki engaging in a pretend game with an imaginary pull toy. For nearly two weeks, Viki not only apparently pretended to pull a rope with something attached, she repeatedly acted as if she were pulling the rope up, hand over hand. In order to probe

Viki's understanding, Hayes pretended that she herself was pulling an imaginary toy. At first, Viki followed her with avid interest, even inspecting the floor where the toy might have been. But soon, Viki became visibly frustrated and exhibited the classic signs of chimpanzee emotional distress. Viki never again pretended to pull an imaginary plaything.

Although researchers other than Hayes have described symbolic play in chimpanzees (Premack 1986), such instances are exceedingly rare. For example, Mignault (1985) studied the play behavior of nursery-reared chimpanzees to look for evidence of pretense. Despite the chimpanzees' exposure to humans, other chimpanzees, and a variety of objects, they exhibited virtually no evidence of pretense in their play. Mignault concluded that low levels of chimpanzee play involving either more than one object or the conventionalized use of objects might account for the difference between chimpanzees and human children.

Thus, there are striking differences in the development of symbolic play in humans and chimpanzees. Whether these differences reflect underlying cognitive distinctions is unclear. The fact that pretense occurs only rarely in chimpanzee play does not prove that chimpanzees lack a capacity for pretense altogether. It is possible, for example, that chimpanzee pretense normally emerges in other, more social, forms. In studying the behavior of a twenty-month-old chimpanzee, one of us (DJP) frequently witnessed what might be called "deceptive pretense," whereby the infant would begin to engage in a prohibited act, but, when caught, would shift to a related but perfectly acceptable activity, as if pretending to be playing. Pretense may exist in chimpanzees outside the context of actual play.

Do chimpanzees teach one another? Can chimpanzees actively teach one another? Are they, like humans, capable of instructing others with an intent to shape their performance according to some predetermined standard of achievement? Premack (1984) argued that chimpanzees may lack the attributional and aesthetic capacities necessary for true pedagogy. In his view, pedagogy requires several components: social attribution, training or planned intervention, and evaluation or judgment. Chimpanzees appear to possess some of each of these abilities, but do not appear to possess the tendency to engage actively in tutelage (Premack 1984). For example, even in the realm of material technology, where what Premack calls silent pedagogy presumably could be most effective, chimpanzees do not display tutelage. An infant chimpanzee may spend hours observing her mother termite fishing, carefully crafting fishing sticks to probe into the mound, and may make primitive attempts at fashioning her own probes. But the mother never pauses to correct her efforts by observing the infant's efforts, molding its behavior, and then finally evaluating what the infant has learned. Isolated incidents, including maternal punishment of infants, may be taken as evidence of one or more of the above components of pedagogy—and indeed, some have been labeled tutelage by some authors (Köhler 1925; Fouts, Hirsch, and Fouts 1982)—but the pattern of pedagogy described above is simply not present in chimpanzee society (but see Boesch 1991 for limited evidence to the contrary).

An absence of active pedagogy poses no special problem for young chimpanzees because adult chimpanzees do not act in ways that are too complicated to learn through observation. Premack (1984) argues that simple material culture may be effectively propagated without pedagogy. It is only more complicated systems, like arbitrary social rules based on abstract concepts, that may require active tutelage. Pedagogy dominates human societies and is a principal force linking human cultures across space and time, indeed providing them with history (Premack 1986). We cannot know for certain when pedagogy arose as an integral part of human culture, but it was clearly present in the earliest known forms of writing in the Old Babylonian period nearly 4000 years ago. Archaeologists have unearthed tablets which show clear evidence of pedagogical instruction (learning to write and to perform mathematical operations, Walker 1987). And it seems obvious that even the earliest forms of writing which appear nearly one thousand years earlier (Walker 1987) must have been propagated through tutelage.

One need only consider the complexity of a "simple" technology such as the making of clay pots to appreciate the importance of pedagogy in propagating techniques (Bunzel 1929). In humans, pedagogy simultaneously develops and constrains achievements, a point that Bunzel (1929) made in her analysis of art in pottery among Zuni and Hopi Indians. One conclusion that Premack (1984) draws from the apparent absence of pedagogy in chimpanzees is that pedagogy creates a unique problem for humans: it creates an intergenerational cognitive gap. The more pedagogy is employed, the greater the intergenerational cognitive gap becomes. For example, in judging young girls incapable of constructing pottery "properly," Zuni women intervene and, through meticulous instruction, bring them to a standard level of performance (Bunzel 1929). Thus pedagogy becomes the solution to the problem that pedagogy itself creates (Premack 1984).

But why do chimpanzees not actively teach others? Perhaps, as Premack (1984) suggested, chimpanzees have the ability to teach, but do not need to do so, given the relatively simple nature of their subsistence patterns. Alternatively, chimpanzees may not possess the cognitive capacity to support pedagogy (Premack 1984). In order to understand the basis for the latter argument, let us reconsider the evidence we presented concerning the nature of chimpanzees' attributional capacities.

The most persuasive evidence of chimpanzee social attribution has emerged through studies of attribution of intention or simple role-taking in which the knowledge possessed by one individual need not be correctly, or even explicitly, represented by the other. Attribution of intention and simple role-taking are clearly present in human 3-year-olds, and, in this context, Premack (1984, 1986, 1988a, 1988b; Premack and Dasser, in press) has argued that chimpanzee social attributional capacities resemble those of 3.5-year-old children. If this represents the limit of adult chimpanzee social attribution, then adult chimpanzees may not possess an accurate theory of knowledge formation. In a replication of the chimpanzee guessing and knowing study using 3- and 4-year-old human children, Povinelli and DeBlois (n.d.) discovered that only half of the 4-year-olds sampled appeared to understand the cognitive results of the differential access to information that the guesser and the knower were given. However, those children who appeared to understand the difference between the guesser and knower demonstrated an immediate comprehension of the task, consistently following the advice of the knower from the very first trials. In addition, rhesus macaques, who differ little from chimpanzees on traditional learning tasks, showed no evidence of discriminating between advice offered by the guesser and knower, even after 800 trials (Povinelli, Parks, and Novak, in press, b). In contrast, the chimpanzees studied by Povinelli, Nelson, and Boysen (1990) showed the ability to distinguish between guessing and knowing only gradually, although they did transfer that ability into another paradigm fairly readily.

However, the analogous task given chimpanzees by Premack (1988a) (requiring them to select the trainer who had seen the food being hidden rather than the trainer who had not) resulted much more quickly in correct performance. This finding led Povinelli, Nelson, and Boysen (1990) to speculate that their task was unnecessarily difficult because it required the chimpanzees to choose between the conflicting advice of two individuals. To complicate matters further, Premack (1988a, pers. com.; Premack and Dasser, in press) remains unconvinced that these tasks really tap the ability to distinguish between seeing and knowing. It is fair to conclude that chimpanzees have not unequivocally demonstrated an understanding of the importance of informational access in knowledge formation.

If chimpanzees do not understand the importance of informational access in knowledge formation, or understand it only weakly, this may explain their lack of pedagogy. As Premack has remarked, "how astute a pedagogue could you be if you were unable to distinguish between what you know and what someone else knows?" (1986:153). Teaching, then, presumes at least some attributional inferences about knowledge states. It may not require a full-blown understanding of the sources of knowledge, but it may well be that pedagogy of the sort humans exhibit cannot occur in organisms that do not frequently or correctly represent the informational states of fellow beings. If informational states of knowledge are more difficult to represent in organisms (such as chimpanzees) that also lack language (Premack and Woodruff 1978; Gallup 1982; Premack 1988a), then pedagogy may never occur to them.

Summary: How noble in reason? Chimpanzees may have a "theory of mind" in that they apparently attribute mental states to others. At present, it would be foolish to attempt to specify the exact nature of the chimpanzee's "theory of mind." However, it is clear that such an undertaking is empirically feasible. We have seen that chimpanzees may share with humans certain attributional processes, including some form of self-awareness, the attribution of intention, role-taking, and perhaps the attribution of knowledge. The evidence is weaker, but chimpanzees may also be capable of some degree of empathic concern, pretense, and intentional deception. Weaker yet is the evidence for second-order attribution and pedagogy.

What do these facts tell us about the evolution of altruism and ethics in humans?

Mind and Morality

Chimpanzees apparently possess some, but not all, of the attributional capacities present in humans. Those attributional skills that chimpanzees and humans do share, and that may have been present in their common ancestor, motivate a wide range of expressed behaviors in chimpanzees. Chimpanzees are socially intelligent creatures, yet they are not ethical creatures. Chimpanzees exhibit elaborate reassurance behaviors which tend to be expressed when conspecifics are distressed or injured. Yet they may not experience sympathy, and they do not have networks of shared values. Ethics, and perhaps even empathic altruism, may require attributional capacities more sophisticated than the specific subset that we have postulated as shared by chimpanzees and humans. This implies that we should consider the evolution of altruism and ethics as a sequence of events involving an initial appearance of basic attributional capacities supporting behaviors completely unrelated to ethics, but without which ethics could never have evolved. The emergence of ethical systems depended on the later evolutionary elaboration of those ancestral attributional capacities.

How absent of altruism? We have asserted that helping behavior in humans is distinct from that of most other animals said to behave "altruistically" in that human helping has a complex motivational base that depends in part on self- and social attribution. The experience of social caring or sympathy emerges through social attribution, and is thus a by-product of the ability to project emotions, needs, knowledge, and so on, to others. Social attribution motivates a wide range of responses, only one of which is sympathy for individuals in need. In humans, empathic concern can motivate helping without any expectation (or realization) of return.

As we have shown, it is difficult to ascertain to what extent chimpanzees experience sympathy. Chimpanzees show patterns of behavior that appear, from a psychological perspective, only weakly altruistic. Much of what might qualify as chimpanzee altruism may be based on the arousal of feelings of emotional distress in the helper, perhaps through emotional contagion, and the role of social attribution is unclear when helping is prompted by emotional contagion. In any case, expressions of helping in chimpanzees resemble those of young human children. Chimpanzees almost certainly do not have the same capacity for appreciating the mental states of others that human adults possess. Thus, chimpanzees may share some but not all of the cognitive underpinnings of human altruism. Ultimately, a better understanding of the chimpanzee's capacity for empathic concern should enable us to understand why chimpanzees behave as they do toward others in distress.

How absent of ethics? Ethical systems require more than a capacity for empathic concern. They cannot exist unless individuals develop and attribute values or personal goals to themselves and to others. They also require that those values be shared. This would appear to require a clear understanding of second-order attribution.

It is in this sense that we believe chimpanzees have no ethical systems. In humans, values are often shared through active tutelage. Chimpanzees may not have the attributional capacities necessary for tutelage, and this could explain their lack of ethical systems. The cognitive skills that underlie pedagogy may have been crucial for the evolution of human ethics.

On the other hand, it is clear that not all forms of helping behavior require tutelage. Tutelage may influence the likelihood that individual humans will help others. Certainly the inculcation of values influences the likelihood of helping, and this inculcation is influenced by cultural norms. But altruism can occur in animals that do not exhibit tutelage, or any social attribution whatsoever, as the eusocial insects amply demonstrate. The weak altruism and elaborate reassurance gestures that exist in chimpanzees may depend on social attribution, but they do not depend on active pedagogy. This suggests that while a "theory of mind" of the type characteristic of chimpanzees may be sufficient to produce helping, it is not sufficient to produce ethical systems.

As a working hypothesis we propose three cognitive prerequisites for the emergence of ethical systems that can be dissociated from the evolution of altruism: (1) the attribution of values, (2) tutelage, and (3) second-order attribution. All of these depend on rather sophisticated capacities for social attribution. We do not yet know whether chimpanzees attribute values or personal goals—that is, whether they make attributions about desired states of existence for themselves and for others. Premack and Woodruff (1978) suggest that chimpanzees may interpret the behavior of others in terms of intentions or wants. And most organisms react in ways which indicate that they seek out certain experiences over others (avoiding pain and retrieving food). However, it remains unknown whether primates in general, or chimpanzees in particular, are aware of these desired states as enduring mental representations (that is, as characteristics that persist in individuals over time). But, even if they do have such mental representations, there is little evidence that they are capable of sharing them. In other words, if chimpanzees do not realize that others attribute mental states (second-order attribution), it is by definition impossible for them to "share" these states with others.

Perhaps chimpanzees do possess values or desired states of existence; perhaps, also, if they attribute intentions to others (as they seem to), they understand that other individuals have values. But such values cannot translate into ethical systems through observational learning alone. Infant apes may learn from watching, but if ethics are produced through active pedagogy, and chimpanzees lack pedagogy, then chimpanzees produce no intergenerational cognitive gap and, therefore, have no intergenerational cognitive gap to close. The weak presence of altruism, coupled with the absence of ethical systems in chimpanzees can, then, might be understood within the larger context of their acquisition of basic social attributional skills, but not of pedagogy, second-order attribution or attribution of values.

Language also seems to be an important ingredient in the evolution of complex ethical systems. Tutelage can exist without language, and many forms of nonverbal tutelage exist in humans (Bateson and Mead 1942; Mead [1928] 1949, [1930] 1953, [1935] 1963), but language is an especially efficient means of explaining values. Without language, it would be difficult to ascertain what other individuals' values really are. Perhaps, one would be able to intuit other individuals' immediate desires, wants or needs, and perhaps even make inferences about their knowledge states. One might observe a certain consistency in their behavior, and conclude that they have certain preferred modes of action, but it would be difficult to infer personal values. And even if one could, it would be difficult to explain one's own values. The ethical meaning that people assign to any behavior derives from accounts that others give of the behavior in question. Deviations from normative standards are pointed out and corrected and individuals are judged according to some shared cultural standard, again emphasizing the link between shared values and second-order attribution.

This returns us to the issue of pedagogy. We speculate that once attributional capacities became sufficiently sophisticated, tutelage could have emerged, in part, as a means to impose normative standards of behavior on others. As Premack (1984) has noted, pedagogy both creates and bridges an intergenerational cognitive gap. As humans began to rely on pedagogy to share values, that intergenerational cognitive gap must have lengthened. Ethics may have emerged as pedagogy both produced and closed an increasingly formidable intergenerational cognitive gap.

Altruism in humans is one expression of a set of cognitive capacities that are collectively unique to humans, and that involve the ability to project mental states onto others. This means that human ethics cannot be described as codified standards of right and wrong that are either genetically or culturally fixed. In figure 1 we sketch our working hypothesis of the relationships between epigenetics, neurobiology, attributional capacities, empathic altruism and ethics. Ethical systems emerge from a complex network of causality that begins with species-specific, epigenetically determined attributional capacities, and that allows for individual decisions concerning values. These individual decisions ultimately generate cultural standards of ethics, which, then, in turn affect individual decisions. It is at the intersection between individual value decisions and cultural expectations that the plasticity of human ethical systems arises. Ethical systems, then, depend on the ability to attribute values, emotions, intentions, motives, knowledge, and, indeed, attribution itself, to others. Without complex social attribution, human ethical systems could not exist. The degree to which social attribution is present in different species will have a direct effect on the existence and expression of altruism and ethics (see fig. 1).

Filling the cognitive gaps. A tension exists—rightly or wrongly—between those who see altruism and ethics in humans as direct products of natural selection and those who see them as culturally determined and propagated. At the extremes are those who believe that all have completely escaped the constraints of reproduction, that behavior is "adaptive" only in its cultural (social, political or economic) context. Most researchers acknowledge that human behavior derives from both biological and cultural forces, but the tension between many sociobiologists and cultural anthropologists still exists. We opened this chapter by suggesting an alternative approach which addresses the cognitive void left by studies that focus on ultimate causation, while retaining an explicitly evolutionary focus. Our efforts point to possible bridges between cultural anthropology,

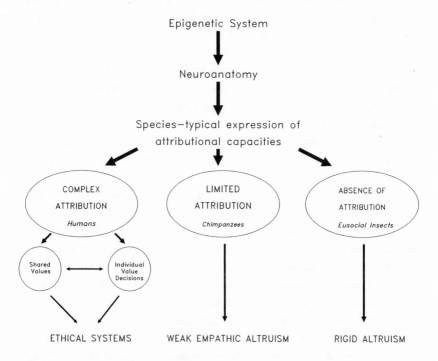

Figure 1. The presence of ethical systems in a species is directly dependent on the presence of complex forms of social attribution, which are ultimately the result of the epigenetic system. We argue that, as a working model, species which lack attributional capacities altogether can show rigid forms of altruism, presumably as the result of kin selection. In addition to such rigid forms of altruism, species with limited attributional capacities may show weak instances of empathically motivated altruism. We hypothesize that chimpanzees are one such species, showing evidence of intention and responsibility attribution, and perhaps certain forms of knowledge attribution, but showing no elaborate signs of empathic concern, pedagogy, attribution of deception, or second-order attribution. Humans, in contrast, display elaborate forms of social attribution including attribution of intention, knowledge, false belief, as well as empathic concern and second-order attribution. Pedagogy, in particular, emerges from such complex attributional processes and allows for the intergenerational transmission of both individual and cultural values. These individual cognitive processes ultimately emerge as both individual and shared ethical systems. The role of kin selection in species with complex attributional processes remains unclear.

developmental, social, and comparative psychology, and evolutionary biology. What is needed is a broad, comparative investigation of the expression and ontogeny of attribution in humans, chimpanzees, and other primates in order to reconstruct the cognitive characteristics of the ancestors of particular clades.

Many questions remain unanswered, but our approach has a number of immediate implications for the evolution of human ethics and altruism:

1. Empathic altruism in humans operates in a fashion that is distinctly different from other forms of helping behavior. Empathic concern exists in humans, and motivates at least some expressions of human helping.

2. We must understand the evolution of social attribution before we can understand the emergence of empathic altruism and ethical systems. In particular, ethical systems cannot exist unless values can be shared. In humans, tutelage supports the intergenerational transmission of values. Its existence appears to depend on sophisticated attributional skills.

3. Because certain forms of attribution exist in primates that do not have ethical systems and show only weak expressions of genuine altruism, it is clear that attribution did not evolve to support ethical systems.

We would guess that altruism and ethics, as they are manifested in humans, were never rigidly mediated by natural selection. Altruism and ethics in humans may well be emergent by-products of the way in which brains capable of complex social attribution work. Complex social attribution may support both helpful and hurtful behaviors, as well as intentional deception. It is possible that these expressions are not genetically separable from each other. This means that any presumed selective advantage of altruism or ethics may not be independent of the selective advantage of the entire neural system that generates social attribution.

A comparative approach to studying attribution helps us to understand the biological basis of human behavioral plasticity. Human ethical systems emerged through the evolution of a suite of cognitive processes, some of which were present in the common ancestor of humans and apes, while others appear to have uniquely emerged in the human lineage. We have arrived at the point where we can begin to reconstruct the sequence by which the cognitive infrastructure supporting ethical systems evolved.

Acknowledgments

We wish to thank Sandra DeBlois, Michael Chazan, John R. Cole, Gordon Gallup, Jr.,

Jonathan Holmes, Jonathan Marks, Stefan Senders, and Ervin Staub for sharing comments on earlier versions of this manuscript and for providing useful references.

Note

1. Duranti (1988) argues that an intentional view of language is not the only one possible. He examined speech acts in Samoan society, and identified patterns of language use that appear to be at odds with the view of language that we adopt here. Duranti argues that individuals are not universally perceived as expressing personal intentions or desires. Local theories of self and the particular task at hand contribute to the meaning of the speaker; furthermore, the audience has an important role in defining meaning. We have no difficulty with his description of intriguing differences between Western and Samoan speech acts. But we also believe that such differences do not contravene underlying intentional components of language use and meaning. Indeed, the transcripts of Samoan speech that Duranti provides demonstrate that, at one level, personal intentions are the very cornerstone of the conversations he examines. The first conversation, for example, involves one individual directing specific allegations of wrongdoing at another individual, and the language that the accuser uses, while crafted according to the influences that Duranti outlines, is clearly a tool to achieve a desired personal goal (the punishment of another individual). Furthermore, Duranti's description of some of the concerns of the observing audience leads us to believe that, for Samoans as well as Westerners, peoples' intentions are critically important. Why else would one of the orators request clarification of whether or not the accused individual is specifically being accused of lying? Duranti's central point that a personalist theory of language is not the only (or necessarily preferred) route to understanding language is well-taken. But this does not imply that there are differences in the cognitive foundations of language among people of different cultures.

References

Alexander, R. 1974. The evolution of social behavior. *Annual Review of Ecology and Systematics* 5:325-83.

Alexander, R. 1987. *The Biology of Moral Systems.* New York: Aldine de Gruyter.

Ashworth, P. D. 1979. *Social Interaction and Consciousness.* New York: John Wiley & Sons.

Asquith, P. J. 1984. The inevitability and utility of anthropomorphism in descriptions of primate behavior, 138-76. In *The Meaning of Primate Signals*, ed. R. Harré and V. Reynolds. Cambridge: Cambridge University Press.

Bartsch, K., and H. Wellman. 1989. Young children's attribution of action to beliefs and desires. *Child Development* 60:946-64.

Bateson, G., and M. Mead. 1942. *Balinese Character: A Photographic Analysis.* New York: New York Academy of Sciences.

Batson, C. D. 1989. Personal values, moral principles and a three-path model of prosocial motivation, 213-28. In *Social and Moral Values: Individual and Societal Perspectives*, ed. N. Eisenberg, J. Reykowski, and E. Staub. Hillsdale, NJ: Erlbaum.

Batson, C. D. 1990. How social an animal? The human capacity for caring. *American Psychologist* 45:336-46.

Batson, C. D., K. O'Quin, J. Fultz, M. Vanderplas, and A. Isen. 1983. Self-reported distress and empathy and egoistic versus altruistic motivation for helping. *Journal of Personality and Social Psychology* 45:706-18.

Bavelas, J. B., A. Black, N. Chovil, C. R. Lemery, and J. Mullett. 1988. Form and function in motor mimicry: Topographic evidence that the primary function is communicative. *Human Communication Research* 14:275-99.

Bavelas, J. B., A. Black, C. R. Lemery, and J. Mullett. 1986. "I show how you feel": Motor mimicry as a communicative act. *Journal of Personality and Social Psychology* 50:322-29.

Bavelas, J. B., A. Black, C. R. Lemery, and J. Mullett. 1987. Motor mimicry as primitive empathy, 317-38. In *Empathy and its Development*, ed. N. Eisenberg and J. Strayer. Cambridge: Cambridge University Press.

Benedict, R. 1923. The concept of the guardian spirit in North America. *Memoirs of the American Anthropological Association* 29:1-97.

Benedict, R. [1934] 1946. *Patterns of Culture*. New York: Mentor.

Bennett, J. 1976. *Linguistic Behavior*. Cambridge: Cambridge University Press.

Bickerton, D. 1987. More than nature needs? A reply to Premack. *Cognition* 23:73-79.

Bitterman, M. E. 1987. Evidence of divergence in vertebrate learning. *Behavioral and Brain Sciences* 10:659-60.

Boas, F. [1940] 1966. *Race, Language, and Culture*. New York: Macmillan.

Bock, P. K. 1988. *Rethinking Psychological Anthropology: Continuity and Change in the Study of Human Action*. New York: W. H. Freeman and Co.

Boesch, C. 1991. Teaching among wild chimpanzees. *Animal Behaviour* 41:530-32.

Borke, H. 1971. Interpersonal perception of young children: Egocentrism or empathy? *Developmental Psychology* 5:263-69.

Bretherton, I., and M. Beeghly. 1982. Talking about internal states: The acquisition of an explicit theory of mind. *Developmental Psychology* 18:906-21.

Brower, L. P., and J. V. Z. Brower. 1962. Investigations into mimicry. *Natural History* 71:819.

Bunzel, R. L. 1929. *The Pueblo Potter*. New York: Dover.

Burke, K. 1966. *Language as Symbolic Action: Essays on Life, Literature, and Method*. Berkeley: University of California Press.

Burnstein, E., and P. Worchel. 1962. Arbitrariness of frustration and its consequences for aggression in a social situation. *Journal of Personality* 30:528-40.

Byrne, R., and A. Whiten. 1985. Tactical deception of familiar individuals in baboons (*Papio ursinus*). *Animal Behaviour* 33 (2): 669-73.

Chandler, M. J., A. S. Fritz, and S. Hala. 1989. Small-scale deceit: Deception as a marker of two-, three-, and four-year-olds' early theories of mind. *Child Development* 60:126377.

Chandler, M. J., S. Greenspan, and C. Barenboim. 1973. Judgements of intentionality in response to videotaped and verbally presented moral dilemmas: The medium is the message. *Child Development* 44:315-20.

Cheney, D. L., and R. M. Seyfarth. 1985. Vervet monkey alarm calls: Manipulation through shared information? *Behaviour* 94:150-66.

Cheney, D. L., and R. M. Seyfarth. 1990. *How Monkeys See the World: Inside the Mind of Another Species*. Chicago and London: University of Chicago Press.

Cohen, R. 1972. Altruism: Human, cultural, or what? *Journal of Social Issues* 28:39-57.

Coke, J. S., C. D. Batson, and K. McDavis. 1978. Empathic mediation of helping: A twostaged model. *Journal of Personality and Social Psychology* 36:752-66.

Cole, M., and B. Means. 1981. *Comparative Studies of How People Think*. Cambridge, MA: Harvard University Press.

Cooley, C. H. 1912. *Human Nature and the Social Order*. New York: Scribner's and Sons.

Davis, M. H. 1980. Multidimensional approach to individual differences in empathy. *JSAS Catalog of Selected Documents in Psychology* 10:75.

Dawkins, R. 1976. *The Selfish Gene*. New York: Oxford University Press.

Dawkins, R., and J. Krebs. 1984. Animal signals: Mindreading and manipulation, 380-402. In *Behavioral Ecology: An Evolutionary Approach*, ed. J. R. Krebs and N. B. Davies. Sunderland, MA: Sinauer Associates.

Dennett, D. 1971. Intentional systems. *Journal of Philosophy* 68:87-106.

Dennett, D. 1978. *Brainstorms*. Montgomery, VT: Bradford Books.

Dennett, D. 1983. Intentional systems in cognitive ethology: The "Panglossian paradigm" defended. *Behavioral and Brain Sciences* 6:343-55.

Desmond, A. 1979. *The Ape's Reflexion*. London: Blond and Briggs, Ltd.

DeVries, R. 1970. The development of role-taking as reflected by the behavior of bright, average, and retarded children in a social guessing game. *Child Psychology* 41:759-70.

DuBois, C. [1944] 1961. *The People of Alor*. 2 vols. New York: Harper & Row.

Dunn, J., and N. Dale. 1984. I a daddy: Two-year old's collaboration in joint pretend with sibling and with mother, 131-58. In *Symbolic Play and the Development of Social Understanding*, ed. I. Bretherton. New York: Academic Press.

Duranti, A. 1988. Intentions, language, and social action in a Samoan context. *Journal of Pragmatics* 12:13-33.

Eisenberg, N., and P. Miller. 1987. Empathy and prosocial behavior. *Psychological Bulletin* 101:91-119.

Ekman, P. 1973. Cross-cultural studies of facial expression, 551-77. In *Darwin and Facial Expressions*, ed. P. Ekman. New York: Academic Press.

Epstein, R., R. P. Lanza, and B. F. Skinner. 1981. "Self-awareness" in the pigeon. *Science* 212:695-96.

Falk, D. 1987. Hominid paleoneurology. *Annual Review of Anthropology* 16:13-30.

Fein, G. G. 1981. Pretend play in childhood: An integrative review. *Child Development* 52:1095-1118.

Feshbach, N. 1975. Empathy in children: Some theoretical and empirical considerations. *Counseling Psychologist* 5:25-30.

Flavell, J. H., P. T. Botkin, C. L. Fry, Jr., J. W. Wright, and P. E. Jarvis. 1968. *The Development of Role-Taking in Communication Skills in Children*. Huntington, NY: Robert E. Krieger Publ. Co.

Flavell, J. H., B. A. Everett, K. Croft, and E. R. Flavell. 1981. Young children's knowledge about visual perception: Further evidence for the level 1-level 2 distinction. *Developmental Psychology* 17: 99-103.

Fouts, R. S., A. D. Hirsch, and D. H. Fouts. 1982. Cultural transmission of a human language in a chimpanzee mother-infant relationship, 159-93. In *Psychobiological Perspectives*, ed. H. E. Fitzgerald, J. A. Mullins, and P. Gage. Child Nurturance Series, vol. 3. New York: Plenum Press.

Gallup, G. G., Jr. 1970. Chimpanzees: Self-recognition. *Science* 167:86-87.

Gallup, G. G., Jr. 1979. Self-awareness in primates. *American Scientist* 67:417-21.

Gallup, G. G., Jr. 1982. Self-awareness and the emergence of mind in primates. *American Journal of Primatology* 2:237-48.

Gallup, G. G., Jr. 1983. Toward a comparative psychology of mind, 473-510. In *Animal Cognition and Behavior*, ed. R. E. Mellgren. New York: North Holland Publishing Co.

Gallup, G. G., Jr. 1985. Do minds exist in species other than our own? *Neuroscience and Biobehavioral Reviews* 9:631-41.

Geertz, C. 1973. *The Interpretation of Cultures*. New York: Basic Books.

Gladwin, T., and S. B. Sarason. 1953. *Truk: Man in Paradise*. Chicago: University of Chicago Press.

Godfrey, L. R., and K. Jacobs. 1981. Gradual, autocatalytic and punctuational models of hominid brain evolution: A cautionary tale. *Journal of Human Evolution* 10:255-72.

Goffman, E. 1959. *The Presentation of Self in Everyday Life*. Garden City, NY: Doubleday.

Goldman-Rakic, P. S., and T. Preuss. 1987. Whither comparative psychology? *Behavioral and Brain Sciences* 10:666-67.

Goodall, J. 1986. *The Chimpanzees of Gombe: Patterns of Behavior*. Cambridge, MA: Belknap, Harvard University Press.

Gratch, G. 1964. Response alternation in children: A developmental study of orientations to uncertainty. *Vita Humana* 7:49-60.

Grice, H. 1975. Logic and conversation, 41-58. In *Syntax and Semantics*, ed. P. Cole and J. L. Morgan. New York: Academic Press.

Griffin, D. 1976. *The Question of Animal Awareness: Evolutionary Continuity and Mental Experience*. New York: Rockefeller University Press.

Hala, S., M. Chandler, and A. S. Fritz. 1991. Fledgling theories of mind: Deception as a marker of three-year-olds' understanding of false belief. *Child Development* 62:83-97.

Hall, G. S. 1891. Children's lies. *Pedagogical Seminary* 1:211-18.

Hallowell, A. I. 1960. Ojibwa ontology, behavior, and world view, 19-52. In *Culture in History*, ed. S. Diamond. New York: Columbia University Press.

Hallowell, A. I. 1971. *Culture and Experience*. Philadelphia: University of Pennsylvania Press.

Harré, R., and P. Secord. 1972. *The Explanation of Social Behavior*. Oxford: Basil Blackwell.

Hartshorne, H., and M. A. May. 1928. *Studies in Deceit*. Book 1. New York: Arno.

Harvey, J. H., and G. Weary. 1981. *Perspectives on Attributional Processes*. Dubuque, IA: Wm. C. Brown Co. Publishers.

Hayes, C. 1951. *The Ape in our House*. New York: Harper and Brothers.

Heelas, P. 1981. The model applied: Anthropology and indigenous psychologies, 39-63. In *Indigenous Psychologies: The Anthropology of the Self*, ed. P. Heelas and A. Lock. London: Academic Press.

Heider, F. 1944. Social perception and phenomenal causality. *Psychological Review* 51:358-74.

Heider, F. 1958. *The Psychology of Interpersonal Relations*. New York: Wiley and Sons.

Hodos, W., and C. B. G. Campbell. 1969. Scala naturae: Why there is no theory in comparative psychology. *Psychological Review* 76:337-50.

Hoffman, M. L. 1975. Sex differences in moral internalization. *Journal of Personality and Social Psychology* 32:720-29.

Hoffman, M. L. 1977. Empathy, its development and prosocial implications, 169-218. In *Social Cognitive Developments. Nebraska Symposium on Motivation*, vol. 25, ed. H. E. Howe and C. B. Keasey. Lincoln: University of Nebraska Press.

Hoffman, M. L. 1982. The development of prosocial motivation: Empathy and guilt, 218-31. In *The Development of Prosocial Behavior*, ed. N. Eisenberg. New York: Academic Press.

Hogrefe, G.-J., H. Wimmer, and J. Perner. 1986. Ignorance versus false belief: A developmental lag in attribution of epistemic states. *Child Development* 57:567-82.

Hollis, M. 1984. Of masks and men, 217-33. In *The Category of the Person: Anthropology, Philosophy, History*, ed. M. Carrithers, S. Collins, and S. Lukes. Cambridge: Cambridge University Press.

Holloway, R. L. 1975. Early hominid endocasts, 393-415. In *Primate Functional Morphology and Evolution*, ed. R. H. Tuttle. The Hague: Mouton.

Imamoğlu, E. O. 1975. Children's awareness in usage of intention cues. *Child Development* 46:39-45.

Kagan, J. 1981. *The Second Year: The Emergence of Self-Awareness*. Cambridge, MA: Harvard University Press.

Kardiner, A., and R. Linton. 1939. *The Individual and his Society*. New York: Columbia University Press.

Keasey, C. B. 1977. Children's developing awareness and usage of intentionality, 219-60. In *Social Cognitive Development. Nebraska Symposium on Motivation*, vol. 25, ed. H. E. Howe and C. B. Keasey. Lincoln: University of Nebraska Press.

Köhler, W. 1925. *The Mentality of Apes*. London: Routledge and Kegan Paul, Ltd.

Krebs, D. 1975. Empathy and altruism. *Journal of Personality and Social Psychology* 32:1134-46.

Krout, N. H. 1932. *The Psychology of Children's Lies*. Boston: Gorham Press.

La Fontaine, J. S. 1984. Person and individual: Some anthropological reflections, 123-40. In *The Category of the Person: Anthropology, Philosophy, History*, ed. M. Carrithers, S. Collins, and S. Lukes. Cambridge: Cambridge University Press.

Langer, S. K. 1942. *Philosophy in a New Key*. Cambridge, MA: Harvard University Press.

Lempers, J. D., E. R. Flavell, and J. H. Flavell. 1977. The development in very young children of tacit knowledge concerning visual perception. *Genetic Psychology Monographs* 95:3-53.

Leonard, E. A. 1920. A parent's study of children's lies. *Pedagogical Seminary* 27:105-36.

Leslie, A. 1987. Pretense and representation: The origins of "theory of mind." *Psychological Review* 94:412-26.

Lewis, M., and J. Brooks-Gunn. 1979. *Social Cognition and the Acquisition of the Self*. New York: Plenum Press.

Lewis, M., M. W. Sullivan, C. Stanger, and M. Weiss. 1989. Self development and self-conscious emotions. *Child Development* 60:146-56.

Lienhardt, G. 1984. Self: public, private. Some African representations, 141-55. In *The Category of the Person: Anthropology, Philosophy, History*, ed. M. Carrithers, S. Collins, and S. Lukes. Cambridge: Cambridge University Press.

Lock, A. 1981. Universals in human conception, 19-36. In *Indigenous Psychologies: The Anthropology of the Self*, ed. P. Heelas and A. Lock. London: Academic Press.

Lutz, C. 1985. Ethnopsychology compared to what? Explaining behavior and consciousness among the Ifaluk, 35-59. In *Person, Self, and Experience*, ed. G. M. White and J. Kirkpatrick. Berkeley: University of California Press.

Marvin, R. S., M. T. Greenberg, and D. G. Mossler. 1976. The early development of conceptual perspective-taking: Distinguishing among multiple perspectives. *Child Development* 47:511-14.

Masangkay, Z. S., K. A. McKluskey, C. W. McIntyre, J. Sims-Knight, B. E. Vaughn, and J. H. Flavell. 1974. The early development of inferences about the visual precepts of others. *Child Development* 45:357-66.

Mauss, M. 1984. A category of the human mind: the notion of person; the notion of self, 1-25. In *The Category of the Person: Anthropology, Philosophy, History*, ed. M. Carrithers, S. Collins, and S. Lukes. Cambridge: Cambridge University Press.

McCune-Nicolich, L. 1981. Toward symbolic functioning: Structure and early use of early pretend games and potential parallels with language. *Child Development* 52:785-97.

McPhail, E. 1987. The comparative psychology of intelligence. *Behavioral and Brain Sciences* 10:645-56.

Mead, G. H. 1934. *Mind, Self, and Society*. Chicago: University of Chicago Press.

Mead, M. [1928] 1949. *Coming of Age in Samoa*. New York: Mentor.

Mead, M. [1930] 1953. *Growing Up in New Guinea*. New York: Mentor.

Mead, M. [1935] 1963. *Sex and Temperament in Three Primitive Societies*. New York: Apollo.

Mignault, C. 1985. Transition between sensorimotor and symbolic activities in nursery-reared chimpanzees (*Pan troglodytes*). *Journal of Human Evolution* 14:747-58.

Miller, P. H., and P. A. Aloise. 1989. Young children's understanding of the psychological causes of behavior. *Child Development* 60:257-85.

Mitchell, R. W. 1986. A framework for discussing deception, 3-40. In *Deception: Perspectives on Human and Nonhuman Deceit*, ed. R. W. Mitchell and N. S. Thompson. Albany: SUNY Press.

Morin, A., and S. DeBlois. 1989. Gallup's mirrors: More than an operationalization of selfawareness in primates. *Psychological Reports* 65:287-91.

Mossler, D. G., R. S. Marvin, and M. T. Greenberg. 1976. Conceptual perspective taking in 2- to 6-year old children. *Developmental Psychology* 12:85-86.

Panksepp, J. 1986. The psychobiology of prosocial behaviors: Separation distress, play, and altruism, 19-57. In *Altruism and Aggression: Biological and Social Origins*, ed. C. Zahn-Waxler, E. M. Cummings, and R. Ianotti. Cambridge: Cambridge University Press.

Perner, J. In press. *Understanding the Representational Mind*. Cambridge, MA: MIT Press.

Perner, J., and J. Ogden. 1988. Knowledge for hunger: Children's problems with representation in imputing mental states. *Cognition* 29:47-61.

Perner, J., and H. Wimmer. 1985. "John thinks that Mary thinks that . . ." Attribution of second-order beliefs by 5- to 10-year old children. *Journal of Experimental Child Psychology* 39:437-71.

Piaget, J. 1929. *The Child's Conception of the World*. New York: Basic Books.

Piaget, J. 1932. *The Moral Judgment of the Child*. New York: Free Press.

Pillow, B. H. 1989. Early understanding of perception as a source of knowledge. *Journal of Experimental Child Psychology* 47:116-29.

Povinelli, D. J. 1987. Monkeys, apes, mirrors and minds: The evolution of self-awareness in primates. *Human Evolution* 2:493-507.

Povinelli, D. J. 1991. Social intelligence in monkeys and apes. Ph. D. diss., Yale University, New Haven, CT.

Povinelli, D. J., and S. DeBlois. N. d. Young children's understanding of knowledge formation in themselves and others. Submitted, *Journal of Comparative Psychology*.

Povinelli, D. J., and S. DeBlois. In press. First, know thyself. *Behavioral and Brain Sciences*.

Povinelli, D. J., K. E. Nelson, and S. T. Boysen. 1990. Inferences about guessing and knowing by chimpanzees *(Pan troglodytes)*. *Journal of Comparative Psychology* 104:203-10.

Povinelli, D. J., K. E. Nelson, and S. T. Boysen. In press, a. Comprehension of role-reversal in chimpanzees: Evidence of empathy? *Animal Behaviour.*

Povinelli, D. J., K. A. Parks, M. A. Novak. In press, b. Do rhesus monkeys *(Macaca mulatta)* attribute knowledge and ignorance to others? *Journal of Comparative Psychology.*

Pratt, C., and P. Bryant. 1990. Young children understand that looking leads to knowing (so long as they are looking into a single barrel). *Child Development* 61:973-82.

Premack, D. 1984. Pedagogy and aesthetics as sources of culture, 15-35. In *Handbook of Cognitive Neuroscience*, ed. M. S. Gazzaniga. New York: Plenum Press.

Premack, D. 1986. *Gavagai! Or the Future History of the Animal Language Controversy.* Cambridge, MA: MIT Press.

Premack, D. 1988a. 'Does the chimpanzee have a theory of mind' revisited, 160-79. In *Machiavellian Intelligence: Social Expertise and the Evolution of Intellect in Monkeys, Apes, and Humans*, ed. R. Byrne and A. Whiten. New York: Oxford University Press.

Premack, D. 1988b. Minds with and without language, 46-65. In *Thought Without Language*, ed. L. Weiskrantz. Oxford: Clarendon Press.

Premack, D., and V. Dasser. In press. Perceptual origins and conceptual evidence for theory of mind in apes and children. In *Natural Theories of Mind*, ed. A. Whiten. Oxford: Basil Blackwell.

Premack, D., and A. J. Premack. 1983. *The Mind of an Ape.* New York: W. W. Norton and Company.

Premack, D., and G. Woodruff. 1978. Does the chimpanzee have a theory of mind? *Behavioral and Brain Sciences* 4:515-26.

Quiatt, D. 1984. Devious intentions of monkeys and apes? 9-40. In *The Meaning of Primate Signals*, ed. R. Harré and V. Reynolds. Cambridge: Cambridge University Press.

Rapoport, A. 1967. Escape from paradox. *Scientific American* 217:56-60.

Romanes, G. J. 1884. *Mental Evolution in Animals.* New York: Appleton and Co.

Rosaldo, M. 1982. The things we do with words: Ilongot speech acts and speech act theory in philosophy. *Language in Society* 11:203-37.

Sachs, J., and J. Devin. 1976. Young children's views of age appropriate speech styles in social interaction and role-playing. *Journal of Child Language* 3:81-98.

Schiffer, S. 1972. *Meaning.* Oxford: Oxford University Press.

Schwartz, R. 1980. How rich a theory of mind? *Behavioral and Brain Sciences* 3:616-18.

Searle, J. 1983. *Intentionality: An Essay in the Philosophy of Mind.* Cambridge: Cambridge University Press.

Selman, R. L. 1980. *The Growth of Interpersonal Understanding.* New York: Academic Press.

Selman, R. L., and D. Byrne. 1974. A structural developmental analysis of levels of role-taking in middle childhood. *Child Development* 45:803-6.

Shantz, C. H. 1975. The development of social cognition. In *Review of Child Development Research*, vol. 5, ed. E. M. Hetherington. Chicago: University of Chicago Press.

Shatz, M., and R. Gelman. 1973. The development of communication skills: Modifications in the speech of young children as a function of listener. *Monographs of the Society for Research in Child Development* 38 5, Serial No. 152.

Shultz, T. R., and K. Cloghesy. 1981. Development of recursive awareness of intention. *Developmental Psychology* 17:465-71.

Shultz, T. R., and D. Wells. 1985. Judging the intentionality of action outcomes. *Developmental Psychology* 21:83-89.

Shultz, T. R., D. Wells, and M. Sarda. 1980. Development of the ability to distinguish intended actions from mistakes, reflexes, and passive movements. *British Journal of Social and Clinical Psychology* 19:301-10.

Smith, M. C. 1978. Cognizing the behavior stream: The recognition of intentional action. *Child Development* 49:736-43.

Smith, N. V. 1982. *Mutual Knowledge*. New York: Academic Press.

Staub, E. 1980. Social and prosocial behavior: Personal and situational influences and their interactions, 237-94. In *Personality: Basic Aspects and Current Research*, ed. E. Staub. Englewood Cliffs, NJ: Prentice Hall.

Staub, E. 1986. A conception of the determinants and development of altruism and aggression: Motives, the self, and the environment, 135-64. In *Altruism and Aggression: Biological and Social Origins*, ed. C. Zahn-Waxler, E. M. Cummings, and R. Ianotti. Cambridge: Cambridge University Press.

Staub, E. 1989. Individual and societal (group) values in a motivational perspective and their role in benevolence and harmdoing, 45-61. In *Social and Moral Values: Individual and Societal Perspectives*, ed. N. Eisenberg, J. Reykowski, and E. Staub. Hillsdale, NJ: Erlbaum.

Stiff, J. B., J. P. Dillard, L. Somera, H. Kim, and C. Sleight. 1988. Empathy, communication, and prosocial behavior. *Communication Monographs* 55:198-213.

Taylor, M. 1988. Conceptual perspective taking: Children's ability to distinguish what they know from what they see. *Child Development* 59:703-18.

Tobias, P. V. 1971. *The Brain in Hominid Evolution*. New York: Columbia University Press.

Trivers, R. 1971. The evolution of reciprocal altruism. *Quarterly Review of Biology* 46:35-57.

Tudor-Hart, B. E. 1926. Are there cases in which lies are necessary? *Pedagogical Seminary* 33:586-641.

Vasek, M. E. 1986. Lying as a skill: The development of deception in children, 271-92. In *Deception: Perspectives on Human and Nonhuman Deceit*, ed. R. W. Mitchell and N. S. Thompson. Albany: SUNY Press.

Waal, F. de. 1982. *Chimpanzee Politics: Power and Sex among Apes*. New York: Harper and Row.

Waal, F. de. 1986a. The brutal elimination of a rival among captive male chimpanzees. *Ethology and Sociobiology* 7:237-51.

Waal, F. de. 1986b. Deception in the natural communication of chimpanzees, 221-44. In *Deception: Perspectives on Human and Nonhuman Deceit*, ed. R. W. Mitchell and N. S. Thompson. Albany: SUNY Press.

Waal, F. de. 1989. *Peacemaking among Primates*. Cambridge, MA: Harvard University Press.

Walker, C. B. F. 1987. *Reading the Past: Cuneiform*. Berkeley: University of California Press.

Wallace, A. F. C. 1952. The modal personality structure of the Tuscarora Indians as revealed by the Rorschach test. *Bureau of American Ethnology. Bulletin 150*. Washington, DC: Smithsonian Institution.

Weber, M. 1947. *The Theory of Social and Economic Organization*. Trans. A. M. Henderson and T. Parsons. 2d ed. London: Free Press.

White, G. M. 1980. Conceptual universals in interpersonal language. *American Anthropologist* 82:759-81.

Whiten, A., and R. W. Byrne. 1988. Tactical deception in primates. *Behavioral and Brain Sciences* 11:233-44.

Wimmer, H., G.-J. Hogrefe, and J. Perner. 1988. Children's understanding of informational access as a source of knowledge. *Child Development* 59:386-96.

Wimmer, H., and J. Perner. 1983. Beliefs about beliefs: Representation and constraining function of wrong beliefs in young children's understanding of deception. *Cognition* 13:103-28.

Wispé, L. G. 1986. The distinction between sympathy and empathy: To call forth a concept a word is needed. *Journal of Personality and Social Psychology* 50:314-21.

Wittgenstein, L. 1953. *Philosophical Investigations*. Oxford: Blackwell.

Woodruff, G., and D. Premack. 1979. Intentional communication in the chimpanzee: The development of deception. *Cognition* 7:333-62.

Yerkes, R. M., and A. W. Yerkes. 1929. *The Great Apes: A Study of Anthropoid Life*. New Haven, CT: Yale University Press.

Yuill, N., and J. Perner. 1988. Intentionality and knowledge in children's judgments of actor's responsibility and recipient's emotional reaction. *Developmental Psychology* 24:358-65.

Zahn-Waxler, C., and M. Radke-Yarrow. 1982. The development of altruism: Alternative research strategies. In *The Development of Prosocial Behavior*, ed. N. Eisenberg. New York: Academic Press.

Zahn-Waxler, C., M. Radke-Yarrow, and J. Brady-Smith. 1977. Perspective-taking and prosocial behavior. *Developmental Psychology* 13:87-88.

Evolutionary Origin of Moral Principles

Adam Urbanek

An evolutionary or largely naturalistic approach to the origin and development of moral qualities of man has been a frequent theme in Western literature since T. H. Huxley's seminal paper (1893; see above). J. S. Huxley and T. H. Huxley's *Touchstone for Ethics* (1947) revitalized the interest in evolutionary ethics (e.g., Raphael 1958; Waddington 1960; Simpson 1966), and a new dimension was introduced by the development of sociobiology. The emerging interface between the naturalistic approach to morality and the social sciences was examined at the 1978 Dahlem Workshop (Stent 1978).

The East European contribution is modest and, perhaps, with the exception of Kropotkin (1902, 1922), little known.

Let me start with a few words on the authors discussed in this chapter. Peter Kropotkin (1842-1921), a Russian anarchist philosopher, was born to one of the most aristocratic Russian families, in fact, a descendant of the first Russian ruling dynasty. After being carefully educated in the School of Pages in St. Petersburg, he chose a scientific career and eventually became a professional revolutionary. His life was full of contrasts. He was arrested and sentenced to prison, and his escape from the Peter and Paul Fortress of St. Petersburg evoked a worldwide sensation. Later he spent many years in Western Europe, especially in France and Britain, where he became a prominent figure in intellectual life. He returned to Russia after the February Revolution of 1917, but had little political influence. During his entire life he was a consistent disseminator of anarchism, with a keen interest in the problems of ethics (Capouya and Tomkins 1976).

I will also present the views of two Polish scientists on the emergence and function of moral norms. The first, Ludwik Krzywicki (1859-1921), an eminent sociologist, ethnologist and anthropologist, who in his earlier years was strongly influenced by Marxism and Darwinism, combined historic materialism with an evolutionary theory of natural selection. Like many of his contemporaries around the turn of the century he was of the radical intellectual left, and was involved in revolutionary movements. With the years his ties with the socialistic movements lessened and he became a sort of "cathedral" socialist—to whom Marxism was mainly a scientific methodology. He published numerous and significant papers on social sciences and anthropology (for

Krzywicki's collected works see Sztumski 1986).

The second is Andrzej Wierciński, a contemporary physical and cultural anthropologist, whose scope of scientific studies ranges from the rate of morphological evolution of man to comparative studies of religion and magical practices of shamanism.

While Krzywicki considered the evolutionary origin of moral norms, Wierciński was concerned with the role and function of morality within the social system.

Cooperation Instead of Competition

Kropotkin's (1902) *Mutual Aid* was a direct reaction to T. H. Huxley's (1888) paper on the struggle for existence in human society. Nature, from a moralist's viewpoint, was shown as an arena of merciless fight, comparable to the gladiator show. Before the dawn of civilization "men were savages of a very low type." Their life was a continual free fight "and beyond the limited and temporary relations of the family, the Hobbesian war of each against all was the normal state of existence." The severity of Huxley's formulations may be partly explained by the fact that he constructed his picture as an argument against the belief that ours is the best of all possible worlds.

In contrast to such views shared by many Darwinians, Kropotkin advanced the idea that *in evolution mutual aid represents an important progressive element.* He based this idea on numerous observations made during his travels in eastern Siberia and northern Manchuria. What he had seen, first of all, was the mass elimination of organisms caused by such adverse natural agencies as frosts, snowstorms, torrential rains and monsoons, which led to enormous periodical destructions of life resulting in underpopulation rather than in Malthusian overpopulation. Thus, Kropotkin concluded that struggle for life means above all the "exterior war against the adverse natural conditions" while "the inner war for means of existence within the species" considered by Darwinians as the main arena of merciless competition, is far less significant. Only rarely do "animals have to struggle against scarcity of food" and even when they do "no progressive evolution of the species can be based upon such periods of keen competition" because the survivors also come out much impoverished in vigor and health. He had observed, instead of competition, numerous instances of mutual aid and support during migrations of deer and birds, in breeding colonies of birds, and in colonies of rodents. This empirical data helped him to conclude that in nature another law, together with that of mutual struggle, namely, the law of mutual aid, is operating. He was far from treating the latter as an expression of such sentiments as love or even sympathy;

for him it was "an instinct that has been slowly developed among animals and men" in the course of evolution.

Today Kropotkin's observations cannot be considered scientifically very sound. Yet he was essentially right in his strong reaction against simplified versions of the "struggle for life" concept as applied by T. H. Huxley and H. Spencer to life in the wild and the early human societies. Nevertheless, Darwinian metaphor, borrowed from current ideas concerning nature rather than based on accurate ecological studies, provided an essentially correct first approximation. Unfortunately, instead of being empirically scrutinized, the Darwinian concept of competition as a driving force of evolution was subject to further speculations. Life, as a continuous Hobbesian war of each against all, was presented as the normal and the only way of existence. This interpretation neglected the entire field of cooperative and altruistic behavior, simply because it does not fit the simplified Darwinian metaphor.

It is clear that Kropotkin's ideas on the role of mutual aid in the evolution of lower organisms bear heavily on his understanding of the origin of morality. First of all, a certain degree of cooperation and mutual aid appeared in prehuman ancestors of man and provided a basis for further sociability. This is because "life in societies . . . offers best chances of survival and of further progressive development." Kropotkin advanced the view that mankind began its life in small societies, bands or tribes. He criticized the view that isolated families were primitive forms of organization of mankind and that beyond the temporary limits of the family the Hobbesian war was the normal way of life. Huxley (1888), following this Hobbesian line of thinking, presented, in Kropotkin's words, primitive man "as a sort of tiger or lion deprived of all ethical conceptions." Kropotkin had no doubt that within the given tribe the peace and mutual support in food sharing, friendship, help, cooperative hunting, etc., were prevailing. Hostilities and competition were the rule only outside the given band or tribe. He insisted also that the first germs of the family appeared only later and were preceded by formation of clans or gens. This conclusion seems irrelevant for the general theory of mutual aid, but Kropotkin used it—in my opinion—to campaign against family chauvinism (nepotism), which he considered dangerous for the socially oriented mentality of man.

Kropotkin used his arguments to defend Darwin from Darwinians. He shared Darwin's belief that the moral sense of man developed from his social instinct and which, with the advances of mind, provided a foundation for the gradual replacement of individual struggle by cooperation. In this situation "the fittest are those who learn to combine so as to mutually support each other."

The Emergence of Moral Norms

Krzywicki's views on the origin and historical development of morality are of considerable interest. To him morality evolved against the background of conflicts between the interests of an individual and of another person and between interests of an individual and of an entire social group. The spontaneities of such conflicts, resulting usually in direct confrontation, have harmful consequences for both sides and are charged with a high risk of defeat. To decrease the severity of such conflicts—which are imminent in solving the life problems—one should create *norms* of conduct or behavior in conflict situations which would alleviate the interindividual and intergroup conflicts and facilitate compromises in their solving. According to Krzywicki, "norms are lubricants" in the social relations system.

Norms of conduct provide an elementary basis for morality. Their introduction, however, requires an understanding of the consequences of behavior as well as an ability to analyze the individual and group experiences. This, in turn, may substantiate a conclusion that conflict situations usually leading to grave consequences should be avoided or solved according to certain steady norms. This in turn implies evaluation of the modes of conduct: They are valued highly if they permit avoidance or alleviation of the conflicts, and some are undesirable as they lead to confrontation.

In other words, the moral evaluation of conduct requires a high elaboration of the mental qualities. The emerging system of norms determines the principle of respect to the rights of others and has the sanction of the entire social group. It is in the very nature of the norm that it usually transcends the existing level of sociability; it is somewhat beyond the human nature but, nevertheless, is commonly accepted as desirable and the right approach. Such norms may be eventually fixed as a spontaneous necessity.

This fixation of a moral norm was to Krzywicki a truly Darwinian process occurring by means of "social selection." He defined social selection as elimination from the group of those individuals who do not obey the given norm, and who introduce disorder into the everyday life of the society (1951:244). This elimination was either expulsion from the group or—as Krzywicki put it—"impeding delivery and survival of the progeny" (1951:284). His choice of strikingly modern wording and his understanding of the phylogeny of morality place Krzywicki, without exaggeration, among the forerunners of contemporary sociobiology.

Although Krzywicki did not develop his ideas further, a twofold effect of his "social selection" principle can be assumed. First, getting rid of the moral deviants could lead to the elimination of those genetic lines which displayed an inborn inclination to excessive aggression or violence. Second, it had a tremendous didactic impact on other members of the group, deterring them from evil-doing. The first assumed effect might be evidence that man, indeed, is genetically responsible for his moral sense—that, in fact, he is a "moral animal." The other didactic assumption may have been the source of numerous myths and legends describing the pitiful results of amoral conduct (Prometheus, Oedipus, Tantalus, Sodom and Gomorrah, Lot and his wife, etc.).

With time a given norm could become so strong that its alienation could occur, that is, its application could reduce the severity of conflicts at the cost of making human conduct automatic. In this way justice becomes more important than man himself, suppressing in him natural feelings of friendliness and sympathy to another human being. What Krzywicki has in mind is when morality is replaced by "fighting of immorality." Enforcement of law is thus understood as a substitute for morality.

In Krzywicki's opinion morality develops through historical crises. Decay of the existing moral system causes periods of "demoralization," followed by the emergence of a new set of moral principles. However, the advance of moral norms is not a self-organizing process, but is secondary to the development of the "material conditions of life." The historical aspect of some moral norms is also the consequence of this relationship, and can best be seen in the approach of moral thinkers to the problem of human rights. Great moralists of antiquity, like Aristotle and Seneca and the Fathers of the American Revolution, defended, or at least accepted, slavery as a natural element of the human condition. Although generally a new norm replaces the old one, occasionally it evolves within the old norm which then acquires an entirely new meaning. Thus, obedience to parents means to us something quite different from the sense it had only a century ago. A leading factor in the evolution of moral ideas is a steady broadening of the meaning of the human being, the meaning following the spontaneous transformations of material and social conditions. The successive stages of evolving meaning are from man as a member of the group, through man as a member of the nation, to man as a member of humanity.

Krzywicki discusses also the controversial relation between morality and religion. To him this relation, although intimate, is secondary. Religion does not exist for morality, nor morality for religion (1951:265). However, religion substantiates morality and usually protects and cultivates moral values. Religious justification of moral norms as God's revelation proved to be very convincing to people of different times and of different ethnic origins. When the eternal redemption is substituted for real human interests and values, this close relation may deform moral norms. Krzywicki remarked that the illusion of a paradise was frequently used to sugar the bitter pill of earthly existence (1951:274). This may be a mild version of Karl Marx's harsh definition of religion as "opium for the people." Undoubtedly, Krzywicki was an advocate of an independent, secular ethics.

Krzywicki defined morality "as a means of pressing the man into the frames of existing ideal[s] of sociability" (1951:251). Our next problem is to analyze how morality and its norms function within the framework provided by social ideas and institutions.

The Role of Morality in the Social Machinery

Wierciński (1988) offers a system approach to the functioning of the moral norms within social structures. These norms are described as a complex system involving information transfer and control based on feedback mechanism (fig. 1). Wierciński delegates crucial roles to the *world view* which on the one hand provides a comprehensive insight into the structure and history of the world, and on the other suggests a deeper sense of human life. The world view implies also the general goals to be achieved by the people, and specifies the admissible means for their accomplishment. In this way, the world view determines the general strategy of human behavior. In turn, the world view itself satisfies those specific human needs which are related to the high level of the development of mental qualities—especially reflective thinking.

To be effective, however, in the steering of the society, the world view should be linked with such *social institutions* as family and educational systems, religious and political organizations, and power structures. It is important that these institutions dispose of some material products, which may serve as *information carriers*, like art, public announcements, the press and other mass media. Both the social institutions and information carriers control and support moral norms expressed in characteristic attitudes and convictions or beliefs. The moral norms, in turn, provide the basis and justification for more specific norms of conduct of individuals and social groups in everyday life as well as the ritualized forms of such occasional behavior as celebrations.

Wierciński believes that all—the world view plus social institutions plus information carriers—interact to produce an *ideological steering system* of the society. Through the education and upbringing of the youth this steering system molds the consciousness of every generation and supports the social bounds of people on the basis of the common ideas stemming from the accepted world view.

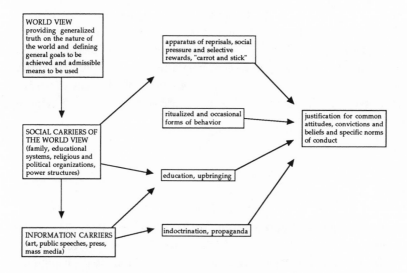

Figure 1. The structure of an ideological steering system. Simplified from Wierciński 1987.

The educational and normative influences of the world view determine a given individual—as Wierciński puts it—not only by his genetic endowment and his experience (i.e., his past), but also by the future as defined by the far-reaching goals set by culture.

The world view and other components of the ideological steering system, as defined by Wierciński, are elements of the adaptive mechanism of the culture. He emphasizes that human culture may be understood as a species-specific mode of psychosocial adaptation of humans to the environment. Culture is expressed through a complex system functioning both in the sphere of material products and in the sphere of consciousness. In fact, culture represents above all the socially organized means of conscious adaptation of man to the environment, including goal-directed activities leading to the changes of the milieu.

The general scheme of interrelations within the sphere of culture remains stable in different stages of the historical development of the society and is valid for "primitive" as well as for "advanced" societies. However, particular components of the system were subject to profound changes, especially the steering system in which the world-view component passes through a number of stages related to the historical development of culture. Wierciński distinguishes three main stages in the development of the world view, namely, (1) magic-religious, (2) philosophical and (3) scientific, the latter forming only today as a result of the progress of science. Each stage offers different cognitive and explanatory paradigms, for example, for the first stage a characteristic cognitive paradigm is *animistic*—assignment of spiritual and vitalistic qualities to all material objects, or distinguishing of a supernatural sphere penetrating entire reality. Advanced religions rely on the meaning of *sacrum*, etc. While the world view may be dominated by different pivotal and crucial ideas the general "cybernetic" scheme remains rather stable.

Comparisons and Conclusions

Kropotkin, with his conviction that cooperation is as much a law of nature as the struggle for life, was an early pioneer of modern sociobiology, which made altruistic behavior the field of systematic and fruitful studies. More than that, Kropotkin was also an early, and surely the most eminent, exponent of a pivotal idea, destined to play an important role in Russian thinking—the idea that it is a tendency of nature to avoid intraspecific competition as injurious to the species and to replace it by mutual aid and cooperation (for a detailed study of this idea, see Todes 1989). Kropotkin mentioned an earlier thinker advancing similar thoughts, namely, Professor Kessler, a zoologist from St. Petersburg University, who in a public lecture in 1880 outlined comparable concepts of the role of mutual aid in evolution. But only through Kropotkin's book did the future generations learn his wisdom, "Don't compete!"—because "the practise of solidarity proves much more advantageous to the species . . ." This, in addition to Marxism, was the second source of his conviction—wrong or right—that rampant capitalism should be transformed or replaced by a system based on cooperation.

In science, Kropotkin's ideas produced two programs: one, of empirical studies of competition (e.g., between seedlings) without necessarily, however, confirming his view that intraspecific struggle is irrelevant as a general factor of evolution; the other was that Lysenko (1948 and later) advanced ideas clearly inspired by Kropotkin, although without quoting him. Lysenko proposed the formation of large belt zones to protect fields from dry winds blowing from central Asia. He proposed that seedlings of trees be planted in great densities thus enabling the mutual support between neighboring plants. Subsequent elimination of the majority of seedlings he explained by "self-sacrifice" of some individuals for the benefit of other conspecific plants. Thus Lysenko introduced a vitalistic meaning to the explanation of the phenomenon—an element entirely alien to Kropotkin's way of thinking.

Krzywicki's views on the development of moral qualities differ distinctly from the classical approach of Darwin (1871) as well as from Kropotkin's (1902) ideas on the role of mutual aid in the origin of ethical norms. Krzywicki—within true Darwinian methodology—saw the source of morality in conflict situations (competition) and assumed a direct involvement of selective mechanism in the fixation of moral norms. Surprisingly enough Darwin was in this respect less Darwinian. He was convinced that the foundation of morality lies in the *social instinct*, a unique kind of instinct leading to strong *sympathy*, or to a relationship between individuals, where in whatever affects one similarly affects the other. Morality, to Darwin, evolved (1) due to the enduring and ever-present nature of social instincts, (2) because of man's appreciation of the approbation and disapprobation of his fellows, and (3) in the results of his mental faculties, especially his abilities to recall past impressions and to improve future actions according to past experiences. The influence of selection is only presumed because of the highly beneficial role of those instincts for the species, and because the leading role is delegated to activity of mind, a feature in turn developed under the control of natural selection. Thus, in Darwin's approach, the moral qualities appeared foremost as an epiphenomenon, as a correlate of the evolution of the mind.

In deriving moral sense from the logic of competition Krzywicki approaches closer to the contemporary neo-Darwinian sociobiologists than to Kropotkin with his firm belief in cooperative behavior as the primary source of morality.

The significance of Wierciński's approach lies largely in the scarcity of analyses of the functioning of morality and ethical norms within the society. He clearly indicates that ethical norms function as components of a larger system, called by him the ideological steering system (or subsystem), of the society and within this system they reflect primarily certain pivotal ideas composing the world view of a given community or society. Now the meaning of the world view, and especially the notion of scientific world view, are frequently questioned in Poland. The notion of the world views was a component of official Communist phraseology, and as such became a target of severe criticism in post-communistic Poland. Yet I am convinced that the world view is a reality, a product of education and individual experience, of myths and scientific pictures of the world, arising in every generation and providing a deeper justification for the way of thinking and conduct of people. As I see them, the enemies of the scientific world view do not in fact deny any form of the general world outlook, but try to replace all previous forms (considered erroneous and untenable) by a fideistic form of the world view based on religious ideology. In today's Poland this tendency might lead to a perilous monopoly of a single doctrine, a reversed analogy to the predominance of yesterday's Marxism. The ideological steering system as a goal-directing institution may serve equally well the needs of pluralistic as well as totalitarian societies—always the monopoly of a single idea may open the way towards totalitarianism.

I share Wierciński's conviction that culture may be understood as an essentially secular institution and that one can visualize some future general or unified scientific theory playing the role of the core in the world view and providing a basis for a modern moral code of entire humanity. However, the majority of Polish theorists of culture would now probably disagree. They believe that religion is an essential and indispensable component of any culture, and that culture is not complete without its religious ingredient and is doomed to degeneration when deprived of its religious aspect.

In this way they pay tribute to the revival of religious sentiments which fill the gap created by the fall of the official Marxist's ideology. Moreover, they draw conclusions from the failure of the former Soviet policy of state atheism and administrative restrictions on the freedom of religion. While their criticisms are well founded, their conclusions are less convincing. A gradual decrease of the significance of religion as the foundation of morality is also a general trend in Western societies. What recent Polish theorists overlook, or neglect, is the role of scientific theories as natural opponents of religious dogmas. This common approach among naturalists is especially true of scientific materialism capable of providing a coherent, interdisciplinary and emotionally attractive world view. Moreover, contemporary religions lost their potential of satisfactorily explaining to modern people the riddles of human existence in relation to the world. The future may yet see the emergence of a universal system of convictions which will combine the rational attitude to the world (so characteristic of science) and human values with strong motivation for actions and doing good—which has so far eluded religious and moral ideologies.

Acknowledgments

I am grateful to the Field Museum of Natural History for the 1990 Visiting Scientist Position, during which tenure part of this paper was written. It is a pleasure to acknowledge my debt to Professor Andrzej Wierciński for his insightful discussions on the meaning and significance of the world view. I also thank Dr. Matthew Nitecki and the anonymous reviewer for their most valuable comments.

References

Capouya, E., and Tomkins, K. 1976. *The Essential Kropotkin*. London: Macmillan Press.

Darwin, C. 1871. *The Descent of Man, and the Selection in Relation to Sex*. 2 vols. London: J. Murray.

Kropotkin, P. A. 1902. *Mutual Aid. A Factor of Evolution*. London: Heinemann.

Kropotkin, P. A. 1922. *Etika. Proizkhozdhenye i rozvitye moralnosti (Ethics, Origin and Development of Morality)*. St. Petersburg-Moscow.

Krzywicki, L. 1951. Rozwój moralności (Development of morality), 233-95. In *Studia Socjologiczne. Wybór (Sociological Studies. A Selection of Papers)*. Warsaw: PIW.

Raphael, D. 1958. Darwinism and ethics. In *Century of Darwin*, ed. S. A. Barnett. London: Heinemann.

Simpson, G. G. 1966. Naturalistic ethics and the social sciences. *American Psychologist* 21:27-36.

Stent, G. S., ed. 1978. Morality as a Biological Phenomenon. *Report of the Dahlem Workshop on Biology and Morals*. Berlin: Abakon Verlagsgesellschaft.

Sztumski, J., ed. 1986. *Ludwik Krzywicki. Czlowiek i spoleczeństwo. Wybór pism (Ludwik Krzywicki. Man in Society. Selected Works)*. Warsaw: Ksiazka i Wiedza.

Todes, D. P. 1989. *Darwin without Malthus: The Struggle for Existence in Russian Evolutionary Thought*. New York: Oxford University Press.

Waddington, C. H. 1960. *The Ethical Animal*. London: George Allen and Unwin, Ltd.

Wierciński, A. 1987. Mit religijny a wspólczesny przekaz naukowy (Religious myth and the contemporary scientific report). *Studia Religiologica* 20:165-75.

Wierciński, A. 1988. Antropologiczna koncepcja rozwoju światopogladu (An anthropological concept of the world view of development). *Seria Antropologia* 12:30-41.

The Complex of Questions Relating Evolution to Ethics

Lawrence Slobodkin

Ethics and Ethical Codes

The meaning of the word "ethics" is slippery at best. Consider the distinction between "ethical laws" and "ethical behavior." The word "ethics" changes meaning in a substantive way in these two contexts, as contrasted with other possible adjectives. If, for example, I was discussing "Roman laws" and "Roman behavior," the meaning of the word "Roman" would not have changed with context. Or consider "physical laws" and a "theory of physics," in contrast with "ethical laws" and a "theory of ethics." Sober nicely analyzes some of the other linguistic problems associated with the word "ethics." On the other hand, most of the other symposium participants, and particularly Ruse and Richards, seem comfortable with the term "ethics"—as if it had a clear meaning in their minds. While they have some differences there seems a general agreement that one can develop a "code of ethics," based on some objective, or at least explicit, set of criteria. After hearing them I still have a problem with the meaning of the word "ethics," which I must clarify before directly facing the central question of the relation between biology and ethics.

Richards and Ruse, for example, seem to agree that any properly formulated ethical code provides information on how to behave under a broad array of circumstances. Ethical codes assign the "goodness" or "badness" of sets of particular acts. It is also apparently possible to consider some ethical codes as better or worse than others. Better codes are the ones that eliminate as many dilemmas as possible, and do not violate our sense of good and bad. It seems possible to choose among ethical codes in terms of their internal consistency, generality, and what their consequences would be under different circumstances, and their agreement or lack of agreement with what seem to be "commonsense" or "instinctive" standards of right and wrong. On one level this seems to imply that comparing and evaluating ethical codes assumes belief in some "instinctive" criteria of good and bad, but this is not the only interpretation.

If "instinctive" is meaningful in the context of human ethics, then an "instinctive" understanding of good or bad would seem to define ethical behavior without any need to formulate an ethical "code." If, on the other hand, one denies the role of instinct in humans, then what is the source of the sense of good and bad, and is a sense of good and bad sufficient for guiding behavior?

Other questions arise. How are we to distinguish between the term "ethical" as applied to a body of laws, a body of articulated sentiments (or "sensibilities" in Jane Austen's sense), a philosophical system defining what laws are just and legitimate, and a very personal guide for making decisions in situations that are beyond the law or involve choices that the laws do not specify. How do we distinguish between a "code of Laws" and a "code of ethics?" Are legal codes based on ethical codes? Might it be the reverse? Do people deliberately violate their own sense of good and bad and, if they do, under what circumstances?

Perhaps there is a layered relation, in which an ethical instinct or (if this seems unfair) a "sense of ethics" stands behind the ethical code, which, in turn, is the basis for a legal code. Perhaps the legal code can depart from the ethical code, because it takes into consideration pragmatic issues that override ethical considerations. The happily vanishing Apartheid laws of South Africa and the former segregation laws of the American South may stand as examples of laws that would seem to violate what most would consider a "sense of ethics" or "an ethical code." Did their developers somehow have a different set of "instincts" than most of us, or were there other considerations?

One possibility is that "ethical codes" are based on some narrative which is taken as having special importance. To say, "That is my ethical code," might then mean something like "I consider that I ought to behave as if I were a participant in a dramatization of this narrative." If this is at all helpful, and it may not be, it would conform with, for example, the South African supporters of Apartheid visualizing themselves as continuing the story of the Voertrekkers. "Evolutionary ethics" might then mean placing oneself in the position of an evolutionary successful organism and would offer ethical sanction to doing the things such an organism would do. This is less explicit in its ethical prescriptions than either the Voertrekker narrative or religious texts, since the ways of succeeding or failing to succeed in evolution are enormously varied and context-defendant (Slobodkin 1991).

Perhaps racial segregation laws are related to mere ethnocentric lack of cultural breadth. Perhaps they arise from economic considerations—assignment of scarce resources, the need for cheap labor—which would override the purely ethical. Ethical codes can combine as expedient. Notice that supposed biological "facts," bolstered by religious arguments, were used to support racism in both South Africa and the United States, although profound conflicts between biological facts and religious arguments are reasonably often manifested in both regions under different circumstances. Is the use of biological facts in support of ethical and legal decisions what is intended when it is affirmed that there is a connection between ethics and this or that biological fact or theory?

My own understanding was that codes of law could be constructed to achieve particular ends. These ends might be fiscal, as laws relating to business and taxation; medical, as laws relating to injuries or sanitation; or purely conventional, as laws relating to standards of public attire. If pressed, it might be possible to rationalize these laws in terms of good and bad, but the rationalization is not absolutely necessary. Why particular ends are chosen is not always clear. The possibility remains open that the ends are at least sometimes chosen for what are believed to be ethical reasons, and at this stage of discussion the source of ethics is left open.

Ethics and Law

Ethics, as such, does not have legal authority, nor is any explicit ethical code the legal foundation for any legal system. If it were, the ethical code would be part of the legal code. But, in any case, the ultimate sources of legal systems are of somewhat narrow intellectual interest since we generally do not initiate legal systems de novo, so that the relation between legal systems and ethics relates with greater urgency to refinement of preexisting legal systems.

It is possible for the laws to be considered as emanations from some authority, but there may in fact be several such authorities in whose names law might be promulgated. These authorities might in their turn be ranked, so that in the United States, each state, city, village and county may promulgate its own system of laws for its own purposes. The general rule seems to be that the laws of any political subunit are subject to the restriction that it cannot deny or abrogate laws relating to any of the larger units to which it belongs. County law cannot deny state law cannot deny federal law. I believe the authority for the law is the same as that for the governing body that created the law, which may or may not immediately reflect beliefs of individual legislators.

But secular law is not the only code for controlling behavior. In religious systems, certain laws, and even certain general statements about what is good or bad, may derive their authority from the belief that they were promulgated by a Deity or the agent of a Deity. In Judaism, which is particularly fond of laws, not every law is seen as directly divinely inspired. Some laws are, but most are seen as decisions by lawyers and judges about how certain cases should be settled, if they happen to arise. For a lawyer or judge to base action on an ethical code without legal standing would result in chaos. On the other hand, outside the law court, legalisms seem inadequate to deal with actual problems. Perhaps what is meant by a code of ethics is the more or less inarticulate informal way of making personal judgments and decisions.

For these reasons, it seems to me that ethical considerations that do or do not violate our sense of good and bad, however that might have been derived, relate to specific cases in which the laws seem to conflict with each other or seem to fail to cover some particular case which must be decided. If these cases can be solved by revision of a legal system, then they move from the category of ethics to that of law. If a code of law is a summary of such cases, then it may be said to be based on ethics. But the problem of the source of the ethics is left unanswered.

The kinds of situations that I understand to pose ethical problems may be illustrated from any newspaper. For example, on May 12, 1990, the day of the Symposium, a superficial examination of the *Chicago Tribune* provided the following examples which seemed to me to pose problems in ethics—problems which seem to require some solution, based on some sense of what is right or wrong, beyond the law.

1. For Americans aged 17-64, the largest share of medical expenditures is for the treatment of injuries (as contrasted with "disease"). Nevertheless, the national research expenditure on injuries and on their prevention is minor compared to that expended for the study of disease. Any increment in research funding for injuries would almost certainly require reduction of expenditures on other medical research, which has greater popular appeal.

2. The United States Secretary of the Interior, Manuel Lujan, who by law is responsible for protecting wildlife, triggered an outcry from environmentalists by saying that Congress should weaken the Endangered Species Act to make it less of an obstacle to development. He was particularly concerned that protection of red squirrels is blocking a $200 million project for the construction of a telescope in Arizona.

3. A mother abducted her daughter from a Chicago hospital, despite the daughter's heart condition, because the mother's beliefs, as a member of Jehovah's Witnesses, prohibit the use of blood transfusions.

Each of these cases involves conflicting needs, desires, or opinions. In each of them there is neither an obvious pure good or pure bad. In each of them we can imagine fighting out the problem in advance and promulgating a law which would declare societies' opinion that one or another of the conflicting parties is correct and the other incorrect. Species might take precedence over development, or medical opinion might take precedence over the "instincts" of parents as a matter of law, but these laws would not embody any sort of absolute ethical codes.

In sum, my understanding is that ethics, in the most useful sense, takes over when laws are inadequate, either due to conflict or to failure of formulation or to violation of popular mores. A code of ethics seems to be a quasi-legal system if it is public, or a set of idiosyncratic opinions if it is private.

Evolution and Ethics

Ethical decisions must take cognizance of the facts of evolution and of evolutionary and ecological law if only because one cannot exclude facts from entering ethical arguments. Whether or not there are ethical criteria for dealing with the biological world in all its complexity, fragility, and diversity leads to real questions of biology and management. Without denigrating the importance of these, I will not pursue them further in this chapter.

It seems to me that there are three obvious issues in the relation between evolution and ethics, but underlying the difficulties in resolving these issues is a less obvious metaphysical assumption about the bases of ethics. Since, in serious discourse, answers depend more on questions than on empirical facts, I will consider, briefly and in sequence, the questions along with possible answers. I will then suggest what seems an obvious hypothesis.

The questions, and my provisional answers, are:

1. *Are human ethical decisions constrained by a "biological human nature" because of either the nature of evolution itself or particular properties of human biology?* To the extent that this question is empirical, the answer is "No!", or perhaps more correctly, "Not in any way which we know about now." This is the question at the heart of the "nature-nurture-sociobiology" controversy, to which this volume also contributes. After a lot of vituperation on several sides, what appeared clear to me from this controversy was that, at very best, it did not seem possible to demonstrate for any primate, and certainly not for humans, any relevant genetic constraints on ethical or, more broadly, political decisions. Specifically, it has not been unequivocally demonstrated that a particular human individual will favor those individuals with whom a greater number of identical genes are shared. This denies a biological explanation for why we might favor one individual over another in making an ethical decision.

In fact, the genetic arguments were based on what particular genes might be expected to do if they existed, rather than on any actually demonstrated genes. The failure to demonstrate a genetic-similarity-driven affection on the personal level, or patriotic sentiment on the public level, or conversely a gene-difference-driven personal revulsion or xenophobia, in no way denies the common observation that sharing of common rearing is a major force in future behavior.

Cultural differences, including language, diet, and economic and educational differences, seem plausible explanations for the various forms of bigotry, xenophobia, and group antagonism, without invoking genes at all. In short, the evolutionarily problematic behaviors of human altruism and kindness do not seem to follow genetic constraints, as Androcles pointed out to the lion.

My arguments for rejecting this model of genetic control of human behavior, and for being extremely doubtful that appropriate sorts of genes will ever be discovered in humans, have been published elsewhere (Slobodkin 1977, 1978, 1983, and 1991). They have nothing whatsoever to do with political considerations. Rather, they are based on my conviction that the intervening processes between the genotype and decision processes in humans are uniquely complex and make it extremely unlikely that what is called ethical or moral behavior has anything to do with measurable genetic differences—except in the special cases in which metabolic disorders contribute to what is considered antisocial behavior, as in porphyria or alcoholism, or conceivably in mental disorders called schizophrenia. Even here the definition of "antisocial" is culture-bound, as can be seen from the existence of well-defined roles in some societies for persons that would be considered antisocial or even evil in others.

2. *Is nature in some sense ethical?* This is a nonquestion. At least within the context of my understanding of ethics, there is a kind of silliness in attributing ethics, good or bad, to nonhumans. It is a projection of human values onto nature, like conversing with a puppy, or better, a turtle. The fact that many animals, from guppies to rats, engage in various forms of nutritious infanticide may be disgusting or, at least, offensive to those of delicate palate, but is no more a demonstration of unethical behavior in nature than snow falling down one's neck.

It is a naive metaphysical assumption to believe that nature, being produced by an ethical Deity, ought to be ethical, and is on a par with being surprised that the good die young, that earthquakes destroy churches full of people, that pigeons soil masterpiece statues, and that piety is no cure against pestilence or equally meaningless death. More sophisticated metaphysics concedes that metaphysical theories are not coercive on a Deity, nor is there any clean way to legislate what its legal or ethical properties "ought" to be.

The primary value of metaphysical naivety is to generate trite literary themes, but trite themes may generate masterpieces as well as potboilers, both scientific and literary. The misbehavior of nature figures in the biblical book of Ecclesiastes, and in Wilder's *Bridge of San Luis Rey* (1927), and I'm confident that before this chapter is printed there will be at least two novels and a film based on the 1989 San Francisco earthquake.

3. *Was the origin or development of the theory of evolution bound by the conscious or subconscious ethical assumptions of the developers?* This interesting question is answered by the methodology of social and intellectual historians and historians of science. My attempt at a reply to the question will consist of a short but important digression, followed by a discussion of the metaphysical bases of ethics.

A Digression on the Real "Two Cultures"

In C. P. Snow's once-chic book, *The Two Cultures*, he declared that there was a cultural barrier between those who had spent their time in the British public school system studying Latin, Greek, and the Great Books, and those who prepared reagents and skinned birds. This, of course, had been noticed earlier by Kipling (1899), and had been set up by the various schoolmasters, like Thomas Arnold, who designed the curricula. Snow's contribution was to point out that these educational dichotomies generated communication barriers that lasted into later public life, impeding decision processes in sometimes dangerous ways. He advocated solving the problem with a few strategically placed courses in science aimed at a nonscientist audience. In the intervening four decades I have been teaching at least one such course per year—probably because both I and the members of various curriculum committees had read Snow.

While I was the only biologist among the resident fellows of the Wilson International Center for Scholars for eight months in 1990, I discovered another barrier dividing the world of the intelligentsia, if not of the intellect. This is the barrier between what may be described, by an obvious analogy with suburban tomato plants, as determinate and indeterminate scholarship. A determinate tomato plant has a limited growth and then it bears fruit. An indeterminate tomato plant continues to grow and bear fruit until it is killed by frost. Determinate plants are smaller and neater, and in normal years may be earlier and more productive. Indeterminate plants will take up all the space they can if external circumstances permit. There is a similar distinction between

an indeterminate kind of scholarship that grows on itself and a more determinate kind
that is tied to a discrete and finite external subject matter.

For example, some philosophers, literary critics and historiographers (as contrasted with historians) use the works of their fellows as subject matter. Once an
assertion has been made, it becomes the subject matter for further discussions, and
these, in turn, are more subject matter. There is the very real possibility of a Malthusian
increase in the subject matter for the field if each philosopher writes about previous
philosophers and, in turn, is the subject for future philosophers.

By contrast, determinate scholarship, which focuses on a process, object, theory,
or event, is ultimately exhausted of its further interest by sufficiently thorough investigation. This does not mean that the subject becomes devoid of value—rather that it
seems so well understood that further study is either pointless, unoriginal, or requires
ever more ingenuity to establish a sense of novelty. It may then become mummified
as a textbook case. All of Euclidean geometry and parts of Mendelian genetics, ecological population growth theory, and classical mechanics, now have, or should have,
this status.

I, therefore, will focus on only a very few examples from the indeterminately
growing field of evolutionary ethics, aware that there are hundreds more fruit-laden
branches I have not explored.

I contend that Spencer, Huxley, and most of the nineteenth-century biological
and philosophical evolutionists have curious metaphysical baggage that they carried
with them into the battles with antievolutionists and metaphysically oriented philosophers and apologists for preevolutionary thought, who carried much the same baggage.

The problem of relating evolution and ethics obviously could only arise given
the historical antecedent of Darwinian theory itself—that is, from the midnineteenth
century on. But this same time period was heir to other ideas, which infused all discourse on this subject by pre-Darwinian evolutionists like Spencer, and which continue
to color our present discourse. This stream of antecedent thought is usually ignored or
denigrated, but at least a brief account of it is vital to leading us out of our indeterminate growth mode.

The problems of ethics, if they are not mere talk, involve serious and conflict-
laden decisions or actions, in accord with ethical standards or guidelines. What is the
source of ethical guidelines? So long as religious orthodoxy was a major force, God,
speaking through religious authority, was the assumed source of ethical judgment, at
least in the Christian nations of Europe which gave birth to evolutionary theory.

For better or for worse, in the ashes of religious certainty, which had burned out by the time of Luther, ethical problems are replaced by problematic. (I think it was very much for the better, but that is arguable.) As the assumption that the world and mankind was "in God" shifted to the assumption that God was in the world, as in the pantheism of the Romantics, or that God was in each individual human, as in the doctrines of many Protestant sects and early scientists, it became more difficult to provide clear answers to many ethical questions because the single text had been replaced by many individual revelations. Ways had to be found for finding answers to contentious questions when there were no God-ordained authorities, with precooked ethics, that were authoritative in the eyes of all the participants in ethical disputes. To prepare ethics from scratch was a new problem, perhaps never having arisen before in all of European and American history.

The civilization that grew out of the Reformation developed a new theology in which God, within each person, provides direct inspiration for words and action. This is seen in a very pure form at Quaker meetings, in which it is assumed in principle that God directly inspires members to say the correct things at meetings. Several American denominations, in the early nineteenth and late eighteenth centuries, forbade the writing of sermons on the theory that the pastor delivering an unprepared sermon was "guided by the Spirit's energy" to speak "the truth in the demonstration of its might" (Cross 1981). The present-day Church of God, Mormons, some branches of the Baptists, and, in general, most of the native fundamentalist Protestant sects, began with the assumption that the voice of God can be found by seeking within one's heart.

In another branch of the river of the Reformation a concern for revealed religion was replaced by a concern for natural law. Science was a lovely way to find non-disputaceous answers. Scientists could learn about the world by direct interaction through observation, experiment and all the other good things we do with the "God in the world." Certainly scientists had no need to have their insights arbitrated by doctors of the church, nor could they be accused of hearing false messages, since in principle their work could all be repeated and verified. Unfortunately for ethics, the terms "right" or "wrong" in their ethical contexts never appeared in the rigorous, universally agreed to, statements by scientists. Scientists themselves, therefore, did not have an important role in solving ethical problems, however the results of their researches may have been used by others. Had sociobiology been valid, it would have verified the insights of the early Protestant divines as to the source of ethics, while demonstrating that science could maintain ethical codes reasonably similar in content to those claimed by the fundamentalists, but without requiring supernatural sources.

Ethics and Cultural Relativism

I suggest that there is no hard evidence that ethics is ingrained in the human brain, or body, or mind, soul or spirit. In fact, the evidence indicates that ethical feelings are remarkably culture-bound. There is no unique narrative of all humanity from which a universal code of ethics can be derived. I suggest acceptance of cultural relativism as a fact, not necessarily a comforting one, but the best that our evidence permits. The reason cultural relativism—which was standard cultural anthropological doctrine in the heyday of Margaret Mead—has fallen into disfavor was, first, the onset of sociobiology, and, more important, that cultural relativism implies ethical relativism. Was Hitler evil, or is the best that I can say merely that I disagree personally with what Hitler did? In other words—is there a way of maintaining a concept of good and evil along with internally consistent cultural relativism?

I think that the dangers of cultural relativism can be avoided in part by abandoning the concept of "code of ethics" and replacing it with the assumption that ethical problems are those that cause us to extend or alter laws. At any given moment we can strive for a legal system that has already considered as many ethical problems as we can imagine arising.

In any case, I see no empirically sustainable way out of cultural relativism. Most actual decisions do not involve ethics, one way or the other. Making purchases, deciding where to go, or what job to take, involve very simple ideas of self-interest in most cultures. If more or less than self-interest is involved, it usually turns out to be politically or culturally determined—for example, keeping to a boycott, hiring or not hiring women or minorities or old or young people, and avoiding products that involve rare species.

Those who do not share my political, religious, esthetic, or even philosophical convictions may be wrong from my standpoint, but cannot be generally labeled as evil. If we can avoid each other by mutual agreement, no ethical issue arises. In most circumstances I do not consider my opponents evil, although they might be a nuisance. Evil arises when values clash in such a way that no possible agreement is possible, given the culture-bound behavior standards of both parties. Even mutual avoidance or the agreement to disagree is not available to at least one of the disputants. But this infers that evil, as much as good, is culturally relative—which I think must be accepted as uncomfortable fact. From my position Hitler was evil—from his own he was not.

Science involves a search for empirical truth, however cold the comfort it provides. The advocates of evolutionary ethics based on sociobiology have accused their opponents of being softhearted, and perhaps softheaded, when we tried to separate ethics from evolution. What I am suggesting is that the format for making behavioral decisions, of the sort that are often subsumed under ethical arguments, derives from cultural indoctrination. This is almost the most hardheaded and least comforting position I can imagine. However, it is the only one for which there seems an empirical foundation. The only unhappier state of affairs I can imagine is if there were biological evidence of a deep lust for evil. Fortunately, the evidence for a natural lust for evil is as weak as that for a natural tendency to follow any other ethical code. We are condemned to step-by-step groping after the ethical, as we see it.

References

Cross, W. R. 1981. *The Burned Over District.* Quoting the *Baptist Register* (Utica) III, 23 June 1826. New York: Farrar, Straus and Giroux.

Kipling, R. 1899. *Stalky & Co.* New York: Doubleday.

Snow, C. P. 1965. *The Two Cultures and A Second Look.* Cambridge: Cambridge University Press.

Slobodkin, L. B. 1977. Evolution is no help. *World Archaeology* 8:333-43.

Slobodkin, L. B. 1978. Is history a consequence of evolution? *Perspectives in Ethology* 3:233-55.

Slobodkin, L. B. 1983. The peculiar evolutionary strategy of man, 227-48. In *Epistemology, Methodology, and the Social Sciences,* ed. R. S. Cohen and M. W. Wartofsky. D. Reidel Publishing Company.

Slobodkin, L. B. 1991. *Players and Pawns: The Role of Simplicity and Complexity in Games of the Intellect.* Cambridge, MA: Harvard University Press.

Wilder, T. 1927. *The Bridge of San Luis Rey.* New York: Boni.

The Kinds of "Individuals" One Finds in Evolutionary Biology

Evelyn Fox Keller and Margaret S. Ewing

Although the usual meaning of the term "evolutionary ethics" is the biological evolution of ethics, we construe the term to mean the ethics of evolutionary biology, or, more generally, the human imprint on our theories of evolution. We turn the conventional meaning on its head not simply out of perversity, but out of principle. We take it as axiomatic that we are social and ethical animals before we are scientists, and thus regard the project of attempting to seek a biological basis for our ethics premature—at least, that is, until we have first reflected on the ways in which our particular ethical, political, and social structures may have shaped our theories of biology. For this reason, our concerns are with a social theory of science rather than with a scientific theory of sociality.

The motivation for the particular remarks here comes directly from Keller's earlier work on language and ideology in scientific, and especially, in evolutionary theory (see, e.g., Keller 1987, 1988, 1990, as well as Keller and Lloyd, forthcoming). The principal thesis emerging from this work is that language serves as a carrier of political, social, and psychological expectations into scientific theory through the phenomenon of polysemy—that is, through the presence of multiple meanings of key terms and the oscillation of reference this multiplicity engenders. If so, it would be of obvious importance to at least document and characterize such semantic multiplicity in the theoretical discourse of evolutionary biology. In this chapter, we will focus on the particular term "individual"—conspicuously important to evolutionary biology—and attempt to track the many meanings that term has acquired in the scientific literature.

The difficulties and ambiguities inherent in the commonsense notion of a biological "individual" are notorious, and have been discussed by many authors, perhaps especially by David Hull. In popular parlance, a biological "individual" is an organism, more or less like ourselves—at the very least, an animal, and usually, a vertebrate. Yet, despite the obvious inadequacy of the popular definition for the range of living forms encountered in the natural world, it is precisely to this commonsense understanding that biologists (and biology texts) tacitly appeal in their most conventional uses of the term.

Some have argued for the elimination of this commonsense notion of "individual" from biological discourse because of its inadequacy; its very ubiquity, however, suggests the need for further examination. It may not be possible either to salvage or to eliminate the "idea of individuality" from biological discourse; it may, however, be possible to sort out the different ideas that the term, in fact, subsumes.

A brief review of the literature of the last 150 years suggests a rather lengthy list of properties on which biologists have focused in their efforts to find a more general, and generalizable, definition of a biological "individual." Even without being exhaustive, such a list would have to include (1) spatial boundedness, (2) temporal boundedness, (3) physiological autonomy, (4) integrated wholeness, (5) indivisibility, (6) uniqueness, and (7) genealogical or genotypic identity. These various properties are not independent, but rather tend to cluster around three axes of meaning: unitarity, wholeness, and singularity. Properties of spatiotemporal boundedness and physiological autonomy (1-3) refer to unitarity; physiological autonomy, integration, and indivisibility (3-5) to wholeness; and temporal boundedness, uniqueness, and genotypic identity (2, 6, 7) to singularity. These properties collectively define the root, "commensensical," individual: a singular, autonomous, and highly structured biological entity developed from a fertilized egg, in short, a being like "man." It might be noted, however, that an extensive literature in feminist scholarship explores the ways in which the "commonsensical" notion of individual may in fact be attached to specific notions of masculinity rather than to the generic human being. (For discussions of "individuality" in psychology, see Scheman 1983; in political theory, Pateman 1988; and in evolutionary biology, Keller 1990.) But, in order to find a definition that might also apply to living forms which do not conform to our own standard, biologists over the last two centuries have sought to ground their definition of "individual" in various combinations of the above properties. Sometimes, properties are only implied in particular definitions; often such definitions vary even within the writings of individual authors, depending on context and purpose.

To illustrate the range of definitions that have been employed since the nineteenth century, we offer a representative sample of attempts to define the biological "individual," schematically characterizing them with respect to the above properties, numbered (1) through (7). So entwined are ideas of "individual" and "organism" that for many authors the two terms are used interchangeably, and in virtually all these definitions, spatial discreteness (property 1) is tacitly assumed as the most intuitively obvious property generally considered necessary to an acceptable description of an "individual" of any kind.

T. H. Huxley (1852:187): The individual animal is the sum of the phenomena presented by a single life: in other words, it is, all those animal forms which proceed from a single egg, taken together. (7)

H. Spencer (1898:250): [I]f the conception of individuality involves the conception of completeness, then, an organism which possesses an independent power of reproducing itself, being more complete than an organism in which this power is dependent on the aid of another organism, is more individual . . . Hence, a biological individual is any concrete whole having a structure which enables it . . . to maintain the equilibrium of its functions. (3)

J. S. Huxley (1912:28): First comes the minimum conception of an individual; the individual must have heterogeneous parts, whose function only gains full significance when considered in relation to the whole; it must have some independence of the forces of inorganic nature; and it must work, and work after such a fashion that it, or a new individual formed from part of its substance, continues able to work in a similar way. (3, 4)

More famously, J. S. Huxley invokes a contrast with inanimate objects to stress the indivisibility of organisms:

(1912:9): Cause half a mountain to be removed and cast into the sea: what remains is still a mountain, though a different one . . . (5)

C. M. Child (1915:1): The individual is not necessarily a single whole organism; it may be a part of a cell, a single cell, or a many-celled organ or complex part of the organism; or, as in most plants and some of the lower animals, a number of organisms possessing certain organs or parts in common, and therefore remaining in organic continuity with each other, may together constitute an individual. (4)

A. E. Emerson (1939:182): An organized biological unit relatively independent of other units is considered a biological individual. (1, 3, 4)

G. C. Williams (1966:195): From the standpoint of evolutionary theory . . . the concept of "individual" implies genetic uniqueness. (6)

M. Jeuken (1952): Thus an amoeba is an individual, but a cell in a many-celled being is not, because in nature this cell can only live in the whole. (1, 3)

M. Ghiselin (1974:538): Species are to evolutionary theory as firms are to economic theory . . . [They] are individuals, and they are real . . . If it is true that only individuals compete, then species as well as organisms can compete just as corporations and craftsmen can. (1, 6)

D. L. Hull (1980:313): Individuals are spatiotemporally localized entities that have reasonably sharp beginnings and endings in time. (1, 2)

R. Dawkins (1982:250): The organism is a physically discrete machine, usually walled off from other such machines. It has an internal organization . . . and it displays to a high degree the quality that Julian Huxley (1912) labelled "individuality"—literally indivisibility—the quality of being sufficiently heterogeneous in form to be rendered non-functional if cut in half. (1, 4, 5)

E. Mayr (1982:46): Population thinkers stress the uniqueness of everything in the organic world. What is important for them is the individual, not the type. They emphasize that every individual is uniquely different from all others, with much individuality even existing in uniparentally reproducing ones. There is no "typical" individual, and mean values are abstractions. (6, 7)

S. J. Gould (1984:30): We tend to call a biological object an organism if it maintains no permanent physical connection with others and if its parts are so well integrated that they work only in coordination and for the proper function of the whole. (1, 4)

If unitarity, wholeness, and singularity are the principal axes of meaning around which the above definitions revolve, then for some authors it is unitarity that is privileged (e.g., Emerson, Hull), while for others it is wholeness (e.g., Child), and for yet others it is singularity (e.g., Mayr, Williams). In part, this difference in emphasis reflects differences in disciplinary interest: for example, for authors on developmental dynamics, wholeness is of signal importance, while for evolutionary biologists, unitarity and singularity emerge as the principal demarcators of individuality. Most definitions, however, combine several properties, usually falling along more than one of these axes.

Among the many controversies in which these differences in definition have been implicated, three biological phenomena pose especially critical dilemmas for evolutionary biology: colonial organization, symbiosis, and asexual reproduction. The first two are perhaps more obvious, while the third is somewhat less so. (Indeed, there may be more than passing irony in the fact that it is asexual reproduction that has been historically problematic for evolutionary biologists, while it might be argued that it is sexual reproduction that, at least by some definitions, logically confounds the category of individual. See Keller 1987.) Colonial organization and symbiosis both blur the spatial and physiological boundaries between the component units, while asexual reproduction confounds the expected conjunction of unity with singularity and may even disturb the clarity of temporal boundaries. Indeed, it is, in part, for just these reasons that the coelenterates, most notably the Portuguese man-of-war, became objects of such intense interest for biologists in the nineteenth century (e.g., Steenstrup, Owen, Leuckart, T. H. Huxley, Haeckel, Agassiz). Furthermore, because the organization and life cycles of these organisms embodied the dilemmas posed both by asexual reproduction and colonial organization, these nineteenth-century debates can be seen as prefiguring much of the current diversity in definitions of "individual."

The nineteenth-century debates, so well reviewed by Churchill (1979) and Gould (1984), may be quickly glossed as follows: Those who were inclined to privilege spatial, temporal, and morphological identity (e.g., Steenstrup, Owen, Agassiz, and now Gould), saw the various component structures of the coelenterates—"the swimming, floating, protecting, feeding, capturing, and reproducing structures"—as individuals. By doing so, they tacitly sacrificed the expectation of physiological autonomy, thereby endorsing Goethe's image of a plant as a community of individuals and extending it to invertebrates (see Churchill 1979:146). Gould justifies this choice by appealing to evolutionary history:

> By history, siphonophores [e.g., Portuguese men-of-war] are colonies; they evolved from simpler aggregations of discrete organisms, each reasonably complete and able to perform a nearly full set of functions (as in modern coral colonies). (1984:24)

But, as Gould goes on to note, appeals to current physiological function lead to a different conclusion:

> The persons of a siphonophore no longer maintain individuality in a functional sense. They are specialized for a single task and perform as organs of a larger entity . . . The entire colony works as a single being, and its parts (or persons) move in a coordinated manner. (1984:24)

Gould's argument here closely parallels that of Lynn Margulis for conceptualizing the eukaryotic cell as a "community" of originally discrete organisms or individuals (see Margulis 1982).

Those who, like T. H. Huxley, began by privileging the notion of physiological autonomy were able to salvage this attribute from the start by emphasizing genealogical identity (*omne vivum ex ovo*) and opting for a "life cycle" designation. It is interesting to note that, for most nineteenth-century authors, an emphasis on physiological autonomy went hand in hand with an emphasis on sexual reproduction as "the primordium of all true individuality" (Burnett, quoted in Churchill 1979:151). Perhaps it could be argued that the requirements of autonomy and genealogical identity could remain a cluster for these authors precisely because of their preoccupation with organisms (like the siphonophores) in which the distinction between organism and colony closely maps

onto the distinction between sexual and asexual modes of reproduction. In the twentieth century, however, other organisms, in which these distinctions are not aligned, have
become more central foci of study; accordingly, somewhat different clusters of attributes have emerged in contemporary discussions of individuality.

Even more significantly, the focus of contemporary discussions has shifted
almost entirely to the question, "What entitities function in the evolutionary process?"
For many authors, this question translates to that of "unit of selection," and, accordingly, concerns with physiological autonomy (or "wholeness") give way to that of
singularity as the *a priori* property required for competition. Thus, a gene might
qualify as an individual relative to other genes not by virtue of any sense of physiological completeness, but simply because of its distinctiveness, and hence from its inferred
"competitive ability"; the same criteria can be invoked to qualify a species as individual
(see the quote from Ghiselin 1974). For Ghiselin, as for many others, the principal
requirement for individuality is the capacity for competitive "self-interest," and it hardly
needs noting that this notion would be meaningless if it did not presuppose uniqueness.
From such a perspective, an organism (or clone) becomes an individual by virtue of its
genotypic uniqueness rather than by properties of unitarity or wholeness. One way to
salvage unitarity and singularity as a cluster for both clones and species is provided by
the suggestion that unitarity be reconceived as a scale-dependent property (Williams
1973). From a sufficiently remote perspective, both clones and species could thus be
seen as "spatiotemporally localized entities" (Hull 1980).

Directly germane to the privileging of singularity is Harper's (1977) distinction
between "genet" (the product of a single zygote) and "ramet" ("the effective units that
are readily counted in the field"), as well as Janzen's (1977) distinction between "evolutionary" and "nonevolutionary" (or "layman's") individuals; both of these can be seen
as being in rough accord with Buss's (1987) focus on the sequestering of the germ line
as the key criterion for evolutionary "individuality." Also relevant here is Dawkins's
proposal of a cellular bottleneck (1982:263), as the condition for individuality appears
to revert to criteria of wholeness and unitarity, but, interestingly, genetic uniqueness re-
surfaces when his discussion turns to selection. In our reading, bottlenecked individuals
seem to become proper subjects (or "rivals") for natural selection only to the extent that
they derive either from fertilization or from a mutational event at the single-celled
stage.

However, concerns about physiological autonomy and functional integration have
not entirely disappeared from contemporary debates. Indeed, we suggest that much of
the debate over levels of selection at least tacitly hinges on the perceived importance of

such properties, and some of these concerns are now beginning to surface. In a self-conscious attempt to rejoin criteria of functional organization with selective criteria of individuality, Wilson and Sober (1989:341) have introduced a definition of "individuals" as "groups of genes that have become functionally organized by natural selection to perpetuate themselves." By so doing, they pave the way for a relative, context-dependent conception of individuality consistent with multiple levels of selection framework. In such a framework, and with such a definition, the properties of "individual" or "organism" are no longer "restricted to single creatures, much less to genes, but rather can be distributed over a hierarchy of units from genetic elements to multispecies communities" (Wilson and Sober 1989:354). It has to be admitted, however, that this is a minimalist definition of "individual," and it will not satisfy everyone.

Given the multiplicity of criteria implicit in different notions of individuality, it comes as no surprise that twentieth-century biologists have not reached a consensus on a scientific definition of "individual." Rather, what has become increasingly clear is the unrealizability of any single definition that would apply either across the spectrum of biological diversity, or across the spectrum of theoretical diversity. For this reason, a consensus appears to be growing on the inevitable relativity of the very notion. Criteria of individuality depend on the organisms one is studying, on theoretical perspective, and on disciplinary (and other) interests. Both what counts and how one counts depend on the spatial, temporal, and conceptual stance of the observer (see Williams 1973); they depend on the theoretical scheme into which one's tally needs to fit; and finally, they depend on the support that particular definitions of individuality can provide to larger conceptual, ethical, and ideological commitments. Just as Haeckel and Huxley had invoked their interpretations of siphonophore individuality to support particular claims about the organization of human societies (e.g., Haeckel compared the structure of siphonphore colonies to the division of labor found in "advanced" human societies, citing modern warfare as an example, "requir[ing] hundreds of human hands, working in different ways and manners" [see Gould 1984: 26]), so, too, do the social commitments and expectations of contemporary researchers find their way into technical debates today. In an earlier paper, one of us (Keller 1988) argued for a particular ideological function that the designation of individuality has served in much of the literature over the last several decades, both in units of selection debates and in mathematical ecology—namely, as a tacit demarcator between two sets of values. In the first set are autonomy, competiveness, randomness, and simplicity; in the second set, interdependence, cooperation, purposiveness, and complexity. It is the properties in the first set that are generally assumed to obtain *between* the units we designate as "individuals," while the properties in the second set are reserved for dynamics internal to these units, operating only in the interior space of the individual. Put in these terms, much of the debate over the proper locus of individuality can be seen, at least in part, as a debate over the proper domain of these two different sets of values that has deep resonances with similar debates outside biology. In particular, the bigger and more complex the individual is, the more scope there is for internal cooperation and interdependence, and for functional and/or purposive dynamics; the smaller the individual, the larger the scope for external competition and/or random interactions between individuals. In the limiting case, the gene as individual, that interior space vanishes altogether. It is at least plausible to suggest that shifting fashions in evolutionary discourse reflect shifting values in the larger political and social arena.

When one considers the many different kinds of issues and interests at stake in designating individuality, the task of finding a single, adequate definition appears hopeless. Even if we were able (which we are not) to bracket these differences, we would have to acknowledge that by no existing criteria of individuality would the resulting tally be unambiguous anyway. Take, for example, that paradigm of common-sensical individuality, "man,"—even this individual is an idealization only approximately realized in nature. The simple fact is that he is neither physiologically nor reproductively autonomous, and particular individual human beings are not even necessarily genetically unique. Rather, we suggest, the task that lies ahead is one of attempting to clarify the character of the work—conceptual, disciplinary, political, or even psychological—that is performed by particular individuals and the particular definitions of individuality they deploy.

References

Buss, L. W. 1987. *The Evolution of Individuality*. Princeton, NJ: Princeton University Press.

Child, C. M. 1915. *Individuality in Organisms*. Chicago: University of Chicago Press.

Churchill, F. B. 1979. Sex and the single organism: Biological theories of sexuality in mid-nineteenth century. *Studies in the History of Biology* 3:139-77.

Dawkins, R. 1982. *The Extended Phenotype*. San Francisco: W. H. Freeman.

Emerson, A. E. 1939. Social coordination and the superorganism. *American Midland Naturalist* XXI:182-209.

Ghiselin, M. 1974. A radical solution to the species problem. *Systematic Zoology* 23:536-44.

Gould, S. J. 1984. A most ingenious paradox. *Natural History* 93(12): 20-30.

Harper, J. L. 1977. *Population Biology of Plants*. New York: Academic Press.

Hull, D. L. 1980. Individuality and selection. *Annual Review of Ecology and Systematics* 11:311-32.

Huxley, J. S. 1912. *The Individual in the Animal Kingdom*. Cambridge: Cambridge University Press.

Huxley, T. H. 1852. Upon animal individuality. *Proceedings of the Royal Institution*. New Series (1851-1854) 1:184-89.

Janzen, D. H. 1977. What are dandelions and aphids? *American Naturalist* 111:586-89.

Jeuken, M. 1952. The concept "individual" in biology. *Acta Biotheoretica* 10(1/2): 57-86.

Keller, E. F. 1987. Reproduction and the central project of evolutionary biology. *Biology & Philosophy* 2:73-86.

Keller, E. F. 1988. Demarcating public from private values in evolutionary discourse. *Journal of the History of Biology* 21(2): 195-211.

Keller, E. F. 1990. Language and ideology in evolutionary biology: Reading cultural norms into natural law. In *The Boundaries of Humanity: Humans, Animals, and Machines*, ed. J. J. Sheehan and M. Sosna. Berkeley: University of California Press.

Keller, E. F., and E. Lloyd. N.d. *Keywords in Evolutionary Biology*. Cambridge, MA: Harvard University Press. Forthcoming.

Margulis, L. 1982. *Symbiosis in Cell Evolution*. San Francisco: W. H. Freeman.

Mayr, E. 1982. *The Growth of Biological Thought*. Cambridge, MA: Harvard University Press.

Pateman, C. 1988. *The Sexual Contract*. Stanford, CA: Stanford University Press.

Scheman, N. 1983. Individualism and the objects of psychology, 225-44. In *Discovering Reality*, ed. S. Harding and M. Hintikka. Lancaster: D. Reidel.

Spencer, H. 1898. *The Principles of Biology*. New York: Appleton.

Williams, G. C. 1966. *Adaptation and Natural Selection*. Princeton, NJ: Princeton University Press.

Williams, M. 1973. Falsifiable predictions of evolutionary theory. *Philosophy of Science* 40(4): 535-36.

Wilson, D. S., and E. Sober. 1989. Reviving the superorganism. *Journal of Theoretical Biology* 136:337-56.

Purpose, Gender and Evolution

Mary Catherine Bateson

It is hard to think of areas where comparisons between humans and nonhumans have created more interesting and confusing comparisons than in ethics and evolution.

It has been traditional for writers exhorting human beings to virtuous behavior to use imagery from the animal world: be as industrious as the bee, as courageous as the lion, as foresighted as the squirrel, as faithful as the stork. The pelican, traditionally believed to feed its young from its own blood, serves in iconography as a symbol of self-sacrifice and of the Christ.

Social Darwinism built on a new perception of the factors determining and determined by interactions in nonhuman species to propose an alternative rhetoric for the validation of particular patterns of human behavior by natural history. With changes in evolutionary understanding, we see this set of analogies as just as inadequate as those of medieval moralists, but only after they were also condemned as omitting central ethical issues of human behavior and as being destructive of human communities to boot. The writings of sociobiologists represent another stage of this debate. Moving beyond the notion of behavior as oriented to individual survival, they have proposed, for instance, that altruistic behaviors in humans and in other animals (in prophets and in pelicans) can be regarded as maximizing the survival of a shared genetic inheritance.

Ethical Discourse

All of these analogies, however, deal with behavior and its evolution. In this discussion I will work on the assumption that ethics is not a characteristic of behavior, but a domain of human discourse dealing with the act of choice between real alternatives. At the same time, I will assume that making choices is a part of the overall pattern of human adaptation, and that the capacity to discuss and make choices has evolved because it has, so far, been adaptive (Waddington 1967). Characteristics resulting in the destruction of a species' environment so that it can no longer survive or flourish in that environment would not be regarded (in retrospect, at least) as adaptive.

To the best of my knowledge, there is no evidence that bees are tempted to sloth, or inclined to hoard their honey and withhold it from the common store, or that there exists a domain of discourse to assist individual bees in these decisions. For human beings, whether or not one concedes individual free will in human decision making, such a domain exists. It has changed over time, increasing in complexity and (slowly) adjusting to new realities in the human situation, and it appears to have some relationship to actual decisions made, although not in a uniform way. These decisions, in turn, may have implications for survival of individuals, or of populations, or even of the biosphere.

Ethics consists not only in what we conclude but in what we are able to discuss, and where and how (and involving who) the discussion takes place. Ethics in this sense is a part of human culture and is variable from one human community to another. It has frequently been argued that for *Homo sapiens* cultural evolution has largely re-placed biological evolution, allowing human communities to adjust their adaptive patterns far more rapidly and to transmit new patterns through symbolic communica-tions that do not need to wait on the turnover of many generations for the dissemination of new possibilities. Human behavior also suggests a preoccupation with the survival of cultural information—creeds, dogmas, traditions, and, indeed ethical systems—passed from generation to generation symbolically as well as through genetic descent. We die for dogmas as well as for DNA, living, for example, in celibacy to produce spiritual offspring through propagation of a faith, rather than producing biological off-spring.

Ethics follows efficacy, but prior to efficacy there is an issue of awareness. The cultural domain of ethics involves those areas where choice is possible, and the ways and criteria whereby choices are discussed and made. This domain is changed by knowledge, by technical capability, and by factors which structure the understanding of these possibilities, particularly attention. The fact that some human beings carry the genetic trait for Tay-Sachs disease or for sickle-cell anemia only becomes a matter for decision making when the nature of these traits is understood, when it becomes possible to test for them, and when there are several alternative courses of action available. The context of such choices varies; at one time, they are seen as matters of individual concern, and at another as matters of community concern.

Some of these issues are raised very sharply by the AIDS story (see Bateson and Goldsby 1988). Human immunodeficiency virus (HIV—the virus that leads to AIDS) represents an apparently new element of human ecology; thus, when we look at efforts to respond to AIDS, a little reflection can remind us that we are watching evolutionarily derived patterns of adaptation in action. The virus is a product of evolution and itself continues to evolve. Its emergence has already had an impact on human culture, including the evolution of biomedical knowledge. In this crisis, there is also a pressure for evolution in the ethical domain.

The potential direct selective pressure of HIV is already being modified by two different kinds of cultural adaptation: individual behavior changes produced by education, and biomedical technology. It is important to notice that these forms of adaptation are not different in kind, for both depend on human capacities to learn and to teach. Adaptation to the existence of the new virus involves a wide range of decisions by individuals and institutions. Individuals must make new kinds of decisions about sexual choices and about whom to inform about infection. Institutions must reexamine funding priorities and modes of functioning. The kinds of information going into these decisions has changed in the course of the epidemic.

The identification of the AIDS virus itself and of its modes of transmission is an interesting example of the way in which knowledge alters ethical discourse. With that scientific step, we moved from an era of amorphous threat (a "gay plague" whose causes were unknown) to one in which effective communication could make the difference between life and death. This created new ethical dilemmas, as did the development of an antibody test and the development of drugs that retard the disease. All of these ethical issues are complicated by the association of the disease with patterns of discrimination and economic inequity and by contemporary sensitivity to ethical issues of privacy and human rights, factors that are regarded as relevant to policy by some and not by others. As with population growth, these ethical sensibilities may be challenged and altered by biological facts.

In the same way, the human capacity to act with ever-increasing impact on the natural environment has led to whole new areas of ethical concern. Interestingly enough, however, once an issue is defined as ethical it becomes important to deal with it symbolically as well as practically. Thus, many environmentally deleterious behaviors are destructive only if performed by large numbers of people, yet bringing these behaviors into the domain of ethical discussion involves a condemnation of their performance by individuals. An environmental ethic is perhaps best expressed in terms of the Kantian Categorical Imperative to act as if one's behavior were to become a rule for the whole society. Thus, preservation of the ozone layer does not depend directly on my decision or yours not to use aerosol products, but bringing such behavior into the realm of ethics does lead to a focus on individual decisions that proposes changes in patterns of human attention and in the formulation of purposes. People of good will are often highly inconsistent in their efforts to evolve standards, proposing that some decisions should be regarded as completely private while others involve not only the community but the entire planet.

Knowledge and attention are by no means synonymous. A theory of what is relevant to that process is implicit in any decision-making process—what factors shall be taken into account, ranging from commandments attributed (in some sense) to revelation, to an assessment (never complete) of possible effects of a given action. Some systems decontextualize as much as possible; others are sensitive to situational differences (see Fletcher 1966).

Several factors of attention affected human response to the AIDS threat. First, the disease was identified because of the institutionalization of epidemiological attention in health monitoring organizations, especially the Centers for Disease Control. Second, mobilization to meet the disease was inhibited by attitudes towards homosexuality and unwillingness to discuss sexual practice, attitudes that mandate inattention. Third, public and media attention has fluctuated between sensation and boredom, suggesting the existence of a cultural pattern of thresholds of attention. Attention has been fragmentary and erratic, rarely including the entire social context of the disease. Finally, narrow problem-solving orientations that ignore broader issues have shown the potential for worsening the situation ("driving the disease underground").

Conscious Purpose and Human Adaptation

Working on this essay has provided an opportunity to reassess a hypothesis put forward twenty years ago by Gregory Bateson and discussed at length at a Wenner-Gren conference (see my account of that conference, Bateson [1972] 1991), namely, that the human capacity for conscious purpose involves a distortion such that, in the service of conscious purpose, decisions are made based on a biased selection of information. The original proposal was open as to whether this problem was a biological problem based on species-specific neurological limitations, or a cultural one based on learning.

"A question of great scientific interest and perhaps grave importance is whether the information processed through consciousness is adequate and appropriate for the task of human adaptation. It may well be that consciousness contains systematic distortions of view which, when implemented by modern technology, become destructive of the balances between man, his society, and his ecosystem . . . It is suggested that the specific nature of this distortion is such that the cybernetic nature of self and the world tends to be imperceptible to consciousness insofar as the contents of the 'screen' of consciousness are determined by considerations of purpose . . . Our conscious sampling of data will not disclose whole circuits but only arcs of circuits, cut off from their matrix by our selective attention." (G. Bateson in M. C. Bateson [1972] 1991)

From a perspective of two decades, this hypothesis remains provocative but must be modified in a number of ways.

1. The availability of some portion of mental process for conscious inspection and reflexivity is apparently a precondition for the elaborate capacities for learning and teaching that underlie human adaptation. Similarly, however, the fact that only a fraction of mental process is so available means the existence of some form of partitioning or selection, and the exclusion from consciousness of the great majority of events must also be essential, if only for reasons of economy (see Bateson and Bateson 1987).

2. Humans resemble all other animals in having the natural sensory capacity to receive and process only a fraction of potentially available information. We must assume that these limitations were at one time appropriate to an early human adaptive pattern. In general, however, as with so many human capacities, the human sensory pattern is wide ranging and not highly specialized, but is subject to substantial learning, including the learning of what to omit. Some of that learning may involve something like Freudian repression, but most of it is a matter of attention, concentration, and focus.

Among the !Kung (Bushman) of the Kalahari (see Lee 1979; for gender differences see Shostak 1981), a great part of hunting consists in tracking an individual animal that has been wounded with poisoned arrows until the poison is effective. The men in a hunting band no doubt have a slightly better sense of smell than an urban American, but their capacity to track game depends primarily on trained attention to visual cues like tracks or crushed grass that are visible to an outsider when they are pointed out. The outsider can "see" the clues to the animal's worsening condition and the signs of its passage, but he doesn't "notice" them. The training of his attention is related to but not identical with the existence of an interpretive system defining the relevance of the various cues. The !Kung are aware, of course, that there are individual differences of skill and talent that benefit the group. At the same time that they focus on particular kinds of information, they must, of course, exclude others—attention is selective.

3. Technology, broadly conceived to include everything from telescopes to the use of dogs—a symbiont with a range of sensitivity to sounds and smell that has been used for millennia to supplement our own—allows an extension of this range. The question of what information shall be deemed relevant to a decision is not today depen-

dent on sensory capacities—it is, however, dependent on cultural decisions about where and how to attribute relevance.

4. Just as survival is not a characteristic of individuals but of populations, so also attention should be considered in relation to whole societies or communities, which include potentially complementary kinds of sensory capacities and attention. In his original discussion, G. Bateson suggested that decisions by various corporate bodies consisting of "part-persons" might be more biased than individual decisions, but the discussions of his hypothesis led to the proposal that the solution also lay in the construction of groups able to incorporate individuals with different kinds of knowledge and sensitivity.

5. In this context, the function of various kinds of division of labor in human adaptation becomes important, for these carry over to patterns of attention and decision making. Of all forms of division of labor, the most ancient and universal is the division of labor between the sexes. Starting from biologically different roles in reproduction and infant care, human communities assign males and females to socially constructed roles which involve extensive learning of contrastive patterns of activity and attention. The roles assigned to women typically involve attention to more than one thing at a time (one or more children still dependent on constant care as well as some subsistence activity).

While the !Kung man is tracking game, with a very highly focused kind of attention, the !Kung woman is likely to be on a gathering expedition with a group of other women, each one accompanied by one or more children, carried or walking. !Kung adaptation depends on women for 60-80% of the food supply, as well as firewood and water. However, the kind of attention needed for gathering is apparently different from that needed for hunting. In both cases a minute knowledge of the natural environment is needed, but the women will be engaged in a broad scanning pattern, rather than in a narrow focus on following a set of tracks, as they look out for signs of the presence of a variety of food sources and keep track of the children as well. The !Kung example then stands here both for culturally shaped patterns of attention and for culturally constructed complementary divisions of labor in patterns of attention, contributing to the overall adaptation of the community. It serves all the better because such a gathering-hunting society exemplifies a very ancient pattern that prevailed for many millennia in the history of our species.

6. We must assume that human divisions of labor are pervasively built on different patterns of attention and inattention, and that these partially carry over outside of working hours. Thus, farmers and factory workers notice different things. Here it

is interesting to notice that farmers are less likely to be bird watchers than are urban people, perhaps because of what farmers learn not to notice as they go about their daily work, and, in fact, many ranchers seem to view wildlife only in relation to their own economic purposes, i.e., as varmints. On the other hand, visitors to cities, unlike residents, look up (much of the architectural ornament in cities is at the top of buildings). The "part-persons" that G. Bateson describes as in charge of corporate (or national) decision making are persons following a pattern of attention believed to be appropriate to doing their job. Until recently, members of Boards of Trustees argued that attention to social policy issues (i.e., apartheid in South Africa) was actually illegitimate when they were acting in a fiduciary capacity.

7. It is still not clear whether recurrent patterns of difference between men and women are biological or cultural, because of the cross-cultural prevalence of learned differences geared directly to biological differences. Interestingly, however, some male-female differences that have been observed in our culture seem to be related to patterns of attention and to be congruent with the differences described above for the !Kung. For instance, research has suggested that women make ethical decisions differently from men (Gilligan 1982). Women are less interested in fixed rules or principles of right and wrong, and more interested in looking broadly at the context and at the welfare of those affected—in effect, their attention is differently structured. There is evidence that women in the sciences publish less frequently than men but may include more in each paper, and that women's performance on various kinds of tests is more "context dependent" on the average than is men's. Women in management situations tend to combine a concern for corporate goals with a concern for the persons they affect and for the feelings of those participating in the discussion. In my own work on contemporary American women (Bateson 1989), I have increasingly been seeing the women's style of action as *responsive* and men's as more generally *purposive*. Where men's purposive focus may lead them to ignore peripheral factors and side effects, women's broader responsiveness makes them vulnerable to distraction and ambivalence. Clearly, both men and women are capable of both kinds of attention, but practice them to different degrees. Clearly, too, a broader, more contextualized pattern of attention offers a potential for including full cybernetic circuits but does not guarantee it.

The multiplex attention of the San woman is similar to the situation in which many women involved in careers find themselves: stirring the soup, holding the baby, and negotiating complex transactions over the telephone, all at the same time, or concentrating on one thing but available and responsive to other needs.

8. In general, as societies become larger and more complex and control greater

technological possibilities, the division of labor also increases. The progressive division of communities into groups of specialists with noncompeting separate niches provides one of the commoner metaphors relating social and biological evolution. Interestingly enough, one common usage of the term "ethics" is to associate it with particular professions within society (e.g., medical ethics). Specific knowledge, specific patterns of attention, and specific modes of action do indeed require different specialized codes of ethics. Arguably, however, just as peace and war are too important to be left to politicians, so also, health is too important to be left to physicians, and the health of the biosphere is too important to be left to engineers and economists. The Waddington argument that ethical discourse can be expected to embody some degree of adaptive wisdom does not apply to specialized ethical codes of groups of professionals, for these are adapted to professional solidarity and to competition within human society.

9. When G. Bateson formulated his hypothesis, he used the gender-biased language of the time, discussing a human problem in terms of "man." But it is possible that he was inadvertently accurate, for today we can consider the possibility of erroneous human decisions resulting from reliance on only a part of the human capacity, because of various kinds of division of labor. Since all human beings, within the range of species-specific capacities, learn patterns of attention and inattention, fully human decisions on ethical matters may require engaging a wide range of possible participants. This becomes an argument for deliberately seeking cultural, vocational, and, above all, gender diversity in decision making in order to evoke a variety of sensitivities. Within the species, increasing division of labor may weaken, rather than increase, the human ethical capacity.

10. Of all the complementary patterns which have characterized human divisions of labor, gender differences may be the most promising in looking for ways of correcting deleterious human misperceptions of the natural world. The !Kung hunter on the track of game, with his highly honed attention to particular cues, does not embody the whole of an ancient human pattern of adaptation, for his kind of attention and his contribution to subsistence are not viable by themselves, but must be complemented by the patterns involved in gathering, most highly developed by the women. A !Kung band, in spite of its division of labor, is relatively egalitarian; furthermore, decision making about issues affecting the whole band in relation to its environment (most typically migration decisions) are not made in a segregated setting of exclusively male discussion.

It remains to be determined whether patterns of attention and ethical decision making characteristic of women might correct for "man's" maladaptive behavior. A similar question might be asked about adaptive or maladaptive attitudes to time. The recognition that women are context sensitive, allow attention to more factors at the same time, and are responsive to issues often regarded as peripheral by male decision makers is suggestive but by no means conclusive. Do women conceive of causation in more cybernetic terms than men, and do they only do so as long as they are locked into traditional roles or can they bring these capacities into decision-making settings? (This cannot be tested by looking at the contributions of token women only, but requires looking at some degree of balanced participation.) Will changes in the social construction of gender roles free men to develop new patterns of attention?

Conclusion

It remains to bring this discussion back to some of the issues raised at the beginning. If ethical discourse is a form of discourse that is important to human adaptation, then it becomes very important to determine who participates in that discourse, how that discourse is linked with practical decision making, and what kinds of awareness are brought into that discourse. Increasing division of labor is typically regarded as progressive in human evolution, yet if it leads to the exclusion of relevant insight from ethical discourse it may represent a form of devolution. The assumption that the human ethical capacity has been a product of human evolution and has been adaptive over millennia does not make it proof against social arrangements that bring only a portion of potential thought and sensitivity into play. The dawning realization of ecological disaster in Eastern Europe where decision making was highly centralized is an argument for pluralistic decision making. This paper proposes the need for a different and even more ancient kind of adaptive pluralism.

References

Bateson, G., and M. C. Bateson. 1987. *Angels Fear: Towards an Epistemology of the Sacred*. New York: Macmillan.

Bateson, M. C. [1972] 1991. *Our Own Metaphor: A Personal Account of a Conference on Conscious Purpose and Human Adaptation*. New York: Knopf. 2d ed. Washington, DC: Smithsonian Institution Press.

Bateson, M. C. 1989. *Composing a Life*. New York: Atlantic Monthly Press.

Bateson, M. C., and R. Goldsby. 1988. *Thinking AIDS*. Reading, MA: Addison-Wesley.

Fletcher, J. 1966. *Situation Ethics: The New Morality*. Philadelphia: Westminster Press.

Gilligan, C. 1982. *In a Different Voice*. Cambridge, MA: Harvard University Press.

Lee, R. 1979. *The !Kung San*. Cambridge: Cambridge University Press.

Shostak, M. 1981. *Nisa: The Life and Words of a !Kung Woman*. Cambridge, MA: Harvard University Press.

Waddington, C. H. 1967. *The Ethical Animal*. Chicago: University of Chicago Press.